JULES VERNE

JULES VERNE

an exploratory biography

HERBERT R. LOTTMAN

ST. MARTIN'S PRESS ❧ NEW YORK

JULES VERNE: AN EXPLORATORY BIOGRAPHY. Copyright © 1996 by Herbert R. Lottman. All rights reserved. Printed in the United States of America. No part of this book may be used or reproduced in any manner whatsoever without written permission except in the case of brief quotations embodied in critical articles or reviews. For information, address St. Martin's Press, 175 Fifth Avenue, New York, N.Y. 10010.

Design by Songhee Kim

Library of Congress Cataloging-in-Publication Data

Lottman, Herbert R.
   Jules Verne : an exploratory biography / by Herbert R. Lottman. —1st ed.
     p.   cm.
   Includes bibliographical references and index.
   ISBN 0-312-14636-1
   1. Verne, Jules, 1828–1905—Biography.   2. Authors, French—19th century—Biography.   I. Title.
PQ2469.Z5L65   1997
843'.8—dc20
   [B]   96-30532
                                             CIP

First Edition: December 1996
10 9 8 7 6 5 4 3 2 1

CONTENTS

ACKNOWLEDGMENTS

I T SHOULD BE CLEAR FROM THE NOTES THAT THE AUTHOR knocked on many doors in writing this biography of Jules Verne. I am especially grateful for the existence of two institutions, the Centre de Documentation Jules Verne in Amiens (Verne's place of death) and, in Paris, the Société Jules Verne, whose president, Dr. Olivier Dumas, was generous with his time. In Amiens, special thanks to Cécile Compère, who knows everything and where to find it, and her deputies, especially Jean-Jacques Nasoni.

Thanks also to Colette Gallois of the Centre d'Études Verniennes in Nantes's Bibliothèque Municipale. I am also grateful for the help of the many people whose names I do not know but who suffered my presence and my questions at the Bibliothèque Nationale in Paris (departments of books, manuscripts, periodicals, and illustrations).

I received help and advice from Florence Roth, librarian of the Société des Auteurs et Compositeurs Dramatiques in Paris, and from the competent staffs of the New York Public Library and the New York Psychoanalytical Institute. Information on conversion of francs from Jules Verne's time to the present came from diligent officers of the Banque de France and the Institut National de la Statistique et des Études Economiques.* Personal thanks to Malcolm E. McLouth of Port Canaveral, to Jules Verne

---

*For a rough idea of the U.S. dollar value of present-day French francs, divide by five.

fan Michel Hourst, Roger Pierrot, Nicole Asquith, Hugh Nissenson, and my readers Marianne and Jérémie Véron.

For better or for worse, I am responsible for translations from the original French.

PROLOGUE

THE BALLOON

THE PATHS TO CREATION ARE MULTIPLE—OFTEN WONDROUS. A seemingly ordinary person from a very ordinary home, a man of unremarkable education, trivial culture, modest ambitions (save for one, an ambition shared by other young Romantics of his time), wakes one morning to find himself famous. Jules Verne had written poetry, plays, and some stories, but nothing—until this moment—worth remembering. He'd have been the first to say so.

And then—one, two, three—comes a succession of stunning achievements. Now all the unspoken ideas, the unconscious preparation of his adolescent years, the self-discipline of his youthful writing seem to come into play. For nothing he had done immediately before this moment offered the slightest sign that he would now create work so compelling that it would become immortal.

ON THE THIRTY-FIRST OF JANUARY 1863, A SMALL VOLUME measuring four by six and a half inches was offered to booksellers in France under an intriguing title. The title page read:

FIVE WEEKS IN A BALLOON
Voyage of Discovery in Africa

By Three Englishmen
Based on the Notes of Dr. Fergusson[1]

The book opens with an account of a meeting of the Royal Geographic Society in London on January 14, 1862, which had occurred one year before the book's publication. The topic at that meeting was a new form of exploration: a flight across yet-to-be-explored central Africa.

At that time geographers were getting first reports of expeditions that sought, with greater or lesser success, to penetrate the most remote regions of that still unexplored continent. Some of the most perilous—and potentially most rewarding—explorations were still in progress, as readers of scientific periodicals and the serious press were aware. But while such enterprises called for arduous cross-country marches and the constant risk of death at the hands of wild animals or startled tribesmen, the new book described an extraordinary flight high above these dangers—in a manned balloon.

Speaking to the assembled geographers on that January day in London, the scientist Dr. Samuel Fergusson had argued that his adventure in the air would confirm what earlier visitors to the Dark Continent, such as Capt. Richard Burton, had only recently reported,[2] and what other British explorers, such as John Speke, James Grant, and David Livingstone, were discovering at the very moment.[3] "This attempt, should it succeed," the society's president declared—to applause and shouts of approval—"will tie together fragmentary elements of the African map, and should it fail, will nevertheless stand as one of the boldest efforts of human genius!" Along the way, the Fergusson team would observe fabulous and rarely seen sites such as Timbuktu, surprising varieties of animal and plant life, uncharted mountain ranges, lakes, and rivers, and fascinating and sometimes frightening glimpses of indigenous activity that could not have been observed—safely at least—from the ground.

Early reader of *Five Weeks in a Balloon (Cinq semaines en ballon)* no doubt were confused as to whether the book was fact or fiction, finding it hard to decide *what* to believe. The author seemed intentionally to have confused them; drafting an announcement for his publisher, Jules Verne presented the book as a possibly authentic travel diary: "The incredible and prodigious details of this journey were placed at the disposal of Mr. Jules Verne, who now delivers them to the curiosity of the public."[4] *Five Weeks in a Balloon* contained a roster of past and recent explorers who had visited one or another region, painstakingly detailed descriptions of natural phenomena encountered, with exact dating and notations of latitudes and longitudes, together with what appeared to be articles from the daily press and scientific journals of Europe and the United States discussing Fergusson's intentions.

One need not have been exceptionally well read or of a scientific bent to have been aware at the time of persistent attempts to improve both the endurance and the steering capability of passenger balloons. While a number of such craft—having in common only their spherical shape—had been released into the atmosphere since the experiments of the eighteenth-century Montgolfier brothers, only in the most recent decade had another Frenchman, Henri Giffard, demonstrated a convincing guidance system for these otherwise-uncontrollable inflated spheres. The dirigible was about to be born.

Dr. Fergusson had conceived the idea for a hydrogen-filled sphere that could be steered by the simple expedient of rising or descending to an altitude at which a wind stream was blowing in the desired direction. In the past, such a technique had required tossing out ballast to gain altitude, then releasing gas for the descent. Of course, neither the ballast nor the gas could be replaced, therefore restricting the maneuverability of the vehicle and the duration of a flight. Fergusson's balloon, in contrast, would rise to the appropriate altitude when the pilot heated water with the newly invented Bunsen burner until hydrogen and oxygen separated; the oxygen would then be channeled into the balloon: To descend, the pilot would let the temperature fall.

In practice, the balloon's mechanical system would not be that simple, as Jules Verne's readers learned while following the adventures of the intrepid Fergusson, his loyal manservant, and a skeptical Scotsman named Dick Kennedy (six feet tall and a keen marksman), with whom Fergusson had served in India. Kennedy had gone down to London to persuade his friend *not* to make the dangerous voyage; Fergusson argued, "Everything in life is dangerous; it can be dangerous to sit at one's table or to don one's hat. . . ." He also reminded Kennedy that attempts to cross Africa by land had not succeeded until now; explorers had died.

Fergusson and Kennedy sailed to Zanzibar, off the southeast coast of Africa, where they began their flight on the heels of the last overland expedition to the still-unknown sources of the Nile, the great African river. Fergusson was determined to complete the observations not only of Burton and Speke but of Heinrich Barth, a German geographer who had spent over five years exploring in central Africa. But none of these predecessors had succeeded in tracing the source—or sources—of the Nile.

Fergusson intended to do that. The specially designed balloon—in fact, two balloons, one inside the other for greater security—was attached to its gondola by netting; it carried every conceivable measuring instrument. A navy ship transported crew and equipment around the Cape of Good Hope. When they reached Zanzibar, the British consul gave them news of Captain Speke, who was reporting severe privations and deadly weather in his overland trek to the Nile's sources (an expedition that had also begun at Zanzibar and was now in its second year).

Fergusson believed his own enterprise would be spared such hardships. Relying on a German atlas containing accounts of recent explorations, a survey of the Nile, and maps published in Royal Society bulletins, he felt himself adequately equipped. Fergusson was all science and rigor, while Kennedy provided the spirit of adventure for adventure's sake. Their resourceful valet cooked up good food from strange ingredients.

Once, when they felt it safe to descend so that Kennedy and the valet could hunt for food to supplement their vehicle's rations, a danger shot from Fergusson brought them rushing back to the balloon, besieged by what seemed to be angry natives—but were, in fact, dog-faced baboons, which were as ferocious in their own way. There were encounters with indigenous peoples, some friendly and awestruck, others angry and dangerous.

Following these initial skirmishes, Verne then took his voyagers over Lake Victoria, one of the world's largest bodies of water, discovered and named by Speke only four years earlier. Speke, however, hadn't seen all of it; he couldn't even find a boat in order to explore it further. Like the real-life Captain Speke, Jules Verne's Fergusson is sure that Lake Victoria contains the secret of the Nile's origins, so he finds and describes it, flying as low as he dares, despite the occasional appearance of hostile natives. He thinks that he is bridging the gap between the expeditions of Burton and Speke on one side and—fifteen hundred miles to the west— that of Heinrich Barth; at that very moment, the Scottish missionary David Livingstone was exploring the terrain beneath them.

But Fergusson's travails were not over; henceforth, discoveries came harder. Observing tribal warfare from on high, the voyagers put an end to the bloodshed when one well-aimed shot by Kennedy kills the bloodthirsty chieftain. They save a missionary, but the missionary dies; while digging his grave, they discover gold nuggets in blocks of shale, scoop up a respectable quantity, only to be obliged to sacrifice it along the way, when emergencies require the release of ballast for quick ascent.

They run out of water—water needed both to create hydrogen and for their personal needs. And their inability to heat gas for ascension to the proper wind flow makes it even less likely that they will be able to guide their craft to water; they risk death from thirst over the Chad desert, but a felicitous windstorm increases their speed, leading them to an oasis—and safety.

In one of the worst moments of their odyssey, rapacious birds—bearded vultures—tear into the balloon, sending it careening toward Lake Chad, thus nearly putting an end to the expedition. Nothing much is left of their craft when it skims the surface of the Senegal River and lands safely among French colonial troops. They then proceed to the coast for a tranquil sea voyage to London.

"UNDER THE TITLE *FIVE WEEKS IN A BALLOON* WE HAVE AN-nounced publication of a book by Mr. Jules Verne that will intrigue the scientific world," noted the Paris daily *Le Figaro*, whose journalist posed the question: "Is Dr. Fergusson's journey a reality or is it not?" Surely the reviewer was playing along with the joke; *he* knew. "All we can say is that it is as bewitching as a novel and as instructive as a book of science," he continued. "Never have the serious discoveries of celebrated travelers been summed up as well."

The date of the article was February 8, 1863—little more than a week after the book's publication. Soon the austere afternoon daily *Le Temps* was eulogizing this work "signed by a name unknown until now but whose success we need not predict, for it is already guaranteed."[5] Indeed, only one other novel by Jules Verne, *Around the World in Eighty Days,* was to sell more copies in the original, nonillustrated edition.

Consecration came in the form of praise from one of the Continent's most distinguished literary journals, the *Revue des Deux Mondes,* which hailed Verne's "brilliant début." "His book will endure as one of the most curious and useful imaginary journeys, one of the rare creations of the mind worthy of the Robinson Crusoes and the Gulliver, with the advantage that it doesn't abandon reality for an instant, grounded even in its fantasy and invention on positive knowledge and indisputable science."[6]

Everything that would be recognized later as typical of Jules Verne's writing is found in *Five Weeks in a Balloon:* descriptions of little-known lands and peoples, descriptions as reliable and accurate as the reference books and magazine articles of the time; the inventive genius of an uncommon hero; foils in the person of a witness, usually a doubter, sometimes a best friend, often an antagonist. There is also the first of a long line of clever and ingenious, if not always courageous, manservants. Evil is depicted in these early books as mindless and innocent, or simply the result of a mechanical accident (later, the dark forces are more often deliberate in nature).

Above all, there is always the intimation of a science that might well exist, of inventions waiting for their inventor. For a writer as visionary as Jules Verne was, the fantasies so easily concocted by science fiction were never employed; machines and materials simply did not come into being at the snap of the author's imagination. Verne's adventurers were forced to rely on actual scientific knowledge, making use of available tools and materials to forge new ones. When Verne sends a manned space capsule to the moon from a Florida launchpad, equipped with retrorockets and condensed food fit for astronauts, then brings his space crew down to splash safely into the Pacific, he is unwittingly anticipating the *Apollo* flights of our time—as recent astronauts, childhood fans of Verne, would remember with delight. Verne's space capsule, as it was rendered, could not have reached the moon; his flying machines could not have flown; his submarines lacked the fuel that would be created for such vessels in modern times. His explosives, had they been detonated, would not have been as effective as he suggested in his fiction.

But he often came close.

pared, at least in spirit, for seagoing travel, exploration, and adventure. In the tenth century, and again in the Middle Ages, Nantes had been the capital of Brittany, France's continental probe into the sea. The town became a hub of the slave trade, thus of the sugar trade, when suitable subjects purchased along the coasts of Africa were shipped to the island colonies of the Caribbean. The money received from the sale of slaves was used to purchase cane sugar, which was then shipped to Nantes. The good people of Brittany preferred to call their slave trade the "ebony trade," the dark African wood serving as an obvious euphemism for their sordid transactions.

In the century before Jules was born, Nantes was France's preeminent port. It was during the eighteenth century that its shipowners and traders built the houses of the town center, as well as the docks, which formed the setting for his childhood. But revolutionary ideals, the revolt of the blacks of Saint-Domingue (now Haiti)—pivot of France's slave-based economy—combined with the rise of a beet crop that supplanted sugarcane—precipitated the end of the ebony trade and the decline of Nantes as a flourishing entrepôt. The location of Nantes, not quite on the ocean but upstream from the mouth of the Loire, restricted the utility of its docks, especially with the advent of larger and more sophisticated ships. Closer to the sea, the port of Saint-Nazaire was developed to serve and substitute for Nantes.

By the time Jules Verne was born, Nantes's golden age had waned, and only the trappings of the fabulous harbor survived, like the wedding gown of an aged lady. Later, when Verne was writing about Nantes, the city had still managed to maintain its rank as the fourth-largest commercial port in France—even though oceangoing vessels no longer came closer than Saint-Nazaire. What remained, Verne did not fail to point out, were the "magnificent" shipyards, and the iron and steel mills that fed them.[1]

THE ILE FEYDEAU WAS THE HOME OF THE ALLOTTE DE LA Fuÿe family. Before settling in Nantes, Jean Isaac Augustin Allotte (the Revolution had excised the noble suffix) had been a trader in Morlaix, a market town just inland from Brittany's craggy northern coast. There in 1793, he married Sophie Marie Adélaïde Guillochet de la Perrière. Their third child, also christened Sophie, was Jules Verne's mother. In February 1827, she married Pierre Verne, a young lawyer—actually an attorney of

I

GROWING UP
BRETON

So you go to nantes in an attempt to understand. It was there, when the little city just upriver from Brittany's Atlantic coast still flaunted the heritage of its years as a prosperous commercial harbor, that Jules Verne was born at noon on February 8, 1828. His family lived in the city's most desirable residential neighborhood, located in the heart of the old town, on an island formed by the Loire River as it completed its undulating journey across France to spill into the ocean some forty miles to the west.

Verne's birth site was called the Ile Feydeau, a city within the city, created by the shipowners of Nantes, who designed houses appropriate to their prosperity on piles over a dried-out sandbar. Nantes's great houses were built to last, outliving the golden age of their builders, and today one can still admire their sculpted facades and ornate ironwork balconies, notably on the rue Kervégan, which bisects the tiny island.

The riverbed has since been diverted, and a canal that cut through the isle, carrying the waters of the smaller Erdre River into the Loire, is now a dryland avenue. So one can only try to imagine how the street looked when it was a quay, with masts standing as tall as the fourth-floor windows of the house in which Jules Verne was born (then 4, rue Olivier de Clisson, now cours Olivier de Clisson, named for a commander in the fourteenth-century wars against England).

A boy growing up in the early nineteenth century in Nantes was pre-

PART I

Nantes Versus Paris

record, more or less equivalent to a British solicitor, a step down socially and financially from a barrister, who takes cases into the courtroom.

Pierre Verne was a newcomer to town and the newlyweds' first domicile was her parents' house—now (and perhaps then) a rather plain structure as Ile Feydeau houses go, situated at the corner of rue Kervégan and rue Olivier de Clisson. The Vernes lived here a full year, until their first child, Jules Gabriel, was born.[2]

The son of a judge in Provins, an ancient town some fifty miles southeast of Paris—no sea winds there, nor in Lyon, to where a paternal great-great grandfather has been traced—Pierre Verne grew up to the law, studied it, and began to work at it in Paris. But in 1825, he set his sights on Nantes, purchasing a solicitor's practice there. Meeting Sophie, marrying, and then fathering Jules followed in quick order. As soon as he could, he moved his new family out of his in-laws' house, but not very far. The new quarters conveniently served both as home and office.

A few yards north of the Ile Feydeau stands a soberly elegant town house with an atypical pediment, located on dry land at 2, cours des Cinquante Otages. Try to imagine it as 2, quai Jean Bart, for the Erdre as it rushed to mingle its waters with those of the Loire flowed beneath its windows. The front yard of the infant Jules, who was to spend the first eleven years of his life here, was a quay.[3]

Pierre Verne's firstborn received a perfunctory baptism immediately following his February birth, the formal christening postponed by authorization of the bishop to the first of May, to allow winter to pass before obliging the paternal grandparents to undertake the long journey from Provins.[4]

Marguerite Allotte de la Fuÿe, an early Verne biographer and a somewhat remote relation, despite the sonority of her signature, created fictional table talk during the family supper following the church ceremony. "He'll be a poet like yourself, mischievous and tender as Sophie," an aunt from Provins announces to Pierre Verne. "My son will be a solicitor like me," he is said to have replied dryly.[5] He may well have said that, for he was to try to make it happen.

It is not possible to understand very much about either Jules's father or mother from extant portraits. Sophie is seated at the piano, her face displays a solemn expression one hopes is not one of sadness, and she is wearing a lace collar and a long robe. There is the identical oval face on Jules's father (by the hand of the same painter, Francisque de La Celle de Châteaubourg, married to Sophie's sister Caroline). Pierre Verne is also dressed somberly, as if a formal portrait demanded such austereness. He sits at his desk in front of a bookcase, holding a sheet of paper in his hand—appearing purposeful, as indeed he was.

Sophie Verne gave her son the river and the ocean beyond. Her husband, an amateur poet, made verse seem a natural accompaniment to birthdays and other family gatherings, and what has survived as verse, his son Jules heard as *music.* ("He wrote songs at a time when songs were still written in France," Verne later told an English journalist. "His songs were sung in the family; very few of them ever got into print.")[6] When the Vernes met friends, they would engage in poetry contests, or they would put on a play in someone's living room.[7] Clearly, the milieu transmitted a respect for articulate speech and writing. Jules's father was also fascinated by the discoveries of contemporary science, and he communicated that enthusiasm, too.

Yet he was something his son refused to be: pious. Pierre's Catholicism meant discipline, wariness of easy pleasures; inevitably, he had been hostile to the lifestyle of actual poets.[8] To remain on good terms with such a father meant either to conform or to demonstrate convincingly that following one's own road did not signify rejection of the only true faith.

⚜

JULES WAS NOT QUITE TEN WHEN HIS PARENTS BOUGHT A hilltop vacation home at Chantenay, a village just downstream, not more than three kilometers from the center of town. Today, Chantenay is only an outlying neighborhood of Nantes, and not a very cheery one. The front garden that sloped toward the river has since been supplanted by a nondescript warehouse, and the house itself has been left to rot. If one goes out to Chantenay now, it is only to attempt to look at Nantes and its docks and shipbuilding facilities and the outlying fishing villages, as a child might have done during holidays over a century and a half ago. But this perspective is no longer possible, given the warehouse in the garden and other large constructions, neither old nor new, on the somewhat-desolate waterfront.

Jules Verne wrote about it in his brief "Memories of Childhood and Youth," written for publication in the United States but apparently never published there or anywhere in his lifetime. At the outset, he prides himself in having grown up "in the center of maritime life of a great commercial city, port of call of innumerable long voyages." He could see sailboats, clipper ships, and three-masted schooners all around him. "In my imagination I climbed into their riggings, raised myself to their crow's nests, gripped the top of their masts!" He would undoubtedly have given much to be able to step onto the deck of such a boat, but a certain shyness prevented that.

Once, just once, he did leap over the railing of a three-masted boat (the *gardien* was making the rounds, but in a neighborhood bar). He took hold of a tackle, slipped it into its pulley, and experienced a profound joy. He smelled sea smells, odors of tar and spices. . . . Mounting to the poop deck, he gave the steering wheel a turn. "It seemed to me that the ship was about to leave its moorings, sails billowing from its masts, and I was the one, an eight-year-old helmsman, who would guide it to the open sea!"

His fascination with America, he confessed, also began at an early age. His uncle Prudent had been to Venezuela, and that, too, was America; later, he used his uncle's name for one of his American heroes.

From his window in Chantenay, he could see the Loire flowing over a distance of six to nine miles (he said two to three leagues), between flatland it often covered in winter. On the other hand, the river dried up in summer, revealing sandbars—"a whole archipelago of shifting islets!"

Later, with brother Paul (his junior by a year and four months), he would pay out the somewhat-awesome sum of one franc for a day's rental of a small sailboat—never going very far beyond the patch of water below their summer house. Once, though, he went out alone on a poorly equipped skiff lacking a keel. He was some thirty miles downstream from Chantenay—on the way to the Atlantic—when a plank collapsed and water poured in; there was no way to stop the leak. The skiff sank immediately. Luckily, Jules was close enough to one of the many small islets of the sandy estuary to be able to scurry to safety among the reeds. Stranded on his islet, he began to imagine how he'd cope, what he'd find to eat (he was already an ardent reader of *The Swiss Family Robinson*). But by then the tide had run out, and he could walk, through ankle-deep water, back to what he called "the continent"—his own right bank of the Loire. He was home in time for dinner.[9]

That was enough to feed family legend, transformed in the usually unreliable biography by Marguerite Allotte into a fugue: Eleven-year-old Jules disappears and the family panics; a witness reports having seen the lad in a dinghy accompanied by two cabin boys, rowing away to ship out on a three-masted sailing vessel headed for "the Indies." But in the Allotte legend, the ship will make a brief stopover at the estuary harbor of Paimboeuf, and by hopping a steamer that served the estuary ports, father Pierre gets there in time to rescue his son.[10]

It's such a good story that it became a favorite of Verne's fans, and many wanted it to have happened. Then why Verne's failure to mention

any such fugue? Lovers of the fugue theory deal with his silence by arguing that as a writer for the young, Verne dared not even hint at such rebellious behavior.[11] And then, reminiscing at the age of sixty-six—and to
a journalist writing for an American magazine for adults—when he described the dreadful leaky boats he and his brother ventured out in, and
"what risks we, no doubt, ran," why (when he could safely do it) didn't he
tell the story of his adventure as a cabin boy about to ship out?

For the obvious reason that it never happened, and during his lifetime
no one even suggested that it had.[12]

At the age of twelve, he still hadn't seen the open sea—the "real sea."
Then one day, he and his brother were given permission to take a passenger steamboat that followed a regular route along the Loire, sailing
past the great shipyards, stopping first on one bank, then the other, at the
widening mouth of the estuary. On arrival at Saint-Nazaire, they dashed
to the shoreline—only to discover, scooping some of it into their closed
palms, that the "real sea" wasn't salty. (It was low tide, so what they tasted
was still river water.)[13]

Myths have sprouted about Verne's early fascination with science. It
was the age of the didactic family magazines of invention and discovery,
magazines no parent would try to keep from children. The Vernes would
have been eager subscribers to Parisian weeklies such as *Le Magasin Pittoresque*. This eight-page paper, which began to appear in 1833, opened a
window on sights as near as Chantilly or as far as Pompeii or Malta. In addition to its illustrated geographical stories, it carried news of science and
industry for the lay reader, in the form of brief didactic pieces on the uses
of anchors, an explanation of thunder, a description of one type of spi-
der, or of a rare Nile fish. The index to the fifty-two issues of 1835—Jules
was then seven—indicates systematic coverage of manners and customs,
history, nature studies, scientific news, reports on trade, industry, mechanics, astronomy, travel, geography, and cities. Of course one saved
these magazines, binding them in sets for home libraries; one could also
purchase bound issues for an entire year. "I was present at the birth of
phosphorus matches, detachable collars, double cuffs, letterheads,
postage stamps . . ." Verne would reminisce. Also "the metric system,
Loire river steamboats . . . railroads, trams, gas electricity, the telegraph,
the telephone, the phonograph! I'm of the generation encompassed by
two geniuses, [British engineer George] Stephenson and [Thomas Alva]
Edison!"[14]

Yet in 1894, Verne confessed to a journalist from *McClure's Magazine*,
Robert Sherard, that he hadn't been particularly taken with science (neither then nor later). But he did like to watch moving machinery, and dur-

ing their holidays at Chantenay, the Vernes would visit the nearby construction yards, where the boy would stand "for hours" watching the machines—machines that were turning out steam engines for the French navy.[15]

Actually, the earliest letter that has been found in his hand—Jules was seven or eight years old—reveals a fascination for one particular device—little toy "telegraphs." The "telegraph" in question was a miniaturized version of the signal post with movable arms invented by Claude Chappe, installed on hills and other heights to relay messages across the country (it lasted until electric telegraphs replaced it).[16]

When he was nine, Jules was enrolled in a Catholic elementary school, Saint-Stanislas. Actually, he was a bit ahead of his class, for he entered the French seventh grade—equivalent to the American fifth, and did quite well at that, receiving mentions in "reciting from memory" and geography; the other area in which he excelled was singing. During the next year, he received honorable mentions in Greek and geography; in his final year at Saint-Stanislas (1839–1840), he distinguished himself in Latin—and in singing again.[17] He remembered geography as his favorite subject—until he caught the literary bug.

After Saint-Stanislas, he was placed in another religious institution (*placed* is the appropriate word, for it was a time when parents sent the youngest of the young to boarding school, where they were confined except for brief sorties—even when their families were within walking distance). This was the Little Seminary of Nantes, whose prospectus described it as "particularly designed to receive young people preparing for an ecclesiastical vocation," although the school also admitted children whose parents would be happy to have them raised "in a house whose religious character offers the best guarantees."[18]

While still in his teens, Jules found a way to make use of his experience in a half-humorous, half-ironic account described in his unfinished novel *A Priest in 1839 (Un Prêtre en 1839)*. The seminary was "a good place to board," but only in relative terms—"alongside a murderer, the simple thief is an angel." He explained further: "The other institutions in which young proselytes were inculcated with pedantry were totally incompetent. . . . Among several nullities one had to choose the least worthless. . . ." As the son of a bourgeois, the young author is certainly laughing to himself as he has the father superior explain: "Our institution is divided into two distinct groups, lay students and ecclesiastics; the ecclesiastics pay only half-board and the outsiders pay double. One group pays for the other."[19]

While such recollections are fiction, an actual letter from son to father has survived, revealing how much a prisoner a boarder could be. "I learned with dismay that you had fallen ill and are confined to bed. . . . A week ago when no one came to see us I realized that someone was unwell, not being accustomed to being without visitors for such a long time. . . . I beg you, dear papa, let me have news of you quickly because I am very worried."[20]

No record survives of the three, perhaps four, years spent at Nantes's Little Seminary (although in a letter of December 1842, the youth—then almost fifteen—tells his mother he is seventh in his class in reciting from memory). A classmate remembers him as "a spirited schoolboy, racing around at top speed as he pushed his hoop ahead of him." (Apparently, teenagers still ran after hoops in those days.) Jules was not, added the classmate, of the studious kind.[21]

His parents could have kept Jules in the seminary, which at the time saw itself as a bulwark against anti-Catholicism (and many churchmen believed the Collège Royal, administered by the state, was the Devil itself). But the parents preferred to remove both Jules and his brother, Paul, a better student, and send them to a state high school, a move that indicated a desire to improve their chances in the national examinations. Jules, after all, was destined for law school, and Paul for the naval academy.[22]

This high school—now called the Lycée Clemenceau—occupies a site upstream from the old center in the city's monumental quarter, beyond the massive ramparts of the castle of the dukes of Brittany and the imposing cathedral, which appears even more overwhelming because it is perched on a rise. Occupying the grounds of an old convent and making use of some of its buildings, the high school today is a sprawling compound, more like barracks in a frontier garrison town. "This handsome and vast institution, located at one of the highest and healthiest parts of the city," so read a contemporary guidebook, "is divided into three sections by age, with no communication from one to the others." Each section had its own dormitory and dining hall. And even this state institution dispensed religious instruction as part of the prescribed curriculum.[23]

We do know that young Jules got through the all-important finishing exams with a "rather good." But if his marks in Greek, Latin, and philosophy were satisfactory, the writer to be was only "passing" in physics and chemistry, French and written composition.[24] He was *never* good in spelling or grammar.

While the boys were at school, the family grew in size. Brothers Jules and Paul were followed by three sisters, Anne in 1837 (that was the year nine-year-old Jules entered Saint-Stanislas), Mathilde in 1839, and Marie in 1842. By then, the family had moved again, finding more space in a somewhat-plain building on narrow rue Jean Jacques Rousseau (which Nantais call rue Jean Jacques). The house at number 6—where Napoléon's general Pierre Cambronne was then living in well-merited retirement—still stands, as do so many structures that were built during previous centuries in Nantes.

2

MINOR POET

THE WRITER CAME BEFORE THE STUDENT. JULES VERNE HAD NO desire to study to become someone or something else. His professed vocation, law, was his father's choice, but it never wholly captivated the son. The revelatory correspondence that began when Jules arrived in Paris to work for his law degree demonstrates that he did not have a good word to say about school, nor is there a hint of passion for the career for which he was supposedly preparing.

Poetry, on the other hand, was a family pastime—almost an obligation in the Verne household. Brothers and sisters, parents and children, uncles, aunts, and cousins exchanged verse as if they were handshakes or hugs. Jules could have taken rhyming as one more family duty; instead, he rose to the occasion. Later, he would tell a journalist that he began to write at the age of twelve—began to write poetry, that is—"and dreadful poetry," in his words.

Don't believe Jules Verne when he belittles his own work. Later, he was to salvage one of his early poems to his future wife and publish it as a love poem ostensibly written by the hero of one of his novels. "Still," Verne admitted to the journalist, "I remember that an address which I composed for my father's birthday—what we call a 'compliment' in France—was thought very good. . . . I remember that even at that time I used to spend a long time over my writings, copying and correcting, and never really satisfied with what I had done."

From the first day, creation was application. Lines, however effortless they may have appeared on the page, were the product of considerable rewriting. "I don't think I have ever done a piece of slovenly work," he boasted (this in the same interview).[1] Perhaps not, but sometimes the effort was all too obvious. The first of his poems to survive has been dated December 1842, when he was almost fifteen. An ode to his mother on the birth of her last child, Marie, it can now be read alongside a letter he wrote to his mother from his school dormitory during the same period.

The letter is affectionate, yet restrained. As usual, he was confined to the school dormitory while great events transpired elsewhere. "I should so much like to see you but, dear mama, don't try to visit me, it's too far for you." He waited impatiently for the time when he would be able to give her "tokens of tenderness"; meanwhile, he wished her "full recovery. . . . And what else could a child desire who loves his mother tenderly?"[2]

In the ode to his mother, he addresses not her but the infant she holds in her arms:

> *To give you life she accepted every sacrifice;*
> *Nine months in her breast your mother carried you. . . .*
>
> *When, despite her travails, her tender labors,*
> *You voice a plaint, she rushes to your side,*
> *Offers a breast, nourishes you abundantly*
> *With food God made for the newly born. . . .* [3]

He would learn soon enough to write in the idiom of spoken speech, but that was *not* the idiom of the lyrical Vernes.

Later, it was puppy love that inspired him to write. Most of what we know about these flirtatious messages comes from two school notebooks containing drafts of poetry Jules addressed to a succession of young maidens—girls who without exception were reluctant to unite their futures to his (or whose parents couldn't for the life of them see the little lawyer's son as a good match). Most of this poetry written before he turned twenty centered on two events. He wooed and lost a young woman named Caroline, and believed that he had found his destiny in one named Herminie.

Caroline Tronson, to believe a family chronicler, would have turned any young man's head—"plump," of a "blinding beauty" (certainly of classic prettiness, as we see her in a portrait by her uncle Francisque de Châteaubourg). That she was a year and a half older than Jules seemed no handicap, at least to Jules. Nor was her kinship: She was the daughter of his mother's sister. Jules and Caroline had been playmates, sharing vacation houses. It is not known how Caroline felt about her first cousin, but we know from his own words that he considered her a desirable fiancée. A poem Jules scribbled into his notebook titled "Hesitation" may have been written to and about Caroline; he hasn't declared his love, nor does he know if she loves him. But she does seem to love *someone.* This troubles him. Will she ever betray him?[4] She will do precisely that.

Family legend has it that his parents arranged for him to go to Paris—his first trip there—in the spring of 1847, at which time, back in Nantes, Caroline was being married off to a local merchant, forty years old.[5] More likely, Jules *had* to be in Paris just then—for law school.

Actually, we can't be sure that any of the surviving poems about a young man's love are addressed to plump Caroline. Unless it be this one:

> *Life is like that! . . . Every young maiden*
> *Has dreamed eternal love, when the world*
> *Seemed closed by a convent gate.*
> *And each of them, coldly, would later behold*
> *Alongside her husband, seated at their table,*
> *Eating, drinking, laughing, the adorable cousin*
> *Who had offered her flowers, and hereafter*
> *Could be separated from her only by death.*

But this isn't a love poem at all, rather dialogue from his first performed play, *Broken Straws (Les Pailles rompues),* staged in Paris in 1849, only two years after Caroline's marriage. Marguerite Allotte de la Fuÿe, his devoted but not always reliable biographer, may well be right when she sees this plaint as a direct reference to Caroline's choice.[6]

Jules would be turned down again and again—seemingly not for boorishness. Surviving portraits show that he was indeed handsome, and his respectful behavior would certainly have endeared him to parents. Nevertheless, the merchant class of Nantes simply expected more from their sons-in-law than he was likely to offer.

Caroline was followed by Herminie Arnault-Grossetièrre—just four months older than Jules—the daughter of landed proprietors presumably seeking someone of commensurate status for their daughter.

This was unfortunate, for Jules was infatuated; his outpouring of verse is sufficient testimony. Olivier Dumas, a physician who studied Verne's life as a second profession, counted some thirty poems dedicated to the young lady, who—for a while at least—returned his love.[7] We know what

Herminie looked like because of the poem "La Fille de l'air," which Jules dedicated to her:

> *I am blond and enchanting*
> *Winged and transparent.*

She is fickle, and she keeps him guessing (or perhaps she has already told him the facts of bourgeois marriage). It is surely for her and not for Caroline that he would write "To a maiden I love, and who does all she can not to know it!!"[8] Or if she knew it, she didn't care—or wasn't allowed to care. Her parents proposed another candidate, and Herminie went along with their choice, flaunting her new suitor for everyone, especially Jules, to see. The new suitor, like her father, was a man of property, and in July 1848, she married him. Twenty-year-old Jules remained under her spell, for he evoked her in poems long after her betrayal by betrothal.[9]

Such was the fate of a young man of irreproachable manners and insufficient prospects that after being encouraged to join the society of his peers at the social dances of the town's best families, he let himself get carried off his feet. Half a dozen years later, writing to his mother from Paris, when he was still a bachelor and unsettled (and not much further advanced in a career, either), he summed up his bad luck on hearing of the marriage of another of the young women on whom he had set his sights, but who, like all the others, had preferred a mature breadwinner. Or, as Jules put it: "white hair mixed with black, the half-century married to the quarter-century."

Disabused but bravely ironic, he added, "This marriage hardly surprises me since I once courted Miss Héloïse, and every young lady to whom I paid hommage invariably married soon afterwards!"[10]

Then there was Laurence Janmar. Jules began to see her at the beginning of the 1850s, when he was attempting to carve out a career in Paris while keeping in close touch with Nantes, for Nantes was the only place he was likely to be able to arrange a marriage acceptable to his family, which was the only kind of marriage he believed possible then (or later, for that matter).

Unfortunately, the very desirable Laurence was then virtually engaged to a local merchant. According to family legend, Jules managed to bow out of a Paris obligation in order to be present as an active suitor. He arrived in Nantes in time for a costume ball given by a local dignitary, where he was able to be in Laurence's company (or at least in the same ballroom); he was disguised as a dandy, Laurence as a gypsy.

A bad joke came out of the soiree: When Laurence was heard to complain to another young woman that the bones of her corset stays were causing discomfort, Jules supposedly said, "Ah, if only I could pick at those bones"—or something close to that. As the story goes, when Jules's father called on Laurence's father, the latter's objection to the match embraced both the pale prospects of Jules and the bawdy little joke about his daughter's corset. (In fact, Pierre Verne couldn't have called on Laurence's father without making a trip to Paris, and he didn't do that.)[11]

Jules saw himself as a victim not only of the parents of the women he wished to marry, but, as he would often see himself throughout his life, also as the victim of bourgeois society itself, certainly in the form it assumed in Nantes. So one of his poems attacks this city of "thousands of empty heads," concluding:

> *Sugar and rice, a trader race,*
> *Knowing how to count its cash,*
> *Which night and day torments it.*
>
> *The women ugly, most of them,*
> *Inept clergy, the governor a fool,*
> *Fountainless city: that's Nantes!!!*[12]

In another of his poems, "Farewell to a lady," he suggests that leaving his home town for Paris might actually be helpful:

> *Doubtless in exile, I'll be a wiser man:*
> *Fleeing the failure that follows temptation! . . .*
> *Yet I can't remember Paradise without longings!*[13]

Later, he would say that he embarked upon his first ambitious work—plays (both tragedies and comedies) as well as novels—at the age of seventeen. Nantes had a first-class theater on place Graslin; its antique temple facade recalled the imposing Odéon in Paris, and well-known actors of the Paris stage (such as the great Rachel at the height of her fame) performed there during provincial tours. Another center-city theater, the Salle des Variétés, offered more popular attractions.[14]

Under the spell of Victor Hugo, France's literary monster, whose verse dramas *Cromwell* and *Hernani* dominated Verne's adolescent years, Jules wrote *Alexandre VI: 1503,* a five-act romantic drama in verse, which centered on the evil Borgia pope Alexander VI, followed by *The Gunpowder*

Plot, whose central figure was the legendary Guy Fawkes. In fact, the manuscript of the Borgia play (discovered by his son after Jules Verne's death) indicates that it was composed between May 8 and June 29, 1847,[15] when the aspiring writer was nineteen, not seventeen. The Guy Fawkes play also dates from that year. Another verse play, entitled *A Drama Under Louis XV,* is a tale of court intrigue and tragic love. The young playwright displayed a lighter touch in a five-act verse comedy entitled *Today's Happy People (Les Heureux du Jour).* These early works reveal considerable effort, a painful striving for effect.[16] "I have always sought after style," Verne told journalist Robert Sherard in his declining, complaining years, "but people have never given me credit for it."[17]

The first of his prose works to survive—owing to that precious family habit of saving things—is his unfinished novel *A Priest in 1839.* Its 124 manuscript pages, written in four school notebooks, come out to some two hundred full-sized book pages when published, for in our own time this adolescent first try *was* published—an example of a not very successful early effort presented as a proper book. Jules probably wrote the first pages when he was seventeen, undoubtedly under the spell of Victor Hugo, going back to it at intervals over the next two years.[18]

The comparisons to Victor Hugo's *The Hunchback of Notre Dame* were obvious; it clearly provided inspiration for the opening chapters. While Hugo takes his readers back to the Middle Ages, his acolyte Jules Verne attempts to recreate the Middle Ages in the Nantes of his own childhood.

It is Lent as the pious citizens of Nantes crowd into the decrepit chapel of St. Nicholas, a chapel that actually existed in the old town center up to the time Jules began writing, when it was torn down and rebuilt in a diligently counterfeit Gothic style.

The crowds have come because a famous visiting preacher is to give the Lenten sermon, and word has spread that he desired that the ceremony be held in this inadequate place. As the hall fills beyond capacity, the old church bell is tolled again and again, until it crashes through the roof of the small church, killing and maiming many within. The young hero, whose name is Jules, saves beautiful Anna. We learn that she was to have been abducted in the panic; the plotters are a defrocked young priest, Pierre, and his foster parents, a criminal couple (she a proper witch). Their crimes include the falsifying of a letter from the famous preacher—for he was not coming to Nantes at all—the wrecking of the steeple, which causes the bell to fall, and the murder of the chapel's sexton, who happens to be the benefactor of young hero Jules.

The parents of the young woman he has rescued are grateful to Jules, but then they dismiss him pitilessly, for he is a patently unsuitable suitor for their daughter. Meanwhile, the witch and her assassin husband plot to wrest Anna away from her parents for their protégé Pierre.

The plot actually thickens at this point, as Jules and a loyal comrade seek to solve the mystery of the sexton's murder. It seems as if much more should transpire before the criminals are foiled and Jules gets to keep Anna, but we shall never know, for the text ends here. Perhaps a mature Jules Verne could have reworked this clumsy, repetitious draft, saving the strengths, such as the Hugoesque atmosphere, but he never did.[19]

The work is a plucky try, even when it irritates. Verne had not yet found his subject, and certainly not his style. Perhaps that is because there was something he needed to get out of the way first.

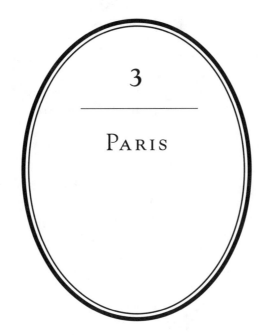

3

PARIS

THE SOMETHING HE'D HAVE TO GET OUT OF THE WAY WAS LAW,
learning the rudiments of it, then finding a place for himself in the profession. Being a lawyer often allowed a young man of promise but with
limited expectations to make his way in the world, even if he only wanted
to be a poet. And in the case of Jules Verne, it was always understood that
as the firstborn son, he would follow the path his father had mapped out;
he was *destined* to take over his father's practice.

For this young man, born and raised in the center of Nantes, there is a
symbol in the location of his high school, the Collège Royal, beyond the
fortified castle of the dukes of Brittany outside the old town walls. It was
the way to Paris, which was where a graduate might go to finish what he
began nearer home. While working as a law clerk under his father's guidance, Jules apparently made a brief trip to Paris in 1847 to enroll and perhaps to pass an entrance examination at the prestigious Faculty of Law.

Once again, family legend has him spending his leisure in Nantes in
the company of other fathers' sons who were pledged to professions they
would temper with occasional forays into the world of arts and letters.
Perhaps he did (as Marguerite Allotte says) frequent an informal literary
salon at a city-center bookshop, perhaps he wrote a tragedy in verse and
tried to have it performed at a local puppet theater. Certainly he was writing plays, and reading them aloud at family gatherings.[1] No matter; he
was pledged to the law.

Brother Paul, *not* a first son, was more fortunate. He didn't make it to the naval academy, apparently for reasons of health, but was taken on as a sailor's apprentice, to ship out on a three-masted vessel as early as December 1847—when he was eighteen. He would go on to a lifetime career in the navy.[2]

All we really know about Jules up until this time comes from love poems, occasional verse, and rare attempts at more ambitious work. Evidence of a serious year between high school graduation and law school appears in a letter Jules sent the mayor of Nantes on December 30, 1847, requesting authorization to borrow books from the town library, "my studies and work duties not allowing me to consult them during normal hours."[3]

"I CAME TO PARIS AS A STUDENT JUST ABOUT THE TIME when the grisette and all that she meant was disappearing from the Latin Quarter," Verne was to tell an English journalist much later—grisettes being young working-class women who were the easiest conquests. "I cannot say that I frequented many of my fellow-students' rooms, for we Bretons, you know, are a clannish people, and nearly all my friends were schoolmates from Nantes, who had come up to the Paris University with me. My friends were nearly all musicians, and at that period of my life I was a musician myself. I understood harmony, and I think that I may say that, if I had taken to a musical career, I should have had less difficulty than many in succeeding."[4] If ever he composed a line of music, there was no witness to it, no auditor, and although many unpublished manuscripts survived him, there is not a line of music among them.

Jules had of course gone to Paris with a specific objective: law studies, financed by a father both frugal by nature and suspicious of what a young man might do in a city whose name had become synonymous with the demimonde. Pierre Verne's concerns were unlikely to have been assuaged by indications that his son really wished to become a writer, nor did it help that young Jules thought he could actually make a living thereby. It is clear that he carried manuscripts in his baggage, plays in verse and plays in prose—most of which would not be published or performed in his lifetime.[5]

The clash in objectives and the inevitable disappointment of Pierre Verne are evident from Jules's letters from Paris; they compose a fascinating record of the beginnings of a career. He was sure that he could succeed. But although he was right to assume that law could never be more than a temporary way station en route to the literary life, he was wrong about the details. He thought money and fame would come to him by way of the theater.

The mid-nineteenth century was a golden age for theater—when the most-admired writers were lending their talents to the stage and theater-going was as natural to the well-bred as dining or dancing. "Theaters are not, as one might imagine, a secondary or a frivolous matter in a capital city such as Paris," explained the author of a guidebook Jules might have had in his pocket; "they are one of the most important things. If theaters are necessary in a rich and flourishing city, they are even more so in a national capital, above all in a population center as vast and as lively as Paris." Theaters were, noted the guidebook, "schools of manners and emotions or distractions, inseparable from ordinary life, and Parisians would rather deprive themselves of food than of their entertainment."[6]

So the young provincial who had grown up in a playgoing family now found himself at the center of a greater theatrical world, alongside fellow students from Nantes also pledged to stable and boring professional careers. Verne and his compatriots wanted to slip their yokes to join the excitement along Paris's Grands Boulevards, that broad thirty-yard-wide swath of avenues that had long since replaced the fortified ramparts demolished under Louis XIV, creating a grand assemblage of magnificent avenues lined with the most popular of the theaters, the brightest of the cafés, the most elegant of the shops.

Especially prominent were the Opéra and the Opéra Comique, the latter a uniquely French theatrical innovation with a less demanding mix of light music and spoken dialogue; it called for the constant influx of new talents. Then there were what the guidebook called the "little theaters," with names still famous today—the Gymnase, Vaudeville, Variétés, Ambigu, Porte Saint-Martin.

The changes that Verne witnessed were not merely cultural. Between Jules's first exploratory visit to Paris in 1847 and his extended stay the following summer, a political earthquake occurred that rocked social foundations throughout Europe. This was a period of seemingly unmanageable economic decline, which resulted in a wave of discontent that toppled monarchies. In France, protest took a form that would become familiar in our own times—an alliance of dissatisfied workers with an avant-garde of students from modest backgrounds. The insurrection became a veritable revolution when troops, remembering their own social origins, refused to serve bone-weary king Louis Philippe, who seemed to personify the worst qualities not of brutal repression but of upper-class indifference.

This event transpired in February 1848, after the banning of one of a series of banquets at which political reform was then being debated. Supporters of the debate movement mounted a protest that ended with a clash on the streets, and soon the disenfranchised classes of Paris were putting up their barricades. In the end, this revolution remained within the bounds of reformism, bearing little or no resemblance to the Reign of Terror during the French Revolution. The new republic that was proclaimed on February 25 would not despoil or behead.

The revolt perpetuated itself. In the absence of a royal faction, it pitted moderates against radicals; order was nonetheless restored after a series of bloody confrontations in June. The new republic soon had a president, Louis Napoléon Bonaparte, until he staged his own coup to become emperor in 1851. Napoléon III—"Napoléon the Little" in Victor Hugo's angry phrase—would rule until 1871.

In July, Jules was obliged to return to Paris to enroll, prepare, and pass his first series of law examinations. Writing to his father on July 17, his first concern was to reassure him concerning his budget—the funds, after all, had been advanced by a family where generosity did not seem to reign. Pierre Verne, perhaps arguing from his own experience in an age when a stable franc made such calculations possible, had budgeted 410 francs for the month; Jules hardly felt the amount was "excessive," with 100 francs for the journey, 2.50 francs a day for food over a thirty-day period, 40 francs for rent; the balance would go to pay enrollment and examination fees, then for out-of-pocket expenses such as postage. (Very roughly, a franc then was worth 20 to 25 francs of our day.)

"In any case, none of this should be a question of figures but of confidence," the young man argued. "This is how I see it, and the monthly accounting will prove it, I think." He would employ much of his time in Paris, then and during subsequent stays, accounting for expenditures, proving his thrift.

Only after discussing his financial situation did he think it necessary to reassure his parents about other issues—particularly the revolution still in progress and the consequences for his personal safety. "I see that you are still anxious in the provinces," he continued. "You're more afraid than we are in Paris." Nothing fearful had occurred on what might have been an agitated July 14th commemoration of the original Revolution. It was being said that Paris would go up in flames on the twenty-fourth, "which doesn't prevent Paris from being as merry as ever." He had inspected the sites of the earlier riots, had seen "houses riddled with bullets and perforated by shells." It was possible to follow the passage of cannonballs along a particular street, as they had ripped into balconies, street signs, cornices—"A frightening spectacle, and which makes it even harder to comprehend these assaults on city streets!" he wrote.[7] There was no political comment here, for between conservative son and conservative father, surely none was necessary.

Some present-day writers have seen Jules Verne as a reformer at this time. The person who knew most about the young man's politics—for he was the editor of his letters home—found not a shred of evidence that Jules was a rebel. On the contrary, he seemed content with "the moderate tranquility" with which the head of the new government, Adolphe Thiers—a determined conservative—was restoring order.[8]

At least once, Jules actually witnessed the workings of government, when a friend gave him an admission card to the constituent assembly. Debate that day centered on the arbitrary arrest of a prominent journalist, Emile de Girardin, and the unduly prolonged suspension of his newspaper, *La Presse*. Many of the legendary figures of that troubled time were present, and a helpful member of the assembly pointed them out to the young visitor from Nantes. In attendance were Alphonse de Lamartine, the celebrated poet and statesman; Alexandre Ledru-Rollin, a radical lawyer; Gen. Louis Cavaignac, famous and feared for having put down the June insurrection; progressive historian-journalist Louis Blanc; the influential socialist Pierre Joseph Proudhon; François Arago, a celebrated physicist before becoming a respected political figure; and Adolphe Thiers himself.

Moreover—wonder of wonders, Jules informed his father—he found himself in the presence of his idol, Victor Hugo. "Victor Hugo who I wanted to see so badly spoke for half an hour. Now I know him. To get to him I crushed a woman and ripped off somebody's opera glasses."[9] Hugo spoke for free speech, of course, and even conservative Jules Verne stood with the reformers on that issue.

Despite the insurrection and its unsettling aftermath, the school system was not wholly disrupted. Jules attended classes and reviewed his notes on a pretrial examination dealing with the penal and civil codes. "The examiners are of remarkable severity," he informed his father. "They are failing a frightful number of candidates." They pulled questions out of a hat—and then claimed to have talked about the subject in class. Jules began to realize that it was difficult to pass examinations at the Paris faculty when one hadn't actually studied there (and of course all the law Jules knew, he had brought with him from Nantes). He wondered whether he ought to do things differently the following year (a hint that he should spend that school year in Paris).

As he prepared himself to face uncharitable examiners who could make or break a career, he slipped in an offhand question to his father:

"Oh yes, I was forgetting, there's something I keep thinking about even when I'm busy in Paris. What could have happened to the marriage of a certain damsel you know well, which was to have taken place Tuesday; I admit that I wouldn't mind knowing how it went." Indeed. The certain damsel was Herminie; in fact, she had gone through with her marriage to the most promising of her suitors.[10] Still, considering how much of a place she had occupied in his thoughts, Jules's casual remark suggested to his family that he might be getting over the crisis.

His family learned otherwise in a very few days, when Jules unburdened himself in a long outpouring of emotion not to his stern father but to his mother. He described a dream, a dream inspired by the marriage of Herminie—whom Jules imagined as unhappy to be standing at the altar with the wrong man. Then he apologized to his mother for his silliness—"but considering the circumstances, my heart had to spill over."[11] He wasn't ever going to snivel again, not for other eyes.

Better news came at the beginning of August. Despite his having drawn some notoriously difficult examiners he passed, which meant that he could continue his schooling in the autumn semester.[12] The Vernes now realized that their son would have to live in Paris in order to succeed. After a long holiday in Nantes in the fall of 1848, Jules left again for Paris on the tenth of November; in the days before railroad tracks stretched as far as Nantes, the usual route of 120 miles to Tours was taken via stagecoach, and from there by train to the capital.

He made the journey in the company of a fellow student from Nantes, Edouard Bonamy, who would subsequently report their adventures to his own parents. Leaving on a Friday, they hoped to reach Paris by Sunday November twelfth, in time for festivities organized by Lamartine for the promulgation of the constitution of the Second Republic. In Tours, they tried to slip aboard a special train reserved for the Garde National. "Where are your uniforms and swords?" a gendarme demanded. "In our luggage," Jules replied brightly. And their travel orders? That stymied them. They reached Paris Sunday evening, Bonamy told his parents, in time to see the dying embers of the celebration. Then began a race around town, with much stair climbing, until they had settled into suitable rooms at 24, rue de l'Ancienne Comédie.[13]

These were auspicious beginnings, for the young men found themselves only a few doors down from the former Left Bank site of the Comédie Française, before it moved across the river to its present site. But for the moment, Jules's mind was filled with more material concerns, such as the cost of getting his trunk delivered, the acquisition of a coffeepot and other cooking utensils, cups, oil, glass for lamps, and other necessities. Their landlady would wash their dishes, carry up food for breakfast; she'd also clean their rooms during the mornings, while they attended classes. Another woman in the building mended clothing, and they thought they had a laundress who would not tear, wear out, or burn their precious clothing.

Jules also began to look about for writing tools, and a dressing gown. He expected to spend 150 francs in all for clothing. "When we said good-bye," he wrote to his father on November 21, "you asked that I try to limit food expenses to two francs a day, from breakfast through dinner. That can be done sometimes, but not always." To find a cheap restaurant, he would have to hike an unreasonable distance—a league, he said (that was an unlikely two and a half miles). "There, for 22 sols [a little over a franc], I can get decent food, which is what I need."

This was the first manifestation of a recurring plaint. He needed sufficient money to buy acceptable food, or else he would suffer from a bad stomach. "Ever since my arrival in Paris there hasn't been a moment without a stomach ache," he told his parents, "and that despite all my precautions. The other night I had a violent fit of vomiting, which happily went away. My stomach, that's beginning to be a nuisance, doesn't allow me to gamble with the quality of what I eat." Thank God, he said, for public toilets—"the inodorous of Paris," as they were called.

Mark these innocent words. The precision with which he described the state of his intestines indicates that the affliction was a new one, unknown even to his solicitous parents. Yet he hadn't been away long enough to feel the effects of poor diet; had there been a sudden infection, a microbial accident in his early student days? Beginning at this time and for the rest of his life, Jules would suffer from stomach cramps and diarrhea, which today might be diagnosed as colitis, inflammation of the colon.

It's impossible that his complaint was not purely physical. The editor of Verne's letters to his family is a physician. He wondered if this and subsequent complaints weren't simply hypochondria; it didn't help that cases of cholera had been reported in the neighborhood.[14] Many of Jules's complaints were accompanied by credible symptoms; not even a modern psychiatrist could conclusively distinguish between psychosomatic disorder and microbial disease, or displacement of vital organs. And a psychoanalyst might associate the adult Jules Verne's anxieties about money—economizing by living far from Paris, for example, or punishing his own son for spending money—with anality, specifically with these early signs of *incontinentia alvi* (fecal incontinence) extending into adulthood,[15] although such issues took on greater significance later.[16]

For the moment, the young man from Nantes was only asking for more money, or understanding when he spent money; trekking a league across Paris in rotten weather to save a few sols just wasn't possible with his stomach. "Most of the time I must dine in my neighborhood; and even if I eat very little, and simply, it's a matter of 40 sols [two francs]." With breakfast and a five-centime tip, he was spending forty-seven or forty-eight sols a day; he hoped his father could understand that. He had to pay out twenty francs for essential law books, and another five to tip the house porter; he also needed shoes, and they cost more in Paris than in Nantes, as did everything else. Room and food alone were going to amount to a hundred francs a month, and that without firewood, clothing, postage—not to speak of "little pleasures," such as they were. He itemized his expenses, then asked his father to do the rest.[17]

When he wasn't writing to his father, his entreaties were addressed to his mother. "My intestines are bothering me, yet I'm not eating too much—is it the quality of the food?" he asked her scarcely a week later. "My accursed watch is costing me six francs in repairs, my umbrella fifteen francs, and I had to buy a pair of boots and a pair of shoes. . . ."[18]

"I'm painfully short of literary works," he told his father. "I can't do without books, it's impossible!" He had gotten a bargain on a complete set of Shakespeare but had missed out on other bargains, such as a complete Walter Scott in thirty-two bound volumes and the plays of Eugène Scribe in twenty-four.

He was about to achieve another ambition, thanks to his uncle (his mother's brother-in-law) Francisque de Châteaubourg, the family portraitist and clearly a person of standing even in the capital. Châteaubourg was introducing his nephew not only to the literary salons but also to the women who ran them. One of these women—so Jules wrote home on December sixth—could introduce him to a young man who was "an intimate" of Victor Hugo—and who would be able to introduce Jules to the great man and thus "make my dearest dream come true."

Such enthusiasm, when expressed by a son who was in Paris to study law, understandably alarmed the good Nantes solicitor Pierre Verne. His son would have to reassure him on that score. Jules replied that he knew what to take and what to leave; he was sure there was more to gain than to lose in the company of these literary lions. "It's a real pleasure not sufficiently understood in Nantes, keeping up with the literary world, following its tendencies, watching it shift regularly from Shakespeare to Racine, from Scribe to Clerville [sic]!"[19]

Clearly he had caught something—an affliction that must have seemed as worrisome as stomach cramps to the family he had left behind, and this new infatuation would be long-standing.

4

THE LITERARY
LIFE

DECEMBER OF 1848 WAS A TIME OF RELATIVE CALM IN PARIS, symbolized by the election to the French presidency (and by an over-whelming margin) of Louis Napoléon. This nephew of the late emperor had only recently returned from London, where he had lived since 1846 as a fugitive, under a life sentence for attempting to overthrow the state—yet he seemed to represent the stability, the continuity, that Frenchmen were newly craving in the wake of the revolts. All the same, in three years he would stage his own coup, ushering in a new autocratic empire, and twenty years of prosperity.

This new period of tranquillity enabled Verne to think of other things. "My health is stabilizing," Jules assured his family back in Nantes. "The at-tacks of colitis are less and less frequent. . . . Eating three meals a day is having its effect. . . . But as you can guess," he reminded his father un-subtly, "this is raising the cost of my food." The association of thrift and intestinal disorder—the one seemingly leading to the other—was a case study Freud would surely have utilized had he known of it.

He was studying for his law examination, a boring job but apparently not a difficult one; this left him time for his real passion (which in writ-ing home he makes sure not to let sound *too* engrossing): "The more I frequent the ladies of the literary world the more I realize how many people they know. . . . Besides, and I'm only saying what has been said to me, I manage to be liked by everybody! Anyway, how could they not like me, when I make it a point to agree with the person who is talking to me!"[1]

The evidence suggests that he had not convinced his parents of his frugality, for his letters reveal a constant need to reassure on that score. At the beginning of 1849, he requested more money again (he wasn't a wastrel; he simply had to pay school fees and Christmas season gratuities, he insisted). These obligations had absorbed most of the money his father had already sent him, leaving insufficient funds to cover examination costs, regular living expenses, and still more gratuities. Then, as if Jules hadn't enough to worry about, there was talk of a new epidemic of cholera.

In January 1849, Verne's father mailed off a detailed list of his son's infractions. Studying law should not entail active socializing, certainly not with poets, Pierre advised. No, responded Jules; he had constantly kept himself at a distance from what might seem "eccentric" behavior. "I was the first to recognize what was worth taking and leaving in the company of artists," he insisted. As boring as they were, he was tackling the Latin jurists, and he assured that he'd get through his examinations, as well as write an acceptable thesis. If he had another career in mind, would he have gone so far in his law studies?

In an earlier letter he had quoted Goethe to the effect that nothing that makes one happy is illusion; Pierre found that rather shocking. So his son was obliged to qualify that. He wasn't suggesting a hedonistic approach to life, he averred; total happiness could be found only in heaven, or else why go there?

Nor was he likely to turn his back on his province. But did his father not remember how irresistible Paris was, and to young people in particular? "It is certain that I'd rather live in Paris than in Nantes. . . . But that is a matter of habit, and with my character, as you know, you can be happy wherever you happen to be!" There would be a difference: In Paris, he wouldn't miss Nantes, but in Nantes, he'd miss Paris a little—which wouldn't prevent him from living in Nantes all the same.

He regretted that the provinces clung to such false notions about the literary world; writers could also keep their heads on their shoulders. Even if he were to pursue his literary efforts, they could only be ancillary. His father had questioned if Jules expected to become a member of the august French Academy, to be an honored poet or novelist. "If I could become anything of the sort, dear papa, you'd be the first to push me in that direction, and the first to be proud of me! Because there is no better status you can have in the world!"[2]

Alas, the wonderful perspective provided by these letters is occasionally obscured by the misguided good intentions of family biographer Marguerite Allotte, who published them, but only after rewriting whole passages and adding or subtracting phrases in order to save the Verne family's honor, religion, and even the reputation of Nantes. She may have done more than that. In the case of eleven of these letters published by her—the originals of which have never been unearthed—Dumas, the editor of the unexpurgated correspondence, found significant details never mentioned in letters whose originals exist and can be consulted.

It almost makes one doubt that the young law student actually met that other literary lion who shared the Paris stage with Victor Hugo—Alexandre Dumas—even though Marguerite Allotte's version indicates such a meeting. In a remark that is almost an afterthought, Verne wrote on February 8, 1849: "You see that old Dumas, who I see occasionally, and his son who gives me tickets to concerts and other things haven't kept me from the delights of Roman law."[3] Fortunately, more palpable evidence exists for these encounters between the literary giant Dumas and the shy young man from Nantes.

A prolific playwright in the 1830s, "old" Alexandre Dumas was known by the mid-1800s as the creator of *The Count of Monte Cristo* and *The Three Musketeers*. He had only recently built his own theater on that favorite promenade of playgoers, the boulevard du Temple, to stage his own plays (among others); he called it the Théâtre Historique. Marguerite Allotte quotes Jules describing the opening of a dramatization of the first part of *The Three Musketeers*. He was seated in the famous writer's own box ("some honor!") and was present to hear the irrepressible author's running comment on his own play. "He couldn't help telling us what was going to happen," Jules wrote home. Everybody who counted dropped by the box to greet the author. Jules confessed that he enjoyed it all.[4]

Verne's actual letters allow us to see through the facade the son has created for his parents' sake; yet sometimes he didn't fear to trifle with their convictions. Jules drew a lucky number in the military lottery—which meant that he would not have to serve in the army. His father seemed to regret this. "You should already know, dear papa, what I think of the military life, and of these domestic servants in livery. . . . You have to abandon all dignity to perform such functions." He never wavered in those feelings.[5]

The letters also reveal that he was not able to rid himself of his hypochondria—and sometimes he seemed to realize that this was what was really wrong with him. "Cholera has definitely arrived in Paris, and I seem to be in the grip of the anguish of an imaginary invalid," he wrote to his mother in March 1849, in an allusion to Molière's famous character. Cases of the disease reported up until then were benign, but the difficulty of being treated immediately, if the situation arose, worried him. He beseeched his mother to send him some courage. "As I thought it wise to protect myself against any possibility of colitis, I've been wearing grandma's rabbit skin on my stomach day and night. . . ."

Unfortunately Edouard Bonamy, still a fellow student and a neighbor, was returning to Nantes, "so that if the sickness catches you at night"— Verne was referring to himself, of course—"one wouldn't know whom to notify right away!"

In early April, he was reassured: The press reported a diminishing of the epidemic. Yet five nights earlier, he'd really been frightened, thinking he'd caught the disease. He had since changed his eating habits. His previous breakfast regime had been causing diarrhea; now he was drinking hot chocolate and taking enemas laced with starch, and eating bread only when it was stale. He had also begun dining out to find good meat—at a cost of 2.50 francs per meal.[6]

❧ ☙

ALTHOUGH ONE CANNOT BE SURE ABOUT THE DEGREE OF IN-timacy between Jules Verne and Alexandre Dumas, there is no doubt that Jules had soon established an auspicious relationship with Dumas's son. Born out of wedlock on July 27, 1824, Alexandre Dumas fils (as he was to be called all his life) was thus Jules Verne's senior by nearly four years. And he was already a successful author. Just a year earlier in 1848, the publication of his novel *Camille (La Dame aux camélias)* made him famous overnight—this even before the successful stage version, and the outpouring of popular plays that followed in the decades to come; he would become *the* dramatist of the Second Empire, and the academician his father never was.

In fact, the son of the great Dumas was obliged early in life to earn his own living because of his father's continually disastrous financial situation (caused by undiscerning generosity as well as badly planned business ventures). Alexandre fils seemed to have inherited some of his elder's generosity. He took up the cause of twenty-one-year-old Jules Verne, and certainly pushed him in the right directions. "I may say that he was my first protector," Jules confessed later.

According to the younger man's recollection, it was Dumas fils who introduced him to Dumas père, this at the time the elder Alexandre was running his own theater. Although Jules Verne's name stands alone as author of the play *Broken Straws,* he acknowledged that the younger Dumas had helped him in the writing, as he would for a later play, *Eleven Days of Siege (Onze jours de siège)*. Soon *Broken Straws* was being rehearsed at the Théâtre Historique.[7]

Charles Lemire, Jules Verne's first biographer, offers an idyllic picture of two young men, Jules Verne and Alexandre Dumas fils, working together on *Broken Straws* at the home of Dumas père. That would be the ill-fated "castle" of Monte Cristo, a confusion of styles and centuries constructed for Dumas not far from Paris at nearby Saint-Germain-en-Laye, but which he would quickly lose (as he'd lose his theater and so many other possessions) in one or another debt settlement. The centerpiece was an outrageous Renaissance-style manor, a touch romantic and a touch baroque, and heavily Oriental, with a minaret outside and arabesque decor within.

The young men worked on a table in the English-style garden; evenings, they'd be joined by a coterie of other young and would-be authors come to sit at their host's feet. The elder Dumas, whose own paternal grandmother had been an African slave in Santo Domingo, would stash away the manuscript of whatever serialization he was working on, then roll up his sleeves to concoct a perfect omelette or whip up a magical mayonnaise.[8] (Dumas was *also* the author of a *Dictionnaire de Cuisine*.)

Most of the time, Dumas père's young guest was very careful about what he put in his mouth, and careful to report the details to attentive parents back home. "I'm quite well!" Jules wrote to his dear mama on a cold, windy, and rainy day in mid-November 1849. "Yesterday, exceptionally, I didn't have a stomach ache all day!" He was taking his meals (expensively) in a café, dining at his favorite bistro. "I don't have a drop of Seine river water in my body!" Instead, he was drinking beer, though not liking it; he felt like a German student, a hero of Schiller: "I lack only a pipe, and a pointed cap, since I already have the beard."

Mornings, his porter on rue de l'Ancienne Comédie was carrying up cold veal (well done) and hot chocolate (made from a chocolate he supplied); the result was a meal costing half what it would come at a restaurant. "Thus for room and breakfast I spend about sixty francs a month. As often as possible I dine for 32 sols [a little over 1.50 francs]. Let papa add it all up for the accounting makes me dizzy."[9]

The point, of course, was to hang on, to survive in Paris, protecting his fragile stomach, getting through law, working at least as hard at the job he preferred—writing. To pursue what he wished to do, he needed to convince his family that he was also doing what they expected him to do—and doing it cheaply.

While Jules felt it necessary to temper his enthusiasm in letters home, his head was full of the literary life, theater life. Plays when successful provided immediate rewards. Authors shared in box office receipts, so that a long run in a crowded theater meant fortune, if not always fame, and a provincial's justification for deserting his province.

Most of his contemporaries were not writing lasting literature, of course, but shallow, stereotyped comedies about money and marital squabbles. In these, the essence of the problem was usually outlined in the opening scene by all-knowing domestic servants who reappeared at intervals for further disabused commentary, occasional comic relief, and more earthy flirtations than their masters would dare. But even if the plays were not irresistible, the consequences of getting them onstage and keeping them there certainly were. A provincial living on borrowed time was unlikely to turn away from boulevard comedy if that might offer the key to independence.

Verne was also pursuing his interest in music. In later years, he would mention his earlier association with two famous composers, Victor Massé and Léo Delibes.[10] Usually, however, he passed his time with lesser-known musical friends who never achieved fame. "The recollections of his friends of the time," remembered a contemporary, "show him as a handsome young man with a small blond beard, in Paris supposedly to study law, in reality to write, but for the moment contenting himself with the writing of words for the music of his comrade [Aristide] Hignard."[11] Another contemporary noted that Hignard's room was then on the same floor as his friend Jules's, and the two would pass from one to the other without bothering to shut the doors.

All of Jules's friends were bachelors, and they seemed committed to remain such. Perhaps Jules's mother felt that celibacy was as sad for women as it was for men, for in a letter attributed to Jules, he wrote that if it's pitiful for women, "I can't imagine a happier condition for a man. . . ."[12]

There is also an oft-quoted letter from Jules to his childhood friend Ernest Genevois, who was getting married in Nantes. In the letter, he wrote, "Anyway, if you persist, despite my formal recommendation . . . to commit the worst of all stupidities a young man can commit, remember that sooner or later I'll be called on to console your wife. You know my tastes; please choose her accordingly."[13] The story has come down to us of the weekly dinner attended by Jules and other young bachelors; these young men gathered to enjoy one another's company and match wits. Verne's specialty at the time was said to be risqué verse.[14]

Whether or not such wit could entertain a paying audience was another question entirely. The time had come to find out; the comedy Verne had been writing under the watchful gaze of the two Dumas, father and son, would provide the means to do so. The Théatre Historique had been built precisely so that the elder Dumas could produce plays he liked—both his own and the work of young hopefuls.

This first public exposure for Verne was hardly likely to enhance the reputation of Dumas's theater, or of his young protégé. It was a one-act play in verse—a demanding medium, but the one in which Jules still felt most at home. Faithful to convention, the flimsy story was introduced by sassy and wise domestic servants. An old count who is jealous of his young wife keeps her locked up, refusing to buy her the necklace she craves. So they "break straws"; henceforth, the first to accept something—however insignificant—from the other loses the wager.

Predictably, there is considerable sparring on the part of each of them to oblige the other to accept some trifle. When the count suspects correctly that his wife has a lover hidden in a closet, he demands the key; when she hands it over and he accepts it, he loses the wager, and so he must give her the necklace. Later, Jules would say that the subject had been suggested to him originally by the younger Dumas; likewise, he said that if it had "some very pretty things" in it, they, too, came from Dumas.[15]

The play got its first airing on June 12, 1850, between midnight and one in the morning, the occasion a fund-raising evening sponsored by a famous actress. Parisian audiences welcomed young playwrights, and thanks to his friends and the hostesses of his favorite literary salons, the twenty-two-year-old Nantais had his supporters. Apparently, the play was considered good enough to continue for an extended run, and the production was moved to the Gymnase theater, where it was performed along with a full-length play.[16]

Of course, there was an audience of one back in Nantes to deal with: His father wanted to read the play at least. In a letter dated June 28, Jules promised to send it just as soon as he could get it printed, which Dumas fils was helping to arrange. "Then you can judge it for yourself. I never pretended that a mother could take her daughter to see it," he added defensively. "I'm not in charge of the education of virgins in France." His father would soon be able to see for himself how the subject had been treated and "rescued"—a clear reference to his helper, Dumas fils. The play had brought in a little money—approximately the sum it had cost him to get it ready for production. "So I sacrificed everything for literary success," he explained to his father, "which was better than financial success—the money will come later."[17]

"The straws," as he'd call it, was staged in Nantes on the seventh of November in a playhouse he knew well, the Grand Théâtre on place Graslin, and the town dressed up for the event. "Our theater offered an uncustomary aspect last night," wrote a local critic. "An eager crowd, anxious to see *Les Pailles rompues,* came to hail the beginnings of a cherished compatriot." The crowd was not disappointed.[18]

5

APPRENTICESHIP

Like a balloon ascending into the sky, shed of its ballast, Jules Verne was now launched. He would still have much dead weight to cast away—the constraints of family and society in Nantes, the relics of a proper education. To rise still higher, he would toss out even more ballast: the legal career to which he was ostensibly dedicated, then certain stock-market work that was intended to provide him with the financial security lawyering could not.

But this came later. At the beginning of the 1850s, his flight had been only a trial launching, the play in Alexandre Dumas's theater the first stage of a slow ascent.

More than ten years of apprenticeship would follow, probably one of the longest recorded for a creative artist. During this period, there would be many false starts, but each would carry its own lesson, offering further training for the great flight.

THE FIRST WEEKS OF 1851 FOUND JULES STILL IN PARIS, AS if he were unable to leave. This was not what his family expected of him; he was to get his law degree, return home, and begin a legal career. "You mention my diploma, dear papa," he wrote casually on January twenty-second, "but I received it quite some time ago . . . ; all that remains is the swearing in process, a matter of fifty francs."[1]

Verne knew that his parents wanted his reply and that they were entitled to it, and before the week was over, he gave it. "I'm working, and if my work leads nowhere right away, I'll just wait!" he declared, with youthful confidence. "Please don't think that I'm having fun; I'm held in place by fate. I could become a good literary person, but only a bad lawyer, seeing only the comical side and the artistic form of things. . . ."

Of course he still depended on his family's money. But the time would soon come when that support would simply be in the form of a loan. For the moment, and perhaps for some time to come, his best hope seemed to be the stage. Later, this error would be blamed on the young man's loyalty to his fellow townsman Aristide Hignard, surely a good and a generous friend (his father was a prosperous shipper back in Nantes) and a capable musician, but not an imposing one. For some time, Jules would link his career to Hignard's in the creation of inconsequential musical plays on which they collaborated, those comic operas or operettas of which mid-nineteenth century Paris could not seem to get its fill. There were also romantic plays and tragedies, leftovers from student days; it seems that Jules had taken them along in his baggage and would have liked to see them staged. Yet he knew he could not count on getting them onto the boards just then, "because they are dramas and there is no place for literary drama today. . . ." If the public wanted comedy, he'd give them comedy.[2]

He continued to remind his parents—especially when writing to his dear mama—of his fragility: He'd been to see his doctor, he reported in February 1851, and had been given charcoal and bismuth, which were prescribed for diarrhea. Still, he could not afford to move into a proper boardinghouse that served home-cooked meals. "When I earn money I'll eat better, and that's that."

In an aside intended for his father, he said: "I'll be sworn in [as an attorney] as soon as papa desires; I'm quite ready."[3] He could be admitted to the Paris bar as soon as he had a place of his own in which to live and work. Thus, he began to make a strong case for a Paris apartment; he promised to consider the money he obtained from home as a loan and pay interest on it, and ultimately, it would be cheaper than temporary student quarters.[4]

Looking at a photograph of Jules Verne from this period is a jolting experience. He appeared so frail and mousy in letters home, yet so affirmative as he posed for the photograph: arms crossed in an aggressive stance, his handsome head held high, a strong nose and mouth, slightly unruly hair. He would always look stronger than he was.

NATURALLY, ANY AND ALL WRITING WAS A HELPFUL EXER-
cise for this young writer. Even those plays written during his high school
years and the inconsequential, instantly forgettable comedies written as a
young adult served to hone his skills, and would later result in the crisp,
impudent dialogue that is a hallmark of his best-known stories, those in
which a small group of friendly enemies would go up in the sky together,
or share a sailing ship, or journey around the world.

By this point, the process by which this neophyte writer would become
a renowned author had begun. The catalyst was a man known by his nom
de plume, Pitre-Chevalier, in real life Pierre Chevalier, another expatriate
from Brittany. He, too, had gone to the Little Seminary in Nantes at a
tender age, then to the Collège Royal. Chevalier had been the publisher
of the old *Le Figaro* when it was a satirical weekly before becoming editor
of a monthly home magazine founded in 1833, *Musée des Familles,* of which
he was also part owner.[5] A purveyor of popular culture and popular science
for adults as well as for educated youngsters, *Musée des Familles* published
such articles as "Physics—Stories and Applications of the Barometer."[6]

On taking charge of the magazine in 1849, Pitre-Chevalier announced
his intentions for the publication: "We've a complete program of contemporary education," he proclaimed without undue modesty. "Who will
be today's best trained young man, young woman, or man of the world?
It will be those at home with religion, philosophy, ethics, and who will
know history from the literature, creation and civilization through travel,
science, and the arts, society by observation of manners and character."[7]
Contributors to *Musée des Familles* were expected to adopt a tone of
high seriousness and demonstrate that their articles were grounded in
personal experience or earnest research; even the fiction was to be instructive.

Jules Verne could accept those guidelines, and he became a contribu-
tor of fictional pieces. In a reference to his first story to be published in
Pitre-Chevalier's magazine, "The First Ships of the Mexican Navy" ("Les
Premiers Navires de la Marine Mexicaine"), he described it to his father
as having been written in the style of James Fenimore Cooper, who had
died that very year—1851—and whose work would be one of Jules's earliest and most lasting inspirations.

He faced a challenge: Could he begin to earn money, to prove himself
in his chosen vocation, before his parents' patience and funding evaporated? A letter written in confidence to his mother in March 1851 is revelatory; she had sent him some money, and he used it to pay his doctor.

"Certainly papa wouldn't have refused to pay for these doctor's visits, but that would have raised the question of my subsistence again, and it's already expensive enough. . . ." Jules did not hesitate to appeal to his mother for pity: "I've been rather ill with intestinal trouble and all these problems have a lot to do with my being sick!"

In the contest between father's rule and son's determination, time seemed to be running out. Before he had a chance to publish or perform further work, he was being asked to choose between law and whatever else he wished to do. "Literature above all, because only in that will I succeed in life, since my mind is set on the subject! . . . Sooner or later, whether I do law for two years or not, if my two careers are pursued simultaneously one will kill the other, and to my mind the bar has little hope of surviving."

To leave Paris now for the two-year apprenticeship his father was offering in Nantes would lose all his contacts. When he came back, he would have to begin all over again, but with less passion and force. And to stay in Paris working as a law clerk meant incredibly long hours—from seven-thirty in the morning until nine at night, and this without hope of earning a cent for a long, long time.

So Jules was not choosing between wealth or penury. "You tell me, dear papa, that Dumas and others don't have a penny. That's because they lack order, not money. Alexandre Dumas earns his 300,000 francs a year. His son, without difficulty, 12 to 15,000 francs, Eugène Sue is a millionaire, Scribe four times a millionaire, Hugo has 25,000 francs in income. . . ."[8] His linkage of "order" and "money" further suggests that "orderliness, parsimony, and obstinacy" are traits characteristic of Jules's anal personality.[9]

He asked for a vote of confidence and sufficient money to enable him to rent an apartment and furnish it. Before the end of March 1851, Pierre had acquiesced, and his son was busy shopping for furnishings—quickly exceeding the budget he himself had drawn up. But he was also writing— he had finished his opera and was making progress on a comedy. Now he could begin to look for a theater.

What in other circumstances might have been bad news was to have no effect on his plans. An attorney for whom he was to have served as clerk died, removing any obligation he may have felt to pursue the law in Paris. The funeral prompted some subversive thoughts about religion, and he felt free enough now to share them with his devout father. "Can it be said that a rich man whose family can pay for lots of prayers, masses, services, etc., has a better chance of getting out of purgatory faster than a poor devil whose decease made nobody richer?"[10]

꧁ ꧂

ACTUALLY, JULES HAD EVERYTHING HE WANTED NOW, AS much as he dared hoped for; he could begin to live *la vie parisienne* in earnest. "At last I'm going to move around," he told his mother, "and I'll be rather surprised if I don't obtain definitive and lucrative results." He could even contemplate marriage again, this member of an inveterate bachelors' club. "I'll marry the woman you find for me," he promised his mother. "I'll marry with closed eyes and open purse; choose somebody, dear mama, I mean it."[11]

Through the mayor of Nantes, Evariste Colombel, Jules was introduced to someone who would have a decisive influence on him. Jacques Arago was not only famous in his own right but was also the brother of other astounding Aragos—the oldest and most prominent of them being the physicist and astronomer François, an inventor known for scientific breakthroughs. Then there was Etienne, a writer, theater devotée, politician and esthete, and Jean, a general who fought for Mexican independence.

No less versatile, Jacques Arago was an indefatigable explorer, a travel writer, and a popular playwright. By the time Jules met him, he had dozens of books in all genres to his credit, including works of history and a true story whose title translates as *Promenade Around the World in 1817, 1818, 1819, and 1820 Aboard the Royal Corvettes* Uranie *and* La Physicienne *Commanded by Mr. [Claude de] Freycinet.* Arago was sixty-one years old, blind, and yet still active.[12]

Surely Jules had read or thumbed through the five volumes of still another Arago work, *Voyage Around the World,* qualified as *Memoirs of a Blind Man,* which was illustrated with detailed studies of foreign faces and costumes. The caption under the frontispiece portrait of Jacques Arago connects him with his more famous brother: "Your name is the echo of the renown of your brother: To François the sky, the globe for the other."

Jacques Arago's style must have spoken to Jules. Eschewing didactics, his descriptions of far-off lands evoked the direct speech of the boulevard plays Arago had composed between journeys. He argued that travel books, when the explorer avoided pedantry, were second only to memoirs as the most interesting of all books, with a minimum of description and a maximum of pithy dialogue. "I have tried to lead you across the steppes, through virgin forests, deep inside black lava thrown into the sky by undersea revolutions," Arago explained in the preface to his final volume. "I accompanied you from one continent to another, from a calm and scented island chain to a rough and wild one. . . ."[13] He actually published a theatrical version of his adventures, in which the letter *a* did not appear once in the text.

Verne and Arago became fast friends, the provocative traveler and boulevardier and the would-be author. Though blind, Arago took pains to guide the younger man through unfamiliar territory, even helping him to collect furniture and equipment for his new flat. Within six weeks of their meeting, Arago suggested that they do a play together. Jules was also writing a play with the editor of *Musée des Familles*. "Pitre-Chevalier is a serious fellow and encourages me a great deal," Jules told his father. "He told me that of the four or five hundred young men who had come to him for advice since he was in a position to give advice, I was one of the three or four he advised to persevere."

By the beginning of the summer of 1851, Jules had not one but two pieces ready for publication in Pitre-Chevalier's *Musée des Familles*. "And so, dear papa," he wrote on June 29, "since I'm destined to contribute often to this magazine I suggest that you take out a subscription."[14]

Jules Verne's first published work of prose was a curious hybrid—a mix of the real and the imagined, much like the novels to come. "The First Ships of the Mexican Navy," with illustrations, filled nine pages of the large-format *Musée des Familles*. Billed as a work of history, it was told in dialogue, like the fiction it really was.

The story contains a date—October 18, 1825—in the opening sentence, a technique its author would use again and again to lend authenticity. Having wrested independence from Spain, Mexico was then a rough, struggling country. The scene is the far Pacific, where two Spanish ships are moored off an island in the Mariana chain. Their ill-fed, poorly paid crews are on the verge of mutiny. One of the Spanish captains, Don Orteva, has been particularly hard on his men; an officer and one of his sailors conspire to kill him, then to seize both vessels and sell them to Mexico, which had no navy at all.

After carrying out their crime they sail to Southern California, the rebel lieutenant and his henchman pursuing the journey overland to negotiate the sale of the ships in Mexico City. But they have been followed by a young midshipman loyal to the murdered Captain Orteva, and he has been joined by a petty officer. Their cross-country adventure allows Jules Verne his first descriptions of a luxuriant, often-hostile landscape, all the while offering lessons on natural features—the precise height of a mountain, the latitude of a mountain chain.

Before reaching his goal, Orteva's assassin has turned on his own accomplice in a mad rage, killing him. He in turn falls to his death when the loyal Spanish officers chop down a high vine-rope bridge over which he sought to ford a mountain stream. Triumphantly, they have revenged their captain, Don Orteva, and all of Spain.[15]

PART II

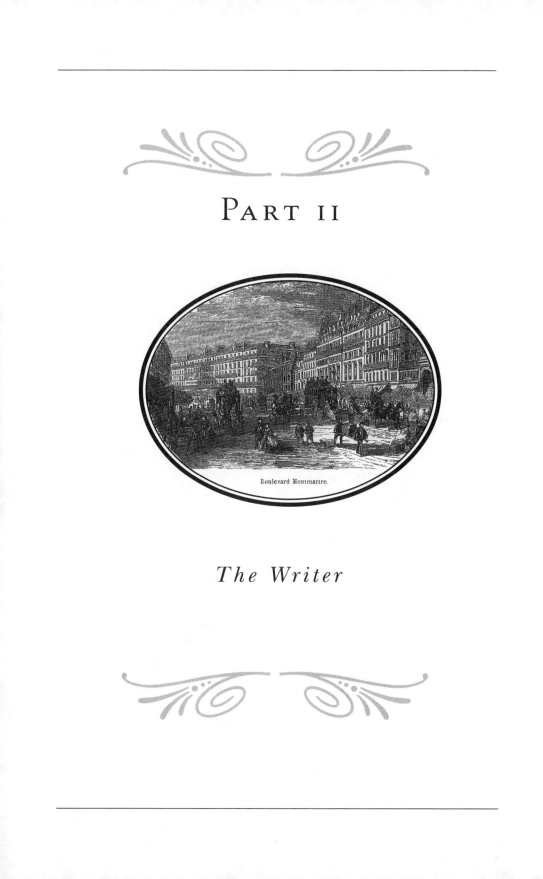

Boulevard Montmartre.

The Writer

6

New Science
and Old Music

L ATE IN LIFE, TALKING TO THE ENGLISH JOURNALIST ROBERT
Sherard about another story he published in *Musée des Familles,* Jules
Verne recalled that this account of "a madman in a balloon" was the first
indication of the "line of novel" he was destined to follow.[1] Interestingly,
he remembers the little horror tale and not the more ambitious "First
Ships of the Mexican Navy," which appeared in the magazine a month
earlier.

Always with the idea of teaching something—in the tradition of most
nineteenth-century family magazines—Pitre-Chevalier ran this second
piece by Verne under the heading "Science in the Family: A Balloon
Trip." It was accompanied by illustrations of ancient balloons designed
for navigation; nowhere was it pointed out that this was another piece of
fiction. On the contrary, a footnote indicated that this "article" comple-
mented, "in a dramatic form," a history of balloon flight previously published in the same magazine.

Again, Verne included a date and a place name in order to add
verisimilitude: "In the month of September 1850 I arrived in Frankfurt
on the Main." The narrator is a pilot who has planned what should have
been an uneventful ascent—until he discovers a stowaway hidden in the
balloon's gondola. The unwanted passenger turns out to be a madman
fascinated by lighter-than-air flight; he has brought along a weighty volume containing a collection of illustrations of earlier flights, and he pro-

ceeds to explain them, all the while capriciously tossing out sacks of sand ballast—causing the balloon to rise higher and higher. Before the odyssey has ended, the stowaway has cut the cables linking the balloon's envelope to the gondola; he falls to certain death, while the hapless narrator hangs on, descending eventually to safety.[2]

It is tempting to speak of influences. Edgar Allan Poe wrote brief thrillers about balloon travel and Jules Verne read them and everything else by the American writer he could get his hands on. Of course, magazines such as *Musée des Familles* were familiarizing lay readers—including Jules Verne—with the most notable scientific advances.

An important difference between the dissemination of scientific information in Verne's time and in our own is that the principal innovations of the nineteenth century could be explained in a family magazine. Turning the pages now, one is virtually seated alongside Jules Verne, for here are reports of discoveries he must have been reading, since he adapted some of them—almost immediately—for his stories. In a single generation, as Jules Verne grew to adulthood, machines were replacing muscle and airwaves supplanted keen eyes and ears. That so many things suddenly became possible suggested to the prescient that more and better inventions lay just around the corner. In the context of his time, Jules Verne's stories anticipated reality, sometimes by only a few years. Hindsight reveals just how advanced his thinking was.

Publishing in Pitre-Chevalier's magazine could not pay the rent, or support a marriage, if it came to that. The theater remained a more promising road to advancement. In the months following the publication of his first stories, Jules can be seen worrying over, perfecting, and refining the slight boulevard comedies he was depending on to justify his decision to stay in Paris. In the autumn of 1851, letters home show what really occupied his thoughts: a one-act comedy. Sending his only copy to his father for comment, he explained: "I've been having stomach aches and cramps for the past few days! Probably I've worked too hard on my comedy, and it exhausted me." There was more correcting to do, but he had high hopes for his play; he felt it had something in it of Molière, and he was going to try to get it accepted by the Comédie Française— Molière's theater.

It soon became clear why he was anxious to have an opinion from his parents in Nantes. Thanking Pierre for his comments on the play, Jules added that his father had been somewhat severe. "That is probably because you think I wanted to make fun of religion, when I didn't have that in mind at all!" he insisted. "I consider religion something respectable, and I respect it." But he had deleted what his father felt to be unhappy phrasing.[3] Expressing impious thoughts and then striking them out would become a habit when he found a publisher sensitive to the sensibilities of his subscribers.

Jules had a new and alarming physical symptom now. Although the precise date is not known, autumn 1851 has been suggested. A description of his initial attack of facial paralysis is not very thorough, but the first known letter that refers to it describes the aftereffects. For a while, it had left one side of his face contorted; then things apparently improved. "My face has reassumed its majestic features," he informed his mother; "it smiles on both sides, pouts at will, and can boo the best plays in the world." He had been cured, he added, by electricity—although the treatment itself brought on a fever.

Olivier Dumas, who as president of the Jules Verne Society and a physician reviewed Verne's medical history from a century's distance, while convinced that there was more than a touch of hypochondria with regard to Verne's stomach complaints, considered these attacks of facial paralysis as real. A motor disorder, this dysfunction of the facial nerve may have been caused by muscular pressure due to inflammation of the middle ear. It was painless, although momentarily disfiguring, and certainly distressing to a young man far from home.[4]

THE POLITICAL CLIMATE IN FRANCE HAD BEEN REASONABLY quiet ever since the return of Louis Napoléon from exile in the aftermath of the 1848 revolution. As "prince-president," the nephew of Napoléon Bonaparte held republicans at bay in the name of the Second Republic. During the elections held in 1849, Louis Napoléon's allies in the aptly named Party of Order showed that they continued to hold the country. But a strong minority of true republicans remained unimpressed, and Louis Napoléon resolved to deal with them the way his uncle might have. By the time of the coup d'état of December 2, 1851, the prince-president gave himself the power to muzzle the opposition.

"Not an instant of trouble in Paris," Jules reassured his family the next day. Street gatherings had been "inoffensive"; the police had not even bothered to break them up. He showed his practical side: "If the stock market falls you'd do well to buy government bonds, dear papa. These are opportunities one is always sorry to have missed."

As it turned out, he had spoken too quickly. There was a thinking minority after all, prepared to defend hard-won freedoms and aware of the inevitable repression to come. On December fourth, Jules wrote from

Paris: "All the shops are closing. Barricades are being thrown up everywhere; people are being arrested and dragged along by horses." Members of the parliament had been killed. He was staying out of trouble, he promised his family back in Nantes, but was very uncertain as to what might happen next.[5]

Jules had the answer before his letter could have traveled very far from Paris. Fighting broke out that very day within the city; on his own street, cannon shot damaged buildings. It was enough to make a rebel even of Jules Verne. "These are shameful things," he told his mother in a letter two days later, "and everyone is angry at the president [Louis Napoléon] and against the army, which in this circumstance dishonored itself. It's perhaps the first time that justice and legality are on the side of the insurrection. Many people have been killed, and they were of the decent kind."

That was a turnaround for Verne son of Verne, lifelong conservative and proud of it (but it was true that Bonaparte was not a proper monarch). Jules was at least as much a libertarian as a believer in law and order, a fact clearly reflected in his novels.[6] But for the moment, he was doing and saying nothing (one could be locked up for loose talk). He had gone out to reconnoiter his terrain—the boulevards—finding the streets lined with soldiers, cavalry, and artillery. Everywhere, facades had been damaged by the shelling. His parents had given him some shopping chores, but he found them impossible to carry out.[7]

In a matter of days, the agitation was over. Just a year after the December second coup, Louis Napoléon would be proclaimed emperor of the French. He pronounced himself Napoléon III and ushered in the Second Empire. France then settled down for nearly two decades of serenity. For the more militant, including some writers and journalists, it was a lobotomized serenity, escape from which required voluntary exile. Victor Hugo was one such volunteer, although when he began attacking the government in pamphlets published beyond French borders, his self-exile became banishment.

Without roots in Paris or a cause to embrace, Jules Verne could hardly be blamed for resuming his routine existence. If there was a threat, it was posed by a well-meaning proposal from Nantes. Pierre Verne, now in his fifty-second year, was offering his son nothing less than his law practice. The offer had serious implications, and it had to be dealt with tactfully. Jules told his father that friends with whom he discussed the matter agreed that anybody not in Jules's shoes would have to be mad not to accept. But he *was* in his shoes; he had come to Paris to write. And he was sure that even if his father tried to protect him from his impulses by settling him in a comfortable office in Nantes, he would find a way to escape again.

In the meantime, he was offered a job as private secretary to the director of the Théâtre Lyrique, also known as the National Opera, which he described to his family as "one of Paris's great theaters." The position would necessarily put him in contact with the directors of other theaters, as well as with journalists and authors. He expected to receive a modest salary, but there he was to be disappointed.

Of course he was grateful to his father for his generous offer, and for having sustained him in Paris until now. "But am I not right to follow my own instincts? It's because I know who I am that I realize what I can be one day. . . ." How, then, could he take on the law practice his father had built up so well, knowing that it would only wither away in his hands?[8]

Jules was right, of course, but he was a late bloomer, and it would take him a full decade to prove that his decision had been a correct one.

Meanwhile he had to be satisfied with small things, and the promise of others to come. Working for Pitre-Chevalier's magazine was almost the best he could do. Waiting for signs of recognition, and knowing how far he would have to go before being able to justify his rejection of a stable career, might have accounted for his constant complaints—violent stomach cramps and fever one day, headaches another, or "a kind of nervous attack," which he blamed on a violent thunderstorm.

Yet he kept working. He contributed new pieces to *Musée des Familles,* including a story entitled "Martin Paz," whose setting in Peru demanded considerable research on topography, customs, and climate. He was using the library a great deal—presumably the national library, a place of "inexhaustible resources," as he would tell his father. Research would occupy much of his time in the preparation of his later *Extraordinary Voyages (Voyages Extraordinaires).*[9]

In June 1852, *Musée des Familles* published the product of his collaboration with the magazine's editor, "Les Châteaux en Californie" ("Castles in California"), described as a one-act "comedy-proverb." The authors were listed as Pitre-Chevalier and Jules Vernes (with a final *s*); the grateful apprentice didn't point out the misspelling, so it was repeated the next month with his story "Martin Paz." This mistake was not as blatant, though, as when his name appeared on the list of collaborators published at the beginning of the year; there his name appeared as Charles Verne.[10]

In this small play, whose story line came from Pitre-Chevalier, Parisian architect François Dubourg has gone to California to prospect for gold, while at home his wife is already spending the money she expects him to bring back. Madame Dubourg has also told Henri, her daughter's suitor, a man of modest means, that since they are now rich, he doesn't have a chance at winning her daughter's hand.

Dubourg returns in rags, pretending to be penniless, but in an aside, he tells the audience that indeed he has become rich. He encourages Henri in his suit, rather than his rival, a Russian prince. Then Dubourg learns that the banker to whom he has entrusted all his funds is bankrupt—so he has lost everything after all. And the Russian prince turns out to be nothing more than his cook's nephew. Henri sums up the situation for the dismayed architect: "Poor and rich twice in a single day, you now know what castles in California are worth. . . . Nothing is lost, since you still have your head, and your family."[11]

It appears there may be more to the play than this simple plot, however. A few of Verne's readers believe they have uncovered in the final scene a series of references to Masonic rite, including the ruined architect's return to "a compass, a square, a plumb line." Such references appear to be more than coincidental, suggesting the possibility that one of the collaborators might have slipped them in slyly. It seems unlikely that it could have been the good Catholic Pitre-Chevalier, for Freemasonry was very much an untouchable subject at the time. One scholar suspects it was Jules, recalling his friendship with Aristide Hignard, an alleged Mason, just as Jacques Arago and Alexandre Dumas were also supposed to be.[12]

So portentous a message in so trivial a play would be surprising, so perhaps it is better to interpret the allusion to Freemasonry as ironic.[13] Most likely, Jules would not have dared to endorse the Masons and run the risk of having his father cut off his funds. He confided his own judgment of the play to his father soon after publication; he was unhappy with it, as with all such puerility. The illustrations had been done in advance, and he had been forced to write a script that fit them, even to add characters unnecessary to the action.[14]

There is no question that he wrote "Martin Paz" alone. It appeared in *Musée* in July 1852 under the imposing title "South America—Peruvian Customs: Martin Paz, a Historical Tale." Introducing the two-part story by his protégé, Pitre-Chevalier expressed the certitude that "our readers will appreciate . . . this work . . . in which all of Peru—its history, peoples, manners, landscapes, costumes, etc.—will be revealed by Jules Vernes [*sic*] in the course of a dramatic story in the tradition of [James Fenimore] Cooper."

The editor confessed to his readers that once again the illustrations had come first. A Peruvian painter then visiting Jacques Arago in Paris had done a series of watercolors depicting life in his country.

The time frame is more or less that of the period; the context is the continued domination of Peru's native population by descendants of the Spanish conquerors, and this after Peru had won its independence. The young Indian Martin Paz adores the typically Spanish beauty Sarah, known as the daughter of the Jewish usurer Samuel, but Sarah has been promised to a half-breed, André Certa. Paz wounds Certa while courting Sarah, then escapes, taking refuge with a kindly Spanish marquis. Meanwhile, Martin Paz's father organizes a revolt against the white ruling class. André Certa buys Sarah from her father, who then reveals to him that Sarah is really a Christian. In fact, she is the daughter of the marquis; the Jew Samuel had saved her from drowning as an infant perfidiously, keeping her and concealing her identity.

Paz persuades Sarah to flee with him, but the marquis thwarts their plan. Paz then joins the rebellion, but when he attempts to protect Sarah from his fellow Indians, his own father turns against him; Martin Paz dies trying to save Sarah, and she dies with him, baptizing him before she expires. Samuel keeps the money obtained from Sarah's would-be husband, "and continued his usury at the expense of the nobles of Lima."

Verne's tale is violent—set in a fictional South America, although one probably close enough to reality. His characters are stereotypes, but their cunning and anger, their revolt, and their motivations seem credible enough. Equally striking is the undisguised vehemence in the author's portrait of "the Jew," who shares the center of the stage with Martin Paz, his traitorous acts the cement that holds the action together. In a chapter entitled "The Jew Everywhere a Jew," Samuel is described as having hands like hooks. "This old man dealt in everything and everywhere; he descended from Judas who delivered his master for thirty pieces of silver."[15]

A student of Verne's political philosophy observed that few of his admirers realize that he was an anti-Semite, since they read only the best-known of his books, over which Verne's publisher exercised strict control. In fact, when that publisher decided to republish "Martin Paz," its chapter titles were eliminated—including, of course, "The Jew Everywhere a Jew."

It also might have been difficult to insert an unsympathetic Jew into the closed universe of *Twenty Thousand Leagues Under the Sea* (for example). Yet by the time Jules Verne wrote *Hector Servadac*, says the same authority, his paranoia was such that he could not restrain himself. He found Jews everywhere, even in outer space.[16]

It appears that no one has come up with a credible explanation for the violence in Verne's portrait of Samuel in "Martin Paz." Considerable intimate correspondence exists for this period, none of it containing a hint of bias. Nor do we have references to incidents, relationships, or even the experience of others among his family or friends involving Jews, and yet there were Jews in the literary and theatrical circles he frequented. The peddler's son Michel Lévy, for instance, published four of Verne's early plays. Writers who inserted anti-Semitism into their books usually manifested it in conversations and letters, but this was not true of Jules Verne.

One is tempted by the astounding hypothesis that the samples of literary anti-Semitism in "Martin Paz" and novels such as *Hector Servadac* were just that—literary. His Samuel in "Martin Paz," Isaac in *Hector Servadac*, and Nathan in *The Southern Star Mystery* have their precedent in Shakespeare's Shylock. In his Romantic period, even Victor Hugo—an idol of Verne's—portrayed Jews without sympathy in his dramas (*Cromwell* in 1827, *Marie Tudor* in 1833), although later he would make amends.[17]

There is also Walter Scott to consider, another of young Jules Verne's favorite authors. In *Ivanhoe*, Scott introduces Isaac and Rebecca—hard father, tender daughter (although, unlike Verne's Sarah in "Martin Paz," she is a genuine "daughter of Zion" and rejects conversion). Scott portrays an Isaac scorned by his fellows, but he also reminds readers that if Isaac is mean, it is because of persecution; he'd be a handsome figure if he didn't remind one of a detested race. Scott's Rebecca is "a combination of loveliness which yielded not to the most beautiful of the maidens who surrounded her." Prince John orders that room be made at the tournament for "my prince of usurers and his lovely daughter." Elsewhere in *Ivanhoe*, Scott decries bigotry; when Rebecca is to be tried as a sorceress, a character points out that Jewish doctors are not accused of being wizards, although they work wondrous cures.

"I'm happy with the article 'Martin Paz,'" Jules wrote home after publication of the second and last installment of the story in August 1852. "It was rather well received, and the end of the tale seemed quite welcome!"[18]

inevitable, an assistant intrudes, escorting a model Leonardo has
seeking for his portrait of Judas in the *Last Supper*. So the painter
ons his almost-mistress in order to set to work at once on the other
t.

rage, Monna Lisa declares her portrait finished and orders it to be
d away; Leonardo philosophizes that henceforth he will be content
he ideal image all poor poets carry in their heads. "This suits me
than reality!" he exclaims.

oung Jules's conclusion (as in his aged grandson's), the smile of La
da expressed both tenderness and scorn—scorn touched by pity—
artist who placed his vision above earthly love.[2]

WEREN'T OBLIGED TO REMAIN IN PARIS, DEAR PAPA, IT
do me much good and make me very happy to spend a month or
Nantes, for I'm quite exhausted after some bouts of fever of recent
. . . ." So Jules was to conclude his August letter. In another letter,
ing an attack of cramps, he wrote, "What a horrible stomach my
r gave me." And yet, he said, he led an exemplary life, apart from
to make do with bad meat.

worked, although he still had nothing to show for it. Despite his
be financially independent, his father's support was as necessary
. In fact, he had to clear up a misunderstanding about his income.
rents were under the impression that he was getting a salary for his
t the Théâtre Lyrique; he swore to them this was not the case. And
nis father seemed to doubt his word, Jules offered to prove his as-
n: The dramatists committee, of which he was a member, forbade a
r director to stage a play written by himself or one of his employees.
rder to get a play on to the stage of the Théâtre Lyrique, he would
remain a volunteer worker.

was clearly hurt by his parents' suspicions. A letter of December 2,
betrays an extraordinary relationship between a provincial father
om money matters appeared to override family solidarity and a son
ad not been able to cut the umbilical cord. Jules regretted that he
go to such lengths to convince his father that he was telling the
bout not getting paid for his work at the theater. Jules was sure that
ne in Nantes had been spreading this falsehood; whoever it was
came his mortal enemy, and he vowed he would have his revenge.
arrangement at the theater was a simple exchange of services. The
er needed Jules and Jules needed the manager—Jules would vol-

7

PENSIONER

seem
been
aban
proje
In
carri
with
bette
In
Joco
for a

"IF I
woul
two i
night
repo
moth
havin
He
wish
as eve
His p
work
since
sertio
theat
So in
have
He
1852,
for wl
who l
had t
truth
some
now l
His
mana

WHEN WRITING TO HIS FATHER JULES
him that he was confident about his career, but wl
provide details it was clear that he still had far to g
expressed high hopes for a comic opera—written t
his friend Aristide Hignard—whose words and m
cheerful."

His father wondered why he was not writing vers
was now hard at work on a play in verse then entit
comedy he described as being in the style of Alfred
one-act play, the manuscript of which is titled *Mo*
more than that.

Yet in scrutinizing Jules's play more than a centur
Jules-Verne, grandson of Jules Verne, thought l
misogyny, or at the very least a readiness to postpor
time as he could perfect his art. In *Monna Lisa* w
gling with his model's smile in a portrait commiss
husband.* As Leonardo labors, painter and mod
stead of declaring himself, Leonardo is distracted l
Monna Lisa's bracelet. When the tension rises

---

*Verne's own spelling is used here for the well-known port

unteer his time, and the manager would produce one of Jules's plays. Jules's work at *Musée des Familles* was the source for rumor: He received so little money for his articles, he was thinking of ceasing to write for Pitre-Chevalier at all.

Was Jules doing only what he felt like doing—as his dear papa alleged? If that were the case he'd have gone to visit his family a long time ago, and he'd be working at home rather than in the theater. The last time he'd been ill, he had nearly had a relapse because he had gone back to work against his doctor's advice. "It's because I knew that a longer absence would be harmful to my interests, and I'd rather die at the task than lose the benefit of all my sacrifices. . . ." He described a daily routine of strict obligation; even his social life was subordinate to dutiful visits. "In the way I go about my work and the means I employ to succeed, you can easily see that I am neglecting nothing that can be of use to me. . . ."[3]

The Théâtre Lyrique, on which Jules had pinned his hopes, occupied a high, narrow building with a loggia and sculpted facade on boulevard du Temple; it had been erected by the senior Alexandre Dumas just five years earlier. Despite a string of successes, Dumas had not been able to make his theater profitable. At that point, a major figure of the Paris stage, the Comédie Française's manager Edmond Seveste, annexed the building for use by what was then called the National Opera, created in 1847 to take some of the pressure from the famous Opéra and the Opéra Comique (hence its formal designation as the third lyrical theater.)[4] Although Jules was not paid, all the hard work fell to him; as secretary of the theater, he was responsible for all the hard work but did not share any of the glory. However, there would be a quid pro quo, the benefits of which were not long in coming. His comic opera *Blindman's Buff (Le Colin-Maillard)*—a collaboration with Michel Carré, with music again by Hignard— was accepted for performance at the theater. "Isn't that something!" he exulted; "It's a result of effort, but let's admit that it wasn't easy, and that even the slightest negligence could have made me lose the benefit of everything I had done until then."

Yet he was still dependent on his parents. Early in 1853 he would have to explain to his mother that he'd had six shirts made to order, for a total cost of six francs, for which he hoped his father would reimburse him, "for times are hard," he wrote. He was sending one of the new shirts to his mother as a model so that she could order a dozen more in Nantes, since those acquired in Paris were of skimpy material and wouldn't survive many washings.

Not long after, he berated her—in a jocular tone—for having lined up a possible fiancée with a splendid annual income; the young lady happened to be a Creole (white and French, but born and raised in France's tropical West Indies). That, he said, would be to unite Vesuvius and Etna (he being the former, the less active of the two volcanoes).[5] However, nothing came of what might have been a turning point in Jules's life.

"Find me a hunchbacked woman who has a good income—and you'll see," he would beseech his mother before the year was over.[6]

Life in Paris in the spring of 1853 gave him no respite. All evidence suggests that he still pursued two careers. First, he was the punctilious secretary of the Théâtre Lyrique, performing routine chores, such as handing out free passes to drama critics, as well as helping to mount a continuing round of featherweight comedies by the second echelon of boulevard authors and composers.[7] At the same time, he was rehearsing his new play, *Blindman's Buff,* a lighthearted skit in which a flirtatious, if mature, baron shares the stage with young couples who more naturally belong together; one fortuitous encounter finds him courting the woman he had abandoned years before; later, they will marry.[8] Jules described the work to his mother as quite "moral"; this time it was not in verse but in "vulgar prose."

Meanwhile, he had moved closer to the theater, renting a flat on boulevard Bonne-Nouvelle, in the middle of the chain of Grands Boulevards. It was a six-flight walk-up (he counted 120 steps)—"it's from here," he told his parents, "that this 25-year-old contemplates the marvels of the Boulevard, and the constant flow of that species of ants that is vulgarly called man."

One imagines him walking home, the applause ringing in his ears, on that April evening following the dress rehearsal of his one-act play, a difficult production to put on, given its cast of nine. Henceforth, he was sure, the doors of the more prestigious Opéra Comique would open for him, despite his father's persistent skepticism. Of course, his parents had focused on the poor reviews the play received, so a theater-wise Jules Verne had to explain that the carping articles were in the minority and an explanation could be found for each. The reviewer for *La Gazette de France,* for instance, had been trying without success to get one of his plays accepted by Jules's theater. Manager Jules Séveste, in any case, was enchanted, and at once asked Jules to give him a second play for the following year. *Blindman's Buff* was to be printed, but that wasn't the important thing; the important thing, or so he informed his mother in May, was to stay afloat. "If next winter I don't achieve something more solid it will be my fault; that would mean I'm just good enough to be a bad lawyer, a shouter, litigious, a first class quibbler."[9] Poor Jules underestimated the road he would have to travel.

He brooked no discouragement. There were good prospects for another production, of a one-act verse play, to be staged this time at the prestigious Odéon theater; he had another story ready for publication by *Le Musée des Familles,* whose editor had commissioned still another.

During the summer, Jules acquired a secondhand piano (getting it for 25 francs, to be paid out at the rate of five francs a month). Late in September 1853, he wrote his parents that *Blindman's Buff* was getting a fourth performance—"it's going quite well, and still pleasing audiences; as for me I rise at six in the morning and go to bed at ten at night; find someone more virtuous. . . ."[10] Before the end of the year, *Broken Straws* was back on the boards, bringing in a little income. Clearly he was wasting no time, and wished that to be known—both by his parents and an exigent theater director. Even to get home to Nantes required a letter from his parents saying that his presence was necessary for "business reasons"; he feared leaving Paris without sufficient reason might compromise his position at the Théâtre Lyrique.[11]

It is likely that the business requiring his presence in Nantes was courtship. Here at last was a candidate who, though not a hunchback, did have an assured income. Her name was Laurence Janmar; she was a young woman just a year his junior. Laurence was then boarding at a convent in Nantes while her parents were in Paris. One wonders whether Jules had some interest in her or if he was merely attracted by her wealth.

Nothing was resolved over the Christmas and New Year holidays. Jules's letters to Nantes in the spring of 1854 were still preoccupied with Laurence, indeed with marriage to anyone his mother could find for him. "I feel remarkably well," he wrote home on April seventh. "Decidedly my good health is quite restored; it's the perfect time to get married, my dear mother, so I ask you to get to work. Find the way to present me as a good husband, perfectly seasoned and cooked just right. . . ."[12]

8

ON NOT BREAKING ONE'S NECK AT AGE TWENTY-SIX

MAÎTRE ZACHARIUS, MASTER CLOCKMAKER, HIMSELF SEEM-ingly as old as time, is convinced that he cannot die as long as the fruits of his art survive. It is he who invented the principle of escapement, with a wheel device that controls the regularity of clock movement. On the rare occasions Zacharius leaves his ancient dwelling in medieval Geneva, it is to regulate his beloved handiworks; otherwise, he can be found in his basement workshop, or in the company of his chaste eighteen-year-old daughter, Gérande, his faithful assistant, Aubert, or his maidservant, Scholastique.

One day, Zacharius's ordered life is troubled. Suddenly, all the clocks created by the master begin to break down. When an owner of one of these clocks brings it to Zacharius, nothing can be found wrong with it. Zacharius is distraught. "Each time one of these accursed clocks stops," Gérande hears her father lament, "I feel my heart cease to beat, for I set them to its movements!"

In fact, pride had turned the head of the old clockmaker, but when his assistant warns him that this is sinful, Zacharius can only admit it is. He is sure that he has discovered the secret of life, the key to the mysterious union of body and soul. Then a curious dwarf, himself resembling a clock, begins to hound the old craftsman. The little creature announces that *he* is the artisan who governs time. In his dialogue with the mysterious stranger, Zacharius manifests more pride than ever; yet try as he might, he cannot repair all the clocks returned to his workshop.

Gérande cajoles her father into going to church; there, during a high Mass, a great clock he built fails to strike noon. Then he and his daughter, with his assistant who is now her fiancé, and faithful Scholastique, visit the Andernatt castle to see all that remains of his life's work. It is a clock modeled to resemble a church; its bells sound prayers. But the clock devil has gotten there first. As the timepiece strikes ten, a message appears on its silver dial in the shape of a church fronton: "Man can become the equal of God," it proclaims. At eleven o'clock, the fronton message pronounces another heresy: "Man must become the slave of science, and for this sacrifice parents and family."

Zacharius can only agree, for he realizes he has taken his daughter from her fiancé to give her to the clock devil, in exchange for this one clock that still works and for eternal life. But at midnight, the clock shatters, after announcing on its dial: "He who seeks to become the equal of God will be damned for eternity." Zacharius dies, and the clock devil disappears. Back home in Geneva, Gérande and Aubert devote themselves to prayer for the salvation of the master clockmaker.

On the surface, this story is an uplifting fable, in the tradition of medieval morality plays. Readers may have thought they were reading a tale by the German fantasist E. T. A. Hoffmann, who died in 1822. Present-day readers might also be reminded of Edgar Allan Poe, who died in 1849 at the age of forty. However, when "Maître Zacharius" was published in *Musée des Familles* (in the issues of April and May 1854), French translations of Poe's work had appeared only in scattered periodicals.

The first of the famous translations of Poe by Charles Baudelaire appeared in July 1848 in a journal launched during the euphoria of the 1848 revolt. The story was "Mesmeric Revelation," in which a doctor questions a patient under hypnosis about God and the universe; the patient continues to respond after he has apparently died. The next Baudelaire translation would not appear until April 1852 (in the popular publication *L'Illustration*). "Berenice" is a stark tale of the narrator's love for a frail epileptic young woman, whom he watches as she wastes away; he is fascinated by her dentition in an emaciated face. After her death, her tomb is violated, her face disfigured, and the reader discovers that the narrator has extracted her teeth. Nearly forty more Baudelaire translations of Poe were to appear in the next decade—published in popular newspapers and magazines that Jules Verne most likely would have seen.[1]

Jules, who was just twenty-six years old when he gave the manuscript of "Maître Zacharius" to Pitre-Chevalier, was proving—first of all to himself—that he could create a credible atmosphere. But he was not to become a Poe or a Hoffmann; he would seldom return to the fantastic.

Writing to his father in April 1854, after having completed "Maître Zacharius," Jules let a phrase drop that more than 140 years later both perplexes and intrigues the biographer. "I'm studying even more than I'm working," he said, "because I'm beginning to perceive new systems. . . ."

What could these new systems possibly be? The next story published in *Musée des Familles,* "Winter Quarters in the Ice Fields", ("Un hivernage dans les glaces"), could well represent this new departure, for it closely resembles Verne's novels.

Yet he hadn't abandoned the stage and its conventions—far from it. The Théâtre Lyrique had closed after a short season but was scheduled to open again, and Jules had been promised an early production of his next play. He'd actually have to wait a full year for the opening of *The Companions of the Marjolaine (Les Compagnons de la Marjolaine),* another one-act comic opera written in collaboration with Michel Carré, with music by Aristide Hignard. Meanwhile, he was counting on the recognition that would come to him on acceptance of a play at the Odéon, and was working with Alexandre Dumas fils on still another one-acter, this one believed to be just right for the Théâtre du Gymnase. "Everything will come in due time," he told his father, reassuring him that in any case, "I work hard and neglect nothing that will assure success."

And still his father wanted more. This is evident from Jules's reply: "Don't push me too hard, my dear father, to do ambitious things; I don't want to break my neck at 26 years of age. The son of Dumas is 31, Augier 38, Ponsard 42, Sandeau 48." (Emile Augier was writing successful plays about Second Empire society, and he would be elected to the French Academy in three years' time; François Ponsard wrote both drama and comedy, and he would enter the Academy the very next year. Jules Sandeau was both a novelist and dramatist, and had become a member of the Academy in 1859.)

Verne's composure was admirable, given the fact he had no definite prospects; it was as if he knew that he had been chosen for greater things.

At the end of June 1854, just a month after the theater closed temporarily, manager Jules Seveste died suddenly, a victim of cholera. Jules and Seveste had been friends; Jules would miss him. "What a horrible disease; fortunately it hasn't become an epidemic," he wrote, summing up his fears in a letter home. "It has become a very ordinary illness, but one must keep away from it, because it gives no mercy." Yet he had found a "happy side" to Seveste's death: It released Jules from the theater in a "natural" way. It also did not affect the prospects for *The Companions of the Marjolaine* adversely, for the next manager would have to respect the theater's commitment to produce the play.[2]

Jules's own health continued to be a problem. He couldn't hide this from his parents, and apparently he had no desire to. It is not evident to what extent his violent stomach disorders had to do with fear of the cholera epidemic sweeping Europe, or with the uncertainty of his professional status, or to what extent it might have represented anxiety over his apparent failure as a suitor for an attractive and dowry-rich bride. "My stomach is not getting better; it is quite upset, and I can hardly eat anything without having painful cramps; I find it difficult to bear."

He reserved the most complete clinical description of his illness for his mother, and in language one would hardly expect in an exchange between provincial bourgeois son and mother. "I'm having cramps and diarrhea again," he told her in a letter of November twenty-fifth. "I gave myself an assload of enema, and now it's all stopped up." But he was tired, he said, of a life "bounded on the north by constipation, in the south by the outflow, on the east by too many enemas, on the west by constipating baths."

He had seen his doctor—his friend Victor Marie, who diagnosed the beginning of a prolapsus, a condition in which the rectum loses its retentive function. When writing to his mother, he explained that "to go" has many meanings. "One goes well, one goes badly, one goes to Paris, one goes forward, one goes backward, and above all one goes from the behind!" But the worst is "to go under oneself," and that was his problem. "You surely know, my dear mother, that the two cheeks are separated by a gap, which is nothing other than the end of the intestinal tract. . . . But in my case this rectum, due to a quite understandable impatience, tends to escape outside, and consequently no longer retains all the charming things stored up."

There was a remedy: a procedure to correct the prolapse. Otherwise, an operation would be necessary to prevent "serious inconvenience to a young man destined to go out into the world and not under himself. For, in a word, my behind doesn't shut very well."

Another letter home betrayed his incessant fears. He was well, he told his father, and expected that his parents were, too. "In any case watch out for scarlet fever, and for all those illnesses that come from mixing with people, such as colds, inflammations, etc." (Here, hypochondria seemed to be giving way to agoraphobia.) "You can only stay well by living in a hole," added Jules, whose stay in Paris had everything to do with contacts, and who was still being supported by his parents back in Nantes. "These reflections," he concluded, "are from a fellow who feels quite well, but who stays home."

He continued to depend on his parents not only for money for food and rent but also for the comforts a mother could provide (in the absence of a spouse). Although his laundry was done in Paris, when a visitor from his hometown announced a return to Nantes, worn shirts were sure to accompany him. "I beg you to look them over carefully," he wrote to his mother. He said she would find that, one, nearly all the collars were worn and needed replacing; two, the cuffs were more or less in the same condition; three, all the button holes were too big for the buttons.

However, he did not fail to mention marriage. In this letter of December 14, 1854, announcing the dispatching of used shirts to Nantes, he mentioned the report of the marriage of one Mlle Héloïse David to an older man in Nantes, and he complained that all of the girls he deigned to consider quickly married someone else. But there is no suggestion that his failure to enter a romantic alliance—even a temporary one—was affecting his nerves. His own analysis, expressed in a letter to his father, blamed poor health and "literary concerns" for his psychological condition.

Voluntary isolation did not keep him away from the theater—for that was his reason for living in Paris. He confessed to his father that he had written more theater pieces than he was showing him—although some were poor and would never be used. Indeed, taken together, there are more surviving manuscripts of unproduced plays than staged ones.

By the beginning of 1855, the play on which he had counted for commercial and theatrical success, *The Companions of the Marjolaine,* was in rehearsal, and *Blindman's Buff* was to return to the boards. But what made him happiest, he told his father, was a new verse play he had written. When he showed it to Alexandre Dumas fils, that expert found it perfect, with not a word that needed changing. In fact, Dumas was submitting it to a theater.

It is sad to follow Jules Verne now, on the eve of his twenty-seventh birthday, pursuing phantasms, writing himself to exhaustion, with nothing to show for it but perishable boulevard comedy. But for Verne, to be a playwright served as an exercise; he was learning to express himself through the crisp expository dialogue of his characters. Later, when he created more down-to-earth characters who traveled to interesting places and had things to accomplish, his readers would become involved in their exploits.

By February 1855, Jules found himself in the grip of another attack of facial paralysis, which this time was treated by electricity. His parents wanted him to see other doctors, but he refused. "Aren't there ten doctors in the theater who'd like nothing better than to treat me free of charge?" (Presumably, they were would-be dramatists seeking his favor.) His mother suggested cauterization. He replied, "I'd rather see my mouth above my nose!" He did make one concession to his malady—which was to shave off his beard so as to be able to massage his jaw more readily.

Dr. Marie applied an irritant to create blisters, this in conjunction with electricity. Jules reported that it had worked for the upper part of his face, "but the bottom part leaves much to be desired!" He then rubbed himself with strychnine—even powdering the blistered area with the poisonous chemical—but the warping of his mouth remained unchanged. Soon his chronic diarrhea had returned, adding to his distress.

His faithful doctor wasn't sure how to treat his friend. "It is likely," Jules informed his father, "that the whole thing comes from extreme irritability and nervous sensitivity; let's hope this doesn't lead to a real nervous disease." Nor, he said, could living in Paris be blamed—"if I wanted to be gruesome, I'd say that it's life itself that doesn't suit me very well."

In February—his birthday month—he informed his parents that he had been confined to his rooms for nearly eighteen days; at least this allowed him to work without interruption. "I believe my work is good, more serious than anything I've done up to now." Possibly he was referring to the five-act play in verse known as *Les Heureux du jour.* Whatever the "more serious" work might be, it would never reach the stage or be published, and that could give anyone a stomachache.

SPRING BROUGHT OUT HIS CHEERY SIDE. HE WAS CHANGING apartments, and that called for a fifty-eight-line poem home, for there was a lot to say, and to ask for. Since he had to give up his flat but could only move into new quarters a week after that, he would have to stay in a hotel. He was expecting payments for an article and a play, but not immediately, and so he requested additional cash from home. Papa replied, also in verse, saying that his son's poem was charming and would be even more so were it not costing him sixty francs.[3]

The Vernes continued to exchange poetry at the slightest provocation, pleasantly insignificant stanzas for births, birthdays, and marriages. One set of impromptu vignettes attributed to Jules was composed during a family gathering at the country house of Jules's great-uncle Prudent Allotte near Nantes. Here, Jules is writing about himself:

> *He's a quite distinguished lad,*
> *Always laughing, never sad,*
> *Who eats well and sometimes feigns*
> *To enjoy his stomach pains.*[4]

9

THE BRIDE

THE BIOGRAPHER IS STILL WAITING FOR THE FIRST DAY. COULD the story called "Un Hivernage dans les Glaces" (Winter Quarters in the Ice Fields), published in two issues of Pitre-Chevalier's magazine in 1855, be the true beginning? Was it the first "Jules Verne"?

"Winter Quarters" does contain many of the features of Verne's earliest book-length tales of exploration, and readers of the long novel *The Adventures of Captain Hatteras* who come upon the shorter piece afterward may well feel themselves in familiar territory. So that none would ignore that his story represented a new departure, and that—even though it was only a short story—its author had invested considerable time in research before writing it, the first installment of "Winter Quarters," published in *Musée des Familles,* bore a prefatory note. In retrospect, one can view it as a manifesto:

> After the martyrs of the faith, the most admirable are the martyrs of science, and among them, the most heroic the navigators of the polar seas. . . . In the history of travel no episode is more curious, no image more arresting, no drama more eventful, than wintering in the ice fields. It sums up all imaginable struggles, surprises, emotions, incidents. This is the subject our collaborator Jules Verne has attempted, in the manner of [James Fenimore] Cooper, within the framework of a haunting story. . . .[1]

An authentic Vernian tale, it begins with a date, "May 12, 187 . . ." (later, in his novels, he'd often specify the year). Dates appear throughout the story, for the seasons and their temperatures are central to it. It is also set in an actual place, Dunkirk, home port of the schooner *La Jeune-Hardie.* As the narrative begins, Jean Cornbutte is waiting for the return of that vessel and its brave skipper, his son Louis. Even more impatient is Cornbutte's niece, the fair Flemish maiden Marie, for she is Louis's fiancée.

The schooner returns, however, without its captain, who has been missing since he sailed away in a lifeboat to rescue another vessel near the Maelstrom, the fierce current off the coast of Norway. Therefore, old Jean Cornbutte must sail in search of his son. His niece joins him, and so does the traitorous André Vasling, Louis's rival for Marie's affection; André will do what he can to sabotage the rescue. On the track of a Norwegian ship that might have picked up Louis Cornbutte, those on *La Jeune-Hardie* must suspend their search with the onset of winter. Laying up as the ice hardens around their ship, they are, of course, subject to the hardships of Arctic frost.

The reader recognizes Verne's style in the diligent description of the crew's preparations for wintering. The author seems to relish the accumulation of details about how a stranded individual—or a group—goes about building a cocoon against the elements. Verne, who in successive stories would return again and again to the myth of Robinson Crusoe, had begun to create his own. He allows the reader to follow the blocked schooner to the bay of Gaël-Hamkes, off Greenland, the farthest point attained by previous navigators. And when at last Jean Cornbutte's conviction that his son is still alive proves justified and Louis is rescued, five more cruel icy months remain until the May thaw.

READING THE LETTERS VERNE WROTE HOME AT THIS TIME, one discovers no evidence that the author had at last found his true path, for he did not convey that. In March, when the first installment of "Winter Quarters" was published in *Musée des Familles,* he seemed preoccupied by plans for the marriage of his sister Anna, and also by his own health. His stomach had been tamed, but the equally debilitating facial paralysis continued. He rejected the remedy his parents had suggested—a stay at a thermal resort. He wrote that Dr. Marie didn't believe in that, and besides, he added, "I don't have the time."

He soon returned to work on the play he would title *Monna Lisa.* By May 1855, his one-act play *Les Compagnons de la Marjolaine* was in rehearsal

at the Théâtre Lyrique. But even though he was working for that very theater, he could not be sure exactly when it would open. That depended on
how soon the public tired of the play then on the boards.[2]

His fragile play went before the public at last on June 6, 1855. In the
tradition of comic opera, it was just another diversion of little consequence and had a conventional plot (the threatened abduction of the
innkeeper's daughter by young rowdies, then a happy ending, with
Marceline safe in the arms of her beau Simplice). It was almost as if "Winter Quarters" had never been written, as if Jules was no longer developing
into a serious writer. Certainly it was advantageous for a writer to have his
work performed (and even read, for this one-act play, all twenty-nine
pages of it, was immediately printed for sale to theatergoers).[3] Learning
the discipline required to create a short play with crisp, witty dialogue was
also beneficial. In addition, it was helpful that Verne had something else
to think about besides finding a bride whose parents would have him.

The absurd situation in which a young provincial could find himself is
suggested by a letter Jules sent his father from Paris. His parents had unearthed another maiden ripe for marriage, and her father had money.
Apparently, she was considered an acceptable mate for either Jules or his
brother, Paul, who was now a young naval officer with prospects even
dimmer than Jules's. "It's obvious that if the arrangement has any chance
at all, it's important to work on it actively," Jules advised his father,
"whether it be Paul or me doesn't matter, if it remains in the family."

The matter at hand involved one Ninette Chéguillaume, a friend of
Jules's sister Anna and nine years Jules's junior. Ninette's father had let it
be known that he was actively seeking a husband for his daughter. The
Vernes found it significant that he confided in Pierre Verne, who was
"equipped with two perfectly marriageable sons," as Jules commented.
He hoped that Anna could learn more about Ninette's prospects without
compromising herself—"for if we try nothing we'll learn nothing, and,
may I repeat, the thing is worth the effort." Jules was certain that his
brother, Paul, would be as ready to say yes as he was.

The letter seems contemporary with another Jules wrote in June 1855,
this one to his mother—hence an opportunity for talking about his
health. He had been confined to bed for some days by a kind of rheumatism that had attacked one side of his body; moreover, he continued to be
tormented by facial paralysis—he could feel the nerves pulling at his features. It was cold in Paris, and that had also brought on another attack of
stomach cramps. He thought that he would need a month to get back
into shape, a month without work, for he was exhausted.

But he was not too exhausted for courtship. Ninette's father was visiting Paris; Jules offered him a box at the Théâtre Lyrique, but he wasn't free to use it. The man sent a thank-you note, but, as Jules wrote, "he didn't offer me his daughter's hand, the ingrate, cotton merchant that he is! . . . as if I were not as qualified as anyone to assure the happiness of this young and rich heiress. The next time I come to Nantes I'll abduct her for sure. . . ."

During this time, Verne worked on projects one can only consider futile; in any case, they were unpublishable, not producible, and not likely to be remembered. Although he didn't seem to realize it, he was going nowhere. Or if he did know it, that explained his physical and nervous complaints. When there was nothing wrong with him, he took precautions nonetheless. "I feel fine, especially concerning my stomach," he would tell his mother that autumn. "That doesn't prevent me from working at home all day, going out only when it's really necessary." He was still worrying about his play *Monna Lisa* and was quite busy with a five-act comedy he had mentioned earlier to his parents—this would become the doomed *Les Heureux du jour,* a satire of the money-mad society of his day.

Attacks of facial paralysis persisted through the final weeks of 1855. His friend and doctor Victor Marie was unable to explain the relapse, but he *was* ready with a vigorous application of electricity. As long as Verne didn't open his mouth, didn't close his eyes, didn't sniff, didn't frown, one noticed nothing. However, he dared not go out and risk meeting people who might say something humorous, for he was not allowed to laugh.

He continued to work from morning to night, seven days a week, despite the paralysis. "My belly is fine, but the tugging at my face annoys me considerably; besides that, since I always have to have something wrong with me, I can't sleep at night—not for a minute," he wrote his mother. He blamed his insomnia on nerves, explaining that he was in a continual state of excitement. Dr. Marie told him that he needed to stop working for a month, but Verne knew he couldn't spare that much time. By the end of December, he assured his parents that he was once again getting enough sleep, thanks to fencing lessons, which fatigued him.

When asked what he wanted for Christmas, he replied, a "tender bride."[4]

THE EARLY MONTHS OF 1856 SAW A BREAK IN THE CLOUDS. Verne's letters bristled with optimism. He wrote that he was dining out. His friend Victor Marie was to marry, and as always for the bourgeoisie, marriage signified new connections, a promise of comfort. Marie's fiancée was the daughter of Théophile Pelouze, a distinguished chemist, the director of the Paris Mint, and a member of the Institut de France, the parent body of the Académie Française. Verne wrote that he considered it a "superb" marriage for Marie. This set Jules to dreaming that he, too, could unearth a Parisian bride—"a rich young girl who had strayed from the right path, for example, or who was ready to do that, and away we go!" Although this was a lighthearted way of putting it, the underlying message was that the only eligible girl he could hope to attract would necessarily come with a handicap.

Marriage was in the air. At the approach of spring, he was able to tell his parents about another one—that of an old Nantes friend and distant relative by marriage, Auguste Lelarge; *that* event would change his own life. Meanwhile, in describing Victor Marie's marriage, he compared the ceremony at Saint-Germain-des-Prés church to "a funeral service." Never, never could he participate in such a ceremony, he proclaimed. In his words, it was "high comedy."[5]

Auguste Lelarge was marrying someone from out of town; the bride resided in Amiens, which was not far from Paris in reality, although culturally it represented a far different world. The ancient capital of the Picardy region, with its own traditions and dialect, Amiens served as capital of the Somme district and the seat of a diocese, with its own criminal and civil courts, and even a small stock exchange. Perhaps Jules had a recent guidebook to entertain him on the train ride north. One such book included this description: "The traveler, transported rapidly by the impetuous locomotive from the banks of the Seine to the plains of Picardy, and who is on his way to Amiens for the first time, will not be able to seize its majesty, its dimensions, or its significance when arriving by rail."[6]

It was a long way to go just to stand alongside a bridegroom whose sister happened to be a cousin by marriage, especially for a young man not in the best of health. But Jules did go, and apparently he enjoyed himself, for he stayed a week.

In a letter to his mother dated May 24, 1856, he described the festivities. He told his sisters that Auguste Lelarge's bride was "rather pretty, quite tall, too tight-lipped to allow the heart to pass through—morally, that is, for I like to think that she throws up occasionally, like everyone else." While in Amiens Jules spent his time at dances, shaking hands, kissing and hugging, thus experiencing the joys of marital bliss, as well as enjoying "Amiens pâtés, stuffed sausages, hearty hams, hour-long breakfasts," and five hour dinners. Despite overeating, he felt well, slept well, and was having a good time in general. He wrote that "more than ever I have my mind set on marriage."

He confided to his mother: "I want to marry, I must marry, I should marry; it isn't possible that the woman who will love me has not yet been hatched, as Napoléon said at Montereau bridge." (Napoléon had been referring to the bullet that might kill him.)

Apparently, he'd found the right family: the Devianes of Amiens (he called them the Deviannes; before the Revolution, they were known as de Viane or du Fraysne de Viane). His friend Auguste had married Aimée Deviane; Aimée had a sister named Honorine, a young widow Jules found to be "quite pleasant"; there was also a brother, Ferdinand, who was Jules's age. Ferdinand was a dealer in securities, which earned him lots of money, and yet he remained "the nicest young man in all the world." Their father was also a good man. He was a retired cavalry captain, but milder than most old warriors, in Jules's opinion. Verne said Mme Deviane was "a terribly witty woman."

It wasn't often that Jules felt so enthusiastic about a family, and he felt sure that his mother would see the point. "I do believe that I'm in love with the young widow of 26!" But why, he wondered, did she have to have two children? "I'm not lucky! I always run into impossible situations of one sort or another," he lamented. Yet he went on to describe this young woman whose husband, deputy to a real estate lawyer, had died only seven or eight months earlier, "consumptive and imprudent."[7]

His letter was written from Amiens on a Saturday; the next day he returned to Paris, and by Monday he was ready to sum up his feelings in a more thoughtful manner, appropriately addressing himself to his father rather than to his mother. He had, he recalled, truly immersed himself in the Deviane family. He had served as the best man, helped to pass the collection basket at church, and performed all the other duties expected of the groom's friends. Therefore, the bride's family had insisted that he stay on for four extra days, "to digest the plentitude of meats and sweets for which that delightful region was known." He had escaped at last by hopping a midnight train.

It was clear from the outset that the young widow was not the only family member of interest. Ferdinand Deviane, brother of the bride and of the young widow, was in business with a friend. They served as intermediaries between stock and bond holders and the brokers of Paris. Thus, without a heavy investment and no risk—since they weren't acting for themselves—they were earning as much as fifty thousand francs a year (over 1 million present-day francs). Deviane and his partner had also invested about 100,000 francs in a Paris brokerage, for a return of at least 20 percent annually—also without risk.

In Jules's opinion, what Ferdinand Deviane was doing in Amiens could

be done even more readily in Paris. There were countless unofficial intermediaries who recruited customers for established stockbrokers. With
no risk and not too much effort, these unofficial agents were earning at
least one thousand francs a month (over twenty thousand francs today),
which was a third of what the official brokerage received.

The job—and Jules had clearly studied the matter during his four extra days in Amiens—consisted in having a lot of friends, and making customers of these friends. It also meant keeping in touch with the stock
market, spending the hours of one to three at the stock exchange each afternoon—leaving him free the rest of the time. There was no office, no
complicated bookkeeping; one didn't even take possession of the stock
certificates being bought or sold, since one acted only as a moral guarantee for one's clients.

Ferdinand was very involved in this world of financiers and agents; he
could easily help a friend establish a working arrangement with a major
Paris broker. Now it was for Jules's father to speak; would *he* put up the
money for Jules's investment in a brokerage house and let Jules handle
his own securities, as well as those of his family and his friends? It would
be the best possible placement of funds. For Jules's part, he said, "I have
a great need to change my way of living, because the present insecure situation just can't continue."

He was placing his fate in the hands of his father, who was already quite
aware of how his son felt. Yet Jules thought it best to remind him just what
those sentiments were: "To be an attorney somewhere, even in Nantes,
leaves me no hope of success or wealth, and I confess that I can't live anywhere else but in Paris." He urged his father to think about his plan—one
that would allow him to live without his family's support, to help his father earn more from his investments, and, of course, to give Jules a better
life.

It was merely coincidental that the stock market was the theme and the
scene of the play he had been struggling with for so long, *Les Heureux du
jour*. In it, he portrayed a financier seeking to triple the capital of a widow
by speculating on a fall in share prices; he could then marry the daughter of the woman he had made rich. A young cousin attempts to foil the
speculator, but what really does him in is a French battlefield victory,
leading to a rise, instead of a fall, in the widow's holdings. Writing about
stocks and bonds was already a genre Jules knew, as he observed to his father.[8]

Now Jules was not debating the merits of a play with his father, as he
had been doing in recent correspondence, but was trying to make an actual get-rich scheme credible to Pierre Verne. His father replied that he

wanted to help Jules settle into a rewarding job but that he still saw his son—so Jules feared—as "a reckless young man who gets all excited about a new scheme."

Jules had no intention of abandoning literature—he would *never* do that. "But while tending to my art," he wrote, "I am quite capable of devoting time and energy to another job." He would simply stop writing brief farces and instead concentrate his efforts on creating one significant comedy each year; this was the only way to succeed in the theater.

He required a position, if only to marry. He added that "this may seem strange, but I need to be happy—nothing less than that. . . ."[9]

He felt that surely his mother would understand.

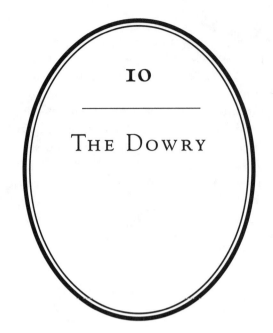

IO

THE DOWRY

JULES'S LETTERS HOME BECAME MORE URGENT. IT WAS AS IF HE had suddenly perceived the direction his life would take. The essential thing was to win his father's approval, as well as his continued financial support. Jules offered every imaginable guarantee that he was serious about the brokerage venture. His father remained wary. Pierre wanted to know more about Deviane and this business scheme. And what had Amiens to do with the Paris stock exchange?

Jules tried a sentimental approach. What he needed was a job that would make him an eligible prospect for marriage, he wrote, "because solitude is truly weighing me down. My heart is desperately empty, and frankly, I can't wait to be married. This proves that I have reached the age when the need for a companion overshadows everything else, and it's better that it be a legitimate relationship. I think you and mama will agree with that. But as long as I am only a stage extra in literature, mothers and fathers will keep away from me, and they'll be right."

He also pointed out (although surely his father knew this) that when he did receive something for the performance of one or another of his short plays, it didn't even cover expenses accrued since the previous money earned. By June 1856, he was ready to admit that the play on which he had pinned his hopes, *Les Heureux du jour*, had little chance of being performed at the Théâtre du Gymnase or at any other serious playhouse, for these theaters were committed to plays written by better-known playwrights.

By early July, his tone was more pressing still. He realized that he'd need time to acquire experience in his new profession, knew that he'd have to start as nothing more than an intermediary, a glorified clerk. But he promised to sacrifice himself to the task. "I'm not giving up writing, but if it's necessary for a year, I'll put it aside. . . ." He was quite certain that with time he would succeed in literature, but he was nevertheless alarmed to think that at the age of thirty-five (seven years hence) he would be no further along in his career than he was presently.[1]

MARRIAGE AND THE STOCK MARKET WERE TO GO HAND IN hand. The proof is contained in a letter written by Julien Deviane, Honorine's father, to Jules's father, Pierre, on September 1, 1856.

> Dear Sir,
>
> When your son informed me of his feelings I thought it my duty to urge him to think about what it was he wished to do. Now that you have given him your consent I can only welcome the request you have made in his name.
>
> The time I have spent with Mr. Jules sufficed to convince me of his worth. The warm and delicate feelings he communicates speak well in his favor. . . . Mr. Jules can count on my family's assistance in obtaining the position to which he aspires; we pray that his efforts will be rewarded.[2]

Obviously, the "position" referred to had nothing to do with literature. While Pierre Verne and Julien Deviane were exchanging courtesies, Jules—recovering from an illness that caused fever and jaundice—was actively reading up on the stock market.

By the seventh of September Jules, still suffering from a recurrent intestinal disorder, was able to forward a concrete proposal to his father. He had met with Ferdinand Deviane and learned that one of Deviane's friends was trying to acquire a brokerage. Jules was hoping that Pierre would purchase a one-fortieth share of this brokerage, an investment of fifty thousand francs. Jules would then either work in the brokerage or independently, receiving commissions on business he brought in. Deviane advised the latter approach.

Fifty thousand francs was a considerable amount of money, but Jules was asking for it not as a gift but only as an investment. If Pierre had bought a law or real estate attorney's practice for Jules, he would have had to spend a comparable amount.

Pierre Verne had suggested his son would be wiser to begin his stock market career by working for a broker in some minor capacity in order to learn the job. "As for apprenticing in a broker's office," Jules wrote back, "Mr. Deviane rejects the idea totally; it seems useless to him. Two weeks of the stock market will teach me more than would six months in brokerage." Starting immediately, he planned to go to the exchange every day to watch the quotations.

Once he became active on the market, he pointed out, he'd be in a position to handle his father's personal investments, thus assuring Pierre a 10 to 15 percent return. As an intermediary between customer and broker, Jules would receive a 30 percent share of the broker's commissions, which could amount to one thousand francs a month in addition to the 15 percent return on the investment.

Pierre remained unconvinced. In his judgment Jules was gambling, or asking him to gamble. In response, his son could only repeat that a broker's practice was as good as gold. Pricing a one-fortieth share of a brokerage at fifty thousand francs signified that the brokerage was worth 2 million francs; Pierre, in turn, wanted to know what would happen if the government took measures that would make such a brokerage less valuable. Jules's answer was, "Napoléon's government, which depends entirely on finance, can't introduce the slightest restriction in the market without losing a pillar of his strength."

Pierre came up with yet another idea: Jules could work for a broker without investing in the company; if his son proved worthy, he would eventually get a minority partnership. Jules replied that it didn't work that way.[3]

There is an element of pathos in a recently discovered letter from Jules to Ferdinand Deviane. It suggests that he had been seeking financial security so desperately in order to be able to marry Honorine, and not the other way around. The letter was written on November 16, 1856, at which time the projected investment was no further advanced than it had been. Jules was then corresponding with Honorine about their future marriage; she was evidently in full accord with his proposal but was also aware of the need to begin by anchoring the prospective groom's financial position.

The letter to Honorine's brother is obsequious; the petitioner treads delicately, for Ferdinand's help is quintessential. "My dear Mr. Ferdinand," it begins. "You do understand how impatient I am to conclude my marriage. . . ." He was only "a poor mortal very desirous, since he has encountered it, to enjoy his happiness."

Ferdinand had thought of giving Jules work in his office in Amiens, a plan abandoned when Jules assumed the role of fiancé, for his future brother-in-law didn't think it proper that Jules reside in Amiens before he was actually married to Honorine. "But," wondered Jules, "is there no way to reconcile propriety and sentiment by celebrating the marriage sooner rather than later? Isn't this what your family desires? Isn't it also my dearest wish?" One of the men in Deviane's office was moving to Paris; if that meant there would now be a vacancy in Amiens, Jules wished to fill it. He would marry and live in Amiens during his apprenticeship, after which he would go to Paris to work for Deviane there.

In any case, Jules wished to make it clear that he had no intention of living at his wife's expense. "I have always felt that the personal wealth of Mrs. Morel should remain in your family where it is safer than anywhere else, and I'd be the one to thank you for taking care of it, as you have done until now."[4]

Persistence paid off, or as Jules put it to his father, he always replied on the day he received a letter (spending a franc a day on postage); he had been writing perpetually to Ferdinand Deviane, and at last he received the reply he wanted. Jules's offer to work in Amiens had only been a means to evoke a response. Clearly, Deviane didn't believe that given Jules's literary and artistic proclivities he really wanted to work at the stock exchange; Jules's proposal to start working in Amiens right away caused Ferdinand to reconsider.

So Deviane came up with an alternative. The man he was sending to Paris would open an office there before the end of the year; Jules would work with him, concentrating on cultivating clients in the capital.

Now Jules turned his attention to the matter of wedding gifts and a dowry. He had been thinking about this carefully; he planned to offer his bride earrings, not silverware; giving silver would make Jules feel that he was giving himself a present. In providing a dowry for his son, Pierre Verne naturally considered how much he would give his son Paul when he married, as well as what he would provide his daughters. Jules expected that wedding expenses, gift included, and the cost of settling in Paris wouldn't amount to more than five thousand francs. He learned that Honorine's dowry amounted to some fifty thousand francs. Eventually, she would inherit sixty thousand more from her parents and another eighty thousand from a rich uncle. (For all these figures, multiply by twenty to get a rough contemporary franc equivalent.)

The marriage was set to take place in Paris in the middle of January, but first the Devianes wished to receive Jules's parents at their home in Amiens. Jules explained to his parents that the reason the marriage had been delayed until January was out of respect for the family of Honorine's late husband. They planned to travel to Essômes—near Château-Thierry, some fifty miles from Paris—to sign the wedding contract. That was where Auguste Lelarge lived, and letting him draw up the papers would save five hundred francs in legal fees. In Paris, they'd have both a church and a civil wedding, as was the custom. Jules wrote his family that he needed some additions to his wardrobe, especially "two pairs of knitted underpants, mine now lacking the seats, the fronts, the legs, and the buttons."

When he paid his courtesy calls in Amiens in early December, the weather was wintry; he made his way around town in a foot of snow. "Today I take leave of this cherished city," he informed his mother on the third of December, and there is no way for us to know whether he was being ironical about that undistinguished little town lost in snow.

The wedding gifts from Jules were to be modest: He spent 235 francs for a decorative chain in gold and quartz, but he did not buy earrings or diamonds, for Honorine apparently had a sufficient supply of both. What jewels she possessed would simply be reset. She already had a proper dress.

Everything about the wedding reflected the frugality of the provincial middle class, who knew when to avoid extravagances. An early-morning wedding mass in Paris was planned. After the ceremonies in church and then the town hall, the families would dine out before going to the theater. This was what the bridegroom desired.

Jules did not tell any of his friends about the wedding except for his old comrade Aristide Hignard, the composer. If he couldn't find an apartment for himself and his new family right away, he planned to live with his wife in his small flat, which was located between the theater and financial districts, until the next rental period began in April. That meant leaving Honorine's children by her previous marriage—five-year-old Valentine, three-year-old Suzanne—with their grandparents in Amiens. "No excitement, no expenses!" he wrote. "The wedding is our responsibility, is it not? How quickly I'm becoming a businessman."

A follow-up note to his father made it clear that in his frugality Jules had the backing of his new in-laws, "who are in complete agreement with me not to have any kind of ceremony or celebration. . . . You won't even have to receive them in Paris; there'll just be a simple dinner at a decent restaurant on the wedding day. . . . I'll order a dinner for so many heads, and that will be that."[5]

ADVISED ON BOTH SIDES BY LEGAL MINDS, THE COUPLE signed a contract specifying that all assets acquired since marriage were to be held in common; this made it necessary to describe and evaluate what each was bringing to the marriage. Honorine Morel's fortune consisted of railroad stocks and bonds valued at 33,500 francs, plus money owed to her and some real estate bonds (another 18,700 francs), together with a personal wardrobe, jewelry, and furniture from her first marriage. Her net worth was estimated at 81,382 francs. Her two children were entitled to 39 percent of that, leaving 49,611 francs for Jules and Honorine (a bit less than one million present-day francs).

For his part, the bridegroom (not quite twenty-nine years old on the day of his marriage) declared no liquid assets, only furniture, books, a piano, and a watch—together estimated at three thousand francs (about sixty thousand present-day francs). To that, he could add his parents' gift of forty thousand francs (approximately 800,000 contemporary francs), which represented an advance on his inheritance; in fact, this was the amount needed to purchase a share of a stock brokerage.

Scholars who examined these papers have also noted that in the event of the death of his spouse, Jules would get his personal library back before the division of the legacy; if Jules died, Honorine would retrieve her sheet music.[6]

The marriage took place on January 10, 1857, in the offices of Paris's third district (the neighborhood of Jules's flat), with a benediction at Saint-Eugène, a church described by a family biographer as "sombre." "I was the groom," Marguerite Allotte, the biographer, quotes Jules's reminiscence. "I wore a white suit and black gloves! I had no idea what was going on, I gave money to everybody: district hall employees, beadle, sexton, errand boy. They called out: The bridegroom, if you please! That was me! Thank God there were only twelve people in the room."

According to Allotte's account the absence of conspicuous consumption on that momentous day saddened Jules's father (although one would have assumed the contrary). Both Pierre and his wife were dismayed by the abbreviated church ceremony and the paltry lunch, a fact Pierre was said to have confided to his wife's brother-in-law, the family portraitist Francisque de Chateaubourg. Marguerite Allotte credits an-

other portraitist, Delbarre, appointed photographer of Princess
Mathilde, a cousin of Napoléon III, with the formal wedding photographs (only separate portraits of Jules and Honorine have survived,
however). Jules was then, Allotte wrote, of "almost perfect beauty."[7] The
photograph of Honorine shows her in a lace collar, a finger to her ear,
looking pensive and somewhat older than her twenty-six years. Jules is
leaning into his raised hand, his beard the beard of a prophet both old
and wise.[8]

OBLIGED TO PROVE HIMSELF, JULES WENT TO THE STOCK
exchange every day, buying and selling for others, and occasionally for his
own account. The assurance he had given his parents—that he wouldn't
gamble—was quickly forgotten in the atmosphere of the exchange,
where money was continually made and lost. Later, Jules would confess
that he had had "dreams of wealth which led me into one or two specu-
lations at the [exchange]. These did not realize my dreams, I may add.
But I derived some benefit from constant visits to the [unofficial market],
for it was there that I got to know the romance of commerce. . . ."[9] Once
again, in a letter home in March 1857, he asked for funds that his father
had promised him, to pay for shares; he was also dealing in securities for
outside clients, one of whom happened to be Pierre Verne. "I'll have a lot
to say to you, dear father, about those of your shares that are worth holding on to, but which nevertheless ought to be sold before the next fall in
the market."

The letter—which he addressed to "Mio caro father"—all but glows
with his new self-assurance; marriage clearly had eliminated the need for
whining. The newlyweds were living in Paris without Honorine's children. "They won't give them to us," he explained, but his tone expressed
no distress about the stubborn desire of Honorine's parents-in-law to
hold on to them. They were receiving friends on Thursdays. In a reference to their finances, Jules commented, "Honorine has her diamond
earrings—350 francs. . . . But enough—I stop the spending here, and
won't tolerate the buying of an inch more of ribbon."[10]

The casual mention of Honorine's young children might lead one to
believe this was a painful situation for Honorine. According to family legend, the parents of Honorine's first husband were unhappy about the distance that now separated them from their grandchildren and they
actively prevented Jules from adopting them, although he did raise them
as his own.[11]

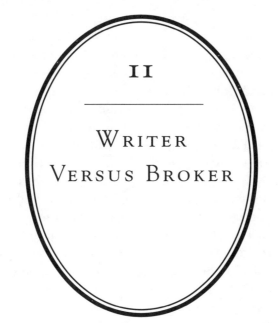

11

WRITER
VERSUS BROKER

JULES'S FAMILY MAY HAVE SAVED EVERY ONE OF HIS LETTERS, BUT many of them have subsequently disappeared. There is a serious gap in the existing correspondence—material relating to the years preceding the period when Verne achieved fame. Much of what we know about the time immediately following his marriage to Honorine has to do with the stock market, and the one surviving letter to his father for the year 1858 contains not a hint of literary achievement. "I'm feeling better, thanks in part to electricity," he wrote, referring to yet another attack of facial paralysis. "Business is better too, thanks to the rise in shares." He was answering a letter concerning his father's investments, and he displayed the experience of one who was now familiar with business dealings. He was actively seeking clients, counting on friends and relatives for help, though, as he told his father, "business coming from Nantes is conspicuous in its absence."[1]

Surviving letters to his brother-in-law Ferdinand show to what extent he had become involved in the stock market. He was preoccupied with the war between Austria and France and with how that might affect the price of bonds. He also mentioned his stepchildren: "Mr. and Mrs. Deviane must be exhausted from having the two little girls—tell them how sorry I am that Honorine didn't bring one of them back here."

The correspondence confirms that Jules was now an active player on the stock exchange. He learned to master the etiquette of the exchange—how to behave in the presence of competitors as well as colleagues. "It's impossible for me to confide in X without being spied upon by Z," he explained, full of his importance, to Ferdinand on March 9, 1859. "But if he sees me doing business elsewhere he's capable of telling X, and I wouldn't know what to do." By now, he was associated with an experienced broker, Fernand Eggly, whose intermediary he became; the correspondence also describes his dealings with new clients in Amiens.[2]

To determine whether Jules was still writing, one must rely on family legend, the vague reminiscences of contemporaries, and the wishful affirmations of admirers, who show a Jules Verne leading a double life. He would rise at 5:00 A.M., slip a pair of trousers over his nightshirt, swallow a hasty breakfast, then sit down to read, annotate, and compose until 10:00 A.M. After that, he would dress, go to lunch, then proceed to the stock market.

During these years, the stock exchange was an easy stroll from his Paris home, as were the principal boulevard theaters. A fellow stock intermediary, who was also a fellow theater man, remembered that Jules "did better in repartee than in business," a fact confirmed by his decision to pursue a writing career. Félix Duquesnel, another broker, saw his contemporary as the nucleus of a group of cronies who divided their lives between market and muse. One of them was Charles Wallut, who would assume the editorship of *Musée des Familles* after Pitre-Chevalier's death. Another was Philippe Gille, successor to Verne as secretary of the Théâtre Lyrique; he would soon agree to stage a minor one-act musical play by Verne. Still another stock exchange regular was Count Fréderic de Cardaillac, owner of the Vaudeville, which would shortly be staging Jules Verne's *Eleven Days of Siege*.

Duquesnel remembered that their little circle of dilettante financiers was regularly mocked by those older and wiser. "Verne was always ready with a reply, teasing or skeptical—unless the subject turned on religion."[3]

In February 1858, the would-be broker had a brief moment of glory when another of his short musical plays was performed: *Mr. Chimpanzee*, the libretto of which he wrote to Aristide Hignard's music. In this bit of nonsense, the hero, named Isidore, disguises himself as a chimp in order to slip into the home of the director of a natural history museum. The director has a pretty daughter, Etamine, who, aware of her suitor's actual identity, plays along with him, telling her father that she is in love with a monkey. When Isidore eventually reveals himself, he threatens that should the father refuse his daughter's hand, Isidore will tell everybody that the man let himself be fooled by a monkey skin.[4]

The play was accepted by the Bouffes-Parisiens, a popular theater under the directorship of Jacques Offenbach, which would soon open its doors to the leading writers and composers of the day. Offenbach was on the eve of his own triumphal musical career, which moved one admirer of Verne's plays to wonder what would have happened if Offenbach had set Verne's work to music, rather than the uninspired Hignard. Perhaps the aspiring playwright would then have accompanied Offenbach through his years of glory.[5]

Offenbach was a German-born Jew, son of a synagogue cantor; Jules Verne did not find it any more difficult to work with him than he had with Michel Lévy, the peddler's son who published four of the five plays Verne wrote before he achieved fame as a novelist.

IN MID-JULY, JULES AND HONORINE TOOK A HOLIDAY IN ES-sômes, where Honorine's sister and her husband, Auguste Lelarge, lived. Here they were surrounded by friends and enjoyed themselves in spite of a heat wave. Aristide Hignard arrived with good news: His brother Alfred, who worked for a shipping company in Saint-Nazaire, was offering Aristide and Jules free tickets for a sea voyage to Scotland. And Jules—despite his marital obligations, stage career, and stock market duties, was going to "grab the opportunity by the hair." It would be a pleasant romp, "whose charm was as tempting as the price."

He had a great need to travel, he told his parents; even during his stay at Essômes, he managed to slip away to Reims to visit the cathedral.[6] "Jules came through here," his mother wrote from Nantes (presumably to a relative), "wild with happiness."[7] He was en route to Saint-Nazaire and his ship.

Jules was at last free to indulge his literary side. For the duration of their journey, he could drink it all in and jot everything down. Then he would lightly disguise his experiences as fiction. The manuscript, however, was not published until 1989, almost a century after his death.

He entitled the manuscript *Traveling Backwards to England and Scotland,* but later he deleted the *Backwards* (it was restored for the posthumous publication).[8] *Backwards* in the title referred to the awkward discovery that rather than sail north to Liverpool the companions had first to travel *south* to Bordeaux to join up with the ship on which they were to sail. Getting to Bordeaux took longer than it should have because of an incompetent skipper; then they wasted seventeen long days in Bordeaux, reducing the time available to them in Scotland. Such are the unpleasant surprises of complimentary tickets. But in this way Jules got his first taste of sailing on a real ocean.

In the fictional account, Jules becomes Jacques Laveret; Aristide, Jonathan Savournon. Their humor is sophomoric, the kind of stories young people tell on return from an uneventful journey, or in letters home: incidents that are entertaining only to those who have experienced them. In Verne's account, much is made of two sailing ships, named, respectively after a countess and a count; Jacques says that he would rather sail the countess. A Scot laughs when one of the travelers is frightened by a stuffed tiger.

The story dutifully follows the actual itinerary, with all the expected boredom of a journey by sea, rail, and coach. From the moment the travelers reach Scotland, Jules's admiration for Walter Scott is evident; he had a good grasp of the work of the famous novelist, and he constantly came upon sites and situations that reminded him of Scott's tales. The book ends with anticlimax—a humdrum visit to London—although it represents a faithful rendition of what actually happened.[9]

Some time would pass before Verne managed to get another of his short musical plays produced. This was *The Ardennes Inn,* written with Michel Carré to music by Aristide Hignard. It is a lighthearted sketch about honeymooners deprived of a bed on their wedding night. The newlyweds discover that the traveler who has gotten there first carries information that will assure their prosperity. The subject appears to indicate that marriage and money were the only things that interested Verne and his collaborators. Performed at the Théâtre Lyrique—then managed by stock market colleague Philippe Gille—on the first of September 1860, the piece had hardly any impact on anyone, including Verne himself.[10]

A family biographer quoted from a letter Jules wrote to his parents at this time. "When I say that I am no longer doing anything, my dear father, it's only a manner of speaking," he wrote. "But at times I am discouraged. . . . I know that I'll reach my goal eventually, but I become frightened—perhaps excessively—to see myself at the age of 32 just where I am, when I thought that by 35 I'd have a fine position in literature."[11]

JULES WAS THIRTY-THREE WHEN HIS FIRST AND ONLY CHILD was born. Michel Jean Pierre came into the world on the night of August 4–5, 1861; for the birth certificate, Verne listed himself as an attorney.[12] Two months earlier, on the first of June, Jules, who still thought of himself as a lawyer rather than a writer, had finally seen one of his more ambitious works produced on the stage. In *Eleven Days of Siege,* a comedy in three acts, the "siege" refers to the hero's attempt to win back his wife. When she discovers that, due to an error, their marriage had never been official, she refuses to allow him into her bedroom; of course, both love and law find a way.[13]

A work in prose this time, with no Hignard music to accompany it, *Eleven Days* was coauthored by Jules's longtime friend Charles Wallut, with whom he had already written the five-act drama *The Tower of Mont-lhéry* a decade earlier, as well as a one-act comedy entitled *An Adopted Son*—neither of which were ever staged.

As time dragged on, there didn't seem to be any reason to assume that 1862 would be any different from 1861. Indeed, at the beginning of 1862, the new father had no prospects of getting a play produced or any of his writing published. All of his attention seemed to be concentrated on the stock exchange, where he expended so much energy between one and five each afternoon.

A rare letter from this period survives. It reveals a Jules Verne devoted to his work as commission agent for Fernand Eggly, with offices in one of the tangle of streets lined with banks and insurance companies in the neighborhood of the Bourse. The letter was addressed to a family member in Nantes, Uncle Francisque, who, like everybody else in the family with funds to invest, was his client. "As for selling your bank stock," the letter reads in part, "I do believe this to be a wise decision. I never thought it advisable to buy it even at 4000 francs—this is horribly expensive. In any case for the past two days everything looks bad, with a horrendous drop in the market. Nobody knows what the government is doing."[14]

At this time, Verne set out on his second travel adventure with Aristide Hignard, a journey once again made possible by Hignard's brother. Now the friends would explore less familiar territory: Scandinavia. The complementary tickets took them as far as Stockholm, and from there they boarded a smaller steamer for the journey to Christiania (now Oslo, the capital of Norway), which at the time belonged to Sweden.

Later, Verne would remember the experience as one of the major events of an otherwise largely uneventful life. They sailed to Christiania by canal, mounting ninety-seven locks—"an extraordinary voyage of three days and three nights. . . ." From Christiania, they traveled by carriage to the Telemark region of hills and lakes, "that wildest part of Norway," and visited a nine-hundred-foot waterfall on the Gausta mountain.[15] No travel diary has survived, although Jules made use of the experience over two decades later when writing his novel *The Lottery Ticket*. The savage beauty of Norway's topography would not be forgotten in his other writings about the far north, either. Actually, this writer of travel adventure had to make maximum use of the little adventurous travel he was to know.

Olivier Dumas, Jules Verne's most diligent acolyte, discovered that in the teeth of the evidence (the evidence being Jules Verne's own dating), bumbling if well-meaning Marguerite Allotte created the unlikely legend that Verne and Hignard had undertaken their journey to Scandinavia a year earlier, in July 1861—thus in the final weeks of Honorine's pregnancy. In Allotte's words, they returned "just in time" for the birth of Jules's son. Later writers, who usually repeated Allotte's errors, surpassed her this time; in some retellings, Jules Verne actually missed the birth of his son.[16] This has been interpreted as indifference on his part, or even blatant hostility to Honorine or to the institution of marriage (or to women in general)—depending on how far one chooses to go.

Marguerite Allotte also told how Honorine, seeing Jules lying on the beach, staring down into the water, asked him, "How do you manage to write such beautiful things since you always look at the sky with your behind?" A bit of meanness, if it came from Honorine, although family legend has it that Honorine's six-year-old daughter, Suzanne, made that insolent remark, not Honorine.[17]

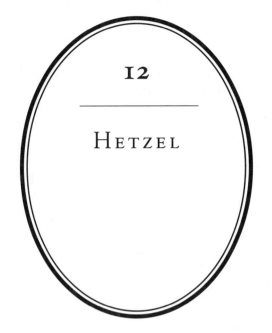

12

HETZEL

THE YEAR 1862 WAS A MOMENTOUS ONE FOR JULES VERNE, AL-though there is precious little documentation or eyewitness testimony to tell us about it. One story, perhaps apocryphal, concerns a statement Verne was said to have made from the floor of the bustling Paris stock exchange. It is the kind of thing he just might have said, the perfect overture to his annus mirabilis.

In this account, Jules, thirty-four, was standing below the exchange's Corinthian columns, talking to friends. "My boys, I believe that I'm about to desert you. I had the kind of idea Emile Girardin says every man must have to make his fortune. I've just written a new kind of novel, and if it succeeds it will be an unexplored gold mine. In that case I'll write more such books while you're buying your stock. And I think I'll earn the most money!"

His friends laughed, so of course he said (or was remembered to have said—"in the same bantering tone"), "Laugh, friends, we'll see who laughs longest."[1] Whether this story is true or false, he actually did write the "new kind of novel," a book so different from anything he or anyone else had done or tried to do until then, it seems an amazing achievement.

We do know something about his intentions. He later confessed that when he sat down to write *Five Weeks in a Balloon*, he had no knowledge whatsoever of ballooning, had never been up in one, nor had he seen Africa.

Why Africa? That unknown continent had always attracted him; he couldn't expect to explore it himself, but he could send his fictional heroes there. And why a flight *over* Africa? He replied that it seemed to him then—and still seemed to him three decades later when he was writing this explanation—"the real way to cross Africa." He confessed that "this means of locomotion allowed him to create a new kind of sensation, a new kind of adventure."[2]

He admitted to British journalist Robert Sherard that at the time he wrote his apprentice novel he didn't really believe in the possibility of guiding a balloon—"except in an absolutely stagnant atmosphere, as in this room, for instance. How can a balloon be made to face currents running at six, seven, or eight metres to the second?" He believed instead in *heavier*-than-air travel, "following the principle of the bird, which can fly, though it is heavier than the air which it displaces."[3]

Indeed, the novelist drew more on fictional balloons than on actual ones as his models. He had read Edgar Allan Poe, of course. Charles Baudelaire published his first translations of Poe's tales in 1856, in a volume including both "The Balloon Hoax" and "The Unparalleled Adventures of One Hans Pfaall." In the first Poe story, a group of Englishmen flying a balloon across the Channel to Paris find themselves blown across the Atlantic instead; the story is told in a realistic manner, as if the report of an actual adventure published in a New York newspaper. In the second story, Hans Pfaall of Rotterdam sells his possessions to construct a balloon containing a secret gas mixture, and then takes off for the moon.

This Poe tale begins in a matter-of-fact style, incorporating pertinent scientific observations, calculations of distances, and descriptions of inventions and techniques employed by the pilot, but fantasy dominates. This, however, was not the path Jules Verne would follow. Poe's hero lands on the moon, to find it peopled with little creatures; later, when Verne's heroes approach the moon, they find no more life there than present-day astronauts have.

Today, we think of Jules Verne as a prophet and a harbinger of the scientific revolution, a writer who described and then perfected explanations of the inventions that define modern times. He was that. But during the age of discovery in which he was writing, the world's remotest corners were just beginning to be explored. A new generation of explorers had begun to penetrate jungles and deserts. Jules Verne's apprenticeship as a writer coincided with early reports of their findings, and a whole literature grew from these roots.

In January 1860, as if he had seized the spirit of his time, Louis Hachette, a pioneer in popular education, had launched a weekly magazine called *Le Tour du Monde—Nouveau Journal des Voyages.* The publisher's prospectus explained its purpose:

> Some travelers represent science, others art, still others commerce or industry; there are those who confront a thousand dangers to propagate their faith, while others are simply observers, moralists, or seekers of adventure. All these preoccupations have their interest and serve a purpose; *Le Tour du Monde* will exclude none of them.[4]

Articles were enhanced by full-page illustrations, maps, portraits of explorers, illustrations of implements and inventions, pictures of sailing ships, indigenous dress, flora and fauna. Each sixteen-page issue opened with a feature story, followed by brief reports on current events. In its first year, the new magazine covered far-off China and nearby North Africa; the controversial geographer Elisée Reclus wrote about New Orleans, and there was a report on the polar explorations of U.S. Navy captain Elisha Kent Kane, including his account of being blocked by ice off Greenland—an account Jules most certainly saved or remembered.

Importantly, for the "new kind of novel" Jules Verne intended to exploit, one weekly issue of *Le Tour du Monde* began with an account of Capt. Richard Burton's mission, under the auspices of the Royal Geographic Society, to explore the great lakes of Africa. The editor reminded readers that "Africa has remained until recently what it was for our ancestors: a mysterious land whose interior tribes continue to live in isolation from the great human family."

An account of the 1858 expedition by Burton and John Speke, during which they discovered Lake Tanganyika, filled three successive issues of the magazine. It was told in Burton's own words, the illustrations based on his sketches. One of them depicted the travelers' point of departure, the port of Zanzibar; of course, Jules Verne's balloon trip would also begin there. Even as Jules worked on *Five Weeks in a Balloon,* Speke was leading an overland team to uncover the source of the Nile, at the time one of the great unsolved mysteries; such a discovery, it was believed, would also answer the riddle of the origins of civilization.[5]

Later, entering the last decade of his writing career, Jules Verne attributed his familiarity with science and its practical applications to general reading, along with assiduous note taking. By then, he was reading such well-known magazines as *La Nature* and Flammarion's *L'Astronomie.*[6] As early as 1856, he would have found a rich source of information, and perhaps inspiration, too, in the magazine *Le Musée des Sciences,* which was sold in weekly eight-page installments intended for lay readers who wished to know more about their changing world. Early issues dealt with subjects as varied as constellations, silver, metallurgy, flying fish, waterspouts, underwater exploration, a new voltaic pile, coal mining, aluminum, and earthquakes—all subjects that would later appear in his work. One issue of *Le Musée des Sciences* featured the account of the construction of a huge oceangoing vessel, the *Leviathan,* later rechristened *The Great Eastern,* a ship Jules would sail on and write about. The same issue included an article on aluminum production, followed soon afterward by an even more substantial report on "Aluminum and Its Industrial Uses."[7] In his books, Verne suggested applications for this little-understood element that his contemporaries could not have imagined.

Indeed, Verne's contribution would be to point to original and often convincing ways in which the new science could be applied. The scientists who were the protagonists of his novels, beginning with Samuel Fergusson in *Five Weeks in a Balloon,* would never venture very far from what was known or being discovered, from existing or conceivable technology. Writing to his father in February 1862, Jules compared his serious intentions with Poe's frivolity in "The Balloon Hoax": "I don't intend to take any ducks on my own balloon . . . but human beings. This airship must therefore be equipped with an infallible mechanism."

The source for this quotation is seemingly omniscient Marguerite Allotte, for the actual letter has never been found, and Allotte was not above writing or rewriting a letter to make a point. One would like to believe that Verne actually made this statement as he began to map out his first major novel. Another letter one must take on faith is that of Honorine to her mother-in-law in Nantes, this one written in May, when the strawberry vendors were out on the streets of Paris. "Do you have strawberries in Chantenay?" she wrote. "Jules is in the process of eating some, while finishing his balloon story. So much paper everywhere. Let's hope they don't all end up lighting the stove!" A unique view of Jules Verne we'll never get again—if it's an authentic one.

He seems more truly Jules in the disabused letter Allotte has him writing to his father in May 1862: "It seems that as soon as I get an idea or involve myself in something, in writing, this idea or this thing goes bad. If I write a piece for a theater, the manager leaves. . . . If I write an article another is published on the same subject, etc., etc. If I discovered a fortieth planet it would blow up to make a liar out of me."[8]

In addition to their aptitude for producing the right machines at the right time, Verne's heroes would also serve as professors, lecturing to readers on physics, chemistry, and advanced technology, as well as nature. Demonstrable knowledge appeared alongside the wondrous—a gigantic battery-powered submarine, for example, or a passenger airplane. Even today, it is not always easy to separate real science and fantasy in a Verne story.

One of his admirers, a literary historian, calculated that far from being the pioneer science fiction writer, Jules Verne was perhaps the 228th. He must have been one of the shyest of the lot, reluctant to "invent" anything that could not actually work—given the science of his time.[9] Verne himself came to understand the difference between his realistic approach and the fantasies of his predecessors. Compare his journey to the moon, based on flawed calculations but uncannily close to the space flights of our time, to Cyrano de Bergerac's totally fanciful voyage two centuries earlier, written in the service of political satire.

Two components were essential to the Verne canon, the body of work published as his *Extraordinary Voyages*. The first was the young man from Nantes himself, who seemed to have been the sole inventor of what would become identified as Vernian—the combining of contemporary and future scientific knowledge with an imaginary exploration of little-known but attainable worlds.

But an author needs a publisher, and in Pierre-Jules Hetzel Verne found one as anxious as he was to reach readers by presenting the new science in a popular, even fictional form. Jules Verne was as important to Hetzel as Hetzel was to Verne.

In 1862, this seasoned publisher was stepping across the threshold of a second career. He was born on June 15, 1814—fourteen years before Jules Verne. The son of an Alsatian father of Protestant stock and a Catholic mother from France's breadbasket south and west of Paris, he spent his school years at the good Catholic Collège Stanislas in Paris, then studied law in Strasbourg. His first job was in the book trade—working for a bookseller-publisher in Paris (in those days, the functions were often combined). Eventually, he became a partner in the firm, which published and sold religious and general books. This indefatigable man created a genre by publishing the animal drawings of the artist who called himself Grandville. These illustrations accompanied stories written by some of the best-known authors of the day. Hetzel was also writing his own tales and novels, publishing under the pseudonym P.-J. Stahl.

Before the mid-1880s, Hetzel was engaged in the production of Balzac's monumental suite of novels called "The Human Comedy." He was also both the publisher and friend of Georges Sand. In the effervescence of 1848, he added political activity to his many endeavors; after the

precipitous departure of King Louis Philippe, he became the chief
deputy of Alphonse de Lamartine, who headed the provisional government. Hetzel also worked with Gen. Louis Eugène Cavaignac, the minister of war.

The arrival of Louis Napoléon Bonaparte swept away Cavaignac's supporters, thus freeing Hetzel for publishing, or so he thought. But when
potential enemies were rounded up after the December 2, 1851 coup
d'état, Hetzel escaped arrest only by hiding. What the new government
really desired was the exile of potential troublemakers, so Hetzel was able
to join other prominent dissenters, such as Victor Hugo, in Brussels.
While absent from France—for eight long years—Hetzel was an underground publisher (with fellow exile Victor Hugo as one of his authors).
He went back to Paris after an amnesty decreed in August 1859, while
Hugo joined a hard core of libertarians who refused to live in France as
long as Napoléon III presided over its destiny.

Preparing for his return to the Paris book trade, Hetzel acquired a
house with a large back garden at 18, rue Jacob. His first authors were obviously going to include exiles whose hardships he had shared. Having
decided to launch a line of books for children, Hetzel turned for advice
to a classmate of his high school days, the educator Jean Macé, another
victim of Napoléon III (although his exile from the capital took him no
farther than the French province of Alsace). Hetzel also published adult
authors, among them another enemy of the empire, pioneer socialist
Pierre Joseph Proudhon; on the lighter side, he published himself—that
is, the fiction of P.-J. Stahl.

By the autumn of 1862, Hetzel was ready to take on the world. With affluent friends, he formed a new partnership under the name Hetzel &
Cie and prepared to undertake more ambitious projects.[10]

There is no documentary support for any of the stories concerning the
first encounter between Pierre-Jules Hetzel and Jules Verne, but publishers and authors always seem to find one another. According to one version—biographer Marguerite Allotte's—Jules simply turned up at 18, rue
Jacob one morning in the autumn of 1862, to be ushered into Hetzel's
bedroom behind the bookstore. This was where night owl Hetzel received morning callers. The shy Verne left his manuscript on the bed,
with hardly a word exchanged.[11] Soon there would be abundant correspondence between Hetzel and Verne, most of which has been preserved, although the very first letters have been lost.

In fact, an intermediary had introduced the two men. Much later,
Verne identified him as Alfred de Brehat (nom de plume of Alfred
Guézenec), a prolific author whose children's story "Adventures of a

Parisian Child," which was dedicated to Hetzel's son, was published by Hetzel in 1862.[12]

But it hardly mattered that it was this person and not that one who introduced Verne's ideal publisher to Hetzel's ideal author; the timing was right. Hetzel envisioned a commercial venture that would appeal to book buyers thirsty for knowledge, above all to their children. In Verne, he found a writer ready and willing to transform the new world of discovery and invention into readable tales.

It seems likely that Hetzel found a nearly publishable manuscript on his bed (if that is where Verne left it), for the time that elapsed between the establishment of Hetzel's new company and publication of the novel was too short to have allowed extensive rewriting. The first piece of evidence linking Hetzel and Verne is a single sheet of paper containing a contract written on both sides of the page, setting forth terms for the publication of what was then called *Voyage in the Air.* The publisher was to pay the author five hundred francs for an edition of two thousand copies in a format measuring four by six and a half inches; that came to twenty-five centimes (one-fourth of a franc) per copy, a rate that would be applied to further editions in the same format. Should the publisher decide to reprint in another format, the royalty would be 10 percent of the selling price for ordinary editions, while for illustrated editions "whose price and cost are higher, royalties will be calculated at five percent of the selling price." (A reasonable clause if one didn't think about it. In practice it ruled out compensation for the books that were to sell best.)

The contracts were signed by Jules Verne and J. (for Jules) Hetzel on October 23, 1862.[13] The book—now bearing its definitive title *Five Weeks in a Balloon*—was ready for year-end holiday gift sales on Christmas Eve.[14] Publishing Verne for holiday sales would become a habit.

LITERARY HISTORIANS MORE LITERARY THAN HISTORIAN often get facts and dates wrong. Some would write, without evidence, that Jules Verne came to know about balloons through Nadar, the pioneer portrait photographer and Renaissance man. There is plenty of evidence that Nadar and Verne were friends and actively shared interests (in manned flying vessels, for instance), although there is nothing to prove that Verne knew Nadar before he began writing *Five Weeks in a Balloon,* or that Nadar inspired or assisted in the writing. Nadar himself said that "it would be exaggerated to say that I was the initiator of Jules Verne; I wasn't even the one who introduced him to airplane navigation. . . ."[15]

It seems clear that Jules met Nadar through Hetzel, thus after he was well into the writing of *Five Weeks in a Balloon,* perhaps when he had already finished the manuscript. Nadar and Hetzel first met in the heady days of 1848, when Hetzel worked for General Cavaignac and Nadar, then returning from Berlin, offered to serve France as a secret agent.[16]

Balloons went up and down, and sideways when the winds were right, but they couldn't be used for purposeful travel. Lighter-than-air vessels going out of control were the bane of serious ballooners, who were convinced—to use Jules Verne's words—that "such a huge apparatus is dangerous to lead, impossible to direct."

The "huge apparatus" to which Verne referred was Nadar's and was appropriately christened the *Giant.* In an article published in *Musée des Familles* in 1863, Verne noted that balloon travel had made little progress since the end of the eighteenth century, when hydrogen gas was introduced. These early vessels had a net surrounding the container to support the gondola with its passengers and equipment, a valve to deflate for the descent, and ballast to be tossed out to make the balloon rise again. Nadar, "this courageous and daring artist," had revived interest in balloons thanks to the good reputation he had among journalists. "At the origin of great discoveries," declared Jules Verne, "there is always a man of this stamp, a seeker of difficulties, in love with the impossible. . . ."

In his article in *Musée des Familles,* Verne pointed to a possible solution for efficient air travel: getting rid of the balloon entirely and replacing it with locomotion—a propeller. Indeed, the use of three propellers was being studied, two to raise and sustain the craft—the latest version of what inventors were already calling a helicopter—the third to guide it. "It's no longer a matter, as we see, of gliding or floating in the air, but of navigating through it," Verne explained, concluding with the slogan attributed to Nadar: "Everything that is possible will be achieved."[17]

Born Félix Tournachon in Paris in 1820, the son of a printer, Nadar exercised his talents early as journalist and caricaturist, for which purpose he adopted his pseudonym. In 1854, he went to work in his older brother's photography studio, then set up as a photographer in his own right. He went up in a balloon for the first time in 1857, the following year becoming the world's first aerial photographer. In the summer of 1863, drawing his own conclusions about the inadequacy of balloon travel, he published a manifesto advocating heavier-than-air flight. This is certainly when Jules Verne entered the picture.[18]

It was during this period of enlightened amateurism that Nadar founded the Society for Encouragement of Aerial Locomotion by Means of Heavier-Than-Air Craft; the letterhead lists Jules Verne as a member of the board, with the function of auditor.[19]

At least one authority sees Nadar's influence on Verne as decisive. Nadar introduced the novelist to his circle of scientific friends (such as the physicist and astronomer Jacques Babinet, an honorary chairman of his society). Theoretical discussions with the likes of Nadar and his distinguished friends most certainly guided Verne through the writing of his early scientific stories.[20] As for Jules Verne, his first and only balloon flight took place a decade later, and it lasted only twenty-four minutes.

PART III

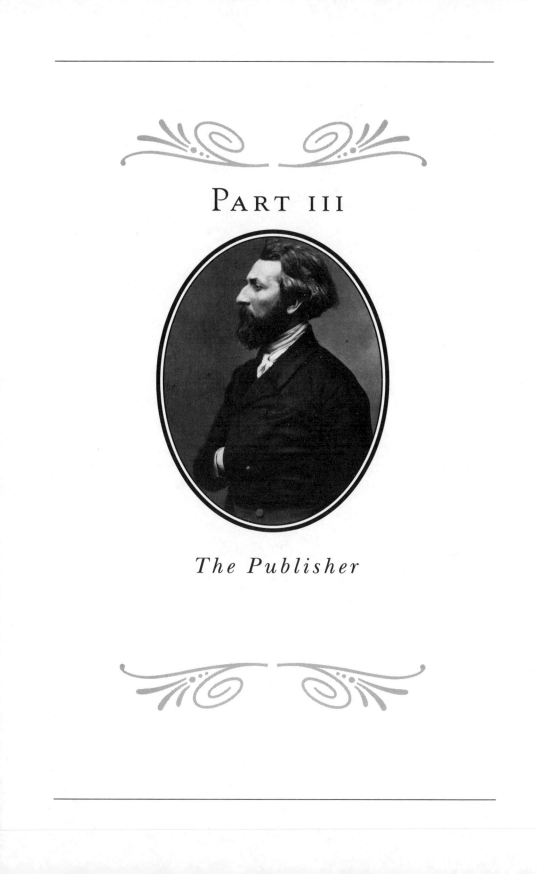

The Publisher

13

CAPTAIN
HATTERAS

THERE ARE FEW PARALLELS IN LITERARY HISTORY TO THE Verne-Hetzel duo: perfect symbiosis—each needing the other, thriving thanks to the other—and both of them knew it from the start. The encouragement, public recognition, and of course the financial rewards flowing from the Hetzel connection became a powerful incentive to the new novelist—not that Jules Verne had ever been a shirker, despite meager returns.

Now, however, the pages fairly flew from his desk. The next decade would see the publication of much of his best and most widely read work. The years 1863 and 1864 were fecund ones.

It is clear that even before the first copies of *Five Weeks in a Balloon* went on sale, its author had to be working on the still more ambitious, somewhat laborious odyssey of Captain Hatteras, describing that tenacious sailor's determination to reach the North Pole, wintering among the ice floes, his triumph—and ultimate tragedy. Before the Hatteras work was published, Verne was deep into yet another of the novels that would make his name, *Journey to the Center of the Earth*. Each narrative took as its point of departure accounts of other people's real-life adventures, news of recent technological developments, both of which called for more than a little familiarity with the books and journals containing these accounts.

For his part, Hetzel was putting the final touches to another of the century's publishing phenomena, a twice-monthly magazine for children and young people that would publish Jules Verne's novels, even the longest of them, in installments. To help him plan this children's magazine, Hetzel enlisted his friend and author Jean Macé, who, in addition to being a Hetzel author, was a determinedly republican educator and the founder of an organization that was to provide the ideological underpinning for advocates of public schools.

Macé was to represent a foil and a counterweight to publisher Hetzel, and, in a sense, to Jules Verne. For one thing, Macé was a Freemason—the bane of devout Catholics. In a France then increasingly divided between church and state, a proponent of public schools liberated from religious influence couldn't have been more different from a Jules Verne, raised as a Catholic. Although perhaps he had lost interest in the practice of his faith, he did not abandon its essential conservatism at a time when the French Revolution remained a painful memory. Somewhere in the middle stood Hetzel, an insurgent who had proved himself in 1848 and who was dedicated both ideologically and for business reasons to universal education. On the other hand, he catered to family audiences, who included a majority of churchgoers.[1]

If the name of Jean Macé on the cover of the new magazine counted for Hetzel, so did Macé's financial contribution (he was an equal partner in the venture). The new *Magasin d'Education et de Récréation* would be published by Jean Macé and P.-J. Stahl, Macé assuming responsibility for the educational part, Hetzel-Stahl for entertainment and literature. Later, a third name would appear on the masthead, that of the new house author, whose novels, published in fortnightly installments, became the backbone of the journal, the best reason for subscribing to it.[2]

What Hetzel needed was a storyteller whose narrative skills would keep readers on edge from issue to issue; to his everlasting credit, he recognized Jules Verne as that man. Henceforth, Hetzel would nurture Verne, making sure that his writing contained just the right mix of erudition and discovery, in conformity with the family morality of the day. A firm believer in lay education, in universal education, Hetzel was not a religious man; his beliefs were closer to those of Macé than to Verne's, and Jules knew that.[3] Yet they had no difficulty working together, and editor Hetzel often served as the author's best counselor on family values.

Their dialogue usually took the form of correspondence, at a time when letters moved faster than they do today. The very first letter to survive from author to publisher—and there are hundreds—bears the date June 26, 1863, written on the letterhead of the Parisian broker Fernand Eggly. Verne had just finished a truly Herculean effort on his book in progress; within a fortnight, he would deliver the first part of the Captain Hatteras saga—which described the long and difficult journey toward the North Pole.

Most of Verne's letters were progress reports, in which he scarcely repressed the joy of having found his way at last. In one letter, he wrote, "I'm in the middle of my subject at 80° latitude and 40° centigrade below zero. I'm catching cold just writing about it." Another letter, dated at the beginning of September, after his return from a fortnight in Brest, informed Hetzel of his progress on the second volume of the Hatteras tale. He was also back at his desk at broker Eggly's; a postscript complained: "I detest my customers."[4]

Hetzel's interventionist approach is revealed in another letter, not from but *to* the publisher; the date is September 16, 1863. In it, Verne assured Hetzel that "I totally approve your remark concerning Hatteras; I'm going to make him quite bold and not a little lucky. His fearlessness will frighten the reader. . . ." At this point, he said no to a request Hetzel had made—something Verne rarely did. Hetzel would have liked to see at least one Frenchman aboard the vessel taking Hatteras and his crew to the far north. But as Verne saw his story, much of the drama derived from the intrusion of an American into what was to have been a British triumph, so there could be no place for a Frenchman.[5]

Captain Hatteras's travails were published as two books, *The English at the North Pole* and *The Wilderness of Ice*, before being combined into a single volume entitled *The Adventures of Captain Hatteras*. Hetzel began publishing the first chapters of the novel in his new magazine before final editing had been done on the last chapters.

The contract, signed on January 1, 1864, called for payment of three thousand francs to the author (a sum equivalent to about sixty thousand present-day francs). This was to cover a printing of ten thousand copies, and the publication of the novel as a serialization in Hetzel's magazine. Further printings were to be paid for at a royalty of thirty centimes per volume; for illustrated editions, Verne was to receive 6 percent of the retail price, 50 percent of the translation rights.

In the contract, the second half of the saga of Captain Hatteras was called *The Robinsons in the Ice Fields*.[6] This abandoned title is significant, for the Robinson myth provides a key to nearly everything Verne wrote. Again and again, he conveyed to his readers his fascination with a closed universe, an island when possible, if not a balloon basket, a spaceship cabin, or even an igloo. Nearly every Verne hero is a Mr. Fixit who can make do with available materials to solve a problem, repair a leak, or cook a meal (often the manservant who accompanies the hero will do the cooking). Some of Verne's heroes attain the status of super-Robinsons, with degrees in engineering (Samuel Fergusson is one of these; omnipotent Cyrus Smith in *The Mysterious Island* is another).

Nearly a century and a half earlier, Daniel Defoe had created verisimilitude in his *Adventures of Robinson Crusoe* by reporting an abundance of detail in the detached manner of an anthropologist, an ethnologist, and sometimes a mechanic. Defoe's narrative, based in part on real events, might have been taken (as Verne's might have been) for history.

THE NEW MAGAZINE WAS READY ON THE FIRST DAY OF spring 1864, with the opening chapter of Jules Verne's new book on the front page. In a preface, the editor called it "the account of a curious and absorbing journey, in which discoveries in the Arctic seas up to our time are summed up with the scientific precision, the expert geographical knowledge, and the persuasive talent of a storyteller whose first book was unique of its kind."

Once again, the narrative bore such trappings of authenticity as a date (a relatively recent one: 1860) and the identification of a succession of real places. As the steamship *Forward* is fitted out in Liverpool for a trip to an unknown destination, its equipment leads bystanders to guess that it will sail to the Arctic Ocean. Its captain, whose identity is a secret, has offered high pay for hazardous work, taking aboard sufficient supplies for a six-year voyage. There is speculation that the captain has chosen to remain hidden because he doesn't wish to frighten his men by announcing their destination too early.

Throughout the book, the reader is informed of time passed, of the *Forward*'s position on the charts, and, when they appear, of the precise nature of the ice fields. As in the earlier *Five Weeks in a Balloon,* the author provides the authentic history of previous explorations of the same sites and a circumstantial account of the fate of ships and crews. In the convincing mix of fact and fancy that pervades *The Adventures of Captain Hatteras,* Verne's hardy seamen come upon tangible evidence of the visit of Sir John Ross, a real-life Arctic explorer. The fictional heroes also pay their respects at the scene of the death of real-life Joseph Bellot, who in 1853 disappeared in a crevice while searching for an earlier explorer.

In John Hatteras—at last the captain throws off his disguise as a member of the crew—the author created one more of his exceptional (but not necessarily well-behaved) protagonists, a man with character flaws and a fixation. Hatteras's self-imposed goal is to plant the British flag at the

North Pole. He had tried to do it before, tried so energetically, so ruth-lessly, that it was difficult now to find seamen willing to sail under his command. But in 1853, an American ship with an American captain had penetrated farther north than any of his predecessors. Hatteras is deter-mined to surpass the Americans at any cost. If nothing else, his steam engine would give him an advantage over previous polar expeditions.

The novelist in Verne shines in his presentation of the crew—notably of the disgruntled, later mutinous first mate, Richard Shandon; and also of the likeable, loyal Dickensian Dr. Clawbonny, invaluable foil to Hat-teras. Tension mounts as Hatteras urges his crew onward in a race against the arrival of winter; the maps show blanks—for no one has gone this far—and the *Forward*'s captain is hoping that the polar region will be sur-rounded by sea to allow a close approach.

When they are unable to proceed farther—which would mean going farther than any previous expedition had—the crew prepares to lay up for the winter. The *Forward* is now encased in thick ice. Soon the ice-bound expedition will come to the end of its fuel supply; crewmen then feed the furnace by chopping up less essential parts of the ship's struc-ture.

Hatteras leads a task force in an unsuccessful search for supplies; on their return, he finds the ship afire, the crew missing. He and his loyal aides salvage essential supplies from the destroyed ship and build a house of ice—still another cocoon.

They find an American survivor of an earlier expedition, one that sought a northwest sea passage. The American is as accessible as Hatteras is somber, but the English captain sees him as a rival. On March 24, 1861, they find the wreckage of the American's ship, which still carries a two-year food supply. Now they will build a proper igloo—they call it a "snow-house," and in its dimensions and comforts, it is that.

With enforced leisure, they set about naming the geographical fea-tures of their new territory. The American insists on calling the new land-mass New America because he had found it before encountering the Hatteras expedition. Through it all, Dr. Clawbonny proves the genial im-proviser present in much of Verne's fiction. He is a well-read man, also a familiar Verne character, who can identify and explain natural phenom-ena, especially when a complaisant fellow character asks him to.

Surely Verne needed no suggestions from Hetzel as to how to fill the pages that would have to be written in order to stretch his story out to run for a year in *Magasin d'Education et de Récréation*. The tale runs on, the nar-rative frame embellished with anecdote, resumés of past explorations, lectures on flora and fauna, and accounts of scientific discoveries. It is a spinning out, a true thousand and one nights, the first of many such by Jules Verne. The author also borrowed a technique from Shakespeare, inserting comic scenes at intervals to attenuate the drama.

When the American is absent, Hatteras informs the remaining crewmen—four in all now, with the doctor—of his intention to pursue the expedition as far as the North Pole; they'll follow him on foot if necessary. Hatteras won't build a small boat with materials from the wreckage of the American vessel, for that would mean "sailing American."

Dr. Clawbonny's ingenuity saves them from attack by vicious bears. In the summer thaw, he plants seeds. During a hunt, the American saves Hatteras's life, and there is reconciliation, the beginning of friendship. On June twenty-fifth, they begin the 350-mile journey to their objective by dogsled, carrying their boat overland with them. On July tenth, they reach water and begin a sea journey.

As they approach the North Pole, the temperature rises, and they find a volcanic island. Hatteras will not rest until he sets foot on the volcano—for that is the precise position of the pole; he climbs through lava, smoke, and ashes to plant his flag. But the excitement unsettles him; he will lose his mind. On the return journey—an easier one by sea—the survivors are picked up by a Danish whaler and repatriated. Their arrival in England is triumphal, but Hatteras cannot share in it. He will end his days in an asylum, each day walking, with the faithful dog that accompanied him to the pole (another repeated Verne device), in the same direction—north.

ON APRIL 25, 1864, OVER A MONTH AFTER PUBLICATION OF the first chapters of Captain Hatteras's adventures in *Magasin d'Education*, the author sat down to review the latest editorial suggestions—corrections, one should say—from his publisher. "You don't know me if you think for an instant that your letter wasn't welcome," Verne began his reply. This was the first surviving letter of a lifelong file of letters responding—usually compliantly—to Hetzel's objections. "I assure you that I'll follow your suggestions, for they are all justified. . . . I am not yet so sure of myself as to be able to do anything I wish." He further assured Hetzel: "It's not a publisher who is writing to me, but a friend in whom I have total confidence."

Verne's original ending bothered Hetzel. Verne had Hatteras leap to his death into the erupting volcano; he didn't say as much, but it took some courage on his part to let the exemplary hero go mad and die. But "how [to] bring Hatteras back to England; what would he do there? Obviously this man must die at the pole. The volcano is the only tomb worthy of him."

They talked further about all this. "Have you ever found me hesitant on the question of cuts or modifications? Did I not follow your advice in the editing of *Five Weeks in a Balloon?*" Hetzel made it clear that he could not accept the suicide of the captain. So Hatteras returned home, if insane.

Perhaps it was imprudent for Verne to let his publisher make such important decisions for him. But this was an author with a decade of failure behind him; now success was within reach. He wanted to assure his benefactor that he was and would continue to be Hetzel's star performer. "Besides, I am going to reveal all my thoughts to you, dear Hetzel. I don't really want to be simply a reporter of fact; consequently, I'll always be ready to make changes for the general good. What I wish to become, above all, is a writer, a laudable ambition you will approve entirely."

He wished, he assured Hetzel, "to become a stylist, a serious one; it's my life-long dream."[7]

By now, publisher Hetzel had a good idea of just how compliant his star could be. For his part, the star knew which member of the publisher-author duo was really the boss. For Verne had gone to the rue Jacob with a third manuscript in his satchel (apparently written during this same year, 1863).[8] However, this new book was vetoed; it would never see publication in his or Hetzel's lifetime. Even the original manuscript was given up for lost.

In this new work, which he had entitled *Paris in the Twentieth Century,* he portrayed a young man living unhappily in the French capital as it might be a century later (more precisely, in 1960). It was a city in which daily life had been enhanced by electricity for street lighting, rapid transportation by elevated and underground urban-transit trains driven by compressed air (and therefore pollution-free), and gasoline-powered horseless carriages: "What would our ancestors have said on seeing these boulevards illuminated with a brightness equal to that of the sun, these thousands vehicles circulating soundlessly on the muffled asphalt, these stores rich as palaces, from which light spreads as bright rays, these avenues as large as squares. . . ." But Parisians of 1960 were not happier for all of that, thinks the young narrator, because their haste and their "American spirit" pushed them forward "without respite or mercy."[9]

In the home were mechanical elevators (not yet invented), again powered by electricity. In the office, stock quotations were sent around the world by telegraph. There were individual telegraph machines (resembling telex), facsimile documents transmitted by what he termed *téléma-*

tique photographique, and giant keyboard calculating machines (resembling early computers).

Of course, the hero, a closet poet named Michel, is miserable, deprived of what he considers essential: his cultural heritage. In his brave new world, humanities have been sacrificed to technical studies (all in one giant school, where 250,000 persons assemble for graduation ceremonies). Victor Hugo has been forgotten, along with Honoré de Balzac, but there is never any difficulty finding books on science and technology. Music, painting, and poetry are virtually underground practices; Michel shares the memory of the great artists and writers with rare fellow dissidents. Plays for the city's fifty theaters are produced in a government drama warehouse, eliminating the need for censorship.

Unable to adapt, Michel finds himself without a roof and without a job. He writes a book of poetry and cannot find a publisher; his clothes are tattered; he is cold and hungry in a wintry city. He spends his last franc on flowers for Lucy, the granddaughter of his old professor of literature, one of the last humanists, but when he proceeds to call on them, he finds that they have been evicted and have left no forwarding address. So he wanders through the heartless, technologically perfect city, until he finds himself in Paris's sprawling Père Lachaise cemetery among the neglected tombs of writers and poets. Saying Lucy's name, he collapses on the snowy ground.

Was *this* the way Jules Verne saw scientific progress? At that moment, Hetzel had only two published books by which to judge his brilliant recruit. In *Five Weeks in a Balloon,* the ingenious Samuel Fergusson and his comrades escape with their lives from a stripped, ripped balloon, despite Fergusson's best science. They had come to the end of a momentous journey, yet Fergusson's inventive mind could not have taken them one more mile. In *The Adventures of Captain Hatteras,* the long-planned journey of an Arctic explorer who thought that determination and a steam engine would take him farther than his predecessors goes awry, and ship, crew, and mind are lost. These books were hardly testimonials to the scientific and industrial revolutions, yet readers (the young and not so young) had too much to marvel at to give much thought to the underlying lessons in pessimism.

Paris in the Twentieth Century, however, was pure gloom. Its characters lead appalling lives, finding salvation only in active dissidence. Certainly Hetzel saw no place for such subversive thinking in a publishing program designed for family reading. He summed up his ferocious marginal comments, scribbled alongside the text as he read, in a letter to this author he prized. Hetzel would have given anything (so his draft letter began) *not* to have to say what he was about to say. He felt that Verne had undertaken an impossible task, and that he could not do better with it than any of his predecessors had. "It's a hundred feet below *Five Weeks in a Balloon*," he declared bluntly. "If you read it again in a year you'll agree with me."

Quite simply, in Hetzel's view, Verne had said nothing new about the dangers of progress; moreover, the book lacked life.

> I am sorry, truly sorry to have to write you this: I'd consider publication of this book a disaster for your name. This would lead people to think that [*Five Weeks in a Balloon*] is a fluke. But I who have *Captain Hatteras* in hand know that [*Paris in the Twentieth Century*] is the fluke but the public won't know that. . . . It's a washout, a fiasco, and if a hundred thousand people told me the contrary I'd send them all to the devil.

Publishing his futuristic vision of Paris now, warned Hetzel, would cause Jules Verne "irreparable harm."[10]

The manuscript—not discovered until 1989—shows how carefully the publisher read the book, and how angry it made him. "For me all this isn't very happy," he wrote in one of his marginal notes. "Measure is lacking, taste also." About one long passage of dialogue, he wrote, "This method is all right in the hand of a Dumas, in a book full of adventure. Here it's just tiring. . . . Try as I might, I can't find any interest in all these criticisms, all these hypotheses. . . . Wait twenty years to write this book. . . . Nobody today will believe your prophecy, nobody will care about it."[11]

The book would receive no further attention in Verne's lifetime.

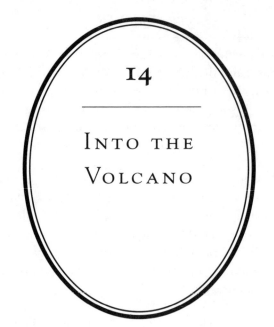

14

INTO THE
VOLCANO

VERNE'S RETURN TO NANTES WAS TRIUMPHAL, ACCORDING TO
Marguerite Allotte, and for once this local biographer was able to quote
a local chronicler, who in this summer of 1864 could barely recognize the
"powerful" new Jules. "Honorine is always the same, fresh and without
pretense."

> Last night: much hubbub. Dance reception on the riverfront in
> the honor of the novelist. The only thing missing at the celebra-
> tion was the hero. Poor Jules was in bed, suffering again from fa-
> cial paralysis, which comes back from time to time. Like
> everybody else Honorine laughed a lot, danced a lot, drank a lot
> of syrups, swallowed a lot of ices in his honor.[1]

The reference to Jules's disabling malady authenticates the document.
It accords with a letter from the author to his publisher; Jules was working even while suffering from "a paralysis of the facial nerve. It's the
fourth time this has happened. One side of my face is alive, the other
dead. One moves, the other can't! Pretty picture. On one side I've the
profile of an intelligent creature . . . on the other that of an idiot."[2]

But he was soon on his feet, and Marguerite Allotte wrote that he became the life of every party, the target of many a barbed stanza.

Take heed, oh writer, one's never sure of glory.
It bursts and you fall, as from a balloon.
The higher you rise, the fall is more gory.
Will Hetzel buy you another pantaloon?[3]

Of course, he worked during the summer visit to the family house on the hill in Chantenay. He was finishing another novel for Hetzel, *Journey to the Center of the Earth*, and this despite the disorder brought on by a houseload of children, reinforced by the presence of his own three-year-old, Michel. Legend depicts the stern author, dressed in the casual way frugality and much indoor living had taught him, appearing brusquely in a doorway. "Blinking his left eye [a reference to his nervous condition], he hurls, with his left eye, a piercing, terrifying, insupportable glance. The noise ceases at once, to begin again five minutes later. . . ."

Chronicler Allotte quotes another neighbor who showed up at Chantenay—actually to call on Pierre Verne. "His son the novelist was there," the visitor reported. "I thought I should compliment him on his success; he was as rude and disagreeable as one can be. I won't be so intrepid as to caress that polar bear again."[4]

Although only one of Verne's novels had been published in book form—the second one was still appearing in magazine installments—he was already a celebrity (and certainly in his hometown of Nantes). Before the year was over, a bona fide geographer, in a respected journal (*L'Année Géographique*), spared no adjectives in saluting this unknown who was making his science popular, notably with *The Adventures of Captain Hatteras*, "[which] one would be tempted to place among genuine travel journals, so accurate is the information it contains." Of course, there had been Defoe's *Adventures of Robinson Crusoe*, and Swift's *Gulliver's Travels*, "but Mr. Verne managed on the first try to create his own niche and to claim the right to invent, thanks to the style with which his work is impregnated. . . . It is difficult to mix science and fiction without weighing down the one and diminishing the other," he explained. "Here they enhance each other in a happy union, which highlights the instructive side of the story while realizing it, careful readers will obtain reliable information that few would have bothered to look for in more austere tomes."[5]

In December the erstwhile broker and minor playwright, suddenly become bard of geography, was presented for membership in the Geographic Society, and voted in (as Jules Vernes with an *s*). A few months later, when he made a gift to the society of his latest work, he was acknowledged as Joseph Verne; according to the minutes, he then stood

before the assembly to "ask the Society's pardon for the role the imagination plays in his works."[6]

The legends would follow. A Parisian memorialist, who claimed to have
gotten the information from the author himself, revealed Jules Verne's
plan to cover the entire world, "without leaving a virgin corner." Later on,
Verne was believed to have kept a map in his office; it reminded the visitor of fireworks, "crisscrossed as it was with lines in red, blue, etc., indicating to the Verne trips already made. . . . ." When ready to begin a new
novel, the author—so said this reporter—would first examine his map to
find a place not yet covered with lines. The visitor imagined that Verne
began by sticking a pin into this virgin territory, then read "everything"
that had ever been published about it.[7] Did such a map ever exist? All that
survived was a small unmarked globe. In interviews, Verne credited sailing as the main source of his geography, although "I sometimes have had
to rely on my reading for my descriptions."[8]

Knowing that Verne never got farther north than Scandinavia or farther south than the Mediterranean basin—apart from a single, brief
transatlantic hop—one is tempted to credit armchair and not seagoing
travel as his main source.

In an armchair, there could be no better company than Edgar Allan
Poe; his tales help to explain the aura of mystery enveloping so many
Verne stories. The difference between the two writers is that Jules Verne
began by puncturing mystery, scattering the aura, in quest of rational explanation; Poe left readers with his hallucinations.

Returning to *Musée des Familles,* the magazine in which he had published
his first work, Jules Verne had contributed an essay on Poe to the April
1864 issue. Now, in addition to the stories published by Baudelaire, including the book-length *The Narrative of Arthur Gordon Pym,* Hetzel published
a collection of Poe stories that Baudelaire had *not* translated. One of these
inspired *Around the World in Eighty Days* (*Le Tour du monde en 80 jours*).

In his long essay, written for readers unfamiliar with Poe, Verne acknowledged this American author (who died in 1849, just fifteen years
earlier) as the master of a school of his own—the school of the strange.
This is not to say that he was insensitive to the calculating side of Poe;
quite the contrary. Verne cited stories "in which analysis and deduction
attain the absolute limits of the intelligence," such as "The Murders in
the Rue Morgue" and "The Purloined Letter." Then there were Poe's
lighter works, among them stories mixing horror with the comic. Verne
mentioned "The Balloon Hoax," yet he preferred "The Unparallelled
Adventures of One Hans Pfaall," even though in each of them "the most
elementary laws of metaphysics and mechanics are boldly transgressed."

As a critic, Verne didn't like that: "This has always astonished me on the part of Poe who, through a few inventions, could have made his stories more believable."[9] This nearly amounted to a declaration of intention on the part of Jules Verne.

It is something of an anticlimax to come upon the shallow stories by Verne that *Musée des Familles* was to publish now. "The Count of Chanteleine," which ran in three successive monthly issues of *Musée,* surely belonged to an earlier time—kept in a drawer, ready to be dragged out when notoriety suddenly made the author's name valuable. The retelling of a historic episode, the resistance of Royalist Catholics in a corner of Brittany to the French Revolution, betrays the author's identification with counterrevoltuion: The count is "one of the bravest, one of the best," who joins a Catholic army mobilizing 100,000 men. He fights against the decision of the Convention, the Revolution's assembly, to "destroy the soil" of dissident western France. When the count is captured and faces execution, the crowd hears of the reversal of revolutionary ardor in Paris, and the execution of Robespierre. The noble prisoner is rescued just before reaching the execution block, then slips out of France until better times. This is a bedtime story for counterrevolutionaries, written in romantic tremolo. Later, when the author wished to include it in a collection of his stories, Hetzel made it clear he had no need of it.[10]

The following year—certainly with the consent of Hetzel—he sold another story to *Musée*. "The Blockade Runners" takes the American Civil War, which had just ended, as its theater. It depicts a Scottish sea captain who forces the Union blockade of Confederate ports. During the ocean voyage, the seaman is won over by an American girl traveling to help her father, a Northerner imprisoned in Charleston because he opposed slavery. The ship slips past the Union blockade successfully, its captain now determined to save the girl's father even at the expense of compromising his cargo and crew. Learning that her father is to be shot for rebellion, the Scot rescues the prisoner, and of course the captain will now marry Miss Jenny, the abolitionist's daughter.[11]

⁂

THE STORIES BELONGED TO THE OLD JULES VERNE. BUT NOW that he had found his true path, he would never abandon it. As soon as he finished a book, he would begin another, which was to be expected of an author who had suffered from a decade of neglect and had been denied the chance to prove himself. He was like a dog with a bone: He had no intention of letting it go.

Verne's next book, *Journey to the Center of the Earth,* was inspired by a science less tangible than that reflected in the earlier books. The fact that in this novel the author indulges in pure speculation about the nature of the planet, and that the quest begins and ends in a volcano—a theme that would continue to tempt him—moved some modern critics to see this voyage of descent, with its hardships and its mystery, as an initiatory rite for the younger of the two protagonists.[12]

This character, Axel, is an orphan. He is working as an assistant to his uncle and guardian, the eccentric chemistry professor Otto Lidenbrock of Hamburg. One day, Lidenbrock finds an ancient Icelandic manuscript; when he shows it to Axel, a soiled parchment slips from its pages. The document contains a text in code from a sixteenth-century scientist. Deciphered, it is an invitation to descend a certain crater in Iceland to the center of the earth, as the dead scientist had done.

Professor Lidenbrock sets off, accompanied by his acolyte. Here, the full sense of initiation comes into force—for by joining this quest with its unknown perils, Axel will become worthy of Graüben, the professor's seventeen-year-old goddaughter. Following the instructions contained in the ancient message, they climb a mountain, then wait there for the sun's rays to indicate the entrance to a tunnel. Along the way, assisted by a guide recruited in the Icelandic capital, they discover fossils of the earliest plants and animals.

Then the perils begin. The expedition is threatened by their failure to find fresh supplies of water; paralyzed by fatigue, the young man collapses, saved by a last ration of water. With his renewed strength, Axel begs his uncle to turn back; never, says Lidenbrock. The two scientists and their guide pursue their exploration through geological layers, but often their route is horizontal, not the rapid descent they had hoped for.

The young hero moves ahead of the others and is lost; soon his lantern fails him; he rushes through dark corridors and stumbles. Then he hears voices, and he is able to communicate with his uncle over a great distance by speaking to the wall. Reunited, the party reaches an underground sea, and finds evidence of prehistoric sea life (monsters threaten the raft they have built to navigate it).

Professor Lidenbrock had discovered the original runic message in Hamburg on May 24, 1863 (so we learn on the opening page of the book). It is June twenty-eighth by the time he stands with nephew and guide at the rim of the Icelandic crater, waiting for the sun to direct their descent. On August twentieth, they calculate that they have covered a sufficient distance under the earth to be positioned below England.

However, they are swept up in a hurricane on the underground sea, then shipwrecked on dry ground. They find a graveyard for antediluvian monsters and discover a human skull, living mastodons, and a human giant. This is a rare example of Verne knowingly proffering a scientific impossibility. Although when Axel later recalls the discovery—for it is he who writes the log of their odyssey—he wonders whether they really saw this twelve-foot-tall superhuman specimen.

Afloat on a makeshift raft, the three explorers find themselves descending into the earth. Their food has run out and heat oppresses them. They detect signs of an imminent volcanic eruption, and, indeed, they are expelled to the outside world—landing on a mountainside. They find themselves on Stromboli, a tiny island off Sicily with an active volcano, twelve hundred leagues from their point of departure in Iceland. By September ninth, they are back in Hamburg. They are acclaimed in their homeland, where, of course, they prepare for the marriage of Axel and Graüben.

Verne's fame would come from the daily press; the critics in the quarterly journals would never show much interest. "This imaginary journey has all the colors and movement of reality," a reviewer affirmed in the Paris daily *Le Constitutionnel,* "and if the author himself hadn't warned us that it was fiction the illusion would have been all but complete."[13] The austere daily *Le Temps* announced: "Mr. Verne is the creator of a genre in our literature, and he will have a place of his own. What Walter Scott's novels are for the teaching of history . . . Mr. Verne's books are for geographical science. . . ."[14]

VERNE HAD ALWAYS SAID THAT HIS THIRTY-FIFTH YEAR would be a watershed. He had turned thirty-five in February 1863, just as his first novel—*Five Weeks in a Balloon*—was launched on its vertiginous career. Now, two years later, on the eve of his thirty-seventh birthday, it was hard to keep up with him. There had been a second book (*Journey to the Center of the Earth*), another (*The Adventures of Captain Hatteras*) currently running in fortnightly installments in *Magasin d'Education,* and still another (and perhaps two) in progress. Henceforth, that would be the pattern, until such time as he could no longer hold a pen in his hand.

15

The Hetzel
Colors

During the U.S. Civil War, some eminent gentlemen of Baltimore, Maryland, impassioned by ballistics (Yankees are engineers, observed Jules Verne, as Italians are musicians, and Germans metaphysicians), founded an association of like-minded souls that they named the Gun Club. When an American has an idea, Verne explained to his readers, he looks for another American to share it; when there are three of them, they elect a president and two secretaries.

Then the war was over; what to do with their science? The drawing room on Union Square in Baltimore is full to bursting on one October evening in 1865. The assembled throng is there to hear the president of the Gun Club, Impey Barbicane, an even-tempered, cool, strict gentleman of forty, director of artillery on the Union side during the late war, as he proposes a vast project worthy of the century, and which the science of ballistics has now made possible—at least in the United States. Could they not fire a cannonball to the moon?

His speech is a triumph; the whole country would soon hear of it by telegraph. No one doubts that Barbicane's plan will succeed. Two days later, the observatory in Cambridge, Massachusetts, replies to a questionnaire from the Gun Club's president requesting technical details, such as the speed at which the projectile would have to be launched, the distance to be covered, and the time it would take (and thus the date at which the shot should be fired to have the moon in the most favorable position).

With Impey Barbicane, and with J. T. Maston, permanent secretary of the club and inventor of a devastating mortar, Jules Verne introduced a new kind of character. It appears that Verne was now more influenced by Dickens than by James Fenimore Cooper or Walter Scott. *From the Earth to the Moon* is an absorbing, occasionally believable story, with a drollery its author hadn't seemed to master until then. It is obvious that Verne had left the artifice of the vaudeville stage far behind.

The new book manifested the author's admiration for things American—American ingenuity and intrepidity—as well as the infinite resources that made bold projects possible. The United States and its people fascinated Verne, and even when he turned against the English, he remained an Americanophile.

He wrote over half of this book before introducing a flesh-and-blood character to accompany his stick figures into space. Until this point, the Gun Club envisaged an unmanned flight. Now, at their Florida base, during the assembling of the mammoth cannon to be christened Columbiad, they receive a telegram from Paris: "Replace spherical shell with cylindro-conical projectile. Shall travel in it. Arrive on steamship *Atlanta*." The message is signed "Michel Ardan."

The Gun Club officers are thunderstruck at the idea of sending a human being on their moon shot—but adventurous J. T. Maston thinks it might not be such a bad idea after all. Ardan's reputation for daredevil feats has already crossed the Atlantic. Ardan is an anagram for: Nadar. "At present," Jules Verne informed his photographer-balloonist friend, "I must invent a character endowed with the best and bravest heart, and I apologize, but I've taken you for the model."[1]

In his flight to the moon, Ardan will be joined by Gun Club president Barbicane and an old rival, Captain Nicholl; the enthusiast Maston is grounded because this old soldier was confined to hobbling on wooden legs.

Read now, when the Apollo space program is already history, the vision Verne displayed in *From the Earth to the Moon* is uncanny. Verne's heroes will dispatch a three-man spaceship—the "cannonball"—to the moon, just as NASA would later do. The cabin will be made of aluminum. The Gun Club enthusiasts solve problems of gravity and resistance that would have to be tackled in reality by future scientists. To launch their shot at the proper angle, the men from Baltimore choose a site in Florida, then largely undeveloped, near Cape Canaveral (this spot actually appears on the rudimentary map in the Hetzel edition).

As a preparatory experiment, Verne's astronauts send a cat and a squirrel into space, retrieving them in the sea—another uncanny resemblance to the tests preceding manned space flight. Not only is the Gun Club team launched from Florida, as American astronauts would be but, like the astronauts, they also splash down in the Pacific.

It is the Frenchman Michel Ardan who suggests the final design of their "wagon-projectile"—the space cabin; to build it, a larger quantity of aluminum has been ordered than had ever been produced for any purpose. The launching will be powered by a formidable quantity of guncotton. The occupants of the cabin are protected from the shock by a layer of water filling the space between the vehicle's double walls. There are thick glass portholes for observation, sealed during the liftoff (and then opened by screws controlled from inside). The air supply will be renewed by oxygen obtained by heating potassium chlorate, a powerful oxidizing agent. Food will be predried to reduce volume.

Their flight was to be monitored from the ground—another Verne anticipation of later events—by a powerful Rocky Mountain telescope operated by the Cambridge observatory.

And so they were off, to cheers from a huge crowd, the playing of the national anthem and "Yankee Doodle Dandy." The story of the dauntless space explorers ends here. "We'll be hearing from them," announces J. T. Maston from his observatory, "and they from us!" Readers would have to wait four long years to learn what happened from the sequel.

From the Earth to the Moon first appeared in installments in the *Journal des Débats,* one of the most serious of Paris dailies, from September 14 to October 14, 1865, and only after that did Hetzel release it in book form. The review in *Journal des Débats* was almost a manifesto: "There is a public for works concerned with modern times, and this is the public to watch."[2]

Verne, who was always writing two or more books at the same time, now felt the need to do it in a quieter place. His choice was a humble fishing port called Le Crotoy, northeast of Paris on the bay of the Somme, a recess in the English Channel, with its somewhat austere shoreline of sandy dunes. The town itself, some forty-five miles from Amiens, had few of the amenities of a summer resort, but Jules Verne, who had spent his boyhood near the Loire estuary, seemed to like it that way.[3]

In the coming years, he would do some of his best work in Le Crotoy, alternating spells of writing with sailing, in borrowed or rented sloops, then in a craft of his own. Once during this first summer, he sailed along the Atlantic coast. "You see that I'm replying from Bordeaux where your letter caught up with me," he wrote to his publisher. "My brother was there, and I couldn't resist the desire to go there to pick him up by sea and to bring him back by sea. And as you know, there is no real journey without a bit of ocean."

Nor did all this activity prevent him from thinking about work in progress: he even planned revisions of a book—*The Children of Captain Grant*—in correspondence with Hetzel. "In fact I'm very anxious to read the manuscript again," he told the publisher. "I'll have it sent to me as soon as I get to Nantes in a few days. It's through your notes, and your pencilled bursts of anger, that I'd understand what doesn't work. I had a wonderful return sail," he subsequently reported, "a spring gale, danger of being washed ashore, a real storm even to my brother—who is a sailor as you know. That's what gives you unforgettable experience!"[4]

And as if it wasn't enough that he was now writing constantly, all the while sending Hetzel his completed work, he was also thinking about one of his most perilous imaginary journeys ever.

The first bit of evidence is a letter Verne wrote to Hetzel from Chantenay; it is reasonable to assume that it was sent during the summer visit to his parents' home. "Today I'm hard at work and lost in New Zealand," he informed Hetzel. This reference is to the shipwrecked protagonists of *The Children of Captain Grant*. "I'm also preparing our voyage under the seas, and my brother and myself are organizing the mechanical side of the expedition. I think we'll use electricity, but that hasn't quite been decided."[5]

The original idea for what may be Jules Verne's best-known book, *Twenty Thousand Leagues Under the Sea,* seems to have come from another novelist. George Sand, a friend of Hetzel's as well as one of his authors in years past, and a fellow rebel in 1848, was already, at age sixty-one, a national hero. Long after their professional ties had dissolved, she and Hetzel had remained close friends; it was normal for this publisher to have a younger author send his first books to Sand.

She had just spent half a year watching her companion, Alexandre Manceau, die; Verne's stories, she confessed in her thank-you letter in this summer of 1865, "succeeded on distracting me from a deep sorrow. . . . I have only one regret concerning these stories, which is to have finished them and not to have a dozen more to read." It was at that point that Sand offered the suggestion that Jules Verne remembered as the origin of the tour de force that was to consume much of his energy over the four years to come: "I hope that you will soon take us to the depths of the sea," she suggested, "and that you will have your characters navigate in diving vessels that your science and your imagination will manage to improve."[6]

FOR THE MOMENT, HOWEVER, VERNE FOCUSED ON CAPTAIN Grant, and above all on his *children*—the characters in a saga that would enthrall readers of Hetzel's *Magasin d'Education* starting in December

1865, then running two full years before it began to fill three published volumes.

When the story begins, Captain Grant, a widower, is missing somewhere along the 37th parallel. This much is known because a bottle discovered in the stomach of a shark by sailors on Lord Glenarvan's yacht *Duncan* carried a scarcely legible message describing the shipwreck of Grant and his crew, who were en route to founding a "New Scotland" in the remote Pacific. Grant was now apparently the captive of "cruel Indians"—or so a scarcely readable phrase seemed to indicate.

The British Admiralty does nothing to rescue the star-crossed sailors, but Lord Glenarvan will risk his life for Captain Grant, whom he doesn't even know. He takes along the lost sailor's children, sixteen-year-old Mary and twelve-year-old Robert. They will also meet up with the absentminded Professor Paganel, secretary of the Geographic Society; it is thanks to this savant gentleman that a new reading of the message in the bottle will take them across the Pacific to Australia. Later, they pick up Ayrton, who identifies himself as one of the castaways from Captain Grant's ship. In fact, he is a bandit, whose intention is to lead the search party astray.

A flirtation develops between Mary Grant and the captain of Lord Glenarvan's yacht, John Mangles. Scenes connecting Mary and John are as thin as the antiseptic trysts of Hollywood cowboys and the daughters of the ranchers they have saved from ruin or scalping. Indeed, there are few successful attempts to render love in Jules Verne's collected works. "I'm very awkward about expressing feelings of love," he confessed to Hetzel. "The very word 'love' frightens me in the writing. . . . So to get around the difficulty I intend to be very sober in these scenes." Apparently, Hetzel had suggested that he slip in a "tender word." "But I can't get it out, this 'tender word,' or it would have been there a long time ago!" Verne replied.[7] In the end, he found a way to maneuver his couple into marriage.

However, much more than this takes place in *The Children of Captain Grant:* escape from the jaws of cannibals, a volcanic eruption, a narrow escape from capture by pirates, until at last a rereading of the message in the bottle leads the rescuers to poor Captain Grant. "I'm still working with considerable energy, and I should add with an equal amount of pleasure, which is a good sign," Verne informed his publisher from his voluntary exile in Le Crotoy. "Young Robert Grant is becoming a daring fellow and quite heroic. Let's hope that generations of children want to imitate him, and read about him, don't you agree?"[8]

This was another book whose first chapters would appear in Hetzel's magazine before the last were written. By now, Verne had assumed the rhythm of the writer who never stops—even if he switches from one project to another on occasion. "I'm still at work here, but for the past fortnight I've given Captain Grant's children a rest. We mustn't exhaust them," he informed Hetzel from his summer retreat. "That doesn't mean that I am resting, and I'm dreaming of a wonderful Robinson Crusoe story. I've got to write one; I can't hold it back," declared this man whose heroes were crisscrossing the Pacific in search of shipwrecked sailors who could well have been Robinson Crusoes themselves.

But he let his publisher know that Grant was not the Robinson he aspired to. "I'm getting some superb ideas," he explained, "and if when it's done it easily brings in the triple of what *The Swiss Family Robinson* earned, you'll be pleased, and so will I. If it's not for us it will be for our children and we won't complain about that." What one can't know, at this remove, is the extent to which the promise of enormous sales was Verne's sole motivation. Or was he simply tossing in a notion that he thought would please an avaricious publisher?[9]

ON THE ELEVENTH DAY OF DECEMBER 1865, JULES VERNE, now residing in the relatively pastoral Parisian suburb of Auteuil (later annexed by an expanding Paris), showed up at rue Jacob to afix his signature to still another contract. Intended to serve as the framework for the relations between author and publisher for six years to come, it called for publication of three books annually, "written in the same genre as those originally published by the same author and directed to the same public and one of the same length." This pointed phrase was designed to guarantee that Jules Verne would continue to write as he had in the past; there would not be another attempt to slip in a *Paris in the Twentieth Century*.

For each of these books, the new contract granted Hetzel a ten-year exclusivity from the date of their respective publications; he could publish them in whatever periodical he wished, with or without illustrations. As for illustrated editions: Since the original woodcuts and engravings would be valueless without Verne's text (so reads the scarcely believable clause), it was agreed that Hetzel would own both illustrations *and* accompanying text . . . forever. This was a truly sly clause, as Verne scholar Charles-Noël Martin pointed out, but to eliminate any possible doubt about what it meant, Hetzel added a statement in the margin: "In a word it is understood between Mr. Hetzel and Mr. Verne that the absolute and indefinite ownership of the works concerned by the present agreement is ceded by Mr. Verne for the exploitation of these works in illustrated editions by Mr. Hetzel."

For his part, the author was to receive 3,000 francs per volume from the publisher, and if he so desired, the money would be available in monthly payments of 750 francs, adding up to the annual total of 9,000 francs (over 170,000 francs today) to which Hetzel was committed. Moreover, during the six-year run of the contract, the author could publish nowhere else without Hetzel's accord. In a final clause, Hetzel insisted that the author give no more than one piece a year to *Musée des Familles,* while Hetzel reserved the right to publish in book form—or not to publish—any of Verne's writings that had appeared in the competing magazine. The terms of the new contract were to be applied to books previously published—*Five Weeks in a Balloon* and the Hatteras books—against a further payment of five thousand francs.[10]

Verne's fame derives in no small part from the famous illustrated editions of his work, and this new and very precise contract paved the way for them. New Year's gift giving was a tradition—long before Christmas became the time for presents—and books were ideal for that purpose. For children, adolescents, and their adoring parents, the discoveries and adventures of Verne's heroes were to prove irresistible. Hetzel's genius was to foresee that.

As soon as the new contract was signed, Hetzel put on sale the first illustrated edition of a novel by Jules Verne—in time for the holiday season. The artist was Edouard Riou, a painter then thirty-two years old, who was just beginning his career as an illustrator of travel and adventure books; Riou's signature would soon become a familiar one to Verne readers.[11] Henceforth, beginning with a reprinting of the Hatteras books in a single volume just a year later—also with Riou's drawings—sales of Verne's books at holiday time would become a tradition. His books became increasingly uniform in appearance, and starting with *The Adventures of Captain Hatteras,* they would be presented under a series title, *Extraordinary Voyages.*

Hetzel's second stroke of genius was the introduction of imitation deluxe touches into these products of industrial-age printing. He designed paperboard books as if they were leather-bound, identifying his series with symbols and enhancing them with showy colors.[12] Jules Verne's fame was now assured, as was Pierre-Jules Hetzel's.

16

———

NEW YORK

ALTHOUGH VERNIANS HAVE SPECULATED ABOUT WHETHER
or not their hero had a secret love life, one must take with a grain of salt
the assertion that Jules Verne rushed his family out of Paris and all but se-
questered his wife on the remote coast of the Somme bay in order to free
himself for infidelities. Much attention has been given to the personality
of a certain Madame Duchesne, described as the author's muse. Subsequently, she has been identified as Estelle Duchesnes (née Hénin), who
died in December 1865 at the age of twenty-nine. Verne's hasty evacua-
tion of Honorine, her daughters, and Michel Verne to Le Crotoy the previous summer has been explained by his desire to be near Estelle in her
final agony. Her name would also throw light on the haunting figure of
Stilla in *Carpathian Castle,* who also died young; Estelle could be the
model for the absent heroine of this novel, one of the most enigmatic
and evocative in the Verne canon.[1]

No one can affirm that Estelle was Verne's muse or one of the mis-
tresses attributed to him, but we can guess that he was unfaithful to Honorine from time to time. Whatever he was doing, he was doing it discreetly.

PERHAPS HETZEL MADE A MISTAKE WHEN HE VIRTUALLY EX-
iled his star author to Le Crotoy so that he could write an illustrated ge-

ography of France to order. Although such a book would benefit from Verne's rapidly growing reputation as a man who could write vividly about travel and exploration, this project seemed to have more to do with burying geography than with reviving it.

Verne had begun the Hetzel assignment in Paris during the winter of 1866, just about the time he accepted the revised contract from his publisher. "I'm working like a galley slave," he wrote his parents in January. "Imagine, dear father—I'm doing a dictionary!" These would be issued district by district, for ten centimes a copy—a very reasonable price. A professional geographer named Théophile Lavallée had begun the job, but he was now believed mortally ill. "What's more, it doesn't bore me," Verne continued. "I nevertheless expect to have the time to do the first volume of [*Twenty Thousand Leagues Under the Sea*], the plan for which is all ready, and which will truly be marvelous. But I mustn't waste a minute."

Verne's enthusiasm is also marvelous. The geographical assignment hardly troubled him, yet he knew that his future had more to do with the epic that was to become *Twenty Thousand Leagues* and that the geographic dictionary could only delay its completion. In this letter, which has been dated January 29, 1866, he lets his father in on a secret: "In truth I rarely go to Eggly's office, and I never set foot in the Stock Exchange, praise the Lord."

He had sent little Michel, not yet five years old if this letter is correctly dated, to boarding school. "He likes it and works quite well," Jules assured his father. Little evidence exists of why Jules's only son became the turbulent adolescent he was later made out to be, but perhaps this early separation from his family might have been a contributing factor. Jules concluded his letter: "I duly sign as your loving son, but who works like a beast of burden whose brain may explode any minute."[2]

In April, from Paris (and still on the stationery of stockbroker Fernand Eggly), Jules wrote to acknowledge yet another poem in his father's hand, assuring him that both he and Honorine had been moved by it. "Father and poet, as Victor Hugo would say," commented Jules, but not without an observation. In the poem, his father had painted an idyllic picture of family life; Jules pointed out that children's screams might be charming in verse but that they certainly were not in reality. "I assure you that you'd quickly have enough of Michel, who combines considerable affection with a frightful character," complained Verne. "He already needs school quite badly."

Pierre Verne had expressed satisfaction with his son's growing success as a published writer; in reply, Jules reminded him that by contract he received a flat fee per book, and no additional benefits if it sold well. "My book sales interests me only platonically," he stated.[3]

Jules Verne's energy and his dogged perseverance in writing a never-ending series of well-tailored fictions, most of them demanding finicky research, are admirable. Less admirable perhaps was his impatience with the hustle and bustle of domestic life. According to one family story, Verne exploded one day when little Michel's screams penetrated the walls of the room in which he was working. Getting up from his desk, he rushed into the living room, shouting, "What is it that he wants?" Meek Honorine replied, "What he wants is the mantelpiece clock!" "Well, then," exclaimed Jules, "give him the clock!"[4]

The remoteness of Le Crotoy seemed essential now. The Vernes packed everything into crates and trunks and moved there at the beginning of spring 1866: "North wind. Storms, low temperature, charming weather," he informed his father—probably without irony, for this man from Nantes clearly enjoyed the climate of Le Crotoy. When he had to or wished to (as he did in early May), he could return alone to Paris; fatigued by his labors, he could abandon his desk to sail his dinghy out into the Channel only a mile and a half beyond the little port, following the line of dunes with their windswept reeds.[5]

Verne could work anywhere. He soon visited his paternal relatives in Provins—"a masterpiece of nature," he told Hetzel. He had taken his geography project with him. "I've finished writing about the Creuse district, and wanted to say hello before beginning Dordogne." He had to admit that he was enjoying the work, getting more pleasure out of it than he thought the reader would.[6]

Jules was doing what he relished most: compiling. That fact helps to explain the joy that leaps from the pages of his adventure stories when he is simply rattling off the names of birds spotted above the polar ice or itemizing underwater flora and fauna. Certainly his readers gladly accepted what might otherwise have been rejected as pedantic description.

In the introductory text he drafted for Hetzel's publication of *The Adventures of Captain Hatteras,* Verne offered this assessment of himself:

> Mr. Jules Verne is the creator of a new genre and has earned a place of his own in contemporary literature. A lively storyteller, the equal of our finest novelists, he is at the same time one of the best scientific minds of our times. No one has endowed fiction with greater realism; in reading his books one wonders whether they are really the product of the imagination. . . .[7]

Hetzel made good use of this draft in his "Notice from the Publisher"; indeed, he embellished it. "We must agree," Hetzel concluded, "that art for art's sake no long suffices in our era, and that the time has come when science has a rightful place of its own in the literary domain."

The standard edition of *The Adventures of Captain Hatteras* appeared in two volumes in May 1866; the large-format edition was issued in November—in time for year-end gift giving. Hetzel made it clear that this first illustrated edition of a Verne novel—"at an uncommon low price and in a genuine deluxe format"—would be followed by a similar presentation of the author's earlier novels. "The works already published and those to come will follow the author's plan," the preface concluded. "His purpose, indeed, is to sum up all the geographical, geological, physical, and astronomical knowledge discovered by modern science, and to present the story of our universe in the attractive and picturesque manner unique to him."[8]

The press picked up on this; Verne received some of his best reviews at this time (later, he would have to be satisfied with the approval of the book-buying public). He came to the attention of one of the Second Empire's leading tastemakers, Théophile Gautier, a respected literary critic who earlier had captured the public's attention with his romantic poetry and prose; in fact, he had been the most vigorous proponent of the doctrine of "art for art's sake" disparaged in Hetzel's preface. He preached from the towering platform of *Le Moniteur Universel,* virtually an official organ of the government. If Verne's adventures never actually happened and remained an impossibility even now, Gautier told his readers, they did hold up scientifically, and the most daring of them would be achieved one day.[9]

Prior to publication in book form, Hetzel put the illustrated *Captain Hatteras* on sale in short unbound installments, sold at ten centimes a copy; at least one critic saw no need to wait for finished books. "Every branch of geographical science is dealt with by this prolific and brilliant author, from ethnology and descriptive geography to geology and cosmogony," gushed a critic of the authoritative *Le Temps.* "The inexpensive edition, handsome all the same, and expertly illustrated by Riou . . . will prove that there is a public, even a vast public, for healthy literature. . . ."[10]

For a moment—but only a moment—the century's master of realism, Émile Zola, came to grips with this creator of fantasy designed to seem real. At twenty-six Zola had yet to make a name for himself; with only one published novel to his credit, he lived on what he could earn from occasional periodical publication. Zola, who would prove to be a judicious critic as well as a prodigious novelist, sized up Jules Verne at once: "He has given himself the task of accomplishing certain things that science believes possible theoretically, but which no one has been able to perform satisfactorily until now."

Children were tired of fairy tales, Zola went on to say. They wanted to learn. Hence, the value of Jules Verne's "scientific fantasies." For Zola, "You find in miniature in these books the grand battle that man has ever waged against nature."[11]

JULES VERNE SELDOM TRAVELED VERY FAR FROM THE OLD world as he knew it. His one big trip took him to New York, but for such a short time! Later, in a memoir addressed to American readers, he sheepishly admitted that "I trod American soil, but—it's shameful to admit to Americans—I spent only a week there! I had a round-trip ticket valid only for a week!" This was akin to his curiously unrigorous trip to Scotland—made possible by a complaisant travel agent, a trip whose time frame was also restricted.

The story of the ship that took Jules and his brother, Paul, to New York is worth a book of its own—and indeed Jules Verne later wrote it (*A Floating City*). It was the longest ship conceivable then—30,000 tons, 210 meters long—equipped with a 1,600-horsepower steam engine driving its screw, a furnace delivering another 1,000 horsepower for its four waterwheels—and six masts for good measure. Designed by an Englishman of French origin to carry four thousand passengers (or twelve thousand troops), the vessel was built over a two-year period, beginning in 1855, and was appropriately baptized *Leviathan*.[12]

By one of those remarkable coincidences that seemed more frequent at a time when travel was less common than it is today, Jules Verne and Aristide Hignard had encountered the ship on their visit to England. Remembering that moment in his fictional travel diary, Jules had written, "To the great regret of Jacques [the stand-in for Jules Verne in the book], one could no longer go aboard this sea monster. . . ." At Greenwich, three miles downstream from London Bridge, Jules managed to lure Hignard into a dinghy to row around "this universe afloat."[13]

Actually the monster ship, originally named *Leviathan,* was now the *Great Eastern,* fitted out for voyages from Britain to its far-off Australian colony. Financial considerations led to a redeployment on the transatlantic route. The ship was descending the Thames en route to the port of Southampton when it had its first accident: an explosion that killed ten crew members in the engine room. The man who had designed the ship died shortly after that, supposedly because he couldn't survive another such blow. In Southampton, the ship's captain drowned.

On its maiden voyage across the North Atlantic, with a crew of five hundred, the *Great Eastern* carried only forty-six passengers; it returned from the United States with seventy. Soon after that, a fierce storm all but destroyed the upper parts of the ship; the steamship line went bankrupt. Then the American promoter Cyrus Field acquired the vessel, white elephant that it was, to lay a telegraph cable along the ocean floor, thus linking Europe to the United States. This arduous task required two years and two tries; in *Twenty Thousand Leagues Under the Sea,* Verne's hero remembers the story as he follows the track of the cable from Captain Nemo's submarine.

After the cable was laid, another group of optimists took over the ship, renting it from its owners in order to transport Americans to Paris for the Universal Exposition of 1867; but first it had to get to America. By then, the renovated vessel was able to take on board close to one thousand passengers desiring to cross to New York. They paid from sixteen to twenty-six pounds sterling for their tickets. This amounted to about 400 to 650 francs (approximately 7,500 to 12,000 present-day francs). Jules and Paul Verne were among these passengers, certainly thanks in part to Hetzel's financial backing, for Jules was going to write a book about his experience.[14]

Arriving in Liverpool for the scheduled sailing, the brothers found themselves among the new victims of the curse that seemed to follow the giant steamer. The departure was postponed for three days, because, as Jules told Hetzel, "the monster wasn't ready; now, however, he has a full stomach and tomorrow he'll move off. In any case our return trip won't be delayed, but this means so much less time in New York."[15]

On the first day out, a capstan pin snapped, throwing the full weight of an anchor on the dozen crewmen manning it, killing one sailor instantly and wounding four others, at least one critically. During the course of the voyage, another sailor died when a wave broke over the deck (although the chief disaster victim, affirmed a chronicler, was the company that had leased the ship; it had been counting on getting three thousand American passengers for the return trip to Europe, but there would only be two hundred.)[16]

Despite all the problems, the crossing was a heady experience for Jules Verne, who more often traveled in imagination. He sized up his early impressions for his publisher and friend during a momentary lull. It was the morning of the ninth of April, a Tuesday; they were in sight of land, but the *Great Eastern* was anchored offshore, waiting for high tide to sail into New York Harbor. "Ah! if you had been with us, your heart would have throbbed more than once because incidents, and accidents unfortunately, were not lacking during this journey." His book on the great sailing ship would be more "diversified" than he might have wished, he said. "We had some fearful gales; despite its size the *Great Eastern* danced like a feather above the ocean; its bow was ripped away by a wave. It was frightening, and my brother confessed that he had never seen a worse sea."

However, this was a wonderful opportunity for the creator of *Twenty Thousand Leagues Under the Sea,* which was not to be the last of Verne's stories about the ocean.[17] As he put it, "I've built up a supply of emotions for the rest of my life." Yet he had found it difficult to go so long without news from home; perhaps he could never have lived the life of a Jules Verne hero.

He was concerned about the return trip. Passengers were informed that their ship would sail back to Europe on the sixteenth of April (only a week hence), which would get him to Paris by the twenty-seventh.[18] If Hetzel had already begun publication of the illustrated geography—one district per each installment—Verne intended to be home in time to continue writing so that the publisher would not run out of chapters.

He wondered what was happening in Europe. "You see, my dear Hetzel, that we don't know what's going on; we are like savages on our floating island. But what an island! What a sample of human endeavor. Never has man's industrial genius been pushed as far." He intended to put it all down in the book he'd intended to write about the *Great Eastern.*

"I don't know if we'll have the time to push as far as Niagara," he postulated. "We really want to see those admirable Falls, but we don't want to delay our return to France a single day in order to do that."[19] He had to get back to his desk to grind out more pages for Hetzel, and a little thing like the North American continent wasn't going to prevent him from that. Later, he recalled what his priorities had been. He would see America—but "incidentally," he said. "First of all the *Great Eastern.* The country of [James Fenimore] Cooper afterward."[20]

He did explore New York, though. He crossed the East River before the Brooklyn Bridge was built, sailed up the Hudson River to Albany, then visited Buffalo and Lake Erie. He marveled at Niagara Falls from the top of a tower before crossing the suspension bridge into Canada.[21] And all along the way, he took note of what he saw—even from shipboard—to use repeatedly in successive books, beginning with the saga he was then in the process of writing. In *Twenty Thousand Leagues Under the Sea,* the sympathetic narrator—the author's eyes and ears—is Professor Aronnax, who is in New York when the reader encounters him, living at the Fifth Avenue Hotel, which happened to be where Jules Verne stayed while he was inventing the professor. Then one of the city's most elegant establishments, the hotel even had an elevator.

Most of what we know about Verne's brief stay comes from an autobiographical sketch thinly disguised as fiction—eventually and appropriately titled *A Floating City*. In it, one reads about Jules's one evening on the town: After a frugal dinner at the Fifth Avenue Hotel (the size of the portions as described by the hungry guest may remind the reader of the latter-day nouvelle cuisine), he went off to Barnum's theater, where he was impressed by a staged fire in the fourth act. The next day, he strolled about lower Manhattan to do errands; the day after that, a cab took him to the docks for the steamboat ride up the Hudson to Niagara Falls.[22]

Along the way, he found himself, perhaps despite himself, in the wonderful land of Cooper's *Leatherstocking Tales*. Even if he never stepped beyond the boundaries of New York state, he could have roamed the lakes and mountains dear to his beloved Cooper's heroes and Indians; a little more time would have helped, but there was that return ticket.

PART IV

Extraordinary Voyages

17

CAPTAIN NEMO

O N THE RETURN TRIP, THE BROTHERS DISEMBARKED AT BREST.
Writing to Nantes from Paris soon after that, Jules expressed regret that
his parents hadn't been at the dock; he said he would have enjoyed
telling them about the "marvelous things" they had seen. As for the fate
of the *Great Eastern,* "the whole business is finished," he wrote. He understood that the shipowners had filed for bankruptcy.

Now that he was back home, another adventure awaited him, for the
Paris Universal Exposition of 1867 was under way. Verne, alone or with
family and friends visiting from Nantes, spent considerable time gaping
at its wonders. Installed on the Champ de Mars, a spacious parade ground
alongside the Seine in western Paris, the central pavilion of this first world's
fair of the Machine Age was conceived as an ellipse, encompassing a suite
of exhibition halls. The largest of these, 75 feet high, 105 feet wide, was the
Gallery of the Machines, designed by the engineer Gustave Eiffel (twenty-
two years before he built an iron tower for another fair on the same site).

Paul, Jules told his parents, had been "thrilled" by it all. He didn't say
anything about his own feelings.[1] He simply didn't have the *time* to appreciate things if he was to keep pace with a diabolic publisher who
seemed to be printing sections of the *Illustrated Geography of France and Its
Colonies* as fast as his author could compile and write them.

"ONE DISTRICT FOR 10 CENTIMES" was the headline above a story in the
sober daily *Le Temps,* announcing this work "conceived . . . to become
everybody's favorite book." The article went on to say: "Accessible to all

by its price and its proportions, it will soon be a book for wealthy homes as well as humble cottages. . . ."[2]

The ingenuity of Hetzel's merchandising was boundless. At the beginning, there were those single fascicles selling for a tenth of a franc. One could also possess a compendium describing all of France and its colonies collected in a single large volume. Hetzel also released a series of paperbound sets, each covering ten French districts, sold at 1.10 francs.[3] Then, when the first half of the book was ready, it was published in one volume in November 1867, the second and final volume to appear in June 1868 (at the same time the complete text was published in a single book).

In his preface, Hetzel introduced his author, "who made a reputation as a geographer in his excellent travel books," but who this time was "giving up the realm of imagination."[4]

But Verne hadn't abandoned imagination for long. In May 1867, Hetzel brought out the first small volume of *The Children of Captain Grant;* the second would appear on July 15, the third at the end of the following January, the large-format (octavo) single-volume illustrated edition later that year. These publications, with the fortnightly serialization in *Magasin d'Education,* guaranteed that there was seldom a day without something to read by Jules Verne.

"Here I am back at my favorite bathing beach," the harried writer informed his parents one fine summer day from Le Crotoy. But lest his family really believe that he was lying idly on the sand, he added, "My stay here is very helpful for [composing] my geography."[5]

THAT AUGUST, DURING ITS ANNUAL ASSEMBLY, WHICH WAS open to the public, the prestigious French Academy awarded a citation to the *Magasin d'Education et de Récréation,* specifically mentioning the contributions of its directors Jean Macé, P.-J. Stahl, and Jules Verne. "The Academy recognizes in this effort an often successful variety of the intellectual activity of our time," read the tribute.[6]

Henceforth, the *Magasin* masthead would bear the proud endorsement "Crowned by the French Academy."

Work on the geography project went on; the Vernes returned to Paris only in early December 1867. Jules had led his parents to believe that he would visit them during the winter. "But decidedly this confounded geography book will prevent me from coming to Nantes. . . ." *He* could complain about the job with which Hetzel had saddled him, although nobody else had that right. "You're always complaining about this geography assignment," he wrote to his father. "But why read it? It isn't made to be read, but to be looked at and consulted when necessary. It's a dictionary!" However, to Verne, it represented more than that: "I tell you again, it's a good deal for me. It may earn me 15,000 or 20,000 francs." (This would be the rough equivalent of 280,000 to 375,000 present-day francs.)

One can see from these letters that Honorine hadn't been spared involvement in the project; she was responsible for copying her husband's scribblings into a readable draft. "Poor woman," commiserated Jules, "I'm having her write 800 lines a day!" Before it was over, he was complaining about rheumatism on his left side, running from his neck down to his elbow. Fortunately, he was right-handed. In addition, Verne mentioned an indisposition suffered by six-year-old Michel; it appears this condition was inherited from Jules. "Michel has a weak spot, his bowels," Jules told his parents, "and we have to give him medication constantly."

By the end of 1867, he had finished the geography commission. "Whew! what a year!" he wrote. "To relax I'm going to work on [*Twenty Thousand Leagues Under the Sea*]. That will be a true pleasure."[7]

⚜

SOON AFTER HETZEL'S PUBLICATION OF *JOURNEY TO THE CENter of the Earth,* in November 1864, the daily *Le Figaro* had published an open letter from one René de Pont-Jest that virtually accused Jules Verne of plagiarism. Pont-Jest had composed what he described as "a philosophical tale," published in the September 1863 issue of the magazine *Revue Contemporaine.* His hero discovers an ancient runic manuscript revealing the burial of a scientist's head atop a Norwegian mountain; the brain encapsuled the secrets of universal science, and he who discovered it would himself possess this knowledge. In Pont-Jest's story, the young man finds the head and is able to interrogate it; then he dies.

Obviously, Verne couldn't see any connection between his exploration of the bowels of the earth and this philosophic tale. He didn't even want to reply to its author, certainly not in the press, so he passed the matter on to his publisher, whose assurances to Pont-Jest appeared to pacify him. No more would be heard of the complainant for the time being.[8]

The repercussions from this incident, however, caused Jules to be more cautious in the future. In October 1867, the daily *Petit Journal* had begun serializing a story titled "Extraordinary Adventurers of the Scientist Trinitus," written by Aristide Roger. In this story an engineer and two fellow passengers employ a small submarine to search for Trinitus's wife and daughter, lost in a shipwreck. Verne, who was now outlining a story that promised to be his masterpiece, had too much at stake to risk future charges of plagiarism. This time *he* took the initiative by writing a letter to *Le Petit Journal,* taking pains to spell out his concerns. A year ago, he wrote, he had begun a book on a "Journey Beneath the Seas." If the book hadn't yet been published, it was because he had been obliged to set it aside momentarily to complete another project. He asked the editor if he would publish this letter, "so as to protect me from any future complaint with respect to the similarity of the two books?"

In his *Magasin,* Hetzel informed subscribers (on the fifth of September): "Let us say that Mr. Jules Verne is putting the final touches to a book that will be most extraordinary of all, 'A Voyage Under the Seas.' Six months spent on the seashore, in absolute retirement, were necessary for this conscientious and talented writer to put together the elements of this curious story."[9]

This colossal enterprise, however, would require far more time than a summer by the sea. *Twenty Thousand Leagues Under the Sea* would be revised again and again; the theme and the personalities of the chief protagonists merited that. "I'm working with fury," Jules Verne reported to Hetzel from Le Crotoy one summer day, obviously with great joy, which was understandable.

> It's important that this unknown character [Captain Nemo] refrain from contact with other human beings, from whom he lives apart. He is no longer on *earth,* he manages without the earth. The sea suffices, but the sea must provide him with everything, clothing and food. Never does he set foot on a continent.[10]

Perhaps Verne envied his character Captain Nemo. Unhappy with the humdrum aspects of his life, a predictable domestic existence singularized only by Michel's disruptive behavior, and confronted by a literary world that had shown no signs of adopting him, Jules Verne may sometimes have wished he could sail out of the bay and never again set foot on a continent. Amateur psychologists could have a field day comparing the curiously withdrawn Jules Verne, who would become increasingly solitary, with this submarine captain whose eccentricity the author had yet to explain.

Twenty Thousand Leagues Under the Sea opens in the year 1866 (at which time Jules Verne was already writing the story). The maritime world is stirred by several reported sightings of a sea monster, larger and swifter than any known whale. Then a passenger steamer is severely damaged after an apparent encounter with the unidentifiable and illusive creature. In New York, where he has gone after a research mission in the American West, young professor Pierre Aronnax of the Paris Muséum d'Histoire Naturelle is invited to join an American government expedition to hunt the mysterious creature. (In the *New York Herald,* Aronnax had offered his opinion as to what the monster must be like.)

The party aboard the frigate *Abraham Lincoln* would include not only Aronnax (who, as drawn by illustrator Edouard Riou, looks very much like Verne himself) but also his loyal Flemish valet, Conseil, an amateur savant who can recite by heart the names of all species of sea life. The foil to these reflective and reasonable men is tempestuous Canadian Ned Land, the harpooner. As they reach the Pacific region in which the monster was last sighted, they discover what appears to be an illuminated animal. The frigate attacks, and Ned makes use of his harpoon; then the monster counterattacks, destroying the vessel's screw and rudder.

After that, the mystery submarine—for that is what the monster turns out to be—picks up Aronnax, Conseil, and Ned Land. The French scientist will be treated as an honored guest, and his host—Captain Nemo—will show Aronnax his treasures, which include a splendid scientific library, old masters on the walls, and luxurious drawing rooms. Nemo also has an extraordinary display of marine specimens—each enumerated with loving care, in the first of many inventories guaranteed to give the most avid reader indigestion. Yet the lists of fauna and flora are essential to the story, for they establish verisimilitude.

Twenty Thousand Leagues Under the Sea has fascinated readers from the day of its publication right up to the present. The spell cast by the incantatory cataloging of underwater life (real and imaginary) has contributed to the attraction of this novel that chronicles the odyssey of the *Nautilus.* This is the name Captain Nemo has given his submarine (a name first used by Robert Fulton for a submarine he constructed and operated, then much later the one given the world's first nuclear-powered sub, the first to sail beneath the North Pole).

Captain Nemo is generous with information, to a point. He reveals that his *Nautilus* is powered by electricity, without disclosing the nature of the batteries. (Verne himself couldn't have explained the technique; even today electricity stored in batteries wouldn't drive Nemo's submarine.) A submarine with portholes for observation of undersea life (and electric lights to facilitate viewing); ingenious Nemo has also invented diving suits equipped with compressed air. Enamored of sea life, he carries out continuous observations of the ocean floor—which sometimes reveal legendary shipwrecks (and lost treasures).

For the involuntary guests on the *Nautilus,* there are manifold mysteries. One day, the captain is inexplicably angry; his captives are obliged to go belowdecks, where they are drugged. The following day, they attend an undersea burial. "Always the same mistrust, fierce, implacable toward human society!" thinks Aronnax. Even the language Nemo speaks to his crew is unknown to the narrator. Yet this opportunity to explore the ocean depths absorbs Aronnax; only Ned, the harpooner, is anxious to escape. Even after Ned saves Nemo from a shark, the enigmatic captain affirms that his captives will never be freed.

They visit pearl beds, another opportunity for the servant, Conseil, to identify and for his master, Aronnax, to explain. Their voyage, sometimes on the surface and sometimes underwater, takes them around the world. Off the Atlantic coast of Europe, they find the sunken continent of Atlantis. Coming upon an ancient Spanish treasure, the passengers learn that Nemo gathers such precious cargo for "suffering beings, races oppressed upon this earth, the wretched needing succor, victims demanding vengeance. . . ." They learn of Nemo's secret port, an underground lake in an extinct volcano. There he mines coal for the needs of the *Nautilus,* which can race one hundred leagues (some three hundred miles) a day and plunge more than fifty thousand feet into the depths.

They hunt, but Nemo refuses to allow Ned to kill needlessly; Aronnax is forced to agree that "the captain was right. The barbaric and thoughtless obstinacy of fishermen will one day lead to the disappearance of the last whale from the ocean."

When they reach the Antarctic, they are blocked by ice. Determined to find the South Pole, Nemo submerges the *Nautilus,* and they attain their goal beneath the ice field; Nemo plants a black flag there.

Dangerous incidents multiply. An iceberg blocks their path, and they risk asphyxiation. They battle a giant octopus. When Nemo again refuses to liberate his passengers, they plot an escape off Long Island, but bad weather intervenes. They survive a hurricane. Off the coast of France, a ship fires at their submarine; Aronnax realizes that Captain Nemo has now been identified as someone who is seeking revenge (but from whom and for what offense?). Nemo reveals that he has lost both his family and his country because of the actions of the nation whose ship that is; then he sinks the ship, whose nationality remains a mystery to Aronnax and his mates. The French scientist, his valet, and Ned Land escape in a small boat just as the sub is swept into the notorious Maelstrom off Norway. The fate of the submarine is unknown, but Aronnax hopes that Nemo has also survived the disaster.

⚘

WHAT HETZEL WANTED FOR HIS *MAGASIN D'EDUCATION*, OF course, was a literature for children and their parents. But *Twenty Thousand Leagues Under the Sea,* like Verne's other ambitious books, seemed to have been written for the author's own peers; we find countless instances of Jules Verne deliberately addressing himself to fellow adults. Yet young people could also understand them. Adolescents who grew up in families subscribing to magazines like Hetzel's attended schools then reserved for the privileged; their level of comprehension was undoubtedly superior to that of children of school age today.

Writing to Hetzel at the beginning of summer 1870, Jules thanked him for his editing of *A Floating City* prior to serialization in the influential Paris daily *Journal des Débats,* then added: "When truly one doesn't write only for children, one mustn't be read only by children."[11] Both publisher and author had good reasons to want to reach the largest possible audience—Hetzel's chiefly financial, Verne's surely including a healthy dose of pride.[12]

The day would come when Verne's fiction would seem too difficult for the age groups originally targeted by his publisher, and prose doctors were hired to adapt him for popular French children's series.[13] This helps explain why today Jules Verne seems to have a readership of children on one hand—encouraged by their grade-school teachers, and sometimes by abridged editions—adults on the other (reading out of nostalgia, or for sheer pleasure), to the exclusion of the adolescent audience Hetzel strove for.[14]

Nearly everything is bigger than life in Captain Nemo's odyssey. An oceanologist later observed that although his documentation is impressive, Jules Verne deliberately sought out the extraordinary. Sea animals and plant life are almost always double or even three times the size of known specimens. The illustrators of the Hetzel gift editions based their sketches on documents found in scientific texts, then blew them up to unreal proportions.[15] Verne managed to deal with the sea, noted a Verne scholar, in some thirty of his *Extraordinary Voyages.*[16] In *Twenty Thousand Leagues Under the Sea,* he had a story and a hero larger than life; gigantic species were only part of the tale, and the lesser part.

⚘

THE WINTER OF 1868 WAS TO PROVE A LONG ONE; BOTH Jules and son, Michel (six and a half years old), were ill. Jules described his own condition: "A violent grippe caught in Paris, embellished with one of those rheumatisms you know so well, from the nape of the neck to the lower back, not sparing the arms." That didn't stop him from shuttling between Paris and Le Crotoy. "I'm waiting impatiently for the proper time to take everybody to the seashore, which means after Easter," he wrote his father early in March 1868. He was then writing *Twenty Thousand Leagues.* "I'm working on it with extreme pleasure, and hope it will prove a curiosity," he informed his parents. He expected to have proofs of the first volume in three or four months and promised to send them to Nantes for possible corrections by his brother, Paul, as well as by his father. "I want very much for this piece of machinery to be as perfect as possible."[17]

His letters to Nantes (and to rue Jacob) reveal that he felt himself, as he celebrated his fortieth birthday, at the top of his form; *this* was what he had been preparing for during the years in the wilderness. One also senses that writing well was a solitary joy, like sailing—the only two pleasures we can be certain he sometimes experienced.

Hetzel, of course, was also aware of Verne's importance to his publishing venture. The evidence is the new contract he drew up early in May 1868. The bait was an increase in the author's annual guarantee from 9,000 to 10,000 francs (close to 185,000 present-day francs). For his part, Hetzel's exclusive right to the original editions of Verne's novels was extended from six to ten years. The important clause for Hetzel, however, concerned the larger format (octavo) illustrated editions, and it left no room for ambiguity: "Concerning illustrated editions of works to come for the next ten years, beginning today, as well as those already published, it is understood that Mr. Verne has surrendered both the right to publish and the ownership to Mr. Hetzel and his heirs, against royalties stipulated in the first article." (That first clause covered the three new books a year, to be paid for at the rate of 3333.33 francs each.)[18]

Far from feeling that he had been shortchanged, Verne was now ready to invest in the publishing house. The company was being reorganized into a limited partnership, with a recapitalization of 400,000 francs to be obtained by sales of shares at 10,000 francs each; meanwhile, Hetzel himself was expected to bring as much as 800,000 francs into the company. Jules was soon beseeching his father to invest with brother Paul, each to take half a share. As for Jules, he was buying a full ten-thousand-franc share. "Although I have an obvious interest in seeing this company definitively organized in a stable way," Jules assured his father, "I don't want to involve you lightly in a bad business arrangement." He didn't think that Hetzel's stock was overvalued. (His own books, which sold at three francs a volume, were listed at no more than one franc.)[19]

Perhaps Jules was so hopeful just now because of the death of Honorine's rich aunt—whose husband had died in 1863. "So we are heirs," he announced to his parents. In fact, Honorine's mother had use of the property for the duration of her own life.[20]

As for investing in the Hetzel company, Jules's father didn't share his elder son's enthusiasm. Pierre Verne was now approaching seventy, had never invested in business, and clearly didn't wish to begin now. There may have been another reason—perhaps the decisive one, as Jules wished to explain to his publisher. Jules suspected that his father's piety had much to do with his hesitation. Pierre was a devout Catholic, while Hetzel's books were *not* Catholic. Christian perhaps—and sometimes of the best sort. Still, some of Hetzel's most successful publications "had nothing in common with Catholicism." Jules was convinced that his father would be upset by the idea of sponsoring this kind of literature.[21]

This was an important consideration, and it underscored the role religion played not only in the elder Verne's life but in relations between father and son. Jules never mentioned religion or Catholicism in particular—certainly not in writing or in any public forum—without respect, even if he seldom went beyond what filial respect required. For his part, Hetzel, a supporter of the lay republican state, was anything but a religious man, yet he knew how important religion was for his readers. *He* was the one who usually added the pious touches to Verne's stories. Even that wasn't always enough, however, as evidenced by a letter to Hetzel from ultraconservative church militant Louis Veuillot, publisher of the Catholic newspaper *L'Univers*. He had not read Verne's books, he told Hetzel, but a friend had, and he found them charming, "save for an absence which doubtless doesn't spoil anything but which removes the beauty from everything and leaves the world's marvels in the state of enigmas." This was a problem with everything else Hetzel published, however worthy it was otherwise. God was missing.[22]

One Verne scholar has pointed out that Verne systematically avoided attributing happy events to God's intervention. Sometimes Verne even inserted an ironic remark about religion, but Hetzel deleted such passages.[23]

SINCE THE *ILLUSTRATED GEOGRAPHY* WAS FINISHED AT LAST, the way was clear in the summer of 1868 for work in earnest on the odyssey of Captain Nemo. Now with everything going so well, and the promise (with the increase in his monthly stipend) of greater rewards to come, the harried author allowed himself a treat.

He had made do with rented or borrowed boats for his cruises out of Le Crotoy; now, he informed a friend, he had been foolish enough (but it was "sweet folly") to contract for the building of his own boat. A letter to Hetzel that has been dated June 1868 reported progress on the construction of the *Saint-Michel:* "The boat is progressing! It will be delightful," he assured the publisher. "I'm in love with this combination of nails and boards, as one is of a mistress at age twenty. And I'll be even more faithful to it. Ah, the sea—what a lovely thing, even at Le Crotoy where she appears twice a day [at high tide, of course]."

Soon it was ready to sail. "I haven't written for a long while," he began a letter to his father early that summer, "but I was taken up by the *Saint-Michel,* which has now been launched and tried out, and is a marvelous craft. With this one we could go to America." He explained the technical details to his brother. His crew consisted of two seasoned skippers—himself and "the best captain on the bay" (now employed exclusively by Jules). Officially, the vessel was registered as a five-and-a-half-tonner; it was twelve in reality, Jules boasted.[24]

Henceforth, his letters would be filled with news of this new joy, his boat, along with the old one, the smooth flow of his writing. "I'm writing to you from Dieppe, where the winds blew the *Saint-Michel,*" he announced to his father in midsummer 1868, "but you can reply to Le Crotoy, where I'll be as soon as the sea permits. . . ." Such delays hardly bothered him, for "the *Saint-Michel* being a floating writing room, I am working as if I were in Le Crotoy." He would soon be done with the first volume of his two-volume saga; he hoped, he said, "that all these impossibilities will seem possible." Then he returned to the subject of his new love: "The *Saint-Michel,* thanks to some corrections of the sails, has become one of the best boats in the Somme bay. . . ."[25]

18

BACK FROM THE MOON

Verne was writing and sailing, doing both well. But Hetzel, his landlubber publisher, wasn't at all sure that he wanted his star author to be risking his life on the high seas. "Don't get so angry with the *Saint-Michel*," Verne admonished him in the autumn of 1868. "You exaggerate the dangers of sailing, and my wife, who was with me on this last cruise, wasn't frightened at any time." Soon he was venturing into foreign waters. "I had set my mind on taking the *Saint-Michel* to London and we're almost there," he informed his publisher in another note. He was writing from his mooring off Gravesend. He had taken time off from working on the final pages of the first half of *Twenty Thousand Leagues Under the Sea* to sail there, but now he was working on it "just as if I were in my office on the Rue de Sèvres [in Paris]."[1] Obviously it was a great joy to be writing about the sea on the sea.

Jules promised to travel to Paris and deliver the first volume of the book soon. "It is definitely very curious, very unexpected, and certainly no one has ever attempted anything like this before . . . There are some sentimental touches of the kind you were asking for, or at least I've left room to insert them," he explained candidly. "I've fashioned the eyes, and you furnish the tears when necessary. . . ."[2]

He was in Paris on September twentieth, but not for long; Hetzel persuaded Verne to accompany him across the Rhine to his favorite thermal resort, Baden Baden; he would take the first volume of *Twenty Thousand*

Leagues, and a considerable portion of the second and final volume, along with him.

Honorine was not joining them in Germany, nor was she staying in Paris. She had returned to Le Crotoy, where Jules himself would go after leaving Hetzel. For Le Crotoy, and not their latest Paris flat on rue de Sèvres, was what he preferred to call home now. Earlier, writing to his parents, he had suggested that their visit to his shore retreat would be appropriate, for it was now virtually their legal residence—and would be their principal residence if they found a suitable house there. "From now on we'll reside in Paris only during the four winter months," he told his father, "sufficient time for business and maintaining relations with people. It's stupid to pay 2000 francs rent for an apartment one never lives in."

This was an important announcement, not a mere domestic detail. Verne, who had given up Nantes for the boulevard life of Paris, where he could see and be seen, was now determined to live and work where he felt most comfortable. Clearly he preferred to live outside Paris, where he could write at least as well and probably better. The excellent French postal system would allow him to keep in touch with the rest of the world.

As promised, he was going to Nantes for the Christmas holidays; indeed, he intended to stay for six weeks, and that would require some planning. "I prefer to sleep with Honorine in the old study," he informed his parents, "and to keep the large bedroom for Michel, Valentine [Honorine's daughter, now seventeen years old], and as the family dressing room. I'll be better there [in the study] for working. . . ."[3]

For year-end gift giving, Hetzel was ready with the deluxe edition of the *Illustrated Geography of France and Its Colonies.* And the authoritative daily *Le Temps* was ready with a favorable judgment. "It's often said, but it can't be repeated often enough to our embarrassment: What do we know about geography in France? Nothing, or very little." This is why Jules Verne's new reference work was so important, declared the writer. "It's a fine gift book, but it's also something else: the last word in geographical science concerning France. . . ."[4]

On December twenty-fifth, the same newspaper published what had become its traditional review of gift books, focusing its attention on the Hetzel line and praising Jules Verne for the very qualities the author himself would have wanted mentioned. "Mr. Jules Verne combines two qualities that it is rare to find in the same man: the precision of a scientist, and the imagination of a storyteller of the first rank. . . . You see the advantages of this system," the reviewer concluded, "geologist, geographer, specialist in natural history and astronomy, all these subjects that seemed so dry in the frightful books that burdened our childhood, now enter the minds of young readers painlessly with the charm of a story."[5]

⚜ ⚜

ONCE AGAIN, JULES VERNE WAS TO DISPATCH THE FIRST chapters of a novel for publication before he had finished the final chapters. In the last months of 1868, then in the early months of 1869, he was completing the first half of *Twenty Thousand Leagues Under the Sea,* which would fill two volumes in the small-format original edition (the first volume to appear in bookshops in October 1869, the second the following June). From Nantes, during his working holiday in December 1868, he commented on the preliminary sketches the illustrator Riou had submitted. He saw at once that they failed to do justice to Captain Nemo's monster submarine. "I think we have to make the characters much smaller and the drawing rooms considerably larger," he told Hetzel. "These [sketches] only show corners of the rooms and so don't give an idea of the marvels of the *Nautilus.*"[6]

He would soon be engaged in a debate about the very nature of his central character, the eccentric Nemo—and this at a time when the manuscript was sitting on Hetzel's desk, awaiting the printer. The cautious publisher worried about Nemo's motivations, feared his violence—specifically, his cold-blooded sinking of a ship he saw as an enemy.

Verne had originally planned that the mysterious Nemo would reveal himself as a Pole dedicated to vengeance against the Russians who occupied and ravaged his land. Hetzel had vetoed that; Russia was a friend of France, and Russians subscribed to his *Magasin.* Therefore, Nemo had to remain an enigmatic figure, his fierce behavior left unexplained—or inadequately explained.

This time, the habitually compliant writer stood up to his bullying publisher. "If Nemo had been a Pole whose wife died under the knout and the children perished in Siberia, and this Pole found himself confronted by a Russian ship with the possibility of destroying it, everyone would admit his right to vengeance." His Nemo didn't kill for the sake of killing; he responded to attacks. "He is a generous person. . . . You understand that if I were creating this character again—which I am totally unable to do because I've been living with him for two years, I would not be able to see him in any other way. Talking it over with you in Paris for a day wouldn't help, we'd need a month. . . ." (This indicated that Hetzel thought that he could win over his author in a face-to-face encounter.)

Then the final revolt came in a letter that has been dated late in May

1869: "If I can't be allowed to explain the reasons for his hatred either I'll remain silent about the causes and about his entire life, his nationality, etc., or if necessary I'll change the ending."[7]

He was as good as his word. He would give the reader no clues as to Nemo's motives, or to his nationality—for this book at least. And when the opportunity arose to introduce the mysterious captain into another novel (*The Mysterious Island*), he would find another nationality for him, and another enemy.

In Verne's capitulation, Hetzel received a poisoned gift. Instead of a rage easily comprehensible to fireside readers, the book would present a major character with an unquenchable thirst for revenge—far more troubling to the good people who subscribed to *Magasin d'Education et de Recréation*.

NOW THAT HIS GEOGRAPHY CHORE WAS BEHIND HIM, JULES could resume doing what he did so well: work on two or even three novels at a time. Although he was still in the throes of writing *Twenty Thousand Leagues*, he was also finishing a shorter novel—comic relief after the tensions packed into Nemo's submarine. A Verne biographer has remarked that he regularly sought to place an amusing book between two serious ones.[8] Certainly he saw no comedy in *Twenty Thousand Leagues*. When Hetzel suggested introducing a light touch—a Chinese youth rescued from Chinese pirates—saying, "He'll liven up the Nautilus,"—Verne simply ignored the heresy.[9]

Around the Moon, the latest project on his writing table, was in fact a sequel to the popular *From the Earth to the Moon*.

That earlier book had left the dauntless occupants of the cannonball in outer space, en route to the moon. At the time of their launching, the two Americans and the Frenchman Michel Ardan had no idea what they were going to do on the earth's satellite, or how they'd leave it for that matter (did their author?). Now, in the sequel, the space explorers seek to land on the moon, but instead find themselves in an elliptical orbit around it. They make use of rockets to modify their trajectory, hoping this will get them onto the moon after all. Instead, they are drawn back to earth and drop into the Pacific Ocean, to be rescued by the faithful J. T. Maston. Upon the successful completion of their adventure, the president of the Gun Club sells his space diary to the *New York Herald*, while a private company will be established to promote future space travel.

Once again, Verne displayed a knowledge of science that was far ahead of its time. As one reviewer put it, when the illustrated edition of *Around the Moon* was finally published, "Mr. Verne's fantasy doesn't lead science astray, it only gives it wings and helps it to fly."[10]

A LETTER TO PIERRE-JULES HETZEL WRITTEN ON FEBRUARY 17, 1869, when Jules Verne was beginning the final fortnight of his working visit to his parents, provides an excellent opportunity to catch author and publisher in the middle of a planning session (something we cannot do when they are together in Hetzel's office at 18 Rue Jacob). Jules had received a letter from Hetzel outlining his project for a book on the transatlantic voyage of the *Great Eastern;* he thanked the publisher, and said he was "perfectly right" about the whole thing. But he was so taken up with the second half of *Twenty Thousand Leagues,* and by the second half of *Around the Moon,* that he couldn't think of anything else just then. He would go from Nantes to Paris; he needed "five or six weeks" of frequent meetings with Hetzel; then in April he'd return to Le Crotoy.

He was convinced that the seaside at Le Crotoy would be good for his ailing son, who would be eight years old in August. "I'm in a hurry to take him to the seaside, for here in Paris he has a small bout of fever every day, and we don't know how to stop it. We're obviously going through a bad time," he concluded.[11]

Hetzel was a severe critic, but he admired his protégé. The proof is his suggestion, in a letter to Nantes, that Verne declare himself a candidate for the French Academy, an elite body limited to forty eminent men of letters, men of state or of cloth; the Academy waited until an academician died before choosing another to replace him. Jules dismissed the Academy as a "dream"—Hetzel's dream. "Anyone without a huge fortune or a significant political position doesn't have a chance."

Hetzel had also spoken of winning Verne's appointment to the Legion of Honor, a much-coveted distinction (and perhaps one easier to obtain, since there were more openings). "You know that I shall undertake no initiative to obtain it," Verne responded. "But if I am to be decorated one day, I confess that I should deeply regret not having given that satisfaction to my father and mother during their lifetime." But he quickly added, "That's a bit naïve on my part." His feelings reminded him of the fictional Joseph Prudhomme, who asks for the Legion medal to make his wife happy, for that *was* how Jules, too, felt about this distinction.[12]

In the absence of correspondence, one can only assume that the Paris encounter between publisher and author was profitable; what is known is that Jules took both manuscripts—that of Captain Nemo's odyssey and *Around the Moon*—to Le Crotoy so that he could work on them further, inspired by Hetzel's observations and marginal scribblings, and then shipped them back to Paris later that spring. "Everything known about the moon, all the questions that remain, are dealt with," he wrote in a letter announcing the dispatch of *Around the Moon* to rue Jacob. "It's rather complete from this point of view, and often rather bold, I think. The final chapter remains to be written, but one discovers a proper ending only at the last minute."[13]

Once again, he spoke with obvious satisfaction about his contribution to scientific knowledge, and *Around the Moon* certainly did contain things his contemporaries would want to know about previous sightings and writings, rendered still more interesting by being placed in the mouths of sympathetic characters.

In the same letter, Verne informed his publisher that he was drawing up a list of replies to Hetzel's marginal comments on the second volume of *Twenty Thousand Leagues*. These ongoing discussions between publisher and author would continue until the book was finished.

LE CROTOY MEANT SAILING AS WELL AS WORK, AND THE gathering up of all the children. Legend has it that local inhabitants referred to feverish Michel as the "terror of Le Crotoy." But if the family was to be together, better to come to Le Crotoy for that. The prospect of this isolation—the remoteness of the fishing village from the nearest railroad line, a long coach ride away, for example—didn't vex Jules Verne at all.

He hadn't totally abandoned Paris. Verne hastened to point this out to Hetzel in a letter that may have been written in August 1869. But if he had had to find an apartment in Paris large enough to accommodate Honorine and himself, their son, and Honorine's two daughters, plus cover all the other expenses connected with family life in the big city, he simply couldn't have afforded it. In Le Crotoy, they could live well; moreover, everybody seemed to like it there. "So do realize that I have three children, and if the future doesn't worry me, the present is often hard."[14]

If the future didn't worry him, it was probably because he expected that he and Honorine would eventually inherit money from their families. Meanwhile, the 10,000 francs he was receiving each year from Hetzel—the equivalent of some 180,000 present-day francs—and this not taking income from subsidiary rights into account, would have been considered a respectable emolument.[15]

True, he was no longer making commissions on stock transactions, and neither he nor Honorine were receiving monetary support from their families any longer. Money obtained from newspaper serializations might represent a quarter of the annual Hetzel guarantee, but there would not be a serialization every year. Although examination of Hetzel's book-keeping doesn't indicate precisely when Verne's royalties were earned, he was paid a total of 3,750 francs for his first four novels, in addition to the original advances (Hetzel received 7,295 francs); for the first five illustrated editions—for which Verne earned a royalty of 5 or 6 percent—he received 18,000 francs (Hetzel got 70,039). Beginning with the contract signed in December 1865, the popular illustrated editions no longer produced royalties for the man who, after all, had written the novels.[16]

SUMMER'S END FOUND JULES IN LE CROTOY; HE HADN'T been able to leave, he told Hetzel—because Michel was there (presumably unwell). But he wasn't wasting his time. He finished correcting the proofs of *Around the Moon,* a set of which was going to the *Journal des Débats,* which began publishing the novel on December eighth, while Hetzel's small-format edition came out a month later.

During the final weeks of editing, Verne was ever more careful than ever about his science. He didn't intend to be rushed by the *Journal des Débats,* for the manuscript of *Around the Moon* had to be read by "a reliable mathematician"—a cousin who was the assistant of Joseph Bertrand, professor of physics and mathematics at the prestigious Collège de France. "This book has passages that are very scientific, very algebraic even," he explained to Hetzel. Later, he was to affirm: "The more I read and revise, the better it all seems, and I have great hopes that the public—despite the strangeness and audacity of certain things—will accept and gobble up the exploits of our three adventurers."[17]

At year's end, he took the family to Amiens for a snowy Christmas. A letter to his parents at the time indicates that he had made a conscious decision to alternate holiday visits between the two families: "Just a year ago we were in Nantes. . . . In a year we'll be back to spend the winter with you."

He reported progress on still another book, *A Floating City.* "Since it's our journey on the *Great Eastern* set to fiction," he explained to his parents, "I expect Paul to make sure not a single blunder gets past him."

Apparently, his father wondered why there had been no reviews of his son's masterwork, *Twenty Thousand Leagues Under the Sea.* Only the first half of the novel had been published (at the end of October 1869); the second would not appear until the following June. He hadn't tried to get critical attention, Jules explained to his father; the first volume alone didn't give the reader an idea of the book's value.[18]

Surely he didn't expect a great many critical articles. Few eminent reviewers ever deigned to mention him, and over most of his career he was treated less as a literary man than as a scientist and an educator.[19]

Was that so bad?

19

LOVE AND WAR

Verne's romantic inclinations can be assumed to have had an effect on his behavior, if not on his creativity. In 1870, for example, something was obviously happening in his life, and Honorine Verne felt its troubling effects.

The first months of 1870 found Jules settled with his family in Le Crotoy, but he made more than one visit to Paris—at a time when the trip was still expensive and exhausting. He did not go there to see Hetzel, for his publisher was wintering in Monaco.

In a letter to Hetzel from Paris—where the temperature had fallen to twenty-two degrees Fahrenheit—Jules explained that he had been there for several days but was now leaving for home, although he would soon return for a couple of weeks. At that time he promised to deliver the first volume of a new project—again a Hetzel commission—*Celebrated Travels and Travelers,* as well as his fictional account of sailing on the *Great Eastern.* Verne's letter began with a report on work in progress: "I'm in the middle of the Robinson [referring to *Uncle Robinson,* which was not published in Verne's lifetime].... I'm burrowing in and can't think of anything else." Then he added, "Except in Paris, where I always arrive *furens amore,* and leave the same way. Oh! nature!"[1]

Scholars have been divided about who had rendered him "furious with love." The name of a translator, Maria Alexandrovna Markovitch (née Velinskaïa), who used the pen name Marko Vovtchok), has been suggested. Then thirty-six years old, she was associated with Hetzel in arranging Russian editions of Verne's books; apparently, she also translated some of them. She had lived in France in earlier years, then visited Paris again at the beginning of the spring of 1870.

Yet Hetzel was involved with this attractive lady ("with her lovely smoky-gray eyes"). Even if she knew and talked to Jules Verne, one assumes he would not have had a liaison with his friendly publisher's sweetheart.[2] Although the object of Verne's affections remains unknown, one can assume that Hetzel knew who she was.

Whoever she was, Jules wasn't afraid to drag in his publisher as coconspirator. In one of his letters that spring, Jules asked Hetzel to send him a letter to the effect that his presence was required in Paris to discuss the illustrations for *A Floating City*. "Which happens to be true," Jules added helpfully. To assure that his accomplice would provide him the alibi he needed, Verne repeated his plea in a follow-up letter. "So urge me on," he pleaded.[3]

"As soon as he arrived [from Nantes]," his suffering wife complained to a friend, "Jules abandoned me. He got it into his head to go to Paris on the *Saint-Michel*."[4] It was indeed an original way to sail into the arms of whoever was waiting for him there. The cruise up the Seine turned out to be easy enough. He moored at the Pont des Arts, in the very heart of Paris, during his ten-day stay there, and thereby "had the honor of drawing crowds."

On his return to Le Crotoy, he found Honorine quite depressed. He (but not she) blamed it on a succession of deaths in her family—the latest being that of the sister of her first husband. "She's very sad and finds it difficult to recover from it all," he explained to his parents.[5]

THIS AWAKENING OF VERNE'S PASSION, ACCOMPANIED BY alienation from his wife, in no way compromised his ability to write. His energies were further whipped up by the likelihood that his book would be serialized in a daily paper, which would augment his income. In a note written from Amiens (during the Vernes' holiday visit there), Jules questioned Hetzel about the fee paid by *Le Journal des Débats* for *Around the Moon*. There had been twenty installments, which at the "very reasonable price" of 125 francs each should have amounted to 2,500 francs, but only 2,250 had been paid.[6]

Despite the failure of the respected *Revue des Deux Mondes* to take his books seriously in its review pages, there had been a surprising overture

Jules Verne.

Jules Verne.

BIBLIOTHÈQUE
NATIONALE DE FRANCE.

*Paul Verne
and his son
Gaston.*

COURTESY OF
BIBLIOTHÈQUE
MUNICIPALE,
NANTES.

*Amiens as Jules Verne
first saw it (from
an 1855 guidebook).*

Théâtre de la Gaite, Paris.

*The North
Station in
Paris when
Jules Verne
began
traveling
to Amiens.*

New York's Fifth Avenue Hotel as Jules Verne saw it (from Miller's New York as It Is (1866).

Théâtre de la Porte, St. Martin, Paris.

Théâtre de l'Ambigu-Comique, Paris.

Illustrated edition of
Five Weeks in a Balloon.
Signed Edouard Riou.

Felix Nadar.

*In the space capsule,
Michel Ardan in center (from
the illustrated French edition
of* Around the Moon).

*The space capsule
(from the illustrated
French edition of*
Around the Moon).

*Splashdown in the Pacific
(from the illustrated French
edition of* Around the Moon).

The Great Eastern
*as illustrated
by Jules Ferat
and Adolphe
Pannemaker in*
A Floating City.

*Grand Salon
aboard the*
Great Eastern *as
illustrated by Jules
Ferat and Adolphe
Pannemaker in*
A Floating City.

Frontispiece for the illustrated French edition of Around the World in Eighty Days.

Phileas Fogg, seated, wearing a top hat, and his servant Passepartout, riding on the back of the elephant (from the illustrated French edition of Around the World in Eighty Days*).*

Frontispiece for original French edition of Dick Sands.

Verne's yacht Saint-Michel III, *illustrated in Paul Verne's account of their voyage to the North Sea.*

Gaston Verne and his father, Paul, attempting to climb down from a Copenhagen church (from Paul Verne's account of the North Sea voyage).

Captain Nemo's last words as illustrated by Jules Ferat in The Mysterious Island.

"Professor Aronnax" in Twenty Thousand Leagues Under the Sea, actually a portrait of Jules Verne.

Jules Verne's fifteen-year-old hero, Captain Dick, in Dick Sands. Illustration by Henri Meyer.

The Sphinx of ice in Edgar Allan Poe's
The Mystery of Arthur Gordon Pym.

*Nellie Bly
(Elizabeth Cochrane
Seaman), famed
around-the-world
traveler.
Her record for
the trip was
seventy-two days,
six hours,
eleven minutes.*

Jules Verne.

The Vernes at home on
Rue Charles-DuBois
(Jules with his dog,
Honorine on the steps).

from its director, François Buloz, whose magazine published Hugo, the elder Dumas, and George Sand. Verne told Buloz that his contract didn't allow him to contribute to another periodical without Hetzel's consent. Nevertheless, the enterprising author thought he should follow up on this offer to publish material not designed for the *Magasin,* "either because of their subject or because, with my doing three volumes a year, the *Magasin* doesn't have the space."

Despite Hetzel's natural desire to hold on to his author, he had given a surprising nod to the idea. That had occurred a year earlier. Verne had thought the story of his ocean voyage aboard the *Great Eastern* might be the right one for Buloz's magazine.

But it was not to be. As Verne explained to Hetzel, the magazine would only pay two hundred francs per manuscript page, which they said was the going rate for new authors; Verne held out for four hundred francs. He wondered if Hetzel would want to try one of the dailies with which he had a connection. He also suggested that the book could run, with a few changes, in Hetzel's *Magasin.* In the end, he would place *A Floating City* in the *Journal des Débats.*[7]

Although Verne's authentic travel diary would have made for interesting reading, he transformed his experiences into a prosaic and predictable shipboard melodrama ostensibly being observed by the narrator (who happens to be a Frenchman much like Jules Verne). The mix of uninspired plot and gushing descriptions rendered *A Floating City* as boring as first impressions scribbled on a picture postcard sent to family members. It was also further proof of the author's own observation that he did not know how to write about love.

In the book, Ellen has been forced to marry the uncouth Harry Drake; because she couldn't have the man she wanted—pale, handsome Fabian—she has lost her mind. During the ocean crossing aboard the *Great Eastern,* her husband confines her to their cabin. By coincidence, Fabian is also on the ship; Drake and he fight a duel in a storm. But when the disappointed suitor spies Ellen, he throws down his sword; just then, his adversary, evil Harry Drake, is struck and killed by lightning.

When the *Great Eastern* docks in New York, the young widow—still in shock—is taken by Fabian to a house near Niagara Falls; it is clear that she is regaining her senses, and this time she will marry the right man. Despite this leaden story, there is a fascinating tour of the giant ship, whose promenades are like boulevards and whose vast spaces are like Hyde Park. The most unexpected scenes are those of old New York—of busy Broadway and the luxurious Fifth Avenue Hotel and its revolutionary elevator (scenes so unexpected that neither author nor publisher seemed to have been able to help the artist who illustrated the story, so the illustrations were omitted).

"I'm killing myself with work," Verne wrote Hetzel early in 1870. "I'm almost finished with 'Travels and Travelers.' I think that my approach will please you." This letter is an interesting one, for it shows that for once the author was holding the reins.

This project took Verne's admirers by surprise. On April 28, 1870, the book was announced—an unusual event, since his books were usually advertised around Christmas. The first volume of *Travels and Travelers,* as he was calling it for brevity's sake—the full title in English would be *Celebrated Travels and Travelers: The Exploration of the World*—covered the feats of explorers from Hanno (sent by Carthage to colonize the coast of West Africa) and the Greek Herodotus to Marco Polo and Christopher Columbus. "Don't think I'm resting when I do these," Verne wrote Hetzel. "Hell, no!"[8]

IN PRINCIPLE, THE SECOND EMPIRE SHOULD HAVE BEEN A time of peace and prosperity; Napoléon III was supposed to guarantee that. But beyond French borders, Europe was in the grip of a new nationalism, which, for France's closest neighbors, gave reunification clear priority over civil peace. Certainly the crusade of Prussia's Prince Otto von Bismarck to rally the loosely federated German states into an empire was causing anxiety in France. In 1870, anxiety soon became crisis, and it appeared that both France and Prussia were prepared to go to war.

The casus belli was found not on the Rhine river separating the belligerents, however, but in Spain. The throne of Spain was offered to a Hohenzollern prince, a relative of King Wilhelm I of Prussia. France now had potential enemies on two frontiers—actually, the same enemy now. The decision of Leopold von Hohenzollern-Sigmaringen to withdraw his candidacy for the Spanish crown ought to have put an end to the crisis, but Bismarck needed a war to complete German reunification.

This man to become known as the Iron Chancellor invented the war he needed. When the French emperor asked Wilhelm for assurances that the Hohenzollern candidacy had been definitely laid to rest, King Wilhelm put him off in measured terms in July 1870, in a meeting with the French ambassador at Ems, a town in the Rhineland-Palatinate. In the Ems dispatch, Bismarck proceeded to toughen the language of Wilhelm's reply so that it was unacceptable to the French. At a time when great powers still fought over insults, Napoléon III could only declare war, which he did on the nineteenth of July.

Even though Jules Verne was now living in the provinces, he knew that trouble was brewing. "People here seem to think that we are going to fight Prussia," he wrote to his publisher in an undated letter, most probably in early July. "I can't believe that—don't believe a word of it—and you?"[9]

Hetzel shared his author's suspicion of jingoist agitation, but he was a realist, and in the end he was right. "We're at war. The Chamber [of Deputies] has just heard the declaration," he informed Verne on July twenty-first. "The European powers are making serious efforts to prevent the shedding of blood. They won't succeed." Hetzel's son and five of their staff were being called up for military service. "My wife weeps all day long," added Hetzel, "and I hold back tears ten times a day, and have stopped sleeping."[10]

Launched on August fourth, the German offensive seemed unstoppable. In mid-August, with the war raging, singular news came to Jules Verne. He had been appointed to the Legion of Honor, an élite society created by Napoléon I in 1802 to honor achievement both by the military and distinguished civilians. Henceforth, Verne would be entitled to display the coveted red ribbon on his lapel. It was the sort of honor he appreciated; his publisher, who knew that, also knew the right people. "You deserved your decoration," Hetzel wrote to him on August fourteenth. "No matter the political circumstances in which it came, I'm glad that you obtained it and to have had something to do with it."

Verne's reply was equally gracious. "I know that my mother and father have been made happy. You are broadminded enough to understand small weaknesses you don't share, for it is certain that with all the positions you have held you could have stuck all the medals in the world on your chest."

Verne knew, of course, that he had received his honor from a collapsing empire—Alsace was already lost, and the capital of Lorraine was occupied on the very day his appointment was announced. "All this is very grave, and you cannot imagine how much hostility I encountered against Napoléon in all the towns I passed through [between Nantes and Le Crotoy]," he reported to Hetzel. "This can only spell the end of a dynasty, but we risk paying dearly for it."[11]

The Legion appointment was a pretext for Honorine to compose a letter of her own to their benefactor in Paris. A letter of gratitude, it then became a long plaint, a confession of despair. Had she misread Jules's symptoms, his longing for Paris, his disengaged attitude at home? The letter sounds as if she hadn't misread them at all. "This morning your good letter brought happiness and perhaps joy back to our home, because you are not unaware that for several months Jules has been sad and not himself," she began. "Is his work exhausting him? Or does he find it harder?—in any case he seems discouraged. And he makes me suffer for all the problems brought on by his discouragement. I note that he sits down to work with difficulty, gets up again almost at once, complains about this and blames me—what to do? What to say? I cry and become desperate. When home life bores and tires him too much he boards his boat and sails off; most of the time I don't know where."

She wondered, pathetically, whether Hetzel, who had done so much to make a distinguished writer of Jules Verne, could also help to make him an acceptable husband. She apologized for opening her heart in this way in a letter intended as a token of gratitude. "Perhaps," she wrote, seeming to beseech the old publisher, "you will find a remedy to deliver us from this tense and trying situation."

Had Jules spoken to him about these things? She begged Hetzel not to let her husband know that she had written in this way. Should the publisher wish to reply with consolation or advice, she said he must write to her care of general delivery. "In my opinion," concluded this most lucid woman, "my husband's worst error was to have left Paris. He is too alone here, left too often to himself. . . . Farewell, dear friend, excuse me and pity me. My husband is slipping out of my hands—help me hold on to him."[12]

FEW COULD HAVE PREDICTED THE FATE THAT WAS IN STORE for France. Prussia was a blustering upstart, and Bismarck's coalition was certainly not expected to be capable of overrunning France and driving out its emperor, occupying every strategic point worth holding, and threatening the glorious capital, all in a matter of weeks. By the beginning of September—only a month after it had begun—Bismarck's campaign was virtually won, with the capitulation of Marshal MacMahon, who was in charge of defending the frontier, and the seizure of Napoléon III himself. After that, the stunned French could only slow down the advance, yielding one and then another province. With the disappearance of the French emperor, his empire disappeared; Paris was now in the care of a republican cabinet prepared to resist.

The Prussian offensive caught Jules Verne in Nantes. He had made his way there despite the crisis—first dispatching Honorine and the children to her parents in Amiens—after receiving alarming news of his father's health. Indeed, old age had suddenly descended upon the seventy-one-year-old Pierre, even though he remained "lively in thought and intelligence." Now there was no joy in this once-joyous family, sobered as it was by the news of lost battles—or the absence of news. "Here the bitterness toward the emperor is at its peak," Jules reported to Hetzel. "Nobody imagines that—winner or loser—he can ever come back to Paris."[13]

By mid-September, with most of northern and eastern France in enemy hands, intrepid Jules—or perhaps he was merely insouciant—undertook the return trip from Nantes to his beloved seaside refuge. It was a difficult journey, with long detours via Le Mans, Rouen, and Dieppe, as he informed his parents after his return on September twentieth. "Here"—meaning Le Crotoy—"the country is still quiet, and I think that we'll decide to stay."[14] His optimism was stronger than his military knowledge: "If Paris resists as it seems to be doing," he wrote to Hetzel, "the Prussians themselves will be obliged to seek peace, because winter will work against them. . . . The countryside asks only to be able to defend itself."[15]

A forty-two-year-old writer would not be expected to serve at the front. As a boat owner, Verne was assigned to coast guard patrol, his companions a dozen veterans of the Crimean War—their arms three flintlock rifles and a small cannon.[16]

For his part, the desperate Hetzel pulled out the chapters on the French territories affected by the war from his star author's *Illustrated Geography* and published them under the title *From Paris to the Rhine*.[17]

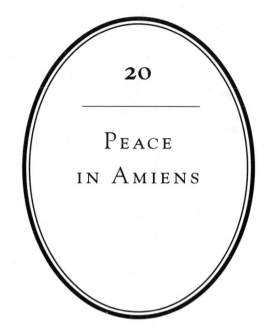

20

Peace
in Amiens

THE UNLOVED EMPEROR WAS GONE. AFTER AN AWKWARD BUT hardly comfortless confinement in a German castle, Napoléon III was allowed to retire to the English countryside. Power in his former capital had slipped almost imperceptibly into the hands of determined republicans, who were intent on pursuing the war. Their instrument was a so-called government of national defense, presided over by an old soldier, Gen. Louis Jules Trochu. While organizing the protection of Paris, the war cabinet also sought, without success, to break through the German encirclement of the city.

Henceforth, half of France, the France of mining and industry, was a battlefield, the strategic map a checkerboard, with pockets of resistance alternating with enemy-occupied territory. The Vernes' Brittany and much more of the western and southern hinterland were spared, the north and east largely held captive. But in those days, one could live in a country at war and not be at war. Even the postal system worked, at least from province to province. One could dispatch a letter from besieged Paris and hope it would reach its destination via balloon, pigeon, or river float.

Thus Jules Verne, national guardsman assigned to Le Crotoy, spent the month of October protecting his territory, and writing a book. A letter his parents mailed from Verne to Honorine's parents in Amiens was forwarded to him in Le Crotoy. He couldn't leave the village even if he wanted to, he told his father. "I prefer being a national guardsman here than in Amiens, but I'm glad that Honorine and her children are in Amiens, in a big city rather than a village. The Prussians have the deplorable habit of burning and looting villages, and it's better for women not to be there."

His own view of the war remained ambiguous. Friends had been called up for military service. By what right, he asked, had this National Defense cabinet—which, after all, was only a de facto government—issued such a decree, and to what extent need one obey it? Only a constituent assembly could give such a cabinet legitimacy. But he was ready to go into battle if called (he had already acquired a gun of his own and 150 cartridges).

Still, he insisted, peace was "in everybody's interest." If the war continued, their district would certainly be occupied; in that case, Honorine and her daughters would go to Brussels to stay with friends. "Then," he predicted, "we'll have a civil war, but that will be nothing in comparison. I hope that they will keep the national guard in Paris for some time, and that they'll shoot down the Socialists like so many dogs. This is the only hope for the republic, and it's the only government that has the right to be without pity for Socialism, for it is the only just and legitimate government."

This was an odd outburst, given the fact that the chief menace still seemed to be coming from across the Rhine; in none of his surviving letters did he express himself with as much violence against Bismarck and his armies. His was an understandable reaction, so his biographer grandson thought, to the angry march of working-class Parisians, who, on the last day of October 1870, had attempted to overthrow the provisional government—on the grounds that it was insufficiently resolved to drive out the Prussians.

"Finally," his letter home concluded, "despite all these worries I've gone back to work, and in the month I've been alone here—apart from two or three trips to Amiens—I've written most of a volume."[1]

In mid-December he was in Amiens again—a significantly different Amiens; the Prussians had reached the Somme. Four enemy soldiers were billeted at the Devianes' and were enjoying it. In a letter dated December seventeenth, written on his return to Le Crotoy, Verne told his parents that the soldiers were eating better in Amiens than they did at home. "They're fed lots of rice so they stay as constricted as possible. It's less bothersome," wrote Verne, a man ever concerned by enteric matters. These Prussians were "mild and tranquil men," soldiers of a line regiment (clearly not the kind you'd shoot down like a dog, as you might shoot socialists).[2]

Throughout this turbulent period, Verne and Hetzel maintained contact—Hetzel's letters following a veritable Vernian trajectory over enemy lines via balloon or carrier pigeon, then by coach into friendly territory—a week in transit from Paris to Le Crotoy, but a marvel all the same. "Yes indeed! I accomplished a lot," he informed Hetzel in the middle of February 1871. "Yes, I had the strength to do that." A fortnight earlier, on January twenty-eighth, the defense cabinet had surrendered the capital; in return for payment of an indemnity, Parisians were spared a Prussian occupation.

Jules Verne could visit Paris at last. "I'll call on you with two finished volumes," he promised Hetzel. These did not include the famous "Robinson" on which he had been working—they'd have to talk further about that. "You know that I stick to an idea like a Breton," he added. "Yes, Paris did a Robinson on a grand scale." This reference was to the siege just ended, whose hardships and deprivations were to become legendary. He did warn Hetzel that the books he had been working on were not among his most ambitious efforts.

The first, as he described it, was "of a terrifying realism"; he was calling it *The Castaways of the Chancellor;* in the end, it would simply be *The Chancellor.* The other manuscript, published in English as *Measuring a Meridian,* would have a more diffuse title in French, translating as *Adventures of Three Russians and Three Englishmen in Southern Africa.* "It's about an Anglo-Russian committee on a geographical mission. . . . It's scientific, but not overly. I think that it will also contain a lot of action." In fact, it would prove to be a *very* scientific book, its equations readable only by the mathematically inclined; for everyone else, it may have been a sleep-inducing book. He had been inspired, he said, by one of the expeditions of his late friend and occasional mentor Jacques Arago—but surely Arago would have livened it up.

"And then I'm just beginning a new project: *The Fur Country,* to fill two volumes. But it's not necessary to talk about it just yet. . . . "

He concluded with another contemptuous remark on the handling of the war by the national defense cabinet, which hadn't really known how to defend the nation.[3] A new national assembly elected on February 8, 1871—formed to comply with Bismarck's demand that the peace treaty be signed by a legal government on the French side—was to count a majority leaning toward the restoration of monarchy (or of a Bonaparte-style empire).

That was hardly the end of the political turmoil kindled by the Prussian invasion. Now came the insurrection of Paris's working class, enraged by the facility with which their leaders had abandoned them to Bismarck and distraught by the country's election of a reactionary parliament. The workers set up an autonomous Commune, in opposition to the new government headed by Adolphe Thiers, who sent in troops to seize the guns of the guard—guns paid for by Parisians in a fund-raising campaign during the siege. Resisting the confiscation, national guardsmen shot two of Thiers's generals, after which the national government withdrew to Versailles. Paris belonged to the insurrectionists.

"The Socialist movement had to happen," Verne wrote to Hetzel, seemingly more resigned than bitter. "Well, it's done, it will be beaten, and if the republican government manifests ferocious energy in putting it down—it has the duty and the right to do that—Republican France will enjoy fifty years of domestic peace."[4]

The Paris Commune elected its own assembly (winning a majority, for the insurrection was simplified by the flight of so many of the well-to-do, who feared it). Revolutionary fervor was maintained thanks to the hostility of the government, now settled indefinitely in Versailles; once again, the city was under siege. But this time the climax, a "bloody week" beginning May 21, saw advancing government forces execute the Parisian insurgents wherever they found them, while the radical resistance killed its conservative hostages; everywhere public buildings burned. The cleanup by the Versailles forces was equally brutal, the consequences more long-lasting.

Hetzel, who had been a rebel once, witnessed these events with growing dismay; illness and the siege's deprivations made him seem older than his fifty-seven years. He slipped out of Paris when he could, first to Monaco, then to Switzerland; now, as the communal government went up in flames, he sized up the dilemma of France in a letter to his wife from Lausanne: "On one side madmen, villains, barbarians: on the other the selfish and indifferent rich who didn't bother to get to the heart of problems and who, when they're not ill, never think of other people's health."[5]

In early June, Verne, who was visiting Paris in the company of his brother, described "these lamentable ruins" for his absent publisher. He tried to reassure Hetzel about his publishing house: "Your Rue Jacob came out of it nicely, I think. It received only a few scratches. But its neighbor, Rue de Lille: what a disaster!" Jules also made it a point to "prowl around the Stock Exchange since I don't know if one can depend on literature in such times and I'm somewhat worried about the future."[6]

He had already raised the matter of his finances in April, when Paris was still out of bounds. Hetzel had suggested that he do a little less work. Writing three volumes a year was too tiring; Verne could reduce that to two and Hetzel would not reduce his annual stipend.

The offer indicated Hetzel's good-heartedness; Jules was of course grateful. "But I must say that in the present circumstances and with the deprivations that are going to last a long time in all sectors, even an income of nine or ten thousand francs will be quite insufficient." His expenses were rising constantly as the children grew older, and what little income had been coming in from bonds had all but evaporated. "Financial hardship is approaching rapidly, I assure you." He now wondered whether he shouldn't be looking beyond writing as a way to survive. "I even wonder if I shouldn't try to return to the Exchange, despite all my earlier disappointments."[7]

Henceforth, money worries would be the leitmotif of Verne's letters home. He revealed to his father that he now had *four* books ready for publication; Hetzel owed him a considerable sum, which naturally worried him. Meanwhile, he had joined his family in Amiens. Le Crotoy was ancient history; if they went there at all that year, it would only be during Michel's vacation from boarding school. He was waiting for the government to return to Paris from its Versailles refuge before going back there another time, although he feared that Thiers wouldn't have the necessary energy to build a strong government on the ruins of the Paris Commune. "Yet it does seem as if only the Republic can save France."[8] He meant, of course, a properly bourgeois republic.

Thiers returned at last, and so did Jules Verne. "Here I am at the Stock Exchange, and the whole secret of the business is absolute punctuality," he explained to his parents, thus offering an excuse for his inability to visit them (although Honorine and the children had gone there for summer holidays). "I'm doing or shall be doing the same job as before. Only instead of working with more or less reliable friends who make you run risks, I'm trying to deal only with the leading banks and credit institutions. But I'll need patience and obstinacy, and I'll have both." He wasn't abandoning writing, he explained. "Far from that. It's only temporary. And instead of doing three volumes a year I'll do at least one."[9]

While he "prowled around the Stock Exchange," he actually wrote to Hetzel on the familiar letterhead of the broker he had worked for in an earlier time, Fernand Eggly.[10] Hetzel got the message; as soon as he could, he put his recent offer in writing—two volumes a year, instead of three, with a rise in his annual stipend to twelve thousand francs.

There was one catch, however: Verne would have to extend the grant to the publisher of exclusive rights for all his books by three years, and this without extra retribution. Verne had no objection, and he signed this rider to their contract on September 25, 1871; monthly payments of one thousand francs were to begin in November.[11]

⁓◌ ◌⁓

PARIS DIDN'T SEEM TO BE THE ANSWER TO VERNE'S PROB-lems. Certainly the stock market wasn't the answer. The financial world was changing, with new kinds of investment in industry, and a new breed of financiers emerged to handle them. Such a market was not for Jules Verne nor he for it. Nor was postwar, post–Second Empire Paris his Paris. "It's impossible to work here now," he confided to a friend. "Too much excitement and too much noise!"

To Charles Wallut, his old friend of theater days, now editor of *Musée des Familles,* he explained the fundamental change in his life that was about to transpire: "At my wife's request I'm settling in Amiens, a well-mannered, organized, even-tempered city; the society there is cordial and well-read. We are close to Paris—close enough to receive its reflection, without the intolerable noise and sterile agitation."[12]

On July 13, 1871—the date on which he made a formal request for a change of his legal residence from Le Crotoy to Amiens[13]—forty-three-year-old Jules Verne was turning away from the only place where reputations were made in his country: Paris was not only France's but increasingly the world capital of arts and literature, not to speak of science. As if he feared the company of his peers, and their competition, Jules Verne would henceforth content himself with the honors one could earn in the provinces—at least most of the time.

Paris had long since preempted France's best and brightest; little remained for the provincial capitals, even the largest of them, such as Bordeaux, Lyon, and Marseilles. By then, the population of Paris numbered over 1.5 million people. "Parisians are lively, witty, and friendly," stated a guidebook published just before the Prussian invasion. "The conversation of high society is refined, delicate, and polite. Workers, quite well educated, live entirely in the present, easily forgetting their sorrows or consoling themselves with song."[14]

In his own *Illustrated Geography,* Verne had of course dealt with Amiens and its 61,063 inhabitants. By the time he drafted the description of the Somme district and its capital, Amiens (some eighty miles from Paris), he had a dozen years of familiarity with the place, thanks to Honorine. "It's a rather interesting city to visit," he had written—a phrase not very convincing in its enthusiasm. "Its modern quarters are well planned . . . but the old sector near the Somme is frightfully ugly; this river in crossing the city divides into eleven arms which provide power for numerous factories." He called attention to the town's pleasant situation, the walks along the inner waterways and the tree-lined boulevards. There were only four historical monuments, but one of them was France's largest cathedral. The library contained 55,000 books and 600 manuscripts, there were the Academy of Sciences, Letters, and Arts, associations of antiquarians and of garden lovers, and the Philharmonic Society.

His adopted city was a manufacturing center, specializing in the production of velvet and cotton—sixteen thousand workers—and wool fabrics—another ten thousand employees; there were wool and cotton mills, carpet factories, weavers' workshops.[15]

Although Verne had described it as an interesting place to visit, living there might prove a different matter.

The chronicler Jules Claretie remembered the visit of the Shah of Persia to Paris soon after the return of the Thiers government. In his honor, Paris put on its first display of fireworks since the war, leading the Shah to exclaim, "Who dares say that Paris isn't Paris anymore?" Verne confided to Claretie: "It is so much the same Paris that I'm going back to Amiens and staying there. This city is too noisy for me!"[16]

Of course, the railroad connected Amiens to Paris. "An exceptional geographical location," a brochure of 1875 boasted; "the obligatory route from Paris to London. . . . "[17] The Amiens station was conveniently close to where the Vernes would finally elect to live. Jules could even read the Paris papers in Amiens, and at long last these publications were talking about *Twenty Thousand Leagues Under the Sea,* which had come out at an awkward moment (the second and final volume was printed in June 1870, on the eve of war). Now, after the peace agreement, Hetzel was releasing the gift edition.

The reviews hardly did justice to Verne's masterpiece; critical acclaim would not come until later. "This *Nautilus* is a rather curious vessel," a nonchalant reviewer told readers of *Le Figaro.* "Life aboard is quite extravagant and naturally serves as a pretext for a considerable number of scientific explanations that the author doesn't spare us, and which he renders interesting thanks to his recognized talent." (If only the review had been as interesting as the book.) "Let no one make a mistake, Mr. Verne is a genuine learned scholar," affirmed *Le Journal des Débats.* "He chooses a fictional framework, fantastic and visionary; but his information comes from the best sources, and except for the hypothetical details that he offers for what they are worth—they lead no one astray—one can rely on him without fear."[18]

VERNE WAS SOON CALLED AWAY FROM AMIENS; IN NANTES, his father, now seventy-two, was dying. Jules arrived in time to say good-bye at the beginning of November 1871. "He was a true saint," Jules wrote to Hetzel.[19]

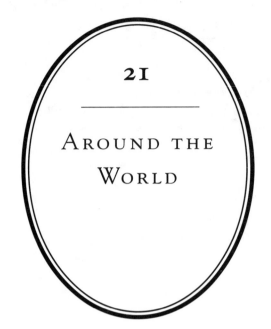

21

AROUND THE WORLD

T HE VERNES HAD FOUND SUITABLE QUARTERS IN A THREE-story redbrick house at 23, boulevard Guyencourt, just south of Amiens's town center, along the railroad line; now and in two successive moves, and indeed to the end of his life, he would live alongside those tracks—not only alongside the tracks but *facing* them, as if he wished to keep his eye on the trains. Often enough, the lumbering locomotives exasperated him, with their signals and their smoke; yet his successive writing rooms would always face them.

The railway followed the line of Amiens's ancient ramparts (long since dismantled), and the city's growing middle class was drawn to recently developed neighborhoods just beyond the old perimeter. It *should* have been possible to find quarters in the same new district yet at a comfortable distance from the passing trains, but the new middle-class residents seemed to want it that way. Jules Verne's new house and the surrounding houses were built after the digging of the railroad trench.

Jules was working as hard as he ever had since tying his fate to Hetzel's. He had long since begun the novel *The Fur Country;* now, in the first months of true peace in 1871, he was finishing volume two. But he had also begun—and was racing to complete—one of his shorter books, another comic novel of the sort he did so well. The new book, *Around the World in Eighty Days,* would live up to its title; if ever a book of his traveled around the world, it was this one.

In *The Fur Country,* he was returning to familiar ground: another hopeless mission to the far north. The protagonists, dispatched by the Hudson's Bay Company, are to set up an outpost on the shores of the Arctic Sea, along the 70th parallel; the year is 1860. The party includes, improbably, an American woman—an intrepid widow traveling with her young maidservant; a third woman, the loyal Eskimo Kalumah, will join their party.

When they reach Cape Bathurst, the explorers build a fort there; it vanishes, along with its occupants, during the long polar night. Unknown to the travelers, their base had been established not on solid ground but over an iceberg; an earthquake tears it loose, and by the time the astronomer attached to the expedition has done his calculations, they have floated north to the 73rd parallel.

Now the danger comes from the thaw. The vast ice field is reduced, and it may soon disappear altogether. The explorers make a raft of it and attach a sail; the clever astronomer finds a way to freeze their floating island with the aid of compressed air. Many familiar elements of a Verne story are found in *The Fur Country,* not the least of which is the lure of the north. "Don't worry," he wrote to his publisher, "I'm working. The two volumes I'm writing for this year are the second half of *The Fur Country* and *Around the World in Eighty Days.* I'm close to finishing, and in two months you will have the complete manuscript of *Around the World.* Next year will be devoted to the Robinson."[1]

His agreement with Hetzel left him free to publish elsewhere, notably once a year in Charles Wallut's *Musée des Familles.* There was every reason to take advantage of this option, for of course it meant additional income. What Verne chose to do now was a long story, which would run in three successive issues of *Musée* (March, April, and May 1872). It is not known whether "Dr. Ox's Experiment" began as an idea for a book and then proved too short or whether Verne did not give it to Hetzel initially because of the story's premise that science could be put to perverse uses.

In "Dr. Ox's Experiment," the scientist of that name offers to provide gaslight to a town—unnamed in the story—at his own expense. Then he takes advantage of the pipes that have been laid to run the gas for an unannounced and mischievous distribution of large quantities of oxygen—thereby livening the behavior of the town's unbelievably indolent citizens; more often than not, the result is embarrassment. In the end, the citizens are so excited by the stimulant that they seek to declare war on the neighboring town.

What begins in "Dr. Ox" as mischief ends on a menacing note, allowing one Verne specialist to read into it the author's anxieties about scientific progress, his doubts about its beneficial contribution, his hatred of war, *and* his growing misanthropy. The problem was that he had glorified science in too many popular stories; he could hardly cancel this message in a single satire in a family magazine.[2]

Hetzel quickly grasped the contradiction, however. When it came time for Verne to offer the story to his regular publisher for inclusion in a volume with four other stories, to appear in 1874, Hetzel removed as much of the deviltry as he dared without eviscerating the plot. Were "virtue, courage, talent, wit, and imagination" simply a matter of oxygen, as Dr. Ox implied? In the revised version, Hetzel guided the author's hand in rejecting this conceit: "and for our part we reject [this theory] from every point of view."[3]

Indeed, a scholar found and published an interesting note Verne sent to his publisher when it came time for a Hetzel edition of the story: "Monday or Tuesday at the latest I'll hand you the text of 'Doctor Ox' myself, and we'll see what needs to be removed for the kiddies."[4]

THE BOOK THAT COUNTED NOW WAS *AROUND THE WORLD IN Eighty Days.* The hero, Phileas Fogg, charges around the globe, after having made a wager with other members of his London club that he'd accomplish the trip in eighty days. Fogg was relying on a story in a London newspaper that estimated the deadline could be met, thanks to the opening of a new section of the Great Indian Peninsular Railway. Accompanied by his faithful French servant Passepartout—whom he had just hired, and who had been rejoicing at the prospect of working for a sedentary master when Fogg announced that Passepartout had ten minutes to pack their bags—the cold-blooded voyager was to employ, as the author summed it up in his final page, "every possible means of travel, ocean liners, railroads, coaches, yachts, cargo ships, sleighs, an elephant." Although Fogg would face numerous obstacles on his journey, these incidents served only to heighten the tension (and the fun, because this would be one of Verne's merry books).

Early on, Fogg's trail is picked up by a Scotland Yard detective who is convinced that the pressed traveler is fleeing after having robbed the Bank of England; the policeman will do what he can to slow Fogg's pace. In India, Fogg and Passepartout save a young Hindu woman from being burned on her husband's funeral pyre; she joins their party. Escapes, improvisations, and increasing speed ensue. In crossing the North American continent, Fogg displays the single-mindedness of his author, who had demonstrated in the *Great Eastern* adventure how indifferent he could be to sights and sounds when in a hurry. Improbable incidents and characters not fully drawn typified *Around the World in Eighty Days,* but the book provided comic relief after the dry adventures of Verne's Englishmen and Russians in *Measuring a Meridian* and the incredibly cold atmosphere of *The Fur Country.*

"Am I working! And can you doubt it!" the author wrote his publisher from Amiens in the spring of 1872. "If you could imagine how amused I am with my journey around the world in eighty days. I dream about it! Let's hope our readers are equally amused. I must be a bit cracked; I let myself get involved with all my heroes' extravagances."[5] Railroads are very much on his mind during the writing of this odyssey. Of course, he now had one beneath his window, but he dreamed about those miraculous American trains he had seen during his journey through New York State. Now he managed to place them advantageously in the new novel.

Verne had given himself a deadline—as recklessly as Phileas Fogg had made a bet; he knew in advance that the novel would be ready at the beginning of October, and he was aiming for serial publication in the daily *Le Temps.*[6] Verne was in the driver's seat now, surely as wise as Hetzel in his perception of his readership.

Even Hetzel's figures—which cannot be verified—would later show that of all Verne's books, *Around the World in Eighty Days* was the one that sold best during his lifetime—and this in the small-format original edition, *without* counting the worldwide publication of the illustrated editions. Hetzel didn't pay his author for these, so they were not included in the sales figures. *Around the World* would be the only one of the *Extraordinary Voyages* Hetzel claimed sold over 100,000 copies in the regular edition up to the time of the author's death (108,000 copies, to be precise). The runners-up were *Five Weeks in a Balloon,* with 76,000 copies, and *Twenty Thousand Leagues Under the Sea,* with an even 50,000.[7]

The new work in progress was so good, Verne read it aloud even before readers could buy it. The opportunity to do that came on his election to the Amiens Academy of Sciences, Letters, and Arts. Its members had taken a bold step in co-opting a relative newcomer to their town, but this seemed justified, given Verne's prominence; he won the seat unanimously on March 8, 1872, but he and the academy only got around to arranging for a formal admission ceremony in June.

It was customary for members to give a formal acceptance speech. Instead of a speech, Verne begged to be allowed to read chapters from his forthcoming book; it was, the society's reporter explained, a "sort of problem whose solution is geographically demonstrated by Jules Verne."

The members seemed to enjoy what they heard of *Around the World in Eighty Days*.[8]

It wasn't often that Verne revealed the origins of one of his stories. But in an interview with journalist Robert Sherard (over twenty years after the book appeared), Verne described how in his reading he picked up all sorts of information "and, as I said, I have a great number of scientific odds and ends in my head." It was thus that one day in a Paris café, scanning the pages of *Le Siècle* (a daily newspaper considered anticlerical and liberal), he came upon an item that indicated one could travel round the world in eighty days. "It immediately struck me that I could profit by a difference of meridian and make my traveller gain or lose a day in his journey," Verne explained to Sherard. "There was my dénouement ready found. The story was not written until long after. I carry ideas about in my head for years—ten or fifteen years, sometimes—before giving them form."[9]

Verne also remembered Edgar Allan Poe's "Three Sundays in a Week," published in the 1862 collection of Poe's stories; Jules had liked it enough at the time to write about it in *Musée des Familles*. In Poe's story, the rich uncle promises a young man the hand of his niece—and a sizable dowry—on the condition that the marriage take place during a week with three Sundays. Subsequently, two naval officers explain that one of them has gone eastward around the world, the other westward; one thinks that the next day is Sunday, the other that it was the day before; but Sunday happened to be that very day. Each of the officers had gained (or lost) twenty-four hours, one hour every one thousand miles, depending on the direction of his journey.[10]

In his new novel, Jules Verne made sure to maintain suspense until the final pages (for all of his ingenuity, Fogg himself doesn't realize what he has achieved, gaining a day thanks to time zones; *he* thinks that he has lost his wager). Then Verne's hero, so much a loner, marries Mrs. Aouda, the Indian woman he has saved—but she must propose to him.

VERNE, A FORMER THEATER MAN, ALSO KNEW THAT IN THIS race around the world he had a perfect subject for boulevard comedy; so did Hetzel, who may actually have thought of it first. They went as far as getting a coauthor, sometime playwright Edouard Cadol, to work on a scenario, but the evidence is that Verne quickly moved ahead and beyond the script. "It is unnecessary for me to say," he informed Hetzel, "that I am putting aside the matter of the play, and in the book itself I often stray from the outline put together by Cadol and myself. I never realized how much a book could differ from a play."[11]

There would be a play—not Cadol's, not quite Verne's, but when it was put on stage, it, too, would circle the globe. Meanwhile, the smaller world of Paris read the serialized version of the novel in the austere *Le Temps*.

It was only fitting that the French Academy think of Jules Verne once again. On August 8, 1872, that body bestowed its annual prize for prose on the collection of books for which Jules Verne was best known: *Extraordinary Voyages*. The prize included a modest cash award.[12] In announcing the prize, the academicians underscored the author's contribution to the "scientific curiosity" of readers. Their recognition, in the words of that institution's permanent secretary, "will be added to that which he has already received, that he receives daily from the public with the great and legitimate success of these books so ingenious, pungent, and at bottom so serious in intent."[13]

The money would have to compensate for the lack of critical applause, for once again the critics who counted were silent.

THE YEAR 1873 WOULD PROVE TO BE A GOOD YEAR FOR Verne. One sign was the resurrection of a play long kept in a drawer: *The American Nephew*, a three-act comedy written in the pre-Hetzel years. Now, with Hetzel anxious to get *Around the World in Eighty Days* on stage, a theater director took a fresh look at this old comedy about the hazards of life insurance. It was only a burlesque, the critic of *Le Temps* reported after the opening at the Cluny Theater on April seventeenth. But he hastened to add that for a play of its kind, it was quite good. On the opening night, from the first lines of the play to the last, there was a "universal burst of laughter."[14]

Perhaps Verne could now afford to relax. The next event in his sedentary existence was a balloon flight—his first, and this a totally gratuitous activity, not one required for his research. Indeed, as a Verne scholar pointed out, he did it *after* writing the first chapter of his next novel, which begins with a balloon caught in a furious storm, then whisked across the oceans to a mysterious island.

The site of his balloon adventure—all twenty-four minutes of it—was his adopted city of Amiens, and he wrote an account of it for the city's in-

dispensable *Journal d'Amiens.* It was a relatively small balloon, weighing
270 kilos, gondola and equipment included; it was filled with a weak mixture "excellent for gaslight," Verne reported, "but for this very reason not
very effective for raising a balloon." He was to have been one of four passengers, with the pilot, a local attorney, and a junior officer. But that
proved to be one too many for the frail balloon, so the officer, who had
flown before, yielded his place.

Then, just as they were to ascend, the pilot's nine-year-old son leapt
into the basket. (The unexpected appearance of an unwanted passenger
should remind Verne fans of one of the first stories he ever published, "A
Balloon Trip.") To rise with that extra weight, they now had to sacrifice
two of the four sacks of ballast, and this reduced the time they could
spend in the sky.

They lifted off at 5:24 that afternoon, the last Sunday of September;
one inhabitant of the gondola who hadn't been counted, a monkey
named Jack, was then tossed overboard with a parachute, to allow a still
more rapid ascent. At 2,500 feet, Jules found the view over Amiens magnificent; in his own neighborhood, the Place de Longueville was "an
anthill with red and black ants, the former soldiers, the latter civilians."
(Amiens was a garrison town.) The spire of the famous cathedral appeared to descend, "and marked the progress of our ascent as if a nee-
dle." He observed that in a balloon there was no perception of
movement, whether horizontal or vertical. Then silence followed, absolute silence, save for the squeaking of the wicker basket that transported them. The sun broke through the clouds at 5:32, heating the gas;
without tossing out ballast, they rose to 3,600 feet—the maximum they
were to attain. The river Somme was "a bright and narrow ribbon," the
railroad tracks "lines drawn with a ruler," the city "an accumulation of
tiny gray cubes."

But they were descending again, against their will; they tossed out ballast to maintain altitude, then threw out papers to test the winds just beneath them. Would they drop into the swampy waters that separated
Amiens from the neighboring locality of Longueau? they wondered.
Their pilot assured them that they would not; lacking ballast, he'd throw
away his travel bag. They flew over a railroad line, then a village; at 5:47
P.M., they dropped their anchor. Bystanders grabbed the guide rope as
they landed gently, without a bump. With an experienced pilot—veteran
of over a thousand such flights—it wasn't even a voyage, Jules Verne
would tell his fellow residents of Amiens; "it's more like a dream, but a
dream that's all too short!"[15]

22

ROBINSON
VERNE

AMONG THE DOZENS OF BOOKS THAT WOULD BE PUBLISHED under the series title *Extraordinary Voyages,* some were written to order and many more to formula. One formula was so obviously close to Verne's heart that no order from higher up could explain it. When the impulse came, he would be ready to write a "Robinson," *despite* orders.

Uncle Robinson, to his misfortune, would be that kind of book. In some of his best books, Verne had already exploited the theme of a man alone, shipwrecked and abandoned on a desert island, or in some other form of a closed universe: balloon, space capsule, submarine. Such situations would require the characters to display an ingenuity à la Robinson Crusoe. Roland Barthes detected a parallel between this theme and a child's need for wholeness, "found in the infant's passion for cabins and tents: shut oneself in and settle down, such is the existential dream of childhood and of Verne."[1]

There is evidence that Jules Verne set out to write a proper Robinson Crusoe–like adventure—and that he resolved to use the name Robinson as part of the title—before knowing precisely what his subject would be. When Hetzel mentioned in 1869 that another author had just written a collection of "robinsons," Verne replied: "There have already been fifty robinsons, and I think mine will be different from all the others." So he began to write his own, starting late in 1869 and continuing throughout the agitated year 1870. By then, he had completed a first part and had submitted it to his publisher; this was the book he wished to call *Uncle Robinson.*

His immediate inspiration was the true account of a shipwreck of five seamen, followed by their *robinsonnade* on an unknown island off New Zealand. In Verne's version of the story, a mutiny erupts aboard a ship bound for the United States; the sailors allow the passenger Mrs. Clifton and her four children to make their way to a nearby island, where they are quickly joined by a loyal French sailor the grateful castaways call Uncle Robinson. Mrs. Clifton's husband, Harry, manages to reach their refuge sometime later. The sailor is an improviser; Harry Clifton is an engineer. Their survival is assured.[2]

Hetzel disliked Verne's new book, and said so—emphatically. It was the first time since vetoing *Paris in the Twentieth Century* that Hetzel took the risk of upsetting his author with a flat no, and this after having announced forthcoming publication of the story in *Magasin d'Education.*

The veteran bookman decried the absence of invention in Verne's new manuscript. "Where is the science?" he demanded in the margin. For the impatient publisher, Verne's characters were simply "too inert!" "Drop all those people and begin with new ones," Hetzel scrawled in his angry script in another place. "You can't put them in a banal cave, when they should be dropped into an underground cavern, an extinct volcano." Again: "It's important that everything be extraordinary, that nothing be repeated." He found the characters "slow," none of them really alive, whereas in Verne's other books, his characters were "life itself." Start over was the message.[3]

Verne got the message. No matter—he'd try again.

⁂

LATER, NEARER TO THE CLOSE OF HIS CAREER AND HIS LIFE, he would confess that the Robinson books had been his childhood companions and that he never forgot them; he never felt the same sensations in any of his later readings. He had no doubt that his taste for this kind of adventure had placed him on the path he was to follow ever after. For him, the important Robinson books were those of Daniel Defoe (how could it be otherwise?) and Johann Wyss.

He also remembered James Fenimore Cooper's *robinsonnade,* a novel entitled *The Crater.*[4] Cooper's tale was translated into French as early as

1850, in a heavily abridged (though illustrated) version, under the title *Le Robinson américain;* if Jules had read it then, he was the neophyte dramatist and storyteller of twenty-two. Two years later, a proper two-volume edition of *The Crater,* filling nearly seven hundred book pages, was ready for publication.[5] Cooper's hero, Mark Woolston, grew up in Bristol, Pennsylvania, on the Delaware River. Big ships didn't usually sail that far upstream, but one did when he was sixteen, and after that he dreamed only of the sea. When the time came, handsome Mark sailed away, but not before marrying his childhood sweetheart. While sailing the Pacific on a freighter, his drunken captain lets the vessel enter a dangerous zone of reefs; the ship is wrecked. The captain is swept away, and the crew vanishes in a longboat; only Mark and a loyal crewman, Bob, remain on board. They are close enough to an island to see the crater of an extinct volcano; Bob thinks with some pleasure that they'll be Robinson Crusoes now.

The two men guide their ship through the shoals to shore. Determined to survive for as long as necessary, they divide their time between the abandoned but well-provisioned vessel and what they can scrape from this desolate island. Sometimes the parallel existence of the amply provisioned ship and their island retreat creates confusion, as when the pigs on board the ship are released on solid ground, where they threaten to uproot the vegetable garden the men have created.

Mark and Bob build a small boat. When Bob sails into a storm, he is lost; now Mark is alone to tend his garden and his animals. There is a volcanic eruption (although not from the placid crater), and a considerable amount of land now appears above sea level. Mark then finds Bob and the small boat. Bob explains that he was picked up by a passing ship, then made his way back to Pennsylvania, where he was able to inform Mark's young bride of his plight. She and friends resolve to find Mark and to settle on his island.

A colony is founded; children are born. The colonists are threatened by savages; the crater becomes their reserve and refuge. When peace is assured, Mark returns to the United States to recruit settlers; now their *robinsonnade* will be organized on a vast American scale. Back on the island, they fight more savages, and pirates, too, but they cannot conquer politics, speculation, or corruption.

Mark, therefore, again takes leave of his former paradise. When he returns later to see if reform is possible on that strip of soil he had grown to love, the island cannot be found. Another volcanic earthquake has submerged it.

ROLAND BARTHES JUDGED JULES VERNE TO BE "A MANIAC OF plenitude," who "never ceases to finish the world and to furnish it." He compared the novelist to an eighteenth-century encyclopedist or a Dutch painter: The world is finished, ready to be inventoried. The artist's job is to compile catalogs.

For this semiologist, the archetype of the Verne dream of closure is his "almost perfect" novel, *The Mysterious Island,* "where the man-child reinvents the world, furnishes it, encloses it, closes himself inside it. . . ."[6] The significance of this novel for Verne is clear from letters showing how much pleasure the very conception of the tale gave him, as if he knew that he was nurturing myth.

He had been helped through the shock of rejection of his first try, *Uncle Robinson,* by his infinite capacity to forget everything else when plunging into a new piece of work. It is also true that he used parts of the rejected manuscript, such as the description of the island refuge, in his new novel.[7] At the beginning of February 1873, he was able to report to the rue Jacob that he was "entirely absorbed by the Robinson, or rather by *The Mysterious Island.*" He was engaged in his usual passion—the research before the writing, spending time with professors of chemistry, visiting factories turning out chemical products (and getting stains on his clothing he'd charge to the publisher). "For *The Mysterious Island* will be a chemical novel."[8]

His interest in science seemed to burgeon as he prepared to attack a theme that excited him. In youth, he hadn't studied science, but he studied it now, reading (as he'd tell an interviewer) with pencil in hand. He carried a notebook at all times, immediately jotting down anything that caught his fancy. In that very year, a new illustrated weekly made its appearance: *La Nature,* presented as a "Journal of Sciences and their Applications to the Arts and Industry."

At home, Verne of course received subscription copies of learned journals such as that of the Société de Géographie in Paris. He had an impressive shelfload of that traditional travel magazine *Le Tour du Monde.* And he'd taken, so he told Robert Sherard, "many thousands of notes on all subjects," some of them based on conversations with travelers and scientists. By 1893, when Sherard interviewed him, he possessed a file of twenty thousand such notes containing information not yet used in his work.[9]

Through most of the new epic, *The Mysterious Island*—it would fill three full volumes in the regular Hetzel edition, running for two full years in *Magasin d'Education*—the shipwrecked protagonists are alone. Gradually, however, they become aware of a deus ex machina who is helping them to survive. In the end, he reveals himself as Captain Nemo, that quasi-mythical hero Verne's readers had taken for lost, for presumably he had gone down with his submarine in *Twenty Thousand Leagues Under the Sea*.

Verne was taking pains, so he told Hetzel, to deal gingerly with the presence—unknown to Verne's Robinsons—of Captain Nemo on their forlorn island, "so as to have a successful crescendo, like caressing a beautiful woman one is trying to lead you know where."[10]

The story begins in March 1865, just a month before Lee's surrender brought the U.S. Civil War to a close. In Richmond, Virginia, a wounded Union officer named Cyrus Smith, a Massachusetts engineer in peacetime, plots his escape from this Confederate bastion with a reporter for the *New York Herald*, Gedeon Spilett. They are to fly over the lines in a balloon, accompanied by Smith's loyal black servant, Nab, a Union sailor named Pencroff, and fifteen-year-old Harbert Brown, son of Pencroff's captain.

But during the escape, a hurricane sweeps in shore, carrying their balloon at terrifying speed across the North American continent and then across the vast Pacific Ocean—dropping them into the sea, although close enough to an unknown island to assure their safety. From the first, they benefit from unexplained phenomena, such as the miraculous rescue of the engineer Cyrus Smith, who had fallen into the sea.

And so the *robinsonnade* can begin—the first firewood (a single match), the first food (from the sea; or pigeon eggs), the first shelter (a cave). The reappearance of Cyrus Smith, natural leader of the group, assures its survival. But young Harbert is also resourceful, *and* an amateur specialist in natural history. It is he who will recite the inventories of natural phenomena dear to Verne and his readers.

These Robinsons—each a sympathetic character—will make of their island, in the words of Pencroff, a little America (as Cooper's seaman Mark did in *The Crater*). Starting with fewer supplies than any Robinson before them, and thanks to their leader's ingenuity and everybody's goodwill they make their own clothing, tools, and cooking vessels.

Of course, Verne being Verne, their island refuge is dominated by the crater of a seemingly extinct volcano: source of mystery but also of salvation. Although the castaways have not discovered the lair of their unknown helper, they experience further signs of his felicitous intervention as the weeks turn into months and the months into years. When pirates arrive, their attack vessel is destroyed mysteriously, the surviving pirates tracked down and killed by an unknown hand.

In the end, after three years of creating an island paradise, the stranded men pledge never to abandon their colony—again echoing Mark in Cooper's novel. "Thus it is in the heart of man," the author intervenes. "The need to create a work that endures, that survives him, is the sign of his superiority over all that lives here below."

At long last, the colonists are summoned—by the telegraph line they have themselves created—to a grotto. There they find a submarine and at once realize who its master is, for Captain Nemo's legend has not escaped the engineer and the reporter, both of whom have read *Twenty Thousand Leagues Under the Sea.*

Captain Nemo is old and dying. For the first time, he reveals to outsiders that he is an Indian prince who detests the English and has sought revenge for what they have done to his people; he asks absolution, and receives it from the stunned visitors. The captain wishes to go down with his submarine, so the *Nautilus* plunges with all its collections and treasures—except for a chest of jewels that has been willed to the colonists for good works. The castaways proceed in haste to build a new ship as the volcano threatens to explode. But they are too late, for the eruption destroys the island and their unfinished ship. They are rescued all the same, and by a character from an earlier Verne novel: the son of Captain Grant.

With the treasure, they found a Utopian colony in Iowa.

IT HAD BEEN HETZEL, OF COURSE, WHO OBLIGED HIS AUTHOR to turn Captain Nemo into an English-hating Indian (since he would not allow him to be a Russian-hating Pole). The publisher's constant intervention is evident in surviving letters, as in this one from author to publisher: "We agree on the ending of *The Mysterious Island.* I'll glue their island back for them on dry land in America."[11] In his original draft, Verne brought his heroes back to the United States, regretful and nostalgic; Hetzel demanded a happier ending—hence the cloning of their island paradise in landlocked Iowa.

Verne could accept such vexations, for he had achieved the important things. It was as if he had also been writing the story of his life, the real and the imagined one, in spinning the saga of the masterful Cyrus Smith and the mysterious Captain Nemo. The evidence that he had all this and more at stake in the new novel is the resistance he offered Hetzel. "I'd need pages and pages to reply to you, and such discussions by mail lead nowhere," he wrote to Hetzel from Amiens, when they were fighting over the middle section of the three-volume book. "I'll be in Paris next week and we'll talk as long as you wish to. . . . But I don't hesitate to say that you're succeeding in disgusting me with the book, and since I'm well into the third volume, it's vital that I keep my faith until the end."

Their quarrel of the moment concerned the traitor Ayrton, a leftover character from *The Children of Captain Grant* discovered by the protagonists of *The Mysterious Island* long years after he had been abandoned by his pirate comrades; Hetzel wasn't convinced that twelve years of solitude would reduce even a castaway to the condition in which Verne presents him. "Several times already you've caused me to doubt about my subject," Verne further protested. "I'm convinced all the same . . . that this book will not be inferior to my other recent books, and if launched as they were, it will succeed. I have a deep feeling that . . . the sum of things imagined in this work is greater than in the others, and that what I call the crescendo builds up in an almost mathematical way."

Never had he marshaled more strength for a protest, nor revealed as much of his intentions; clearly he saw his art as art and not as work for hire. Hetzel had to be impressed, had to be conciliatory—if only for tactical reasons: He wanted to keep his author, and keep him on an even keel. How else could he deal with Verne, who warned that he was working on the climactic scenes with Captain Nemo in the final section of his story, "and I ask you whether I need to be in possession of all my composure"? They would soon have an opportunity to discuss these things face-to-face, for Jules was going to Paris. Meanwhile, he wrote, "It's important that my faith in this contraption remain firm, so as not to doubt a single instant."[12]

This time, it was going to be *his* book.

PART V

Celebrity

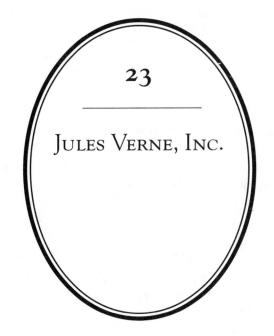

23

Jules Verne, Inc.

Writing *THE MYSTERIOUS ISLAND,* A BOOK THAT SEEMED TO mean so much to Verne, hardly signified that he was now committed to art for art's sake (and he would have been the first to say so). *The Mysterious Island* was, in fact, only one of the books Verne was working on at that time. While completing his dream book, he was also writing *The Chancellor,* which he described as the archetypal shipwreck story. He was also working with Hetzel to revise his slightly ribald story "Dr. Ox's Experiment" in order to make it suitable for inclusion in a collection published by Hetzel. Almost incidentally, he was pushing forward with a strange, and ultimately unsuccessful book, *Hector Servadac.*

He had been working this way for years—call him Jules Verne, Inc.— although he wasn't the first or the only writer-cum-businessman. His peers and predecessors, such as the elder Alexandre Dumas and Honoré de Balzac, hadn't always combined the two roles successfully; both Gustave Flaubert and George Sand resorted to third parties acting as literary agents (before the professions existed) in order to obtain better terms from their publishers. Jules Verne hadn't known he could do that, and if he had, he probably wouldn't have dared to try.

During the winter of 1874–1875, he seemed to be abandoning everything else to go to Antibes, and not for the Mediterranean sun. Plans for a stage version of *Around the World in Eighty Days* were close to realization, and this time no amateurs were involved. His host in Antibes was the fa-

mous d'Ennery, as he preferred to be known—in real life, Adolphe
Philippe Dennery, a theater genius. A specialist in melodramas, admired
for his stage adaptations of such best-selling novels as Eugène Sue's *The
Wandering Jew* and Harriet Beecher Stowe's *Uncle Tom's Cabin,* he was respected as a play doctor who often worked with the original author of a
book. He was described, not necessarily as a compliment, as "a major
manufacturer of plays," and sometimes as many as five different comedies
or dramas bearing his name might be running at the same time in Paris.[1]
In the Verne-d'Ennery collaboration, the veteran theater man was clearly
the senior partner; he was also seventeen years older than his guest.

The partnership hadn't come easily. For in order to write an adaptation with d'Ennery, the author of *Around the World in Eighty Days* had to
forget that he had previously worked on a stage version with a relative
neophyte, Edouard Cadol, and Cadol had taken the precaution (or the
liberty) of registering the title. Now Cadol was demanding half the proceeds of the play, taking his case to the public in a letter published in *Le
Figaro.*

In his accusation, Cadol went so far as to say that he had not only
worked on the scenario but had also contributed to the elaboration of
the original novel. In a letter to Hetzel, Verne protested that he had conceived and written *Around the World* alone. "Cadol didn't invent a single
detail. . . ."

All the same, Verne didn't want the affair to drag on. Not dreaming of
how much the stage adaptation was going to earn over the years and
around the world, he reduced the complaining Cadol to silence by sign-
ing over half of *his* half of the author's royalty in perpetuity.[2]

Verne had made another bad deal, although he didn't know that he
had. He told Hetzel that he hadn't really been fighting for recognition of
prior authorship—only for the financial rewards that *came* with authorship. "I attach *no* literary importance to this use of my book for the stage.
For me it's a matter of money, and nothing else!" he wrote.[3] On those
terms, Verne had come out of this affair badly.

Pierre-Jules Hetzel also knew what counted in life, and he was more
successful in achieving it. Prior to his departure for southern France,
where he was to meet up with his author in Antibes before settling in for
the winter at his own villa in Monaco, Hetzel thought fit to leaf through
his files to review the status of his agreement with Verne. Then, as if writing a last will, he summarized the situation for his own son and heir, Jules
Hetzel. He reminded him that "we have the right to exclusive publication
of illustrated editions of all the books (published until now, and to be
published until 1881) *forever.*" For nonillustrated editions, Jules Verne re-

gained possession of his rights ten years after publication, although the Hetzels had preference over other possible publishers (for an equal sum of money) for further printings.[4]

⚘ ⚘

THE FIRST OF HIS WORKING HOLIDAYS WITH THE D'ENNERYS began splendidly. Their villa was magnificent on the outside, and indoors "a veritable museum," so Jules reported to Hetzel. From his window, his view encompassed all of the coast of Golfe Juan, an extension into the Mediterranean of dense vegetation and isolated villas. The weather was splendid, ingratiatingly warm, blue sky, blue sea, and green everywhere else. He was being treated as an honored guest, and the work with d'Ennery was going well. "I'm learning things I didn't know before. It's not simply a matter of cutting up the book—it's a *play*."[5]

Soon, however, the troubles began. For one thing, Mediterranean weather didn't suit everybody; Jules Verne was a child of the Britanny drizzle, and he had *chosen* to live in the northern city of Amiens. On a later working visit to the d'Ennery villa, he couldn't resist complaining about his inability to adjust to the sunny side of France. "Again I pay tribute to this magnificent climate," he wrote Hetzel then. That meant neuralgia, a sore throat, even an abscess in the ear. "I've been in south France three times, and three times I've caught all these things. . . . This place hardly suits a man of the mist."[6]

Perhaps when the play opened in Paris early in November 1874, Verne felt all his suffering had not been in vain. Behind its neoclassical façade, the two-thousand-seat Porte Saint-Martin theater was one of the largest and most successful of boulevard playhouses, a stage for the likes of Victor Hugo. "We walked out of the theater at one in the morning, dazzled and charmed," exclaimed Francisque Sarcey, the hard-to-please critic of *Le Temps,* in a postscript to his regular column. "The play is entertaining and splendid. Without any doubt it will be an immense success. I shall return to it with more details."[7]

Sarcey did return, dealing with *Around the World in Eighty Days* as the main subject of his column the following week. By then the cautious critic had had sufficient time to temper his judgment. He even wondered why he needed to write anything at all about the Verne-d'Ennery play, since everybody else was talking about it. A success in Paris, it would surely be a success in the provinces, too, and then abroad. If there was something to criticize, Sarcey went on, it was the garish colors of the sets. He quoted Zadig's maxim from Voltaire: "Too much pleasure is pleasure no more."

He acknowledged that such excesses seemed to be the current trend in the theater. "The more we progress, the greater the taste of the public for vulgar displays of costume and scenery." To believe Sarcey, spectators barely comprehended the story of Phileas Fogg's wager; they simply waited for the elephant to come out on the stage (to try to discover whether it was a real one).[8]

Such curious theatrics couldn't be avoided, however, and Sarcey again returned to the subject of them early the following year. Yes, he agreed, the new play was a success, and it was earning nine thousand francs in gross receipts, but he warned, "*Around the World* is an industrial enterprise, a fantasy in which a man of spirit—and we're grateful for that—lent a touch of his originality. . . ." That didn't make for greatness.

"I remark with sorrow," he concluded, "a whole company of excellent actors engaged in talking to scenery."[9]

Thanks to a set of carefully preserved account books, it is possible to discover just how much could be earned from a successful play in those days, particularly how much Jules Verne earned. The standard royalty for authors was 10 percent of the gross receipts from nightly ticket sales. In the case of *Around the World in Eighty Days*, the total royalty was actually 12 percent. Seven percent was earmarked for d'Ennery; the remaining 5 percent was divided between Verne and the miscast but fortunate Edouard Cadol. In November 1874, gross receipts averaged 8,215 francs per evening, 205 francs of which went to Verne. When multiplied by the twenty-three regular performances that month, the total (4,715 francs) was nearly as much as he received from Hetzel for a new novel. And in a full month, his share would come to 6,000 francs, less perhaps 10 percent for the agent's commission—some 105,000 present-day francs—a sum considerably greater than Verne was receiving from his publisher.

The new play grossed between 8,700 and 9,000 francs each night until the tenth of December, and from 7,600 to 8,500 each night for the rest of that month. At the end of the run, in November 1875, gross receipts were still averaging 7,000 francs each evening, or 175 francs for Verne (some 5,250 francs per month before the agency fee).[10]

Verne's new fame brought some inconvenience, however. A voice from the past was heard again, that of René de Pont-Jest, who earlier in Verne's career had created a minor scandal by alleging that in *Journey to the Center of the Earth* Verne had plagiarized a story of Pont-Jest's.[11] Now a minor slight led to a major scandal.

Apparently Pont-Jest had wanted only a couple of free tickets for the opening performance of *Around the World in Eighty Days*. He didn't get them. (One can imagine that half of the theatergoing elite of Paris wished to be invited that night.) Soon, he fired off a letter to his "dear colleague" Verne. There are wounds, he began, which, even if not deep, render the skin sensitive, so that the slightest shock is painful. "It's this pathological phenomenon that affected my pride yesterday, when my request for a seat at the opening of *Around the World* was turned down."

It just happened that in Pont-Jest's pathology, the cure called for legal action. He was *now* going to sue for the literary theft that in his opinion made Verne's journey to the center of the earth possible. His complaint was based on incidental similarities between his story and Verne's. Both of their heroes were German; the ancient manuscripts at the origin of the quest are found in old books, written in runic characters; in Pont-Jest's story, moonlight—and in Verne's story, sunlight—indicates the precise point at which the search is to begin.

Those were the only parallels. Summing up the case for his and Hetzel's lawyers, Verne saw them as fortuitous; finding a manuscript in an old book was so common, it could almost be considered in the public domain. As for the sunlight-moonlight parallel, Verne could only swear that it was pure chance. But if the plaintiff insisted, he would be willing to recognize Pont-Jest's prior claim. The chief argument for Verne's defense, as a close reader of the trial documents observed, was that Pont-Jest's hero never went to the center of the earth—nor did he ever intend to. Or, as Verne phrased it to Hetzel, "Mr. Pont-Jest's story ends just about where mine begins!"

There was a hope—apparently Hetzel's—of reconciliation. Pont-Jest let it be known that he would drop the complaint if Hetzel would publish his work, give him a complete set of the works of Jules Verne, *and* three hundred francs. Arbitration was suggested by the Society of Men of Letters; Pont-Jest rejected that. In fact, he had recently been accused of plagiarism himself by that organization's arbiters.

The affair dragged on, and—against all reason—was taken to court, the complainant arguing that Jules Verne's book had closed the door to a literary genre Pont-Jest had wished to exploit. The case was not heard by a Paris civil tribunal until January 1877, over two years after Pont-Jest failed to get tickets for the opening-night performance.

Pont-Jest's arguments didn't look any more convincing in court than they did on paper. He demanded ten thousand francs in damages, but he lost the case. "There was a silly quarrel," a report who attended the trial told his readers. "Mr. Pont-Jest found the publicity he wanted; but was he right to look for it?"[12]

⊰⊱

ON THE TENTH OF SEPTEMBER 1874, THE FIRST OF THREE
volumes of *The Mysterious Island* had appeared, under a title, *Dropped from
the Clouds*, as if it could somehow stand alone. This first volume ends on a
note of suspense: The sailor Pencroff, eating a small wild hog the castaways have trapped, breaks a tooth on a lead pellet, an incident that
makes the stunned group of Robinsons aware they are not alone on their
island. Then, at the beginning of November, came that smash hit at the
Porte Saint-Martin. A month later another new novel, *The Chancellor*, was
serialized in *Le Temps*; the first installment appeared on December seventeenth, just in time to remind readers that Hetzel had many more books
by the same author available for year-end gift giving.

Chancellor was the name the author gave to the three-masted cargo ship
in the novel. Its hold filled with cotton bound for Liverpool, the ship is
unlucky almost from the day it sails out of Charleston, South Carolina.
The cotton catches fire; the half-mad captain sails south instead of across
the Atlantic. Somewhere in the Caribbean, a storm sends the ship
hurtling against a reef; as it sinks, the crew and a handful of passengers—
including the narrator—escape on a hastily assembled raft.

Prior to the ship's sinking, there had been a series of near disasters, opportunities for revealing the true nature of each of the principal seamen
and passengers—the stalwarts and the sly ones; one of the latter, an
American businessman, escapes in the ship's only usable lifeboat—a
whaleboat—with three sailors he has corrupted.

The supplies carried on the raft run out; a sick man dies, and his foot
is surreptitiously chopped off as bait. Later, the survivors choose one
among them to be sacrificed for food. At that point, the bravest of the
brave, Captain Kurtis and narrator J. R. Kazallon, protest: It is when Kazallon is thrown overboard that he discovers fresh water, which means they
have reached the mouth of the Amazon.

The ending is as happy as it can be; a brave young girl will be wed to a
brave, handicapped young man. They have been adrift for a month and
a half; of the thirty-two passengers and crew, only eleven reach shore. In
relating their trials, Verne betrays more emotion than we expect from
him. Unlike cool Phileas Fogg, Kazallon is a real person, moved as he
should be when people around him fall in love or suffer.

Surviving letters in the Amiens archives show how closely Jules Verne
was following his second stage career—not only the productions of his
plays but also the politics of theater managers (after all, he had had a
decade of experience with them). At the same time, he was the most com-

pliant of authors when a still-more-experienced man of the theater pointed the way; it hardly upset him to add or subtract a character at d'Ennery's behest.[13]

In the winter of 1875, Verne traveled to Antibes to see d'Ennery again. A letter Verne wrote to a railroad ticket agent on January 8, 1875, indicates precisely when he mapped out this new trip. He had been encouraged to solicit a free pass from the Lyon Railway Company "in the event further literary work took me to southern France." That time had arrived. "I am returning to Antibes to write a travel play in the style of *Around the World,* and would be most happy if you could grant me a pass, that would facilitate my journey immensely." If such a thing was possible, added the closefisted author, he wished to be able to stop off in Lyon, Marseille, Toulon, Antibes, Nice, and Monaco.[14]

The new project was a stage version of *The Children of Captain Grant,* and this play would be nearly four years in the making—none of them fun, apparently. He wrote to Hetzel's son that he was beginning to see the faint outline of the play, "but the house here is so unbearable that I shall leave as soon as the scenario is done. I wouldn't write the play here for anything in the world. And your father reproaches me for not having gone to see him in Monaco. If he thinks that I'm enjoying myself and that I'm here for my pleasure he's quite mistaken!"[15]

A Vernian scholar who pored over these letters sent from the d'Ennery villa paints the portrait of a writer unhappy to be where he was, unhappy both with his host and the work he was obliged to do with and for him. D'Ennery was a businessman as well as an artist, and he was one of the nouveaux riches: Verne would come to despise all the d'Ennerys, not excluding Mme d'Ennery and her blasphemies (her favorite apparently being "for God's sake").[16]

In any case, Hetzel had no intention of letting his peripatetic novelist stray *too* far from the rue Jacob. It was time for another contract; the new one made it clear that Hetzel had exclusive book rights to his star author's plays as well as his novels. Actually, the text of the agreement began on a positive and seemingly generous note: "Mr. J. Verne's success having grown following the publication of *Around the World in Eighty Days,* J. Hetzel & Co., wishing to see the author share in the new prosperity. . . ."

In a word, Verne would in future receive royalties based on a percentage of copies sold instead of a fixed annual stipend. All of his books up to and including *The Mysterious Island* in the illustrated gift editions remained Hetzel's exclusive property; for new books, the author would receive 5 percent of the selling price of the illustrated edition on the first twenty thousand copies, ten percent after that; for original, small-format and nonillustrated editions, he would receive half a franc for each copy sold. All earlier books in small format remained Hetzel's property until 1882, after which the same half-franc royalty would apply. Moneys received from newspaper serializations and translations would be divided equally between author and publisher.

Hetzel retained exclusivity over all of Verne's writings present and future, Verne to submit two new works a year, and the publisher to be sole judge of which newspaper or magazine would be the "most useful" or the "most profitable" outlet for each.[17]

This was probably a better contract for an author with ever-increasing sales, although not so good when sales declined. "I shall make only one remark," he replied to Hetzel on receiving the proposed agreement, "and this concerning payment for *illustrated editions* in the future, 5% on the first 20,000 copies, 10% after that. This, I think, should be where I earn the most. But 'The Czar's Messenger' [the original title of what was to become *Michel Strogoff*], for example, which will sell at seven francs the copy like *Hatteras*, will bring me, at 5%, only 35 centimes, or seventeen and a half centimes for each of the two volumes. . . ." Ever reasonable, he added, "I know that your costs are considerable on an illustrated edition, but these should also be the editions that earn you the most money. And they are the ones that give me the least return."

Then he made this surprising observation: "Besides, I don't even know how many copies you published of my illustrated editions up to now."

His modest hope was to see the fifty-centime royalty apply to illustrated as well as ordinary editions. He did appreciate Hetzel's gesture in offering a new contract, and a better one, he assumed, even though the previous contract still had half a dozen years to run.

Verne's was a cry in the wilderness. Hetzel sat down with him in Paris a few days later and convinced him that he could not do better. Their signatures were then affixed to the new document; the date was May 17, 1875.[18]

HOWEVER UNPLEASANT, THE D'ENNERY CONNECTION CONtinued to pay off. A triumphant letter from Amiens in the spring of 1875 informed Hetzel of the twelve thousand francs for a single night's receipts at the Porte Saint-Martin—the 155th performance of *Around the World*. Honorine had traveled to Belgium to see its fiftieth performance on the Brussels stage, where box-office receipts were averaging four thousand francs each night.[19]

This was clearly a play with worldwide appeal—a fact evidenced by the history of the American adaptation. The catalysts for the U.S. production were a dynamic team of Hungarian-born impresarios, the brothers Bolossy and Imre Kiralfy—Bolossy, the younger, would eventually become known in the United States as "the Napoléon of the stage." Within a year of the memorable production of *Around the World in Eighty Days* in Paris, the brothers were rehearsing the American version—which faithfully executed replicas of the original scenery and stage effects. Soon they were ready to open at the American equivalent of the Porte-Saint Martin, New York's Academy of Music on Fourteenth Street, a splendid auditorium with old-world gilt ornaments and chandeliers, and sufficient seating for four thousand spectators.[20]

But this was before the United States took intellectual property seriously. One could be a law-abiding citizen and a pirate of other people's literary work at one and the same time. The Kiralfys learned that this play whose rights they had purchased was also scheduled to open at the competing Bowery Theater. The story is that the director of that establishment had liked the Verne-d'Ennery play so much that he had taken a box at the Porte Saint-Martin night after night until he could copy the whole thing down. Now the law was brought in; the Napoléon of the stage prevailed.[21]

The Kiralfy brothers didn't do things halfway. With the approval of Jules Verne, a balloon flight was added to the script, and a live elephant was rented from the Barnum circus menagerie. The success of this one play assured the fortune of the Kiralfy brothers, and it couldn't have hurt Jules Verne's (even with his small one-fourth of the author's share).[22]

In the same year, 1875, an illustrated edition of *Around the World in Eighty Days* was released by Verne's regular London publishers, Sampson Low, with an eulogistic introduction by one Adrien Marx: "I might write a volume about this eloquent, witty, affable, and sympathetic man, whose biography may, however, be included in these words: 'A Breton, a Catholic, and a sailor.'" Marx helped to promote the conventional image of the author—not very different from what is known about him today.

> The author . . . leads the laborious, regular, and sober life of a student. Wherever he may be, he works from five in the morning till one in the afternoon, passes the day visiting shops and factories, where he carefully studies the machinery, and goes to bed at

seven o'clock. Extended on his bed, he devours all the scientific publications till midnight, and when they fail him he looks over books of travel and tourist adventures. He has no need, however, of borrowing ideas of travel or geography from others, for he has himself travelled much, and is quite familiar with Scotland, Ireland, Denmark, Norway, and Sweden.[23]

As early as 1877, Pierre-Jules Hetzel was able to declare, exaggerating only slightly:

> The complete works of Jules Verne are translated and published simultaneously in Russia, England, Austria, Italy, Spain, Brazil, Sweden, Holland, Portugal, Greece, Croatia, Bohemia, Canada. Some of these books have even been translated into Persian.
>
> No writer until today had carried a French name and seen it accepted and loved in a greater number of countries and as many languages.[24]

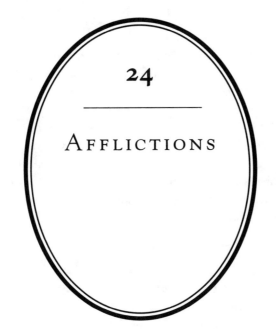

24

AFFLICTIONS

THIS WRITER WHOSE CHIEF CONTRIBUTION TO LITERATURE WAS to turn the world upside down, creating characters who flew over it before that was a feasible thing to do, dug further inside it than anyone actually could, and even attempted to redress its axis, actually wanted nothing more than peace at home. That meant having a very private space that allowed for long, uninterrupted spells of work, as well as a compliant wife unlikely to be troubled by his silences or abrupt, insufficiently explained departures. It also meant having quiet children.

Lacking evidence from anyone other than Verne himself, it is difficult to decide what to make of his constant complaining about Michel, his only son (and the only child engendered by him), a son who in 1875 was to celebrate his fourteenth birthday. Jules saw himself as the unfortunate parent of a child gone bad, and he made no attempt to hide his feelings. There is no evidence of parental tenderness, and yet he must have cared for Michel. He called his successive dream yachts *Saint-Michel;* the French hero of *From the Earth to the Moon*—written when his son was a toddler— was Michel Ardan; now he was about to call one of his most dashing heroes, the czar's messenger, Michel Strogoff.

Verne, who seldom painted fully rounded characters and whose best-known heroes were one-dimensional, had just published *The Chancellor,* among whose shipwrecked protagonists are a caring father and a dutiful son—Monsieur Letourneur of Le Havre, and lame twenty-year-old André, the only French passengers among the Americans. "The father adores this child [*sic*], and one senses that his whole life is centered on this poor being," Verne wrote.

After their ship goes down, the survivors cling helplessly to their raft, weakened by thirst and hunger; now the elder Letourneur will make touching sacrifices. He manages to pass his own rations to his son through the narrator Kazallon (so that André won't refuse them). Later, when it seems necessary to sacrifice one of the group as food for the others, father Letourneur arranges to call out the names so that he and not his son is chosen to be cannibalized.

IT IS NOW, AS MICHEL VERNE REACHES PUBERTY, THAT HIS parents were to decide to look for help. But there were no halfway measures in those times. Earlier, the Vernes had tried a strict Catholic boarding school in Abbeville, not too close and not too far from Le Crotoy and Amiens; but, in the words of Jean Jules-Verne, the severity of a priestly education hadn't sufficed to break Michel's rebellious spirit. The next step was the nineteenth century's closest approach to modern psychiatric treatment, a consultation at the mental clinic in Passy run by the alienist Antoine Emile Blanche, who succeeded his famous father as director of this establishment favored by artists and writers, among them the notorious syphilitic Guy de Maupassant. (Michel's third son thought his father might actually have been treated at Dr. Blanche's or a similar clinic in 1873 and 1874, when he was between the ages of twelve and thirteen.)

What possible crime or crimes had his son committed? Family legend affixes the year 1875 to a letter Jules Verne sent Georges Lefebvre, husband of Honorine's daughter Suzanne; since it speaks of Michel's drinking, it most certainly was written later, but it shows how carefully the father kept track of his little saint: "Michel leaves with his professor for Amiens tonight. . . . It is possible that tomorrow he will ask you for spending money. I beg you to see that he doesn't *drink* too much and also that he come home at the *agreed-upon hour.* . . . Don't give him money, or half a franc at the most." Family tradition also has it that Jules later lent his son (and his stepdaughter Suzanne) considerable sums of money—and he always had them sign an IOU.[1]

Was it Michel's money problem, or his father's? It is tempting to attribute Verne's violent reaction to what, at Michel's age, could only have been minor money problems to his own irrational behavior. A psychoanalyst might call it neurosis—the young Jules Verne's fascination with defecation now replaced by worry over money. Indeed, everything that is known about Verne's adult life recalls the qualities Sigmund Freud attributed to an anal character—"avarice, pedantry and obstinacy"[2]—no matter that some of the same qualities help account for the wondrous detail of his geographical and ethnological descriptions in the *Extraordinary Voyages*. Even the signs of persecution complex: The anti-Semitism that Verne displayed at various times throughout his life and the expressions of bitterness toward a literary establishment he felt conspired to refuse him recognition are traits a modern psychiatrist might associate with anality.[3]

Freud, in any event, would have been fascinated by the intestinal difficulties young Jules Verne described to his mother in such fascinating detail. In the course of life, Freud argued, "money . . . attracts to itself the physical interest which was originally proper to faeces, the product of the anal zone."[4]

At the time, Verne was simultaneously writing a stirring odyssey of czarist Russia, *Michel Strogoff,* and a tiresome and depressing book entitled *Hector Servadac,* a novel few remember. Perhaps family problems weighed heavily, but *Michel Strogoff* is proof that he was writing as well as he ever had.

He was also sailing, thereby convincing observers that he was relaxing. One such observer was the writer who signed his articles Charles Raymond. Raymond was invited aboard the *Saint-Michel* on August 12, 1875; he describes what was still a smallish boat (weighing in at eight or ten tons), with a small pit for the two-man crew, a room (measuring six feet by five) at the stern for the host and his passengers with a low (four-and-a-half-foot) ceiling. Behind the stair ladder, the visitor found a miniature library containing the schedule of tides, some naval charts, three or four dictionaries, and a few travel books.

Raymond told readers of *Musée des Familles* that the celebrated author used this library, limited as it was, for research; he also reported—a fact one assumes his host must have told him—that half of Verne's books had been conceived right there on the *Saint-Michel.* "Attired in a pea jacket of coarse blue cloth or in a knitted striped sweater, his head covered with a tarpaulin hat or beret depending on the weather, he would take in a reef, lower a sail . . . captain and sailor in turn. . . ."

This was a picture of Verne at forty-seven: "His lightly curled hair began to show gray, as did his beard."[5]

⁓ ⁓

IN THE FALL OF 1875, VERNE RECEIVED A LETTER THAT RE-lated a strange story. A man born a Jew in Poland had migrated westward, making a new life in France; for good measure, he converted to Catholicism and proved ardent in the practice of his new faith. Although his mentor, a French priest of Polish origin, continued to use his original Polish name—Father Pierre Semenenko—he encouraged his convert to Frenchify the unpronounceable Olszewicz.

The root of that name, *olcha,* pronounced *ols'ha,* was Polish for alder tree; in French, that would have been *aulne,* or *vergne,* even *verne* in old French. Quite innocently, presumably, the reborn Julien (or Juliusz) Olszewicz had adopted the name Verne, or perhaps *de* Verne, Julien de Verne.

One day in September 1875, Jules Verne opened this letter mailed from Poland. His correspondent, one Herman Olszewicz, greeted Jules as his long-lost brother. He said they hadn't met since the latter's departure from Poland thirty-six years earlier. Jules Verne took the letter for a joke. Two months later, on November 28, he received a second letter—this one registered—from the same man, this one in Polish. Verne sent it out to be translated, but not before reminding Hetzel that he, Jules Verne, was born in Nantes of a father from Provins and a mother from Morlaix. "My family never had any relations with Poland," he told Hetzel."[6]

The second letter related the rest of the story. Marguerite Allotte, a family biographer, thought Verne received a visit from a Polish journalist who was convinced that the famous author was in fact a Jew who had been born in Russian-occupied Poland. The visiting reporter affirmed that Julien de Verne, after his conversion, had been engaged to be married to a Polish princess in exile. According to family legend, the French Jules Verne laughed the whole thing off.[7]

At the time, Verne was in the process of composing his most vitriolic caricature of a Jew, slipped into his novel *Hector Servadac,* in which it would seem to have no place. As if to justify this, some Verne scholars later suggested that he had made this new contribution to anti-Semitism in reprisal for the Olszewicz affair, saying it was a way for him to *prove* that he couldn't be Jewish—since he was an anti-Semite.

Vindictive as he often was, Jules Verne may well have done what his apologists asserted he did. But the evidence is that he had completed the first half of *Hector Servadac*—containing some of the worst of his caricature—*before* hearing from Herman Olszewicz.

This new novel proved to be a long time in gestation, and when it was completed, Hetzel seemed in no hurry to publish it. Verne was working on it as early as 1874, while mapping out the final chapters of *The Mysterious Island.*[8] Then in a letter from Amiens dated March 29, 1875—six months before the first letter arrived from his supposed Polish brother—he informed his publisher that volume one was ready. He said he was going to read it over before sending it on to Paris so that Hetzel could assign an artist to illustrate it. The finished manuscript of the first half of the book—the copy destined for the printer—bears the date December 6, 1875.[9]

In order to accept the argument that Jules Verne inserted an anti-Semitic caricature into *Hector Servadac* as retaliation, one also has to believe that after finishing the first half of the novel he hastily added a character who would play a leading role in it.

⁊◎ ◎⹁

IN THE NOVEL, A COMET FLASHES PAST THE PLANET EARTH, shearing off a slice of Mediterranean coast from Gibraltar to Mostaganem, on the Algerian side, and scooping up at least one French, one Spanish, and one Russian ship—not to speak of the inhabitants of Gibraltar and Ceuta, the Moroccan enclave belonging to the Spanish. This time, the main characters are Frenchmen, while the Englishmen are decidedly unpleasant and perfidious (they get their comeuppance when, after profiting from the breakdown of order when seizing Ceuta, they are plucked away and lost in space).

The real nastiness begins with the introduction of Isac Hakhabut. Hetzel's *Magasin d'Education* had begun to serialize the new novel in January 1877; Isac appears in chapter 18, which was published in June. A Jewish traveling merchant, Isac quickly becomes the scapegoat of Captain Servadac's orderly Ben-Zouf (who, despite the sobriquet, is a working-class Parisian from Montmartre). Not only is Isac a Jew, exclaims Ben-Zouf—worse, he's a German Jew! "He was a man of fifty who seemed to be sixty," Verne begins the characterization of Isac as seen through Captain Servadac's eyes. "Small, sickly, with alert but false eyes, hooked nose, yellowish beard, untamed hair, large feet, his hands long and crotched hands, he presented the well-known type of German Jew, recognizable anywhere."

Is it Servadac who thinks this, or Verne? Knowing the author's anguished feelings about money, the heritage of early adulthood, when impressing his parents with his parsimony and fighting loose bowels were his daily lot, the reader may be tempted to see Verne's fear of Jews as a fear of resembling Jews, or what the provincial bourgeoisie imagine Jews to be. It is hard to imagine anyone Verne had actually met as the model for Isac; the Jews known to have crossed his path were rather eminent contemporaries, such as the composer Offenbach or the publisher Michel Lévy.

Indeed, no one resembles Verne's caricatural Jew as much as Jules

Verne himself does (the oddest example is in *The Will of an Eccentric,* whose "scalpers of Christians" in their closefisted travel around the United States recall Verne's own penny-pinching trip). "He was the obsequious usurer," his description of Isac continues, "heartless, clipper of coins and skinner of flints. Money attracted such a person as a magnet did metal, and if this Shylock had managed to be paid by his debtor he would certainly have sold the flesh retail."[10]

When Ben-Zouf remarks that the Jewish merchant is multilingual, his captain replies, "Yes, but whether he expresses himself in French, Russian, or Spanish, in Italian or in German, it's always Jew that he speaks."[11]

Isac Hakhabut has entered the story on a small single-masted sailing boat known as a tartan, its hold filled with merchandise. He is, of course, the exploiter seeking to gain advantage from the situation in which the castaways find themselves—for they have lost contact with Earth as they hurtle through space. Another indication that Isac is not a last-minute addition to the story is that his supplies will be essential to the survival of the protagonists.

Not much else happens in the book; as if running out of ideas for his final chapters, the author utilizes Isac as the pivot of his story, as the others enjoy extracting vengeance. When at last they desert this patch of land and sea that they have christened Gallia and board a hot-air balloon that will take them back to earth, they make sure that the gold Isac has accumulated by selling scarce goods to everyone cannot accompany him— because of the weight.[12]

IT WOULD HAVE BEEN A STRONGER BOOK, ONE OF VERNE'S BI-ographers once observed, if only Verne himself had believed in it.[13] Fortunately for Pierre-Jules Hetzel, he did not have to decide what to think of *Hector Servadac* just then, or wonder what his readers might think; there were earlier Verne novels awaiting publication. Unlike *Hector Servadac,* one of them was a story that would be remembered. Once again, the author had understood from the beginning that he had a good idea.

Indeed, if he had put away the first half of *Hector Servadac* back in March 1875, it was for *Michel Strogoff.* "I'm in the middle of it and can't think of anything else, and this excites me to a rare degree," he exclaimed to Hetzel. "The subject is magnificent and offers the opportunity for lovely scenes!"[14] In April, he wrote, "I'm off in Siberia and can't ever be stopped! Yes, I think this is going well, and I make it go with passion. . . ."[15] There are no such letters about *Hector Servadac.* Equally certain that this novel was a good one, the always-interventionist publisher contributed his own suggestions—suggestions strongly motivated by a feeling that the hero's single-minded mission needed to be softened by the introduction of amusing characters and incidents; Verne managed to keep Hetzel and his amusing characters at bay.[16]

For his epic narrative, he had imagined an invasion of Russia's far-off Siberian territories by Tatars sweeping north from Turkestan. In his capital of Saint Petersburg, the czar chooses a messenger who must at any cost reach Irkutsk to warn the garrison. For the rebels have cut the telegraph lines, and a traitor is en route to Irkutsk to offer his services to the grand duke, the czar's brother, who commands the region.

The czar's hardy messenger is Michel Strogoff, and he shows himself to be well worthy of confidence. Before his ordeal is over, he will be caught by the rebel chieftain, who orders him blinded; henceforth, brave Nadia, the young woman Michel had taken under his protection, will guide him until his mission is accomplished. This messenger had been presented to the czar as fearless, resistant to frost, hunger, thirst, fatigue, the hero par excellence. Although he doesn't have the science of a Vernian engineer—he wouldn't have found the need for it on the steppes—he does possess a gift for improvisation; mainly, he is strong and silent.

While the author took pains to make his sweeping panorama of czarist Russia authentic (except for the imaginary uprising), Hetzel—who had great hopes for the book—also remembered his subscribers in Russia, whom he wished to please, and feared to offend. Ought one to exploit the exalted Russian ruler in the title of a book? He thought better not to call it *The Czar's Messenger.* Just to be certain, Hetzel solicited the opinion of the Russian ambassador to Paris, Prince Orlov, concerning both the title and the general tenor of the novel. The diplomat appeared relaxed about it all. "The mountain will give birth to a mouse," he told Hetzel, adding, "Still, better to change the title."[17]

Hence, *Michel Strogoff,* but Strogoff, despite all, *is* identified at the outset as the czar's messenger. Verne proved to be as concerned as his publisher about potential difficulties. He accompanied Hetzel on a visit to the Russian ambassador, willingly submitting proofs for approval. He also had the privilege of a reading by the well-known writer Ivan Turgenev, who happened to be Hetzel's longtime friend and literary adviser. For his part, Verne used the best contemporary sources; when he did stray from reality, it was to soften the critical remarks of travelers concerning the autocratic Russian regime.[18]

Hetzel being Hetzel, even that wasn't enough, although it was enough for Jules Verne. Picking up a pile of letters from his publisher, Verne replied from his sickbed (he had, he said, "an enormous cold") "after having thought about it thoroughly." He felt that it would have been better at the outset not to have planned republication in Hetzel's *Magasin,* "which would have spared us much misery." He had accepted the change in title, "however regrettable." But concerning the Tatar invasion, which provided the novel with its scenario, "first of all," he declared, "it's the novelist's privilege." Hetzel wanted a preface in which readers would be warned that the invasion was imaginary. As far as Verne was concerned, such a preface could appear in the magazine, even, if necessary, in the Russian translation of *Michel Strogoff.* But Verne would not accept any such note on the book published in France.

"Did I warn the public that *Hatteras* or *Twenty Thousand Leagues* wasn't a true story?" He agreed to the elimination of anything in the book that would seem to refer to the present Czar Alexander II, or to his father, Nicholas I, but he fought for the right to publish material he knew to be true. "Turgenev, who knows Russia as well as these gentlemen do, didn't find so much to say," he protested in a final outburst. "Only the invasion seemed to him unrealistic. And the invasion of France in 1871, did that seem realistic?"

Hetzel had the last word, it would appear. A reader who pored over the original manuscript of *Michel Strogoff* noted material added by Hetzel—in Hetzel's hand; all the appeals to la divine Providence, notably, were written by Hetzel.[19]

The new novel appeared first in the *Magasin,* beginning with the first issue of January 1876 and running until Christmas of that year, while the book itself was published in two volumes, the first that summer, the final one in autumn. Before that, Verne fans would be able to buy, at last, the third and final volume of *The Mysterious Island,* aptly titled *The Secret of the Island.* It was in the bookshops at the end of October 1875, before subscribers had read the final chapters in their magazine.

The Mysterious Island was, as a reviewer in *Le Temps* put it, one of the most curious of all the author's works. "For it holds a secret," he wrote. Readers of Hetzel's fortnightly had been waiting breathlessly for the solution to the enigma—almost as avidly as they had for the final episodes (during its newspaper serialization) of *Around the World in Eighty Days.* They would not be disappointed, promised the journalist, for the climax of *The Mysterious Island* would please everybody—particularly readers of *The Children of Captain Grant* and *Twenty Thousand Leagues Under the Sea,* "that I have always considered . . . Jules Verne's masterpieces."[20]

Before the year was over, the pertinacious author allowed himself a moment's respite. He took his recreation in the form of a piece of work that he wouldn't be paid for doing. The gray old Academy of Sciences, Letters, and Arts in Amiens had chosen him as president for 1875; at year's end, a speech was expected.[21] He chose to make a story of it, a rare piece of futurology on the part of this author of "science fiction" who usually kept at least one foot on the ground. *Paris in the Twentieth Century,* after all, had been put away, seemingly forever.

His subject for the speech was "An Ideal City," the city being Amiens, a century and a quarter into the future—the year 2000. He explained to the attentive academicians that recently, after what had seemed to be an unusually long night's sleep, he awoke to find himself in a strange place. Suddenly, Amiens had a lot more people, longer streets—so long, he couldn't see to the end of them—and big new buses, too. He walked to the bridge over the familiar railroad tracks; a train passed. Nothing had changed *here,* apparently: "The chauffeur shook the air with the blast of his whistle and purged the smoke from his cylinders with a deafening din." But the train's cars were American-style, meaning that there were walkways allowing passengers to go from one car to the next (something one could not do in French trains).

As he moved through the new-old town, the narrator noticed other things, such as a new cleanliness and a better-dressed populace. He heard curious mathematical music without melody, measure, or harmony, and he discovered a concert broadcast from Paris via electric lines. A new theater with a polychrome façade resembling Garnier's Paris opera house had replaced the uncomfortable playhouse he was used to. He learned that doctors were paid only if they kept their patients in good health, lawyers—well, there were no more lawsuits.

The ideal city had acquired new industry. Bachelors were heavily taxed, the rate rising as they grew older. Schools taught only science, commerce, and industry. He visited the regional fair, with its display of new techniques and inventions, including American machines that processed live pigs into York and Westphalian ham, babies were nursed by machine, one such apparatus replacing five hundred Norman wet nurses.

Everything had changed—ideas, manners, industry, commerce, agriculture; only the speech given at the fair by a government official sounded as it always had. At that point, Jules Verne woke up.[22]

25

HECTOR
SERVADAC

Perhaps *HECTOR SERVADAC* seems oppressive because the author was under so much stress during the writing of it. Just then, at the beginning of 1876, Verne's worries about Michel were compounded by his own illness. "I'm not well at all," he informed Hetzel in a letter that has been dated sometime in January. "Forbidden to leave the house, barely eating, almost constant fever, and this for nearly a month. I can't do any work at all." It was nothing terribly serious: inflammation of the gums, muscular contractions, a throat abscess. Just "quite painful and profoundly disgusting," he wrote. He was begging Hetzel *not* to reread the first part of the book because he wished to make changes in it first.[1]

Then, as soon as he was on his feet, he had to leave for Nantes—a long journey, and one perhaps less motivated by the desire for a holiday or filial affection for a widowed mother than by the urgent need to be close to his son. In Nantes, he was working, but slowly. "I'm still rather ill, unable to eat, and continue to run fevers. I don't go out. I feel quite weak. . . . The succession of throat abscesses just doesn't stop."[2] Following his usual procedure, he had submitted a final version of the first half of *Servadac* to his publisher, although he was only a third of the way into the second half.

He was pleased, he said, with the corrections he had made on the proofs of volume one. "You'll see that I have cut and lightened the text. It's pure fantasy, and one must avoid a heavy hand!"

Curiously—but that was the man—he had not lost sight of his long-term goal: to be respected as well as read. Occasionally, Hetzel encouraged this ambition by talking of an appointment to the French Academy, and now it was the potential candidate's turn to remind Hetzel that because of death, two chairs had been vacated in that institution; obviously, he hoped to be considered for one of them. "You made my mouth water a bit," he wrote. "You have lots of friends in that illustrious body."[3]

Soon Hetzel was able to give his friend reassuring news. He said Jules wasn't likely to be chosen to fill one of the present vacancies; they were already spoken for. But Jules's old friend Alexandre Dumas, himself a member of the French Academy since 1874, had been talking to his colleagues. "Your turn will come, dear friend, that's for sure," Hetzel told Verne. "But one must be a candidate as seldom as possible; and a single time, with success assured, is the way I see it for you."[4]

Sometimes Hetzel's true feelings were most apparent not in his responses to his cherished author but in asides to his own son, Jules. "Here's a fellow set on the idea of the Academy," Hetzel confided to his son. "It won't happen this time, and with every paper mentioning the candidates it wishes to, his name isn't cited and immediately he is astonished and blames the genre in which he works."

Verne was indeed convinced that because he wrote adventure stories about travel and fantastic scientific inventions, and also because he trained his sights on young readers, he was practically ineligible for election to the French Academy. Hetzel didn't quite agree, as he explained to his son: "You don't get into the Academy with books for children, says he? But the books he produces are the only ones he can write and he can *only* succeed with those, and I know that he will succeed. But if he thinks that a member is created in ten years' time and only through his work he is fooling himself. Let him be patient." Wise old Hetzel had a final word for his heir: "The Academy is a disease."[5]

The solicitous publisher was also concerned by the problems Verne was having with Michel. From this mother's hillside country house in Chantenay, Verne had written to thank Hetzel for some thoughtful advice concerning his son—although he was sure Michel wouldn't even comprehend the advice. "His obstinate vanity, his total lack of respect for everything respectable render him deaf to all such guidance," Verne informed his Paris friend and counseler. "But in consultation with my family I intend to act in the most forceful way possible, and if he won't give in, he'll be shipped off for several years."

The reference was to an occasional expedient of helpless parents: a recourse to the complaisant shipping industry. One simply signed one's son over to a skipper, and behavioral problems were resolved on the high seas. "He doesn't know that he's moving in that direction," added the very angry Jules Verne, "but he'll find out if necessary."

That Verne chose to confide this threat to Hetzel instead of shouting it to his son should alert the reader that it was a serious one. "We shall see," he summed up the subject in his letter to Hetzel. "I am not fooling myself with any hope of improvement, because there is a precocious perversity in this child who at the age of fourteen behaves as if he were twenty-five. But I'll have done my duty until the end."[6]

He was also keeping close watch on his finances. He had hoped to sell *Hector Servadac* to the daily *Le Temps* for another serialization. Hetzel set him straight about that. Without quite saying so, he made it clear that the new novel would attract readers. He feared, he said cautiously, that *Hector Servadac* would not have the same effect of "curiosity" that had assured the success of *Around the World*. "After a few chapters the reader senses the nature of the disaster, so the mystery, the secret, no longer supports the story line." Yet, he added hopefully, the book *would* succeed.[7]

SOME WRITERS HAVE PROPOSED A MORE INTRIGUING EXPLA- nation for Jules Verne's visits to Nantes during this period: pederasty. It isn't clear how the notion arose, but Jules Verne's own guardedness about his personal life and his occasionally conspiratorial dashing about opened a door to conflicting interpretations. One could also say that af- ter starting out in life as a prolific author of romantic verse, Jules Verne's subsequent inability to deal credibly in his books with the relations be- tween men and women abetted this theory.

Apparently the object of Verne's affection, then or in subsequent visits to Nantes, was none other than Aristide Briand, often a prime minister in the Third Republic, winner of the Nobel Peace Prize, and future world statesman (as a Socialist party politician, he fought for separation of church and state). Just a year younger than Verne's son, Michel, Briand was a high school lad in his Nantes birthplace in the late 1870s. Nobody can deny that Jules Verne was a frequent visitor to his own hometown in those years, with his mother there, and often his son.

In a later reminiscence, the elder statesman remembered meeting Jules Verne—whose name was already well known to Briand and his school- mates—in 1876 or 1877. As he recalled it half a century later, one of his friends took him along on a visit to Verne's boat—presumably the *Saint- Michel II,* acquired just about then (Briand remembered that there was a cook aboard). "Jules Verne, a nice daddy with a gray beard, seemed to

love food," remembered Briand. "He was a fine man who took an interest
in me and took care of me on my holidays from boarding school," he recalled. Briand remembered seeing inside the cabin of the *Saint-Michel II*
a large blackboard covered with algebraic formulas he didn't comprehend.

"Despite that," added Briand, "I admired him for his books and I was
grateful because he sometimes took me to the theater on Place Graslin.
That was a treat!"[8]

Up to a point, this seems an understandable relationship. With his own
son unable or unwilling to share pleasures—boat or theater—with him,
Jules Verne had found surrogates in Briand and a comrade. Family legend
suggests that Verne had agreed to serve as Briand's temporary guardian,
a kindly mentor watching over a minor attending boarding school at
some distance from his parents' home.[9]

One of Briand's biographers gave a more intricate interpretation: The
comrade who had taken Briand aboard the *Saint-Michel* was a young Creole whom "an old man, with the air of a placid middle class gentleman,
came to pick up on holidays"; the old man was of course Jules Verne. And
Verne, suggested Briand's biographer, was not indifferent to Briand's
charms.[10] In another version, there is no young Creole; Briand meets
Jules Verne through another school comrade—who happens to be Michel
Verne; they share outings with Michel's father.[11]

Jean Jules-Verne, Michel's son, added to the controversy, misreading a
key letter from Verne to Hetzel concerning Michel, written in the summer
of 1877. "I am in Nantes, in the country [presumably the house in Chante-
nay], where I've taken Michel for a few days. I've brought him some tranquility in this family as united as it is large, and he had never known a
family until now," wrote Jules Verne. But his grandson replaced the name
Michel with that of Briand.[12] In fact, the name Michel is quite legible, and
it is repeated a few lines later, in a context where his identity is indisputable.

This misreading, with its suggestion of Hetzel's complicity, seemed to
reinforce the story of Verne's particular interest in young Aristide Briand.
The story, however, has always called for a suspension of disbelief, since
Briand didn't even enter the school in Nantes until February 1878, some
six months after this letter to Hetzel was written.[13]

What is one to make of all this? One could simply call it another
enigma, for there is no other suggestion of a homosexual encounter in
the life of Jules Verne. One could also take a categorical position, as
Verne's admirer Dr. Olivier Dumas did, saying that it would have been difficult for the prominent Jules Verne to be going around with a high
school boy without creating a stir, if only in the family, especially since he
and Briand lived in the same place—Nantes—for only seven months,

which would have been in 1878.[14] One could also make the point that during this visit to Nantes in the early spring when Jules would have seen young Briand for the first time, Honorine was also there.

Another literary scholar, Marc Soriano, considering the sad truth that Jules was tired of Honorine, concluded that he presented a typical case of bisexuality. And since Honorine wasn't able to satisfy him, "the other tendency" was reinforced. All the same, Soriano assumed that Verne's homosexuality was latent. If it surfaced at all, it was in his books—where women count for little and attention is often directed to a "charming adolescent who wins all hearts."[15] The skeptical reader may prefer to see in these adolescent heroes the author's longing for the perfect son he didn't have, or believed he didn't have.

WHILE THEY WERE IN NANTES, HONORINE BECAME ILL. Jules accompanied her back to Amiens, and she was put to bed; her condition worsened. "Successive losses of blood over a two-week period, losses we believed without seriousness," Honorine's son-in-law Georges Lefebvre informed Hetzel, "have brought on such total anemia that for the past week my dear mother-in-law is considered by the doctors to be in danger." Lefebvre was writing to Hetzel because Jules Verne could not. "Her poor husband, although very courageous, is in a fearful state, he loves his wife so much! He didn't have the strength to write to you. . . ."

The date of this letter is April 23, 1876. Two days earlier, Honorine's condition was such that she had asked for a priest to hear her confession, then received the last rites, this before a blood transfusion, which seemed to have succeeded. Then her condition worsened again, "and the doctors, including the one who treats her regularly, stays at her side, simply abandoned her—giving her forty-eight hours to live." When at last he could sit down to write Verne told Hetzel, "If the doctors still have a little hope, in our opinion there is no hope." Honorine, whose illness, whatever the origin, must have been aggravated by the behavior of their son, Michel—and by their perception of that behavior—pulled through.

Jules did try to work. His brother, Paul, had joined him at Honorine's bedside; Paul was now going to Paris, where he would deliver the manuscript of the second volume of *Hector Servadac* to Hetzel. It was "entirely finished, except for the style," Jules explained to his publisher. "I don't have the peace of mind necessary to review the style."[16]

There is considerable evidence that style *was* a problem. The subject was partly to blame, of course: Clearly, the author had not been at ease with his scenario. Now, in addition to nursing Honorine, he became involved in a sparring match with Hetzel over a book that probably shouldn't have been written in the first place. Examining the battered manuscript today, a careful reader can find evidence of Hetzel's constant input. He had slashed a page with an angry "No, no and no" and he had flatly refused to consider the original ending. Verne had his comet crashing back to earth, its survivors receiving heroes' welcomes. (The gold content of the comet they have christened Gallia, in Verne's original draft, immediately depreciates the value of all the gold on Earth.)

Hetzel's main argument was that this incredible event would not be credible to the inhabitants of Earth who hadn't taken part in it. "I'd prefer that they not be believed," he explained, revealing his own unhappiness with the fable. Once again, the author caved in; he rewrote his ending. When asked by his major where he had been, Captain Servadac (in Verne's draft) replied, "I took a ride in a comet!" At Hetzel's request, Verne rewrote this; now Captain Servadac replied, "If I told you that I came from the moon you probably wouldn't believe me." "From the moon?" "Well, friends, I'm back from a trip still further away, but I don't ask you to believe me."[17]

In the final version, as published in Hetzel's magazine, Servadac concludes, "Let's say that I only dreamed it."

When a new book by Jules Verne was finished, it was usually serialized in Hetzel's *Magasin d'Education,* beginning in the first issue of January, always as the lead selection. Subscribers opened their magazine at the beginning of January 1877 to read a note initialed by the publisher at the bottom of the first page: "The new work of Jules Verne, whose first readers will be our subscribers, is divided into two parts, in size similar to *Michel Strogoff.* The general theme will become apparent only with the fourth chapter. The prologue leading to this fourth chapter is only the frame of a picture offering young readers a subject as interesting, in a different field, as *Twenty Thousand Leagues Under the Sea.*"

Hetzel, in this curious intervention, which reads almost as a disclaimer, was saying that the book would get off to a slow start, but that the reader should persevere. He was reminding readers of two very popular novels by the same author to recommended the new one. Without question, he was expressing doubt—not necessarily concerning the worth of the new book, but about the reaction of subscribers.

The author didn't appear to be put off by his publisher's disclaimer, if he realized it was one. The year 1877 began well for him. In January, his "Dr. Ox's Experiment" was adapted as a musical, and this with little or no effort required of him—above all, no forced labor at the d'Ennery villa in

Antibes. Indeed, this "Doctor Ox" wasn't quite *his* fantasy, but a comic opera based on the story, the music by Jacques Offenbach, who was also the director of the Variétés. Offenbach and his librettists made sure to eliminate the boring moments of the story (Verne had intentionally made the Flemish town boring so that Dr. Ox and his oxygen could liven it up). They also added a love interest, in the person of an Oriental princess who was mad about the doctor.

The real added value was to be found in the costumes and scenery, apparently the most elaborate Offenbach had ever put on the stage.[18] In *Le Temps,* an anonymous reviewer regretted the violence done to the original, noting all the same that the most amusing scene did come directly from Verne: the episode in the tower, when townspeople on the lower levels are intoxicated, while up above them Dr. Ox remains immune—because oxygen is heavier than air. Observing that the play failed to move opening-night viewers, the unkind critic said that it was too bad Jules Verne hadn't suggested that oxygen be leaked into the audience.[19]

The adapters got their comeuppance: The play quickly ran out of oxygen; with box-office receipts declining rapidly, it closed after forty-two performances—precious few for the popular Offenbach.[20]

Still, the stage, with its promise of quick and easy returns, proved irresistible to Jules Verne. "I've just completed a big deal with the Odéon theater," he informed Hetzel. "*Michel Strogoff* without a co-author, for May 1878, meaning during the Universal Exposition. I'll have a royalty of 12 percent and 6 percent of the new profits."[21] Alas, this project never got off the ground; when *Michel Strogoff* was adapted for the stage, it was in collaboration with d'Ennery. This time Verne and d'Ennery worked together by mail, not in Antibes.

First, Verne did his own draft of the theatrical version of *The Children of Captain Grant,* then sent it on to d'Ennery. It was not a masterpiece, Verne warned his collaborator, only "a scenario in dialogue"—into which the experienced showman would have to breathe life. "Tedious parts here, abbreviated parts there, bad jokes, feelings lacking development," Verne wrote, belittling his own work. "You are the best judge of all these questions, and your judgments must be without appeal," he added judiciously, for of course he wanted this play to work.

However, he didn't want to travel to Antibes unless that was absolutely necessary. Honorine was ill again, with what appeared to be a recurrence of the same dangerous condition. Of course, he also had to deal with Michel. "At 300 leagues from Amiens," which is where would have been if he had gone south to the Mediterranean, "I wouldn't have a minute of tranquility."[22]

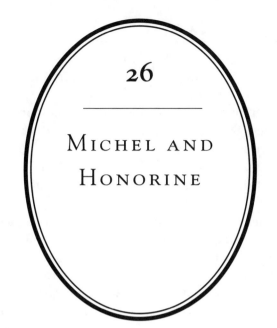

26

MICHEL AND
HONORINE

WHEN THE LIFE OF THE VERNES SEEMED TO HAVE REACHED A
new low—Jules devastated by his wife's chronic illness, his wife by her husband's remoteness, both by seemingly endless, insoluble problems with
their son—they decided to try music. And why not a fancy-dress ball, a
glorious night of dancing amid dazzling colors, an event that the residents of Amiens, Jules and Honorine included, would never forget?

After some investigation, the Vernes discovered that there hadn't been
a costume ball in Amiens in a generation; theirs was set for Easter Monday, April 2, 1877: "700 invitations dispatched, 350 acceptances at least,"
the host announced triumphantly to Hetzel. "The whole town is talking about it." Today, we know something Jules Verne's fellow residents
couldn't have known: The party was an act of desperation, and a costly
one; by his own estimate, this frugal man spent four thousand francs for
that evening (a sum equivalent to about 70,000 present-day francs). The
figure included the rental of a hall vast enough for fifteen hundred rev-
elers, and decorations worthy of a carnival.

Then Honorine had a relapse. Jules's letters to Hetzel—his one confidant—revealed that Honorine, now forty-seven years old, was hemor-
rhaging again. The bleeding soon stopped, and in a matter of days there
were signs of recovery. "But the prospect of this costume ball that we are
giving on April 2, a ball for which it's said that guests are spending a total
of 100,000 francs [today, that would represent over 1.7 million francs], a

ball which can neither be called off nor postponed, that's the complication." And it was already March twenty-first. "I'm frightfully afraid that my
wife won't be able to attend!"

He was, he said, more annoyed than inquiet (Honorine would come
out of it in the end, but too late to greet guests at the party). "I'm terribly
embarrassed," Verne repeated in another worried note. "Her [Hon-
orine's] ball takes place in one week's time—will she be able to be there?"
In the end, Honorine's daughter Suzanne would replace her mother at
the door.

"An élite public poured into the large Saint-Denis hall," an Amiens
daily, *Le Progrès de la Somme,* reported. "It was a truly magic sight, these
splendid costumes sparkling beneath the chandeliers and almost blinding one in their contrast with the formal black coats worn by the sober."
Knowing its readers, the local paper made another point: "If the guests
came away from their evening with wonderful memories, it wasn't a loss
either for local tradesmen who had been badly served this winter by the
limited number of balls and official receptions."

Although the invitations didn't specifically call for it, many guests had
the good sense to come dressed as characters from Verne novels (for example, as Hindu women—a reminder of Mrs. Aouda, the young widow in
Around the World in Eighty Days). The ball ended at six in the morning with
a lively cotillion. "When you live with provincials you must howl with
provincials," Verne wrote to Hetzel, summing up his feelings by borrowing from an old proverb. With unconcealed pride, he declared, "Only I
could put on such an event in Amiens, in this form. There hadn't been a
costume ball in this town in thirty-five years. My name, being neutral,
brought together a brilliant crowd that no political or industrial name
could have attracted."

Then, as if Hetzel needed the reminder, he stated, "You know why, in
part, I live in Amiens. Life in Paris with my wife, as you know her, was impossible. So, I hurled with the wolves, but I don't have to be sorry that I
did. Two hundred costumes for 250 guests present . . . magnificently decorated rooms it would have been almost too much—if my wife had been
able to be there. . . ."

He had wanted to make a splash, but he swore to his publisher that he
was in no way responsible for the stories about the ball published in Paris.
"I gave it so that my wife and her children would have the position they
ought to have but don't have in this town. . . . Now they've come out, and
no one will invite me by myself anymore, as has happened. Personally I'd
rather have spent the 4000 francs on a trip!"[1]

Hetzel had the final word, but he reserved it for his son, who was increasingly his confidant, before becoming his successor. "One mustn't, one simply cannot, take one's wife everywhere. There is a world of family friends, and the private world of the husband's public relations."

Then, as if the costume ball symbolized everything that was wrong about Amiens and Jules Verne's decision to live there, he concluded by saying, "It's pure provincial—and it's in this sense that I say that Verne manages to make provincial life as useless to him as life in Paris; and that he finds a way to see so many people but not the people who might be useful to his mind."[2]

⚜

THE COSTUME BALL MAY HAVE BEEN GIVEN FOR HONORINE, but surely Jules's sights were still set on the French Academy. Letters from 44, boulevard Longueville, where he now lived in Amiens, to Pierre-Jules Hetzel on rue Jacob show that he was not too far away from Paris to follow developments in the corridors of the French Academy on quai Conti. "About ten days ago in Paris, at the auction house, I met Dumas the younger," Verne reported to Hetzel. "He approached and immediately spoke to me, on his initiative, of the Academy. He offered to press my candidacy vigorously if I were willing. He believes it will work, with his friends joined to your friends—they aren't necessarily the same. He was very firm, and very warm." Jules wondered only whether Dumas was motivated more by hatred of rival dramatist Victorien Sardou, a candidate for a vacant chair, or sympathy for Jules Verne. Literary legend has it that Alexandre Dumas, speaking of his prominent father, confided to a fellow author, "Since papa wasn't a member of the French Academy, Verne—this scientific Dumas—should be elected. I'd have the feeling they were voting for my father."[3] Perhaps he didn't quite say that.

Still, Dumas's offer seemed an opening not to be ignored, and Verne wanted his publisher and benefactor to know about it; with Dumas on his side, he might be able to prevail over Sardou. He did wish it to be clear that he had not taken the initiative.[4]

In fact, he did not have a chance of election. Perhaps he hadn't (or Hetzel and Dumas hadn't) tried hard enough; perhaps one couldn't win a seat if one didn't offer oneself publicly. "Academic candidacies are like asparagus," veteran academician Ernest Legouvé, a novelist and playwright, admonished Hetzel. "They are happy only when they show the tiny tip of their nose and raise the layer of earth themselves. But Verne's candidacy isn't showing the tip of its nose."[5]

The reluctant candidate took pains to assure Hetzel that he was not "stung by the academic tarantula as much as all that." What vexed him was the apparent deprecation of his kind of writing by the French Academy: "On the literary scale, the adventure story is lower down than the novel of manners." He accepted the ranking, however; it was certain, he said, that "the study of the human heart is more literary than a narrative of adventures."[6]

"Concerning *genre*," he explained to his publisher, "I return to that discussion that always makes you jump: the little importance that books written for young people have in our literature. . . . Recently a newspaper listing novelists who might have a place in the academy spoke of [Alphonse] Daudet, [Edmond and Jules] Goncourt, [Ferdinand] Fabre, [Paul] Féval, etc., everyone except me."[7]

What Hetzel *really* felt about the matter, he saved for his son's eyes. "Decidedly the Academy is stupid and renders people stupid. It is enough to be a member or to desire to be one to lose one's good sense. Verne has already reached that point."

One must not forget that Jules Verne was above all a prolific writer and Hetzel a successful publisher. The year 1877 was no less fruitful than preceding or succeeding years. Under Hetzel's firm guidance, Verne applied finishing touches to his novel *Black Diamonds,* while composing the novel then being called *A Fifteen-Year-Old Hero,* which was published as *Dick Sands the Boy Captain.* For his part, Hetzel was serializing *Hector Servadac,* publishing the small-format first editions of *Black Diamonds* and *Hector Servadac,* and preparing the year-end illustrated gift volumes of *The Chancellor* (a short novel to which was added the early story "Martin Paz"), *Black Diamonds,* and *Hector Servadac.* The Verne-Hetzel partnership remained an assembly line.

It was now standard procedure, for example, that each Verne manuscript be treated as a draft, which would then be shaped into a commercially viable story by the publisher. "Not enough work had been done on the last three chapters [of *Black Diamonds*]," Hetzel told his son and associate. "I worked very hard on them, for they aren't written in a way to allow inserting the many things that lacked." Now that he had added "more blood, flesh, and heart," he thought the book would be easier to sell. Still, he was under no illusion. "This will make a passable book, not one of the good ones, not one of the bad." In fact, the story had been rewritten four times, and Verne had told Hetzel that he didn't recognize it. From Hetzel's point of view (so he confided to his son): "so much the better."[8]

As published, *Black Diamonds* is the saga of an obstinate Scottish working family, the Fords, who after the depletion of a coal mine that had been both their life and their sustenance, not to forget the life and sustenance of their forebears, resolve to live in the closed pit. For ten years, they seek new veins. When they find one, Simon Ford and his son Harry exploit their mine with the help of the resourceful engineer James Starr, also a veteran of the abandoned pit.

They are troubled by a succession of threatening, inexplicable incidents. At one point, they are trapped below, when a mysterious visitor blocks the passage. When their mine becomes profitable, they build an underground town illuminated and heated by electricity—a marvel that puts Coal City in the guidebooks as a tourist attraction.

Another character is the mysterious young Nell, half-wild from having grown up underground. The reader finally discovers that it is Nell's crazed grandfather who has been trying to sabotage the efforts of the Fords and their friends; the old man is convinced that the mine belongs to him alone. Nell intervenes to save her new friends; in a last desperate act, her grandfather tries to blow them all up, but a great white owl that has been Nell's protector saves the day. Nell then marries Harry Ford.

Le Temps liked the new book, and it began publishing the novel in daily installments on March 28, 1877.

ONE CAN IMAGINE JUST HOW HETZEL FELT WHEN HE OPENED an envelope to find a letter from Zadoc Kahn, the Great Rabbi of Paris, reacting to the violence of *Hector Servadac,* for the chapter introducing the terrible Jew Isac Hakhabut had just appeared (in the installment of *Magasin d'Education* published at the beginning of June 1877). "I read with genuine sadness the latest issue of 'Magasin d'éducation et de récréation,'" the rabbi's letter began, "in which Mr. Jules Verne decided to reproduce one more time the portrait so new and so original of the Jewish usurer; I should have thought that an ingenious and inventive talent like his would have refrained from such worn-out means of amusing readers. But it seems that the habit is too ingrained, all writers must pass that way."

Rabbi Kahn said he had no wish to restrict the freedom to write or to make fun of one's neighbor, but he suggested that what might appear in a book or on the stage had no place in a magazine read by young people. Hetzel's fortnightly had the merit of being addressed to readers of all faiths, Kahn wrote, as it was to all ages, thanks to its generous, noble, and uplifting moral positions. But how could he give the magazine to his children—who had long been faithful subscribers—now that it was publishing a story "so insulting to all Jews"? And how could he distribute it to pupils in Jewish schools, for whom he had subscribed to the magazine? "And youth of other faiths—is it wise, sir, and fair to give them such ideas about a large group of fellow citizens, and to breed prejudices that will come out later in life?"[9]

"I warned Verne," Hetzel assured his son, "I had attenuated more than one passage, but he tore into these pitiful people in such a way that there could only be difficult attempts at attenuation but no remedy for the unfortunate effect produced. We have to realize that there are Jews everywhere." The publisher had received other protests from Jewish subscribers and he said he would have liked "to place a bandage on their wounds." He did intend to insert a phrase at the first appearance of Isac in the novel, to make clear that his behavior harmed all Jews.[10]

Once again, at this remove we can only marvel at Verne's tenacity. For the anti-Semitism displayed in Verne's novel does not exist in his personal correspondence, just as it is absent from the recollections of those who knew him.

The fact that the veteran publisher had not prevailed over his author—had not even tried to until it was too late—indicates the strength of Verne's conviction, and the weakness of Hetzel's. "Jules Verne was an anti-Semite," one of Verne's biographers remarked, "as one was in middle class and Catholic circles of the last century in France."[11] In the opinion of an ardent present-day Vernian scholar, the author was simply following public opinion, as he did when he expressed anti-British and anti-German feelings.[12]

Hetzel, if one believes his letter to his son, had tried but not succeeded in warding off the defamatory chapters in the magazine; he would be more successful with the book version, the first volume of which was published only six weeks later. A close comparison by Olivier Dumas of the magazine serialization and the book uncovered a number of changes for the better: The ugly references to "the Jew" are replaced by "Isac" or "the renegade."

In one particularly harsh passage, which says that no matter what language Isac uses, he was always talking "Jew," the book version replaces "Jew" with "money." Elsewhere, when Captain Servadac exclaims that Isac was a Jew and his orderly replied that he was worse—a German Jew—the book softened the reply: "A Jew, that would be nothing. . . . I've known some who didn't shirk from doing good; but this one is a German Jew. . . ."[13]

Early publishers of Jules Verne in the United States, immune to copyright, didn't have to worry about what the author thought. In the first American publication, just a year after the book appeared in France, the

Jew Isac became Dutch Isaac, although one might assume from refer-ences to the god of Abraham and the Gentiles that he was a Jew all the same.[14]

All previous novels in the *Extraordinary Voyages* series were credited with having sold more than 25,000 copies, but *Hector Servadac* in its original small-format edition sold only 18,000 over the life of the book; later, it would simply be dropped by publishers of Verne collections (such as the children's library published by Hachette, Hetzel's successor).[15]

"Have you arranged the affair of the Jews in Servadac?" Verne would ask Hetzel at the end of summer.[16] It was as if he was counting on his pub-lisher to undo what he'd done.

～◎ ◎ん～

"I'LL SEE YOU IN PARIS EITHER TUESDAY OR WEDNESDAY evening," Jules Verne informed Hetzel.[17] "But explain to me why apart from the Jewish affair you want to see me. Has it to do with Michel's situ-ation? I need to know before seeing Mr. Blanchard in Mettray again."

The reference to Mettray, northwest of Tours on the right bank of the Loire River, indicates Jules Verne's state of mind at this moment. The very mention of the place was enough to arouse dread in the sternest of par-ents. Somehow, the Vernes had been advised to investigate Mettray for their son. In the account given by Jean Jules-Verne, ever the conciliator, Mettray was a reform school; the *Grand Larousse* more properly identified it as an "agricultural penal colony for young inmates." In Jules Verne's time, a minor was committed to Mettray by court order, in a procedure called "incarceration as paternal punishment."[18]

"Verne is in Tours at present," Hetzel told his son on June sixth. "He dined with us last night. He had just received horrible news of his unfor-tunate son and told me about it. What sorrow to be hurt so badly and by one's son." He went on to describe a father deeply affected but who kept his control. Yet before the evening was over, Verne was sobbing, Hetzel re-lated.[19]

Evidence about Michel's situation is scanty; family legend speaks of "nervousness," of "character disorders," and adds that Michel spent a full eight months at Mettray—a stay that, in the words of Jean Jules-Verne, "only aggravated a condition that had become increasingly alarming, threatening to end in madness or suicide." Coercion served only to exac-erbate the boy's rage. Even the director of Mettray felt that the warmth of a family environment would be preferable.[20]

Nantes somehow seemed a better environment than Amiens, both for

Michel's and for Honorine's health, and it was also nearer to the country house at Chantenay. That autumn, the Vernes would rent a flat of their own in the center of Nantes at 1, rue de Suffren, just one street up the hill from the family home on rue Jean-Jacques Rousseau; a plain house, it was surely well within the budget for the longish stays occasioned by keeping Michel in tow.[21]

The Vernes spent August of 1877 with Michel in Chantenay. Jules was finishing the first half of the novel he was still calling *A Fifteen-Year-Old Hero*. Michel had just turned sixteen. In the story, young Dick Sands, an apprentice seaman, is obliged to take over a whaling ship when captain and crew are lost at sea; he succeeds nobly in that and successive challenges.

For the moment, Verne, the watchful father, reported that Michel was only at the stage of swaggering about, "but it is possible that serious things will take place and at that point he'll be shipped out. . . . He'll find the whole family united against him. He's a bad character, a flaunter of vices, and at the same time a head absolutely voice of common sense."[22]

Nothing alarming happened that summer, however. A letter to Hetzel that has been dated September eleventh reported the good news that there was "nothing really serious to reproach Michel with if it isn't his reckless wastefulness and his ignorance of the value of money. This is hardly believable. But in other matters the family notices a certain degree of improvement."[23] Indeed, as he assured Hetzel after taking Michel back to Mettray at summer's end, the holiday with his family had been good for the boy; he would find life harder in the penal colony, though.[24]

There are no concrete examples of Michel Verne's prodigality, only his father's word for it. There did seem to be little an adolescent could buy in those days, no speciality shops for teenagers, no businesses that thrived on selling games or soft drinks to young adults. On the other hand, Michel's father was about to pay a colossal sum for a newly constructed yacht. "What folly" Jules exclaimed in a letter to Hetzel, "55,000 [approximately 965,000 present-day] francs!" The thirty-eight-ton solid-iron steam yacht *Saint-Michel III*, as Verne would christen it, could do nine and a half knots an hour, ten and a half when sails were also used. Its engine was "absolutely perfect," Jules's brother, Paul, told one of his brother's biographers. Amenities included a dining room, a mahogany drawing room, a bedroom for two, with adjacent dressing room, servant's room, and quarters for the crew; the salon could also be equipped with bunks. "On the whole," wrote Paul, "nothing could be more gracious than this steam yacht with its tall inclined masts, its black hull relieved by a light stroke at the water line and the ribband . . . and the elegance of the line from the taffrail to the stem."

Originally, the yacht had cost its marquis owner 100,000 francs. Jules offered to pay half the asking price in cash, half in a year's time; a contemporary noted that, with four hundred performances of *Around the World in Eighty Days,* he could afford a luxury yacht. What his contemporaries didn't know was that Verne had received a "gift" from his publisher in the form of payment for a second *Celebrated Travels and Travelers.* Verne's name would appear as the author, but a collaborator would actually do the work. . . . And this gift, Verne told Hetzel, "induced me to some extent to commit this folly."

His prodigality was also a form of health insurance, according to Paul Verne. "I shall only say that this indefatigable worker sometimes ends up being fatigued." He contested the story (one propagated by Jules himself) that his brother wrote while sailing. In his letters to Hetzel, Verne was effusive about the trips he could make now: "The Mediterranean, the Baltic, the northern seas, Constantinople as well as Saint Petersburg, Norway, Iceland, etc. And for me what an opportunity for new impressions and new ideas! I'm sure that I'll make back the price of the boat—which in any case will still be worth what I paid for it."[25]

He did need a sea change. At the end of this terrible year, in the first December issue of *Magasin d'Education,* a letter signed Jules Verne, ostensibly addressed to publisher Stahl (Hetzel, of course), explains that the first installment of *Dick Sands* was to have appeared in the magazine on January 1, 1878. "Unfortunately, and contrary to my habits, I was ill.'" Something "captivating" written by Stahl himself would appear in its place.[26]

Actually, he hadn't been ill at all. But it had been a bad year all the same.

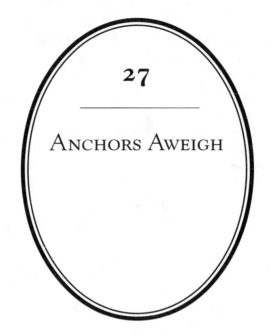

27

ANCHORS AWEIGH

TODAY, IT MAY BE DIFFICULT TO BELIEVE THAT A FRENCH FA-
ther once had the power to order the incarceration of a minor son, then
his transfer to dockside, under the escort of gendarmes, for forceable
embarkation on a ship that would be at sea for the next eighteen months
to two years.

To his credit, Verne had chosen this ship, *L'Assomption,* with care. From
Nantes in mid-January 1878 Verne wrote Hetzel, informing his publisher
that the ship was a "magnificent new three-master of 1200 tons." The itinerary would take Michel, who was sixteen and a half years old when he
sailed, to Mauritius and Réunion in the Indian Ocean, then on to India
(Pondicherry and Calcutta). Verne also said the ship was under the command of a good captain, forty-five years old. "We couldn't have found better" he wrote. Moreover, Michel was pleased by the prospect of an ocean
exile—he "is terribly excited, he dreams only of this voyage," Jules Verne
assured Hetzel.

Nevertheless, explained Verne—becoming the stern father once again—
Michel "will leave the house of detention only to be escorted to Bordeaux, where I shall have preceded him by a few days. I shall therefore be
present at his sailing. Michel will have seen only me and his uncles." One
wonders whether Verne had conceived this merciless plan to head off any
attempt at escape that Michel might make. Certainly Honorine's absence
assured there would be no last-minute reprieve. Verne asked Hetzel to

send him a complete set of his novels in the small paperbound format, to be charged to his account; his son wished to take the books to sea.

"Michel will be an apprentice seaman, registered on the roll of the crew," Verne explained. "But since he won't be expected to learn the trade, having his room at the stern and dining at the captain's table, he will pay 200 francs a month. In other words it's a journey." Then, resuming a grave tone, he added, "What will become of him? I don't know, but the doctors here agree that during a fit this child lacks all responsibility for his acts. Will the sea cure this mind?"[1]

L'Assomption sailed from Bordeaux on February 4, 1878. Jules Verne waited until late in March to draft a letter to the captain. The point, of course, was to elicit news of Michel. He asked what the captain thought of Michel, how he was bearing up under shipboard conditions, and whether he had been "obedient and considerate to you, as it's his duty to be." After this expression of concern, he offered a warning: "In any case it's when you go ashore that things will doubtless become more difficult."

Jules now judged it wise to reveal to the captain just what it was that had moved him to call in the law. Whatever high crimes Michel had committed or was capable of committing had to be spelled out so that the captain would be in a position to deal with them. No mention was made of excessive drinking or of other forms of deviant social behavior, nor did Jules refer to petty thefts, extortion, or other criminal acts. "The greatest defect Michel has is being a spendthrift. He has no idea of the value of money. He'll spend 50 francs as if it were five. He'll probably want to buy things in India or elsewhere—and expensive objects too—as souvenirs of his trip. But that would be useless, and some trinkets typical of the country will suffice perfectly."

Verne left it to the captain to decide how to disburse his son's pocket money, but he made it clear that he felt about fifty francs a month would be reasonable for minor amusements while on land.[2]

What the captain thought about all this is not known; being a skipper, he surely approved of a year or two of life at sea for any young man—regardless of the reason. Had there been other high crimes on the head of Michel Verne that his father communicated only in whispers? The letter suggests that there had been no such communication. Perhaps the captain simply chalked it all up to Jules Verne's avarice? We'll never know.

IN THE SPRING OF 1878, VERNE BEGAN TO USE HIS EXPENsive steam yacht, the *Saint-Michel III.* There are tales of visits to Le Tréport, one of the more elegant Channel resorts of the time. There, the Vernes met the future pretender to the throne, Philippe d'Orléans, whose title was Count of Paris, and his countess, Isabelle. Jules reputedly gave the count a manuscript of *Twenty Thousand Leagues Under the Sea*. Verne was also seen strolling on the pier of Le Tréport with Antoine d'Orléans, the Duke of Montpensier, son of King Louis-Philippe, and with the Count of Eu, Gaston d'Orléans. "These Orléans are good, open-minded people," Jules Verne is quoted as having said. "They do me the honor of liking my books and to some extent my person."[3]

The time came for a real test of Jules's new toy. His crew had been taking the yacht out to the Channel, along the coast of Brittany as far as Brest; it was actually from Nantes that he would embark with his brother, Paul; Hetzel's son, Jules; and a prominent Norman lawyer and former member of parliament, Hetzel's friend Edgar Raoul-Duval.

Almost at once they encountered rough weather. Opting for prudence, they took refuge at La Trinité-sur-Mer on the southern Brittany coast.[4] Paul Verne later remembered that his brother—who had just celebrated his fiftieth birthday—bore their several days of rough weather with courage.[5]

Then after crossing the Bay of Biscay and rounding Spain's northwestern point, they headed out into the Atlantic, but soon they turned back, making for Vigo—in Galicia—their first port of call. A letter from Raoul-Duval, published in his hometown of Rouen a few days later, explained this unexpected change in their itinerary. "Yesterday at one o'clock," he wrote on June fourth, "we were on the open sea, receiving huge waves that covered half the deck. We had both wind and sea against us, and had we pursued our route we'd be pitching heavily right now, painfully trying to stay on course."

Hence, they sailed to Vigo, which turned out to be so endearing "that it's possible none of our other ports of call will give us as much pleasure. . . ." The *Saint-Michel* entered the harbor just as a large French warship was arriving there; soon the Verne party was invited aboard for a tour of the harbor and lunch with the captain. They had arrived just in time for Vigo's annual festival; with the help of the French consul, *and* because of the reputation of Señor Julio Verne, they enjoyed all of the events—a performance of sword dancing, outdoor concerts, fireworks, a torchlight parade.

Later, Jules Verne remembered that the French officer invited their party to make use of a diving suit in order to explore the depths off Vigo, just to see whether Captain Nemo had forgotten any of the galleons that had sunk while carrying gold and other treasures back from the New World. At fifty, Verne was considered too old to plunge, but Jules Hetzel was allowed to try his luck (he had none).[6]

On June fifth they reached Lisbon, where Verne visited his local publisher, attended the theater, and gave interviews aboard the *Saint-Michel.* A journalist described the famous author as "extremely gracious, deeply sympathetic in his appearance, the once-blond beard now a little gray, the eye lively, clear and intelligent." It was three o'clock in the morning on the seventh of June when they sailed out of the harbor to begin the voyage south.[7]

It was hot all the way, and Jules did not like the heat. They called at Cádiz for an overland journey to Seville, than sailed across the straits to Tangier (docking on June tenth) and Tetuán, putting in also at Gibraltar, Málaga, Oran, and then Algiers (from June twenty-fourth to the twenty-sixth). They reached Sète on the French coast on June thirtieth, then made their way north by coach and train while Paul Verne stayed aboard the *Saint-Michel* for the return to Nantes. There would be more sailing that summer: from Nantes up Brittany's craggy coast to the Channel and Le Havre in August, then a return sail to Nantes at the end of that month. After another brief cruise in September, the yacht was moved to its berth in Nantes for the winter.[8]

ABOARD THE *SAINT-MICHEL* THAT SUMMER, VERNE MADE FI-nal proof corrections on *Dick Sands,* which was published in Hetzel's *Magasin* during 1878.

Dick is an apprentice seaman, born of unknown parents (probably from Albany, New York, a city that had been part of Jules Verne's American itinerary); he was given his family name, Sands, because he was found near Sandy Hook, at the entrance to New York Harbor. In every way a hero, "his seafaring trade had already prepared him for life's struggles. His intelligent features breathed energy." When his captain and crew disappear while hunting a whale, Dick must take over the ship, becoming responsible for the safety of its passengers, who include a mother and child, and combating both the elements and an evil man aboard. He prevails, of course.

It is obvious that young Dick is the ideal boy, also the ideal man: "At fifteen he knew already how to take a decision, and to carry through to the end." Not only is he dependable; he is also both generous and frugal (he offers to purchase the freedom of some slaves with "his meager savings"). He is familiar with modern geography. What more could one ask of a fifteen-year-old? Any father, even Jules Verne, might wish to have a son like Dick.

THE MONEYMAKER THAT SUMMER OF 1878 WAS THE REVIVAL of the stage version of *Around the World in Eighty Days* at the Porte Saint-Martin. It really *was* a lot of fun, admitted the difficult critic Francisque Sarcey, and the new run would be a success, just as the original run had been.

"Nothing shows better what's wrong with the theater than the history of *Around the World in Eighty Days*," Sarcey told his readers. For if the idea for the play, and the most amusing details, came from Jules Verne, the adaptation had called for collaborators more familiar with theatrical productions. And then when d'Ennery agreed to take over from the original writers, he received a higher royalty than all the others combined. "That's because in the theater everything is in the dramatic form," explained Sarcey on page one of *Le Temps*. Even Jules Verne, with all his ingenuity, his verve, and his gift for dialogue, could not have succeeded alone.[9]

Willingly accepting his role as a commercial writer, Jules Verne now entered a new phase of his relationship with Hetzel, one that would not make the front page. He was going to sign his name to another writer's work.

Enter a mysterious individual to become known by his pen name, André Laurie. In corresponding with Hetzel from aboard the *Saint-Michel* at Brest, Verne made reference to "the priest's novel." But no churchman was the author of the manuscript they were discussing. In fact, the author was a fugitive from justice, a rebel leader of the Paris Commune, which had so horrified Jules Verne in 1871. Laurie, condemned author, now lived in London, where he survived by writing for friendly Paris editors under a pseudonym. A benevolent priest in Paris allowed Laurie to use his address to receive mail.

Alerted to the existence of a manuscript very much in the spirit of his favorite author's *Extraordinary Voyages*, Hetzel agreed to read it.

The "priest" story was a promising one, although the writing was not up to Hetzel's standards. This manuscript needed more than the editorial skills Hetzel brought to each new Verne manuscript; it called for total revision. Hetzel knew Verne could do such a revision. In order for Laurie to sell his book to Hetzel—for the modest sum of fifteen hundred francs—the exile had to agree that the book would be published under Verne's name only. Laurie agreed, as did Verne.

Laurie was born Paschal Grousset in 1844 in Corsica. Although destined for a medical career, he was seduced by journalism and politics. A virulent enemy of the Bonapartes and the rich man's paradise they had made of their Second Empire, he was a prolific author in all genres.

After being attacked in the press by the emperor's cousin, prince Pierre Bonaparte, Grousset challenged the prince to a duel, sending fellow journalist Victor Noir as one of his seconds to arrange the details; the enraged Bonaparte promptly shot and killed Grousset's man. Victor Noir's funeral in January 1870 became the occasion for a silent march against the regime.

When Parisians rose up against the conservative government formed after the fall of the Bonapartes in 1870, the Paris Commune appointed Grousset delegate for external relations, a position equivalent to foreign minister. Then when the Thiers government swept through the capital, defeating the short-lived independent republic, Grousset was prosecuted on seventeen counts of treason, then sentenced to life imprisonment in a forced labor colony in France's remote Pacific possession of New Caledonia. Grousset failed on his first two attempts to escape, but he succeeded on a third try—two years and six months after his conviction.[10]

In the form in which it was submitted to him, the "priest's" manuscript seemed a total loss to Jules Verne. "The novel, if it can be called a novel, is hardly written," he warned Hetzel. "Action and struggle, and consequently reader interest are totally absent. I never saw anything so disjointed. . . ." But the story was there, somewhere. The title of the manuscript, *The Langevol Legacy,* would become *The Begum's Fortune.* This story of the fight between a good Frenchman and a bad German over a legacy became a favorite among Verne's readers.[11]

Verne set to work on the manuscript, which would be published at the beginning of 1879 in Hetzel's *Magasin,* then in book form the following September. Soon everybody seemed to be reading the story of the benevolent French blood specialist Dr. Sarrasin and the German protagonist, Professor Schultze. These two men were obliged to divide a disputed legacy; Sarrasin employed his new wealth in the conception of a model city in the American West, while evil Herr Schultze despoiled nature with mines and smokestacks in nearby Stahlstadt, where he built a secret arms factory that manufactured weapons intended for the destruction of France-Ville, the model city.

The Schultze character was a reference, of course, to Alfred Krupp, founder of the German industrial dynasty that armed the victorious Prussians in 1870. Grousset had written a fictional Krupp into his story, and Schultze-Krupp survived Jules Verne's rewriting. The real Krupp was known as the cannon king; Schultze is the steel king. In the Grousset-Verne story, valiant Marcel, an Alsatian who hopes to marry Dr. Sarrazin's daughter, finds a way to spy on the German and escape. Schultze fires his cannon all the same, but the inordinate power of the explosive sends the shell beyond its target and into space as an earth satellite.

A danger remains: the shells filled with liquid carbonic acid that can be fired from smaller, more conventional guns. Thus, the ideal city finds itself in greater danger than ever.

Good triumphs, all the same. When the arms factory suddenly ceases to show any sign of activity, Marcel returns to investigate. He discovers that the accidental explosion of a carbonic-acid shell has killed its inventor, thereby removing all danger to France-Ville. "Herr Schultze based his plan on totally erroneous information," Dr. Sarrasin explains to his future son-in-law. "In truth the best government is that in which the chief, after his death, can be most readily replaced, and that continues to function precisely because there is nothing secret about its mechanics." One must attribute the patriotic coloring of *The Begum's Fortune* to Verne's collaborator as much as to Verne. After remarking that Jules Verne had not until then portrayed a *French* engineer, one astute reader has credited Laurie with that.[12]

❦ ❧

WORK ON THE THEATRICAL VERSION OF HIS NOVEL *THE CHILdren of Captain Grant* had been dragging on; now it was time to move the book to the stage. During his summer cruise around Brittany, Verne kept in touch with his formidable coauthor by mail. A letter to d'Ennery dated August 27, 1878, displays Verne's acute sense of the business side of theater. Why, he wondered, should they withdraw *Around the World in Eighty Days* from the Porte Saint-Martin stage while it was still earning money—just to put on *Captain Grant?* The new play could very well wait until the end of the year.

He and d'Ennery were also mapping out the scenario of the musical version of *Michel Strogoff*. Here, Verne collaborated with d'Ennery on the staging as well as the script. "I know that you don't like moving panoramas," he wrote at one point. "If everything is possible in a novel, I see that not everything is possible in the theater, and yet if one wanted to, one could go further." For example, he wondered what to do about the wolf scene. He didn't see how it could be brought to the stage, "failing wolves, even false wolves." For the climax of the story, he suggested they show a burning city on the stage—at the point when the Russian traitor has released tons of naphtha gas into the rushing river, which when ignited sets Irkutsk aflame. And then dauntless Michel Strogoff could sail to the rescue on a sheet of ice or a raft on this fiery river.[13]

⁓

HE SEEMED TO BE EVERYWHERE THAT YEAR. AND YET IT WAS precisely now that he was supposedly carrying on with a beautiful Romanian, Luise Teutsch-Müller, born in a Transylvanian village thirty-three years earlier. She had recently arrived in Amiens with her third husband, a Swiss German whose cousin (the very French Louise) was a friend of Honorine's daughter Suzanne Lefebvre. Her marital history suggests that Luise was an attractive woman with a talent for seduction; she supposedly said, "Just for my voice, all men fall in love with me."

She may have been the model for the beautiful Romanian with blond hair and dark eyes in Verne's novel *Claudius Bombarnac* (both the real Luise and fictional Zinca Klork had worked as milliners); it has also been remarked that this was when Jules Verne began to use Central Europe as the setting for his stories. A tenacious family legend, possibly encouraged by Suzanne, also connects Luise with the mysterious La Stilla, a singer, in *Carpathian Castle*. When the real Luise returned to Bucharest with her husband, she gave birth to a daughter, Eugénie Jeannette, who at the age of fourteen or fifteen went to Amiens for teacher training; supposedly, she frequented the Vernes' home then. Some of her relatives believed she was Verne's daughter. Gossipy Verne biographers have made allusions to a Verne "family secret."

On the Bucharest side, descendants of Luise and daughter Eugénie took pride, they said, in displaying scale models of ships given to them by Jules Verne—models that survived up to the eve of World War II.[14]

Actually there isn't a shred of evidence to link Jules Verne, who was so busy elsewhere, with the charming Romanian; to accept the story of their liaison, one must imagine the celebrated author finding ways and means of trysting in that very provincial city of Amiens, with Luise's husband and Jules's wife never far away. The year 1878 was *also* the time when some say Verne was involved with Aristide Briand, the schoolboy in Nantes. As for Luise, one can guess that in dull Amiens a youngish Romanian woman could have been a distraction, a source of inspiration, without also having been a temptation; or if a temptation, she might have remained an unrealized one.

IN NOVEMBER, VERNE MUST HAVE BEEN REMINDED OF MICHEL
the apprentice seaman when the second and final volume of *Dick Sands
the Boy Captain* was published. At the time, he was embarking on what
were surely the busiest weeks of his year: attending rehearsals for another
complicated play, *The Children of Captain Grant*. While he was virtually
camped out at the Porte Saint-Martin theater, a letter from Michel, forwarded from Amiens by Honorine, caught up with him.

Michel had written his parents previously; in recent letters, he had let
them know that the captain of *L'Assomption* planned a voyage to Le Havre
and Bordeaux. Then on November twenty-seventh (Michel's letter was
written on November 28, 1878, from Calcutta), the captain had announced a change in plans; there was no longer any immediate prospect
of a return to France. "The disappointment was even more painful because the anticipation had been so great," wrote Michel, who had turned
seventeen in August. "It is very sad to be dragged against one's will, with
no chance that effort or any other thing will lead to a change in the situation, far from one's family, one's country, from everything one loves. Of
course it was my fault, and I can't say anything about that." The enforced
absence was a "tyranny" he said he would have to accept, since he deserved it. (Here he added, "I no longer deserve it," then struck that out.)
"But if I could end this exile I would know how to prove by the use I'd
make of my material freedom that I am worthy of my moral freedom."

In his ten months on shipboard at sea, he said it had never occurred to
him to find that the sea was beautiful. "My mind doesn't need to
be . . . developed; it's too developed for my seventeen years. What I need
is education and I ask you whether I am getting that here."

What father was getting from son here was straight adult talk, of a
kind Jules himself had never tried on his father in those letters between
Paris and Nantes permeated with an unbending father's strictures and a
son's compliancy—when it wasn't simply puerility. "As for my feelings,"
Michel's letter continued, "they needed this but only in one way." Perhaps he had required the distance from his father to appreciate him and
return his affection. But this was accomplished now. "Do you think that
it was turning the wheel or washing the deck that did it? I had time to
think about things, ten months have gone by—that's the solution to the
riddle!"

He said he wanted his father to know that no "recrimination" was intended. "I'm not even asking you to bring me home, even though I see
no need to continue a cure on a man who is healthy again, first because

you'd be unhappy if I asked, and then because you'd refuse my request. After all, I might be mistaken; perhaps the sickness is still there! Perhaps the madman still needs his medicine!"

He closed with kisses for his mother, and a wish to hear from her. In forwarding her son's letter to Jules in Paris, Honorine added a word of her own about Michel's disappointment on hearing that his ship was not returning to France for a visit. "Write to raise his morale," she begged her husband. "I'm afraid he'll go back to his old ways." She concluded, "Farewell, I kiss you as I love you."[15]

Possibly Verne had Michel's letter from Calcutta in hand when he declared to Hetzel, "I've just received from Michel the most *horrible* letter a father has ever had from a son! This is killing us." He told Hetzel that he was going to show the letter in question to Blanchard for "an expert judgment."[16]

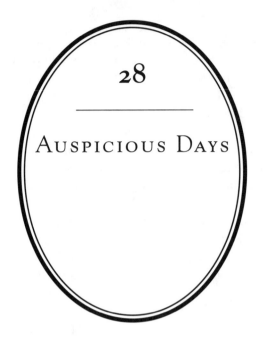

I T WAS MORE THAN LIKELY THAT ONE COULDN'T DO AN *AROUND the World* twice, yet play surgeon d'Ennery had attempted it, and with the earnest collaboration of his coauthor. But even for theatergoers responsive to pageantry the musical version of *The Children of Captain Grant* seemed too much.

The first notice in *Le Temps,* a brief unsigned one, warned that the new play was quite long, as was the novel. Cuts were recommended. Indeed, suggested the pitiless journalist, Verne and d'Ennery could take hints from the head colds observed among spectators. Whenever there was a slackening of the dialogue, the coughing and nose blowing began; the reviewer felt as if he had walked into a hospital ward.[1]

Francisque Sarcey, the exacting and subtle critic of the same paper, compared the adaptation of *Captain Grant* to the stage version of *Around the World,* but in a negative way. "A pretext for scenery succeeding another pretext for scenery," he began. "Isn't this rather sad? Of those fine novels, these jolly books by Jules Verne, almost nothing remains on the stage." The original story, Sarcey said, "is without doubt one of the liveliest and most moving Jules Verne ever wrote. . . . But when it came time to adapt it to the stage one realizes how theatrical lies are thin compared to the ones we tell ourselves at the fireside, with a volume in our hands."

The play went on until 2 A.M. the night Sarcey saw it.[2] And the public continued to cough and blow noses. Later, Jean Jules-Verne, Jules Verne's grandson and biographer, blamed the failure of this play on senseless trafficking with the original story ("I still wonder how the author of the book can allow his work to be defaced in this way.").[3] While box-office receipts were good and the coauthors' 12 percent share—this time divided equally between d'Ennery and Verne—came to between 650 and 1,100 francs each night in January 1879, this share fell to between 400 to 800 francs in February, between 400 and 600 in March. At the end of that month the play was withdrawn from the boards.[4]

The theatrical contretemps coincided with a rare attack on Jules Verne's books by an esteemed literary figure. More often than not, Verne's work was ignored by the literary world. Although Emile Zola, a famous novelist and reputed critic, had written kindly about Jules Verne's fiction in the past, he now chose to attack Verne's very genre in the columns of *Le Figaro Littéraire*. Some had seen this as an act of vengeance, for Hetzel had refused to publish Zola's work.

"The public appears to favor these amusing popularizations of science," wrote Zola. "I don't wish to argue about the genre, which seems to me likely to distort the information acquired by children." The critic said he much preferred simple tales, such as "Sleeping Beauty." But Zola could not overlook the popularity of the type of book Verne was writing; he acknowledged that Verne was "certainly the writer who now sells best in France." (Zola assumed that each of his books sold 100,000 copies.) But what had that got to do with literature? Books that teach the alphabet and prayer books also sell in high numbers.[5]

HETZEL WAS WORRIED THAT VERNE WAS TOO INVOLVED WITH the theater at the expense of his books.[6] In fact, Verne was working as hard as ever. The novel bearing the curious title *The Tribulations of a Chinese Gentleman*, which he had begun in 1878, was all but ready. Originally this was to be a story of a rich American who, thinking himself ruined, asks someone to help him commit suicide. This seemed too fatalistic an act for the American character.[7] Verne made his hero Chinese. Finally, even this character changes his mind and the wise man he has asked to carry out the deed confesses that he would not in any case have helped the rich man go through with the act of despair. It turns out that the hero hasn't been ruined after all; in fact, his fortune has doubled.

A letter from Hetzel to his son indicates that the latter was doing the editing on *Tribulations*—when he could get away with it, for at times Verne proved recalcitrant. "Don't insist too much," Hetzel cautioned his son, letting him in on the secret of handling Verne. "What you do will leave its mark anyway, and it will always be possible to return to the problem when correcting the proofs." On the positive side, he added, "When something must be gotten into Verne's head it's right away; he is quite conscientious in his work and does listen to good ideas."[8]

Verne was also working on the equally curious *The Steam House* (whose subtitle in French translates as *A Journey Through Northern India*), which would be ready for publication in *Magasin* at the end of 1879. In this story, a group of Englishmen travel through India in a mobile home drawn by a locomotive in the shape of an elephant—smoke pouring from the elephant's raised trunk. They confront adverse weather, an assault by real elephants, and native rebellion; in the end, Colonel Munro finds his young wife, who was believed to have been murdered by rebels.

The editing of *The Steam House* led to a rare flare-up on the part of this habitually cool author. He was ready, he assured Hetzel, to throw in the sponge. "If it is demonstrated that the public is tired either of me or of my kind of book I won't be the last to recognize it." As it was, he continued, he was thinking of turning out only one volume—which would have filled only half a year's issues of Hetzel's magazine. Evidently, he was getting tired. Yet he truly believed that *The Steam House* would appeal to his readers. It was full of action, full of local color specific to India. If he was mistaken, he warned, it meant that he could no longer write fiction.[9] One can assume that his association with d'Ennery led him to the increasingly exotic locales of these stories.

Verne's rewrite of André Laurie's *The Begum's Fortune* was serialized in *Magasin d'Education* starting in January 1879. A shorter text, "Mutineers of the *Bounty*," his own version of the authentic tale of a rebellion at sea, appeared in Hetzel's magazine to fill out the year (since *Begum* was too short). Even when Verne was not working, Hetzel was busy on his behalf. Verne was also paid for use of his name on the second volume of the *Celebrated Travels and Travelers*, this one devoted to the eighteenth century. It would be followed in 1880 by a volume on the nineteenth century.

The year 1879 was doomed, however. It was impossible for Verne to forget that he had a son on the high seas. One day Michel, who had seemed so reasonable recently, touched off a seaboard crisis. In an ugly exchange, he struck the first mate—a mutinous act. Both Michel and the ship's officer took up their pens to inform the Vernes. "You understand," the stricken father wrote to the captain of *L'Assomption*, "that we consider that the fault was all on Michel's side, and that the first mate was right."

He then revealed to the captain that Michel had struck a superior before—and more than once. "And according to the doctors," Verne wrote, "he is subject to such crises during which he is not entirely responsible for his acts." In saying these things, of course, Jules was also hoping to curry the captain's favor. He was worried because the first mate had informed him that henceforth he would be "very severe" with Michel. So Jules, now very concerned, beseeched the captain: Without compromising shipboard discipline, could he not intervene in any future incident so that the voyage could be concluded "the least badly possible"? In order to convince the captain, he saw no other way than to darken the shadows: "I repeat that at certain moments he isn't in his right mind, and that could go very far!!"[10]

In letters dated that spring to the builder of *Saint-Michel III,* Verne discussed preparations for another cruise—a new paint job, but not an expensive one, and some minor improvements. In any case, he wrote in mid-April 1879, he didn't think he'd use the yacht before the middle of June or early July, given that his son was returning from India early in June. In a second letter, dated early in May, he repeated his preoccupation with the cost of the work being done on the vessel, "for times are harder than the breasts of pretty little girls, and we mustn't commit ourselves too far." He intended to wait until the following year to do some necessary work on the deck.[11]

What Michel Verne was to return to after eighteen months aboard a ship was another sea voyage, but this time it was a family occasion. Among the passengers, he found cousin Gaston, the eldest of Paul Verne's four sons (in fact, Gaston was Michel's senior by a year). They headed north, to a climate Jules much preferred to the Mediterranean, and to landscapes and seascapes that had delighted him as a young man: southern England, Scotland, and the Hebrides, islands off Scotland's west coast—scenery he would make use of in his novel *The Green Ray* (*Le Rayon vert*).

In late summer, Jules was off once more, sailing to Brest, again with Michel and Paul's sons—and Paul this time—to witness French naval maneuvers from close up. They pursued their voyage in stormy seas as far as Saint-Nazaire, which is as close as they got to Nantes. Anchored in the roadstead, they settled down for a peaceful night among the parked boats, but then the wind rose. A particularly violent gust sent a large three-masted schooner crashing into the *Saint-Michel III;* by the time the Vernes, who were still in their night-clothes, could climb to the deck, they could only assess the damages.

The stem and bowsprit had ripped away and they had lost their anchors. With deck lights ablaze, they had to tack among heaving, menacing vessels to a safe haven. "What a night!" exclaimed Verne in describing the episode to Jules Hetzel. "If the schooner had struck our flank we'd have gone down and your father would have had to finish *The Steam House* all by himself!"[12]

Sharing this experience should have helped bring Michel and Jules together—certainly that must have been one of the compelling reasons for all the sailing since Michel's return. "No serious complaint about Michel, apart from his prodigality and ignorance of the value of money," Verne confided to Hetzel when they were all safely on dry land and in Nantes. "And that is hard to believe. But in other respects the family here has noticed remarkable improvement."[13]

It was now time for the true test—to reintegrate Michel into the family circle in Amiens, where a normal high school would replace boarding school, clinic, and reform school, too.

But obviously, this attempt to bring Michel back into the family came too late. "All my fears are coming true," Jules lamented to Hetzel in early October. Michel's professor had told Jules that his son could pass final examinations as early as the following April but that "already he has stopped working." The catalog of his faults was familiar. "Dissipation, incredible debts, theories which are frightening in the mouth of a young man, the expressed desire to get money any way he can, etc.—all of it has come back." Verne called it "cynicism," a "slight touch of madness," and, worse, a "horrible *perversity.*" This was exactly what the doctor at the Mettray penal colony had diagnosed.

Jules felt that he could accept all of this as long as his son continued to study; when he ceased to do that, the family would have to make a decision. That meant "chasing this wretch from my home. . . . So at eighteen and a half he'll be in Paris, left to himself, with three hundred francs a month, three hundred francs that will be gobbled up in three days."

Jules confessed to Hetzel that he was miserable. "What would you do in my place? Throw him out and never see him again! But there's nothing else I can do. You can't imagine how I suffer!"[14] He wasn't getting any work done (or so he confided to d'Ennery).[15] Perhaps that is why he carried out his threat; he ordered Michel out of the house. Many years later, Jean Jules-Verne, although sympathetic to his grandfather's impossible situation, saw that as throwing out the baby with the bathwater. Michel had flatly refused to go to Paris, so his father, albeit with misgivings, had set him up in Amiens. "It's the first step on the way to life in Paris," he explained to Hetzel. "Or rather a step on the way to the madhouse."

Jules was now certain that Michel suffered from a form of madness—since "perversity alone can't explain all this." So the concerned father called on the law—the prosecuting attorney, the mayor, the police commissioner; each of them promised to keep an eye on his son. Jules himself had cut off all contact, but he had no doubt that Michel was up to his worst tricks, "being connected with the worst characters in town."[16]

For his part, Michel soon had a very good reason to remain in Amiens. Her name was Thérèse, and she was a singer in the company playing the Municipal Theater that season. In the stage tradition, she was known as "the Dugazon"—the generic name for young heroines in operetta (there had once been a flesh-and-blood singer of that name, a good and proper lady, as it happened). Only in our day did a persistent Verne scholar discover that her full name was Clémence-Thérèse Taton, and that she was twenty-two years old (nearly four years older than Michel).

As the bleak year of 1879 came to a close, Jules and Michel found themselves together in the office of the police commissioner. Michel was asking his father to take the formal step of emancipating him—declaring him an adult free of parental tutorship—so that he could lead his own life. Clearly, he was preparing the ground for a proposal of marriage to his Dugazon. This meeting only reinforced his father's conviction that Michel was mad.[17]

Apparently, the young actress was not a dissipated wench at all; the worst thing one could say was that she was an actress. (She was also the daughter of an orchestra leader in Biarritz.) "I said only that when he had fulfilled his voluntary military obligation and reached the age of twenty-one I'll decide what I must do," Verne informed Hetzel early in March 1880 (by volunteering and paying a tax, a young man could reduce the duration of compulsory service). Still, Michel Verne was hooked. He planned to leave town with Thérèse when her troupe moved on at the end of the month.

"I can only oppose that by sending him to jail," explained Jules Verne. "I used this method once and it only made things worse." Hence, the momentous decision: "Out of fatigue, disgust, and powerlessness, I've given him his freedom, at the age of nineteen!"[18] Sagely, he let Michel go, let him abduct the young woman, as Jules put it. Michel and Thérèse were now in Le Havre, where her troupe had begun a repertory season. "I don't think that now, when she is certainly his mistress, he'll go to England to marry, although he had them publish the religious bans in Amiens," Jules declared. "Debts and complaints from everywhere, I can't do anything about it. He's going straight to the madhouse, with misery and shame on the way."[19]

Michel's moods and his seemingly irresponsible acts would continue to upset his father—his liaison now, and later, and paradoxically, his rupture with Thérèse. He was his father's albatross, a bad boy all around. Later, his behavior improved. But at no time did he appear mad.

≈≈ ≈≈

JULES'S WORK WAS GOING BADLY. A CANDID REPORT OF A long talk with Verne that Hetzel compiled for his son's benefit revealed that fact. The meeting took place in early September 1880 and the manuscript they were discussing was probably *The Jangada,* although Hetzel's report may be misdated and therefore refer to a different book. No matter, the document provides an excellent opportunity to observe their relationship up close and to witness Verne's mood.

From the publisher's point of view, the new project simply didn't stand on its own feet; together, they agreed on a number of significant changes that, when made, could turn the manuscript into a good book.

Publisher and author had spent a long day together; then, after dinner, Verne urged Hetzel to look for other authors who could write Vernian books, in preparatory for the day when he would not be able to fill the opening pages of each new issue of *Magasin d'Education.* Hetzel was stunned. How many authors in the same situation would want their publishers to look for successors?[20]

Certainly *The Jangada* contained all the elements of a good Verne novel, including new, superbly exotic locales—the jungles of South America, Brazil, and the Amazon (the jangada of the title is a long raft designed to carry one hundred passengers on the river). The story introduces a planter who in youth was unjustly accused of theft and murder in Brazil; now peacefully settled in Peru, he takes his family to Brazil for the marriage of his daughter. He is recognized by someone who could have him hanged or exonerated, for this person possesses the encrypted confession of the real assassin. In the end, an astute and patient magistrate will break the code, saving the planter'slife.

The story allowed the author to describe a world he had not previously explored, but Verne thought the book's most important feature was the mysterious encrypted document. The plot hinges on it and its eventual decoding. He pointed out to Hetzel that in Edgar Allan Poe's "The Gold Bug," a story only thirty pages long, codes fill ten of them—"and Edgar Poe realized that this was the most important element of the book, even though nobody's life was at stake."[21] Like Poe, Verne was clearly taken by the possibilities cryptography offered: enhancing the mystery and bewilderment and inviting the reader's involvement.

◦≫◦ ◦≪◦

IN THE AUTUMN OF 1880 VERNE WAS INVOLVED ONCE AGAIN with a theatrical production—this time the adaptation of his novel *Michel Strogoff*. It was no accident that the doors of Paris's biggest theater, the Châtelet, with its 3,600 seats, had opened wide to receive the new play. The heroic stature of the central character, the importance of Strogoff's imperial mission, the dangerous and unpredictable enemy, and the vast area of Russia as a setting provided rich theatrical material. There was hardly any need to adapt or change the novel.[22]

Michel Strogoff opened on November 17, 1880—having been announced as a "great spectacle in five acts and sixteen scenes"—and even the blasé were stunned. "It isn't possible for staging to go further!" exclaimed the early review in *Le Temps*. "The splendors of these ballets, these parades of Tatars, of Gypsies, across a Siberia as sunny as India." The anonymous critic noted how the stage was crowded with soldiers—even mounted horsemen—and he described the trumpets, the shelling, and a battle-field strewn with dead warriors. D'Ennery himself was quoted in the review: "We'll be criticized for the production, but didn't Hetzel publish Jules Verne's *Michel Strogoff* in an illustrated edition? Well, the scenery is the illustration of the drama!"[23]

Nothing could stop *Michel Strogoff*. In its first run—which lasted until November 13 of 1881 (just four days short of a full year)—the theater was reputedly filled to capacity at each performance, which would mean a box-office take of twelve thousand francs per night.[24] A report in the authoritative *Le Temps* on the eve of the one hundredth performance of *Michel Strogoff* claimed that the play had already earned 1 million francs, d'Ennery's share totaling 75,000 francs and Verne's 55,000.[25] This indicates that the authors divided—unequally—a total royalty of 13 percent. Assuming 350 performances in the first year, Verne's share would have amounted to 192,500 francs, less an agency fee—perhaps 10 percent—bringing the total down to 173,250 francs—nearly 3 million present-day francs. And this was for the Paris run *alone*.

That was enough to herald what his grandson would later call "auspicious days."[26]

29

At Fifty-Five

A VERITABLE STROGOFF CRAZE GRIPPED PARIS. THE DISPLAY of pyrotechnics on the Châtelet stage had everything it took to stir the imagination. Nor did it hurt that relations between France and Russia were warming, the warmth actively encouraged by the French government. On the lighter side, the Russian look took hold: That winter, one simply had to go around in a fur hat. The craze crossed frontiers. In New York, the Kiralfy brothers, who had done so well with the stage version of *Around the World in Eighty Days*, were moved by a *New York Times* report on the play's European triumph to solicit exclusive rights for the United States (the *Times* noted that the dancers at the Châtelet had worn very short skirts and that American modesty would require some alterations.)

Once again, the Hungarian-born impresarios came up against the American tendency to treat matters of copyright offhandedly. By the time the Kiralfy production was ready in the fall of 1881, three competing versions opened at the same time (but only the authorized one—modeled carefully on the Paris original—lasted long enough to make business sense).[1] Jules Verne would surely have liked to have been there to see it. Writing to an American admirer at the beginning of October, he wondered whether he would have any success giving a series of readings in the United States. We don't know what Mr. C. B. Lockwood replied, but Verne did not make the trip.[2]

Another time, in Amiens, a local club called Cercle de l'Union held a party for its most eminent member, who had now surpassed himself with *Michel Strogoff* on the stage. "You return to us today," the Cercle president declared in his greeting, "after a new success acclaimed nightly in the theater by very welcome 'bravos.'" He wished it to be known, he said, that Jules Verne was "one of us."

In his reply, Verne noted that just three days earlier an English newspaper had announced his death as "occurring in truly deplorable circumstances." Verne quipped, "I have some reasons to believe that this news was premature, to say the least."[3]

<hr/>

"I'M RATHER CURIOUS TO KNOW WHAT YOU'VE ACCOM-plished on your new book," Hetzel wrote Verne in April 1881, implying that Verne hadn't given any recent sign of activity.[4] In fact, he was writing, although the end result would be one of his slighter tales, *The School for Crusoes* (*L'Ecole des Robinsons*). This novel was published at the beginning of 1882 in Hetzel's magazine. The Crusoe of the title is twenty-two-year-old Godfrey Morgan. Betwitched by the Crusoe myth, he longs to visit the farthest corners of the earth before marrying (marrying his uncle's ward, as it happens). So his uncle, a wealthy San Franciscan named William W. Kolderup, arranges for a mock shipwreck on a Pacific island that he had recently acquired in an auction. On his desert island Kolderup makes sure to provide not only proper food and other amenities but fake savages and fake wild animals; one of the natives becomes Godfrey's man Friday.

Alas for his nephew, some truly wild animals mix in with the tame beasts provided by Kolderup. These creatures have been introduced by the unsuccessful bidder for the island, who hopes thereby to render it uninhabitable. But Kolderup comes to the rescue in time.

As soon as that book was completed, Jules began another, equally challenging. *The Green Ray* had to be ready in the spring of 1882, when it was to appear as a serialization in *Le Temps,* before being published in book form in July. As if digging into old notes, the novelist drew on his memories of Scotland for the setting. Two inveterate bachelors who have raised their niece, eighteen-year-old Helena Campbell, now warmly encourage her marriage to the pedant Aristobulus Ursiclos. But first Miss Campbell wishes to see the famous green ray, the legendary atmospheric phenomenon sometimes visible at dusk along the sea. As her uncles take her sailing along the coast in search of what they think will be the right spot, they come upon a sailboat in difficulty. Miss Campbell urges them to go to its rescue, and thus she meets the young painter-poet Olivier Sinclair. He joins them on the search for the green ray, although the uncles make sure that their dull candidate for Helena Campbell's hand is never very far away.

Then, on an excursion to a deserted island, it is Olivier's turn to rescue Helena from a sea cavern—the legendary Fingal's Cave. When at last the green ray appears Helena and Olivier fail to see it, for they can look only into each other's eyes.

"The heroine," Verne explained to his publisher, "must be young but quite uncommon, even eccentric, all the while remaining proper; this has to be written with a light touch."[5] No reader can deny that the result is light; it was also the right size for newspaper publication.

That summer of 1881 the author himself embarked on another northern cruise. With his brother Paul, Paul's oldest son, Gaston, and a lawyer friend from Amiens, Robert Godefroy, Verne set sail for the North Sea, docking at Rotterdam. On the next leg of the voyage, they followed the German coast to the broad estuary of the Eider, navigating upriver and along a waterway cutting across the Jutland Peninsula to Kiel. At the time, the Kiel canal had not yet been dug, and sailing along the smaller Eider required passage through locks—some of them too narrow for the *Saint-Michel III*. "No matter!" Paul heard his brother say. "It won't be said that Bretons aren't obstinate when faced with an obstacle! The *Saint-Michel* is too long? So we'll cut off its nose!" That meant removing the bowsprit—and even after that it was a tight squeeze.

From Kiel they sailed north again on the Baltic Sea to Copenhagen. During the week they spent in the Danish capital, Paul and his twenty-one-year-old son, Gaston, climbed to the famous Baroque steeple of Our Savior's Church (Vor Frelsers Kirke), a feat that even today necessitates hauling oneself up the outer stairway that snakes around it. "You need a solid heart to do that climb," Paul noted in the log he kept of the voyage. "We didn't have enough with our two hands gripping the guardrail to maintain our balance and resist the violent gusts of wind." His son, less hardened than this seasoned sailor, began to show the effects of the tremors—"unpleasant enough when you feel them at a height of 330 feet." Gaston became greener by the minute, as if seasick; his eyes couldn't focus. It was definitely time to go back down.

On the descent, father and son encountered a German woman climbing up with a flock of children. The newcomers insisted on pursuing their ascent, but when Paul pointed to the drawn face of his son, the woman relented.

Paul Verne's account of these days spent with his eldest son is the only reliable document placing young Gaston and his uncle Jules together.[6]

⁓⃝ ⃝⁓

WE CAN GUESS THAT JULES WORKED ON *THE GREEN RAY* WHILE sailing; its episodic character—tailored to daily installments—would have made that possible. And for once, Hetzel (when at last he had the manuscript in hand late that winter) found almost nothing to say. "I read it thoroughly," he wrote to his author from his winter home in Monte Carlo in February 1882, "and of all your books it's the one that yields everything one can expect from it on the first try." Perhaps Hetzel had become mellow with age or was it illness and fatigue? "It's a smooth and agreeable piece of writing, very simple and delicate, which will appeal to readers of quality rather than quantity."[7]

Possibly the conviction that his future lay in the theater—in the bountiful theater of the d'Ennerys—explains Verne's apparent disaffection for the meaty books that had made his reputation. Those vintage Vernes also happened to be the books that *sold* best, so that if he felt that he could afford to turn away from them, it was surely because he thought that he had discovered a richer vein.

Or was it—and Verne himself would soon think this—that he had exhausted the possibilities? That there were no new worlds to conquer.

⁓⃝ ⃝⁓

FOR THE FIRST TIME IN HIS CAREER AS A NOVELIST, WITH HIS next theatrical project, Verne would invent a play rather than adapt it from an existing book. Hetzel, writing to his son in the spring or summer of 1882 in another of those confidential asides concerning their most valuable author, made it clear that Verne couldn't be budged from his present theatrical scheme—he took it to d'Ennery, not the other way around.

The title of this new play was *Journey Through the Impossible* (*Voyage à travers l'impossible*). Hetzel felt that what was needed was the *extraordinary*, not the *impossible*. "But you can't get this Breton to change a preconceived idea," he wrote.[8]

In the conception of their new musical extravaganza, Verne and d'Ennery were returning to the earlier heroic years of the *Extraordinary Voyages*. The play not only evoked but also anthologized some of Verne's best-known heroes, such as Captain Nemo and his *Nautilus,* Michel Ardan of *From the Earth to the Moon,* and single-minded Professor Lidenbrock of *Journey to the Center of the Earth.* Episodes were threaded together by a central character (new to the Verne corpus), Georges de Travental, described as the son of crazed old Captain Hatteras. Georges, also seemingly mad, is fought over by God and devil in his quest for the "impossible." (The devil is incarnated by another familiar character, Dr. Ox.) In his craving for travel, Georges most likely reminded spectators of the hero of Verne's recent *The School for Crusoes.*[9]

Opening night was an event, as were all first nights of Verne-d'Ennery productions. After that, however, came mixed reviews. The new production was called a hodgepodge, and d'Ennery was blamed for its "Catholico-reactionary mysticism which seeks to elicit tears of holy water from the audience." The critics had no way of knowing that d'Ennery had resisted this project at first.[10]

The most telling put-down was from Francisque Sarcey, who dismissed *Journey Through the Impossible* in the most eloquent manner he knew: He allotted precious few lines of his theater chronicle to it. For Sarcey, all the other plays of the week, whatever their defects, were "far more interesting and entertaining." *Journey* was a fantasy, the lighthearted genre that usually matched good and bad fairies; only this time, the creatures of the forest had been replaced by two men in dark suits talking about chemistry. "I didn't quite see what we've gained by the substitution," commented Sarcey. He did admire the conviction with which the cast uttered its stupidities, but that meant having to listen to talented actors repeating nonsense from eight o'clock until midnight. "It is to weep."[11] Even the text of the play vanished soon after its last performance; a researcher found it only in the 1970s—and then only in the archives of the theatrical censorship agency.[12]

But since theatergoers didn't easily turn down the opportunity to see a new d'Ennery play, not to speak of a d'Ennery-Verne production, *Journey Through the Impossible* ran for ninety-seven performances. The collaborators shared a 10 percent royalty equally this time. What they shared ranged from 600 to 1,000 francs in the first days, between 600 and 900 francs early in December, then between 400 and 500 later in the month; the high dropped to 800 in January 1883, then to 600 in February; on the play's final night, February 11, 1883, the authors divided 437 francs, representing their 10 percent share of the box-office take.[13]

By the time *Journey* closed Verne had written another novel, which would move to the stage in the same year it was published; in fact, the play opened just as the second and final volume of *Keraban the Inflexible* was being dispatched to booksellers. The subject of the novel lent itself to the kind of theater Verne's admirers had come to expect. A stubborn Turkish businessman named Keraban refuses to pay a new tax levied for the crossing of the Bosporus strait connecting the Sea of the Marmara and the Black Sea. Instead, he invites a Dutch associate to cruise with him around the Black Sea—ample pretext for exotic adventures. Keraban has a nephew he wishes to marry to a wealthy banker's daughter, but she is abducted, destined to be transported to a rich man's harem. En route, a storm upsets the vessel she is traveling on and the girl is saved by Keraban's nephew. But in order to see his nephew married within the time limit stipulated for him to receive a legacy, Keraban must cross the Bosporus all the same. He accomplishes it in a wheelbarrow on a circus performer's tightrope.

This play was presented in the late summer of 1883 at the Gaité Lyrique, its nineteen hundred seats placing it in a slightly less grand category than the theaters Verne had been used to, although it was still too large for a play with a small audience. And this time d'Ennery, Verne's famous partner, was not involved. Even that did not suffice to content critic Sarcey, however; he saw *Keraban* as another mindless pretext for pretty scenery, despite the fact that the staging lacked the dazzle of *Michel Strogoff* or *Around the World*.[14] Verne believed these hostile reviews—for Sarcey was hardly alone in his scorn—were due in some degree to d'Ennery, who this time had not been called in as coauthor. "We've had absolute proof of the pressures that were applied to obtain bad reviews," Jules Verne complained to Dumas fils. "To have dared do without a coauthor, what a crime!"[15]

Even without having to share, the author's pickings were poor, averaging some three hundred francs per performance in the first fortnight, then 200. *Keraban* closed just over a month after opening night.[16]

⁓ ⌇

THE NEXT BOOK STARTED OUT AS AN EASY JOB. FOR PASCHAL Grousset, who was now publishing his work with Hetzel under the pen name André Laurie, had begun this novel on his own. At some stage in the process Hetzel decided it was a natural for Jules Verne, so he paid Laurie two thousand francs and took the project away from him.

The book, entitled *The Southern Star Mystery*, was to be published under Jules Verne's name alone, and evidence exists that he made considerable changes in the Grousset text. "This will be an immense job," he told Hetzel, "but it doesn't displease me and I intend to use the matter of the false

artificial diamond right through to the end. . . . This changes the plot entirely, eliminating unlikely situations, and the result will be better."

Sending Hetzel another batch of manuscript, he asked that it be set in
type as quickly as possible, for he needed the galley proofs in order to estimate the book's length. "Once this is done I'll develop certain episodes
or eliminate them. . . . I'll use all the good events. Only one or two require some polishing." Given these letters to the rue Jacob, it appears
Verne made the book his own. Still, much of what readers liked in the
story existed before Verne became involved in the project.[17]

The setting for this novel is a new one for the *Extraordinary Voyages:* the
diamond mines of the Transvaal. The Southern Star of the title is the
world's largest diamond, a splendid jewel that has gone missing. The story
of the search for it and what becomes of the diamond once it is found
provide the plot. As the book opens, the original discoverer of the diamond, the good French engineer Cyprien Méré, is led to believe that the
outsized stone is nothing more than the result of his own experimental
production of artificial gems. No matter, he offers it to young Miss Alice,
daughter of mine owner John Watkins. When the Southern Star vanishes
suspicion falls on the natives, until it is determined that the jewel was only
swallowed (along with a great many other things) by an ostrich. Cyprien
Méré's African assistant confesses that this jewel once considered a counterfeit is in fact the genuine article, which he had hidden in his master's
oven.

Then a landowning neighbor of Watkins, the Dutch diamond cutter Jacobus Vandergaart, arrives with proof that some of Watkins's land actually belongs to him—including the parcel on which the fabulous gem was
discovered. Watkins is ruined, but faithful Cyprien Méré is ready to wed
Miss Alice all the same. Finally, Vandergaart offers the diamond as the
bride's dowry; he and Watkins, longtime neighbors and enemies, are rec-
onciled at last. Even when the Southern Star dissolves into powder because of improper handling after cutting, the young couple remains
resolved to marry. Cyprien's land claim is found to be valuable; with the
proceeds of his share, he and Alice will be able to live happily in France.

It was this book that convinced Jean Jules-Verne that his grandfather
was quite capable of portraying a sympathetic Jew in his fiction; Jean, a
well-meaning but not very astute reader, assumed that Jacobus Vandergaart, the generous benefactor, was a Jew. Verne doesn't say anything of
the kind; he identifies Vandergaart only as a Boer patriot. There does
happened to be a Jewish merchant in the story, but "the Jew Nathan," as
Verne calls him, is as evil as all the other Jewish characters in Verne's
work; by his "secret manipulations," we find him plotting the undoing of

the sympathetic hero. This bit of nastiness stands out in a book notable for its anticolonialistic and antiracist tone—which may, after all, have been the contribution of Paschal Grousset.

~~~ ❧ ☙ ~~~

WITHOUT ANY DOUBT A NEW JULES VERNE WAS EMERGING; success on the Paris stage had something to do with that. In Amiens, he had taken an important social step in October 1882 by moving to a splendid manor at the corner of the rue Charles-Dubois, only a few hundred meters along the railroad tracks. With its own watchtower, the house offered a lordly view over the old city, a garden, a winter garden, and space aplenty for receiving guests as well as for family living. Wonder of wonders, there were no visible railroad tracks beneath Verne's windows now; instead, there was a landscaped park covering a tunnel roof.

And Verne's name was beginning to count in Paris. In the space of a single year, 1883, he was to sit for portraits by a number of boulevard memorialists. Surely the most meticulous was published by the chronicler Georges Bastard in the late summer of that year. Bastard did what studio photographs of the time, solemn and standardized, could not; he presented a lively picture of Verne. "Average height, broad chest, his bearing upright and assured, hurried gait, graying beard and hair," he began "with the best-known name and least-known face that you might run into on the street."

For a popular weekly, this author described Verne's "delicate features, regular and sympathetic, illuminated by transparent blue eyes whose tiny pupils suggest a look of deep penetration and astonishing sharpness." Bastard observed that Verne's left eye often remained closed, and he suggested that it might be Verne's way of scrutinizing detail. More likely, this was a disability connected with his earlier attacks. "Finally, a cool expression, a stern appearance, if more preoccupied than somber—brightening on seeing an old friend." He was not a *young* man of fifty-five, Bastard commented: "His face is tanned by south sea [*sic*] storms, wind from the open sea, with a squint due to long winter hours working by lamplight."

Bastard went on to reveal his subject's attractiveness to women, to whom he seemed "a dream type, an adventurous knight"; as a consequence, they fell madly in love with him. Bastard knew this, for Verne had told him or showed him that he received "heaps of letters, declarations of affection, perfumed love notes." Verne was, in Bastard's view, "a mix of dryness and sweetness, coolness and friendliness."

This account portrayed Verne's life as quite ordinary—that of an average citizen: early to bed, early to rise. "In Paris you just can't find him. . . . He usually stays at the Louvre Hotel; but by eight in the morning he has dodged unwelcome visitors, slipped away from nagging solicitors, and the bores. He leaves the hotel after getting his mail at the porter's desk, outwits the cleverest of the hangers-on, climbs to the top deck of a horse-drawn omnibus, and hastens off to his affairs wearing a small round hat."

This observer had been able to keep up with Verne all the same, for he knew that Verne would go to rue Jacob to see the Hetzels, to the theater for rehearsals, to a bookstore, then out for an evening with friends. Bastard calls such a typical visit to Paris by Verne "an obligatory stay."[18]

In his own portrait of Verne—also written in 1883—Jules Hoche saw his subject as "one of the literary celebrities least known to the public." Even though his books had spread his name around the globe, his personality "contents itself with the recognition of a small provincial city." In Paris, said Hoche, giving a surprising impression, "Jules Verne leads the sad life of a derelict."[19]

Remarkably, the troubled personality lurking behind the surface of the false bon vivant was detected by a woman chronicler—a rarity for that time. Summing up his character in a "silhouette" portrait, one Olympe Audouard dared to observe that "his mouth has something hard and bitter that astonishes me, for life has been good to him. He is one of the rare men of talent who did not have a difficult start in life. He should smile at the universe and at human beings."[20]

※◎ ◎※

PERHAPS THE HARD AND BITTER MOUTH HAD TO DO WITH the French Academy. For, contrary to the observations of one of these chroniclers, who found Jules Verne devoid of jealousy and of "the petty passions of literary rivals,"[21] he continued to nurture a secret strategy. In 1883, when so many literary colleagues were calling attention to his renunciations, Verne was overlooking no opportunity to gain the consecration represented by election to the French Academy. Surviving letters sent by Verne from his small provincial city to Alexandre Dumas, friend and academician, reveal how much energy he could devote to planning his attack.

"My dear friend, and even more than friend," Jules began a letter dated April 29, 1883. In it, he thanked Dumas for his contribution to Verne's plan. Verne was now seeking through third parties the support of six other members of the French Academy. (Hetzel was obviously going to be the most instrumental.) Already, Verne had written to the Count of Paris "to ask his intervention with academicians connected by blood or by career to the Orléans royal line." Above all, he counted on Dumas for support; Verne said he was ready to rush to Paris at his friend's call, should his presence be required.

On May nineteenth, he dashed off another note to Dumas; he said he would be in Paris toward the end of the month, and he asked for five minutes of Dumas's time. Before the beginning of summer, Verne was back in Paris to do his own campaigning; he saw the dramatist Victorien Sardou (who had won a seat that Verne had coveted); Sardou seemed all in favor of a Verne candidacy. But he had a rival in François Coppée, who was seemingly backed by Duke Albert de Broglie, so Verne found an intermediary who could introduce him to the duke (who did *not* discourage him).

Writing to Dumas again on July fourth, Verne called attention to an event that could well change his fortunes. The Count of Chambord, Henri de Bourbon, who might have become King Henri V, was dying. In this case, the pretender to the throne would no longer be a Bourbon, but a member of the Orléans dynasty, specifically Jules Verne's friend the Count of Paris, Philippe d'Orléans, "and the *new king* has always displayed so much sympathy toward me that his support, I believe, will not be lacking."

Then came the disastrous opening of *Keraban* and the hostility of "a certain part of the press," as the author lamented to Dumas. In these circumstances, given the campaign that had been directed against him, he thought that Dumas would agree that he put aside any attempt to gain admittance to the French Academy for the time being. It would have been difficult enough to win election without this new handicap. "I've therefore returned to my corner, and to my work as a simple storyteller, less likely, I hope, to arouse the hatred of the critics."

Even with the death of the Bourbon pretender and the raising of his friend the Count of Paris to royal status, Verne feared that "the bad will of these detestable republicans will make his situation extremely difficult." He thought it better not to bother the count with a personal problem just then.

But in December, he was all flame again. Two more academicians had died, and another had been dead since April, with no replacement. Even if two candidates previously bypassed were successful this time, that still left a third chair. "If you think that I should resume the campaign that we abandoned, you will tell me," he wrote Dumas.[22]

30

LAST CRUISE

MICHEL VERNE, WHO IN 1883 HAD ARRIVED AT THE RIPE old age of twenty-two, was behaving the way his father expected him to behave. In a curious turn of events, Michel was about to walk out on his wife and their bohemian lifestyle to take up with a young middle-class girl. Jean, Michel's son, later described the family drama of Thérèse and Michel as a conflict between the demands of a professional singer obliged to travel and Michel's more sedentary way of life. The young couple was then living in the southern French town of Nîmes, (where they had finally married on the fifteenth of March 1884), living thanks to a monthly stipend of one thousand francs that Hetzel was remitting from Jules Verne's account. One can guess that after being shuttled from boarding school to reform school and then by ship half across the world, Michel was happy to have a home.

According to Jean Jules-Verne, temptation presented itself to Michel in the person of adolescent Jeanne Reboul, a talented pianist who was already giving lessons to help support her family. Her head was easily turned by the elegant gentleman on horseback who deliberately passed beneath her window regularly. When Michel ran off with Jeanne, who was nearly seventeen, she still had no idea that her elegant suitor was already married.[1]

By the time Jules Verne warned his son to avoid this new drama in his life, Jeanne was pregnant. Michel took her to Paris, along with his furniture and, as Verne confided to Hetzel, debts amounting to thirty thousand francs (the equivalent of more than half a million present-day francs).

During Jules Verne's long cruise in the summer of 1884, young Jeanne's mother and uncle traveled to Amiens and saw Honorine. "I refused absolutely to intervene," Verne told Hetzel. "Let them file charges for abduction of a minor if they wish to. Then I'll present my case. It will all end in an asylum, and if it doesn't end that way, and soon, there will be horrid scandalmongering in those Parisian circles I've avoided until now." He expressed a wish to talk to Hetzel about all this—including the possibility of arranging police surveillance.

Despite the upheaval in his personal life, Verne was writing. "You see that I am working, dear Hetzel, and doing it in the middle of the most frightful distress."[2] During his "miseries," as he called them in further notes to Hetzel, he was moving ahead with a book intended for serialization in *Le Temps*—*The Archipelago on Fire*—while getting *The Southern Star Mystery* ready for publication and working on the more ambitious *Mathias Sandorf*, which would fill three volumes.

The stress showed in his work. Hetzel had hoped that in the short novel *The Archipelago on Fire* his author would provide a panorama of the heroic Greek revolt against the Turks that had occurred in the 1820s; Verne preferred a smaller canvas, but he used the war as a backdrop for thwarted passion, piracy, and slave traffic. In the story, the slave dealer Starkos intends to marry Hadjine, the banker's daughter, who in turns hopes to marry a young French naval officer who has rallied to the cause of Greek independence. Hadjine is supposed to be sold into slavery, but the Frenchman rescues her; then both are captured by the traitorous Starkos. In the end, the good couple is saved by the navy; they marry, while, of course, vile Starkos is killed in the combat.

This was not quite what Hetzel had intended for the *Extraordinary Voyages,* and he voiced his disappointment. Reacting to his publisher's comments, Verne wrote Hetzel in December 1883, saying that he had come to a difficult turning point in his career. "You understand my situation with respect to our public," he explained to Hetzel in a moment of extraordinary self-analysis. "I don't have any more subjects we can consider extraordinary, such as the balloon trip, Captain Nemo, etc. So I must try to interest readers by a combination of things. And *Archipelago* is such a combination."

He said he was now working on another "combination novel"—"without rape or adultery or extraordinary passions"; he was calling it his *Count of Monte Cristo,* a reference to the wondrous adventure novel by the elder Alexandre Dumas in which a hero unjustly imprisoned escapes from an island fortress to gain riches, influence, and, above all, revenge.

"Obviously," Verne wrote, attempting to reassure Hetzel, "I shall always and to the extent possible hold to the geographical and the scientific, since this is the purpose of the whole body of work but whether it's the theatrical instinct that is pushing me, or because I want to tighten my hold on our readers, I shall be spicing up future stories as much as I can, using everything I can draw from my imagination in the rather limited range in which I'm obliged to work."

As if overwhelmed by this solemn declaration of artistic principles, he asked his friend, adviser, publisher, "Am I on the right track?"[3] It is interesting to note that at this point Verne had written fewer than half the novels that he would be published under his name in his lifetime.

VERNE DEFINITELY NEEDED A RESPITE FROM WORK AND FAMily trials. He had planed his escape since January, when the stress caused by Michel's latest crisis was at its height. First, though, he had to be in Paris to assist in the staging of a revival of the venerable *Around the World in Eighty Days,* then he would go to Nantes to prepare the *Saint-Michel III* for a Mediterranean cruise.

"Don't mention the trip to Raoul-Duval," he begged Hetzel. "I won't have room for him." There would be a boatload of passengers on this cruise—including Michel. "I didn't want to turn him down," Verne wrote."[4]

This would be the last such voyage on the steam yacht, announced a gazetteer. "Verne found motors too easy, too lacking in the unexpected"; the reporter let on that the following year, for a trip whose destination had not been revealed, Verne would trade the steam yacht for a large sailing ship that would take him where he wished to go—if the wind was right.[5]

Actually this was to be Jules Verne's last cruise.

Although Michel didn't make the first leg of the voyage with his father, Jules was accompanied by his brother, Paul, and one of Paul's sons. But which son is uncertain. Even family biographer Marguerite Allotte, who quoted liberally from Verne's unidentified nephew's chronicle of the voyage, did not know. Grandson Jean, who never got his hands on this logbook, just assumed that Paul's second son, Maurice, was its author; others with as little to go on have suggested that the chronicler was Maurice's older brother, Gaston, then twenty-four.[6] Since Gaston would be the protagonist of the next family drama—two years hence—it would be interesting to know whether he was the passenger and the author of the ship's log.

The party, however composed, boarded the *Saint-Michel III* in Nantes on May 13, 1884, sailing south along the Atlantic coast to Spain, then putting in at Vigo, as Jules had done half a dozen years earlier (but this time, a minor engine problem, not rough seas, was the excuse). Verne's nephew remarked on the beauty of the daughters of the French consul there, who, he said, had eyes only for Uncle Jules, virtually "a demigod!"

Then they sailed onward to Lisbon, where they spent a day with Verne's Portuguese publisher, who hosted a lunch attended by a group of artists and writers. The dinner that evening was given by the Portuguese naval minister. "At dessert," the nephew's log reads, "they gave Jules Verne his own works in Portuguese, piled up on a platter of Majorcan earthenware decorated with shellfish motifs, meant to be kept as a souvenir." The nephew carried away the crocker while his father and uncle took a walk with a young Parisian actress who happened to be on tour.[7]

On May twenty-fifth, the yacht docked in Gibraltar, where Verne was recognized and acclaimed by British sailors based there. "Their officers led him in triumph to their club. Punch, ovation, repunch. On the way back uncle claims 'not to be able to stand up straight on his hind legs.'" The next stop was Oran. Sailing into that harbor on May twenty-seventh, Jules found not only his wife but his wayward son, Michel. Michel was participating in this pleasure cruise of unspecified duration with his parents' blessing, leaving an abandoned wife in one town and a pregnant mistress in another.

A local newspaper documented the visit to Oran. The day after their arrival in the Algerian port, the local geographical society threw a party, to which officers of a moored frigate, local dignitaries, and the press were also invited. Jules Verne's entrance was greeted by the playing of the French national anthem. For his part, Verne promised to include Oran and Algiers in a book to be called *Journey Along the Mediterranean Coasts*.[8] Calling at Philippeville, the cruising party was invited to yet another punch party hastily convened by local notables. "If I am here," the author explained, "it's because the damned compressed fuel I took aboard had nothing of a combustible except the name. My yacht was adrift at the entrance to your bay." But he blessed the happenstance that had brought him there, for he had seen so many marvelous things.

In offering a toast, the mayor expressed the hope that the celebrated author would speak of Algeria in a future work; *Hector Servadac* could have been the book but its hero was drawn into space instead. Verne replied that Philippeville would indeed have a place in the book he was engaged in writing.[9]

The pursuit of the journey to Tunis seemed risky, for the sea was rough, and a ship had been lost near Bône. Honorine begged her husband to make this part of the trip overland and let the crew take the *Saint-Michel* to La Goulette, the port for Tunis. The railroad line was unfinished, and the old dirt track made for rugged going, until there was no going at all. They lunched and then dined at Sakhara in what Jules's nephew called a "bedbug inn." "We ate unnameable things, and everyone became ill. My uncle blamed my aunt who had forced him to travel through this dirty country." From Sakhara, they proceeded by coach on a painful journey over rocky roads and through dry hills. Alerted by a French official in Bône, the bey of Tunis dispatched a luxury train to wait for them at the next segment of rail line, and so they continued on to Tunis, with a side trip to fabled Carthage.

Then they departed aboard the steam yacht for Malta. They were forced to halt behind Cape Bon, northeast of Tunis in Sidi-Youssouf Bay—a deserted region. "My uncle pretends to be shipwrecked," reads the nephew's log, as cited by Allotte. "He is delighted. We take a dip in the sea; he does a savage dance around an imaginary stake. Michel, who is on board the yacht, fires a shot. Arabs invisible to us think they've been attacked and fire back."

Marguerite Allotte wondered whether this was the kind of adventure Jules Verne had waited for all his life. This candid view of Jules Verne acting up, if not acting out a story or two, is a splendid one. When the bad weather appeared to have subsided, the party made another attempt to cross to Malta, only to be delayed by another storm. To hear Allotte tell it, there was genuine danger now, a risk of smashing against hidden reefs and rocky cliffs. But daybreak brought respite, and a pilot guided them through the channel to Valletta, where they received another royal welcome.

There was a somewhat abridged itinerary for the return journey via Sicily and the volcano of Etna, then the Bay of Naples and, after that, Genoa. But Honorine had had enough of choppy seas, so the Vernes debarked on the lower Italian coast at Anzio, arriving overland in Rome on July fourth. The press was there to greet them, as were the port authorities, who confiscated their baggage, convinced that they had come from Toulon seeking to avoid a quarantine. The passengers were allowed to proceed to Rome, where they expected to find their baggage at the Hotel d'Angleterre. This did not prove to be the case, however. Only during the night did the authorities accept the evidence that the boat hadn't come from a suspect port, but from Sicily, so the baggage did not turn up until the next day.[10]

These were not ordinary tourists. They were invited to a Donizetti opera, where they were seated in the box of the prefect of Rome, and feted at the French embassy's ornate Palazzo Farnese. On July seventh, Verne and his party were given a private audience by Pope Leo XIII. In Allottte's book, the Pope is quoted praising the visiting celebrity: "The scientific part of your work doesn't escape me. But above all I appreciate their purity, their moral and spiritual values. I bless them and urge you to persevere." Paul Verne's diarist son commented, "A vision from on high" when giving his account of the impression the frail old pope—then seventy-four—made on their group. "Even my uncle is in tears."

The group then traveled north to Florence for an incognito visit. They intended to visit Venice in the same fashion; indeed, Verne registered at the Hotel Oriental under the name Prudent Allotte. But word got out. There were fireworks, and banners proclaiming EVIVA GIULIO VERNE! Another tourist, the savant Archduke Louis Salvador of Austria, called on him. After Venice, they headed for Milan, where legend has it that Jules Verne poured over Leonardo da Vinci's drawings and notes on manned flight.[11]

By the time the Vernes reached Paris, people were reading *The Archipelago on Fire* in *Le Temps,* which had begun daily publication of the short work on June twenty-seventh. It would run until August third, and the small-format book version would be released by Hetzel just eleven days after that, followed that autumn by the illustrated gift edition. *The Southern Star Mystery* was also nearing book publication, although it still had half a year to run in *Magasin d'Education* (this time, Hetzel would release both the original small-format book and the gift edition in November).

One piece of unfinished business Jules could handle in Paris was to put his initials to an extension of his contract. He did it despite failure to obtain a satisfactory response to a long-standing objection, a claim for justice expressed in a letter to Hetzel's son. The problem involved the illustrated editions of his work, from the very first in 1863 to those in 1875, for which he received no income from sales at all. "I do understand that you kept the ownership of these editions, since without the text the illustrations are worthless to you." This indicates that Verne still accepted Hetzel's logic, or rather the gibberish he employed to convince Verne that he couldn't be paid for illustrated editions, which made most of the money.

But since the ordinary editions of the same period now earned royalties, thanks to a later contract, Verne could not understand why illustrated editions did not. "It's painful to see that their books are dead for me." Verne wasn't complaining, though. He willingly accepted the fixed annual fee during those early years, but he said he wished to call attention to this "anomaly" for the future—*if* the Hetzels thought his argument had merit. "In the contrary case, we won't talk about it again."[12]

Apparently, the Hetzels chose not to discuss it again.

BY NOW, IN AUTUMN 1884, VERNE WAS WELL INTO MATHIAS *Sandorf,* that behemoth of a book (though a Lilliputian compared with its inspiration, Dumas's *The Count of Monte Cristo*). But if the Dumas opus provided him with a framework, this time Jules Verne had a virtual collaborator not in André Laurie but in old warhorse Hetzel, who in this last year of his life was to impose his will with more energy than ever. If Verne feared that inspiration and theme were failing him, Hetzel would show him the light. Letters fairly flew between Paris and Amiens, the longer ones from the rue Jacob.[13]

Verne's Dumas-like tale centers on a plot by Hungarian patriots— among them Count Sandorf—to extricate themselves from Austrian domination. They are found out when their traveling pigeon is caught with a coded message, quickly sentenced to death. The Hungarians escape, are recaptured—all except Sandorf.

Fifteen years go by, and Sandorf appears in the guise of the good doctor Antékirtt; ruined after the death sentence, he has made a new fortune, devoting it and himself to tracking down those who had denounced Sandorf and his friends. The action moves from Trieste down the Adriatic coast, to Sicily and the shores of North Africa, which had only recently been explored by the author. "In this novel," Verne declared to his publisher, "I wish the reader to learn everything he should know about the Mediterranean, which is why the action transports him to twenty different places."[14]

The cast of characters is endless (an index would have been helpful here). There is complicated matchmaking, the rise and fall in fortunes, immense risks, and an eventual victory for Sandorf, who leads the vile traitors to a legal execution, finds his lost daughter, then sees her married to the son of his deceased coconspirator. All this provides opportunity for vast geographical leaps, descriptions of the skillful piloting of electric-powered launches worthy of the best inventions of the *Extraordinary Voyages,* and an introduction to Sandorf-Antékirtt's private island, a scientific colony based on Utopian principles.[15]

The good people in *Sandorf* being Hungarian and the setting being

Italy, it was inevitable that Verne's villains would be Italian. Hetzel worried about that, so Verne reassured him, saying, "Please don't worry. I'm remaking a Sandorf desiring justice, not vengeance." But when he sent one of his many letters about *Sandorf* to Hetzel, he signed it "Your old Berquin," an allusion to a moralistic writer of eighteenth-century children's books—thus seeming self-deprecating. Perhaps, though, Verne was really saying it was Hetzel's fault if his bold tries were reduced to *berquinades*—insipid tales.

If so, Hetzel pretended not to notice. "You're rather kind to Berquin," he replied. "If from the heavens he read your letter over your shoulder he would be flattered by the comparison and your humility."

To familiarize himself with the Italian landscape, Verne was rereading Stendhal, notably *Promenades in Rome;* he told Hetzel he had opened *The Charterhouse of Parma* for the twentieth time. "How this novel grips me each time! And how superior it is to everything being written now."[16]

PART VI

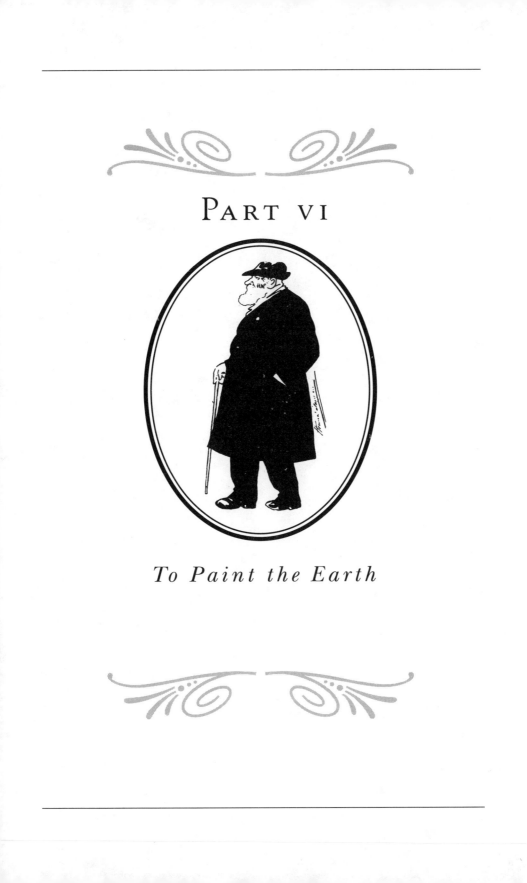

To Paint the Earth

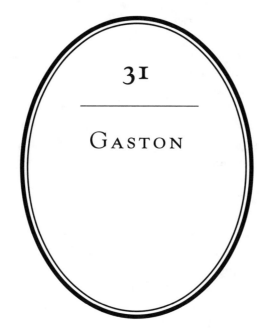

31

GASTON

THE COMPARISON OF *MATHIAS SANDORF* WITH ITS MODEL, *THE Count of Monte Cristo*—the senior Alexandre Dumas anchored his story in France, while Jules Verne set his along the Adriatic and Mediterranean Seas—demonstrates that Verne was fascinated by geography—the more exotic, the better. His attention to detail was reflected by an incident that occurred early in 1885, when he was confronted with a joint protest from the inhabitants of a Greek island mentioned in *The Archipelago on Fire*. The islanders were angry because Verne's novel had propagated the idea that they had harbored pirates during the war of independence waged against the Turks. Defending himself in a Paris newspaper, Verne pointed out that he had based his story "on the most reliable documents." One of them happened to be a popular account of Greek history in a series called *L'Univers pittoresque*. The other was a geographical magazine designed for family reading, *Le Tour du Monde*.[1]

He did seem to be turning his back on science, however, and no matter that invention and the anticipation of scientific discoveries had inspired his first successful works. With regard to Verne's changing attitudes about science, one Verne scholar distinguishes between the first Hetzel decade, when Verne seemed to glorify technological progress, and a second phase, during which he revealed "ironical detachment." Then came years of patent hostility toward present or future inventions, as well as an unwillingness to believe that progress made things better.[2]

Of all places, Verne chose the Academy of Sciences in Amiens to read a story he had just written for *Le Figaro illustrée*. In "Frritt-Flacc," the protagonist is a hard-hearted, rapacious physician who refuses to care for impoverished patients. Then on a wintry night, when a poor family offers all the money it possesses, the doctor agrees to call on a sick man. On arrival at his destination, he recognizes both the house and the sickroom as his own; it is he who lies abed after a stroke, and he who dies.[3]

THE BEGINNING OF 1885 FOUND JULES VERNE AS ANXIOUS AS ever to win election to the French Academy. A letter he wrote at the end of January to the younger Alexandre Dumas, ostensibly to ask his support for the production of a Dumas play in Amiens, ended with a reminder: "I see many candidates crowding around the door of the [French Academy]. You will tell me if I should join the crowd, even at the risk of being crushed."[4]

Meanwhile, he would cultivate his own garden. In a celebration to mark mid-Lent, the Vernes threw another grand party on March 8, 1885, this one in their own generously proportioned house on rue Charles-Dubois. Guests were invited to come in costume. Jules presided, dressed as a chef, and this time Honorine was able to be present, receiving guests in their grand salon decorated as a tavern. And was observed stirring the pot-au-feu in a huge kettle. In fact, a distinguished caterer had been engaged, and a reporter for the local newspaper found some of the guests still on the premises at seven the next morning to enjoy his food and drink.[5]

What the press didn't say was whether Michel Verne's lawful wife took part in the festivities. Early in June, poor Thérèse was still living with the Vernes—although "that wretched Michel" wasn't supposed to know it. The former singer, Verne told Hetzel, was "loved by all." Meanwhile, Michel continued to complicate his life and those of his loved ones. His companion, who would become his second wife, Jeanne, had just given birth to a son, Michel—"a child born of adultery," in Verne's words. Jules was convinced that his son was running up debts in Jeanne's family, which he referred to as "a family of crooks." Michel's property might be seized at any time, Verne informed Hetzel. Jules sought protection by putting the whole affair in the hands of one of the best lawyers in Paris. "How will it all end? I really don't know, and it keeps getting worse."[6]

Jean Jules-Verne, Michel's last son, born to Jeanne Reboul when at last she became Michel's second wife, said that his father was sinking money into businesses about which he understood nothing. Jean's summary of his father's subsequent career portrays him as a gadfly, prospecting for oil in Russia and Romania, working for a paper mill and then a bank in France, still later engaging in a pioneer venture in cinema although he was prepared for none of these careers.[7] Honorine's daughter Suzanne contributed to this view of Michel by recalling that Jules Verne made Michel sign IOUs. A stack of them accumulated, but they were later burned by Honorine.

Each time Michel threw himself into a new endeavor, he went to his father for support. "I'd prefer it if Michel did nothing; he costs me less that way," Jules confessed. "He never did anything useful," Suzanne's granddaughter later remembered, "except to be charming. Everybody adored him."[8]

<hr />

MONTHS EARLIER, JULES HAD RESOLVED TO DEDICATE *MA-thias Sandorf* to Dumas. Of course, Verne was still seeking election to the French Academy, and he needed the support of this academician, who was also his friend. "In this work I tried to make Mathias Sandorf the Monte Cristo of Extraordinary Voyages," Verne declared in his prefatory tribute. "I beg you to accept this dedication, as testimony to my deep friendship."

"You were right, in your dedication, to associate the memory of the father and the friendship of the son," Dumas replied in a letter that must have touched its recipient. "No one would have been more enchanted than the author of *Monte Cristo* by reading your luminous, original, and lively fictions. There is such an obvious literary consanguinity between you and him that, from the point of view of literature, you are more his son than I am. I've loved you for so long that I'm quite happy to be your brother."[9]

Before the year was over, Dumas once again thought there was an opportunity for getting his new "brother" into the French Academy. And Verne was ready to jump on a train for Paris. "You had told me: don't budge, and I didn't budge. You give a contrary order today: I obey."[10]

Verne had plenty of other things to keep him busy at the time. There was a new Grousset manuscript, which required only the master's finishing touches. In fact, Verne felt he deserved whatever compensation he received for rewriting Grousset's tortured prose. This time, however, the finished novel, *Salvage from the "Cynthia,"* was (at Grousset's insistence) to bear the names of both authors, Grousset using his nom de plume, André Laurie.[11]

Salvage has a lot of Verne touches in it—but Laurie often wrote Vernian stories. The novel harkens back to *Captain Hatteras,* with a northeast as well as a northwest passage around the polar circle. It also features an abandoned infant of unknown (but seemingly Celtic) origins, benevolent Norwegian foster parents, and an American capitalist villain. Thanks to Laurie, perhaps, the handsome and skilled (and eventually wealthy) orphan is French. It is a fast-moving yet predictable story, sufficiently padded to fill the twenty-four issues of *Magasin d'Education* in 1885.

BY THE BEGINNING OF 1886, VERNE WAS READY WITH HIS own shorter and slighter *The Lottery Ticket,* whose sole interest is its setting, a touching tribute to the author's timid explorations of the Norwegian hinterland at an earlier time. Here the reader is asked to believe that a lottery ticket used as a farewell note to his fiancée from a man drowning at sea is recovered by him after his rescue and makes him rich—a rich bridegroom. If the book has been forgotten, its fate was not undeserved.

Meanwhile, Verne was more seriously occupied with what was to be one of his most uncanny pieces of anticipatory fiction—this when supposedly he had turned his back on science. It was as if the author's fascination with technology had run up against his growing pessimism about the future. For *The Clipper of the Clouds* launched the flying machine whose concept he had promoted when he joined Felix Nadar in an association of like-minded souls to spread the gospel of heavier-than-air flight.

The new novel opens in Philadelphia, where officers of a gentlemen's club are debating the feasibility of balloon travel. They are convinced that the future is in lighter-than-air transport, once the proper motor is invented to steer it. Already they are putting together an "electric dynamo machine" that will enable their aerostat to become a dirigible.

Their meeting is interrupted by a mysterious visitor calling himself Robur; he scoffs at their balloon scheme, and when he announces his faith in heavier-than-air vehicles, he is all but lynched. In revenge, he abducts the club's president, Uncle Prudent, together with its secretary, Phil Evans, carrying them off in the *Albatros,* a flying platform drawn by propeller engines and maintained aloft by smaller helicopter blades. The adventure has begun.

Until then, innovators in Jules Verne stories had been well-meaning men of science, if at times they lacked tact. Until now, there had not been a Vernian genius of evil intent. Now, in Robur, there was one. The mad scientist intends to hold on to his prisoners, all the while revealing to them the marvels of the world as seen from the air. By what right? The "right of the stronger!" In the end, the captives find a way to destroy Robur's airship, however marvelous and monstrous. But the single-minded engineer quickly rebuilds it, and when Uncle Prudent's club launches its pathetic balloon, Robur attacks it (without harm to our heroes). Then Robur disappears, carrying his secret with him. But his day, and the day of heavier-than-air locomotion, will come. It is Jules Verne and not Robur who concludes, "As for the future of air travel, it belongs to the airship, not the balloon.

"It's the *Albatros* and its successors that will conquer the air!"

Once again, Hetzel got involved with the plot. The ailing publisher accepted Verne's sure science but wanted more of a story. Nobody now doubted that man would eventually conquer the atmosphere, even outer space, Hetzel argued. But that wasn't enough to make a book; the flight of the *Albatros* had to be "disturbing." The new novel would include an attack from the air, anticipating the horrors of twentieth-century warfare.

Robur was evil, but his airship was a work of genius. Evidence exists that Jules Verne considered his book an act of advocacy; he expected to hear "yelps from balloon partisans."[12] Clearly, he was stepping out of his role as a storyteller. Yet in sending instructions to his illustrator, the popular Léon Benett, with whom he had worked on *Around the World in Eighty Days* and *The Steam House,* he was at once precise and mysterious. He actually provided his own sketch of a cross section of the craft, adding some technical detail; then he added, "As for the general effect, fantastic and *cloudy,* I find it excellent. You will be right to show it only under these circumstances, so that readers can't examine it too closely."[13]

"I did an enormous amount of work on Robur," he reported to Hetzel when the book was ready at last. "How I wish I could allow myself the pleasure of writing, of living in fictions and forgetting reality!" exclaimed Hetzel. "But on that side my role is finished. . . . Yet it was the best of my life." He was en route to his winter quarters on the Mediterranean, but without enthusiasm, for it seemed a long journey now. Perhaps he knew that he would not have to make the return trip.[14]

IN FEBRUARY 1886, JULES VERNE COMMITTED ONE OF THOSE acts that cries out for interpretation: He sold the steam yacht *Saint-Michel*

III. At that point, nothing about his health would explain it, and he got the worst possible deal. The selling price was 23,000 francs, somewhat less than half of what he had paid for what was still a very technologically advanced vessel.[15]

Given Verne's problems with Michel, it is likely that he urgently needed cash to deal with his son's creditors, and the consequences of Michel's divorce and remarriage (that same year). It was also Jules's decision to continue to provide a regular living allowance to Michel's first wife.[16]

Another odd occurrence was Verne's attempt to make a writer of his son. Suddenly, in correspondence with the Hetzels, Michel became Michel *Jules* Verne (he was born Michel Jean Pierre Verne). In a letter of February twenty-third sent to Monte Carlo, Jules told his ailing publisher that he would soon be receiving a manuscript written by Michel: "Take all your time, my dear Hetzel, and don't fatigue yourself. . . . The important thing is to see if there is really something to this, and whether he should be encouraged."[17]

※◎ ◎※

ON TUESDAY, MARCH 9, 1886, VERNE SPENT THE AFTERNOON at his club, surely reading the latest periodicals and making notes. He was on his way home at half past five and inserting his key in the lock at 2, rue Charles-Dubois when there was a sharp report behind him, then another. He turned to look, and faced a young man with a revolver. At the same time, he felt a sharp pain in his left leg.

Accounts of this event are confusing, but apparently Verne, assisted by a neighbor or by a servant, attempted to catch the mysterious assailant. Only then was the attacker identified as Gaston, Paul Verne's son who had accompanied his father and his uncle to Copenhagen five years earlier, and who *may* have been the diarist on that Mediterranean cruise. Now twenty-six, Jules's nephew had been under treatment for monomania and a persecution complex. An employee of the foreign ministry, Gaston had been on a visit to Blois for the marriage of a cousin; on return to Paris, he had slipped away from the family, on the pretext of going to the barber. When he failed to show up again, everybody rushed around looking for him, but he found his uncle Jules first.[18]

Local doctors assessed Jules's injury, and soon a specialist was on the way from Paris. Fired from a 9-mm gun, a single bullet had entered the lower part of Jules's shinbone, just above the foot. It has been suggested that the bullet ricocheted after it struck the stone frame of Verne's front

door. In any case, it proved impossible to extract the bullet, and the prob-
ing only heightened his suffering.

There was no hesitation about what to do with Gaston; he was put under guard in a hospital. On the advice of the doctors, who said he was not
responsible for his acts, a judge ruled that there were no grounds for
prosecution. Therefore, he was confined to a mental asylum, and stayed
there all the rest of his long life.[19]

The news of the attack made the next day's Paris press, and the world
press the day after that.[20] Jules's Amiens friend and occasional sailing
companion Robert Godefroy was enlisted to inform the Hetzels, "This afternoon at five thirty Gaston, suffering from alienation of the mind, fired
two revolver shots at Jules Verne. Happily, only one shot attained him. . . .
I only have time to throw this in the mail so that it arrives tomorrow
morning," Godefroy wrote. Upon arrival, the news was quickly passed by
telegram to Pierre-Jules Hetzel in the south of France.[21]

Families have a way of interpreting events to suit their needs. In a letter sent to Nantes soon after the shooting, Paul Verne reported to his
brother-in-law: "He [Gaston] says that he wanted to draw attention to his
uncle to help him enter the Academy—it's the only explanation that we
can get out of him."[22] Family legend has it that Honorine and her daughter Suzanne were near the scene of the assault; after firing his bullets,
Gaston supposedly fell into their arms, babbling, "I wanted to kill uncle
Jules because he is so good that he must go to Paradise right away, so he'll
be very happy." In this version, passed down by Suzanne's granddaughter,
Jules Verne had been miserable because of an accusation that he was a
Jew.[23] Of course, Paul Verne, eager to find the best possible asylum for his
son, was now miserable. "It's a frightful sorrow for the whole family,"
Michel told an aunt.[24]

Half a dozen years later, when presumably Verne had had the time to
assess conflicting reports, he reminded a British journalist of "the sad
story of how a nephew of mine, who adored me, and of whom I was also
very fond, came to see me at Amiens one day, and after muttering something wildly, drew a revolver and fired at me, wounding me in the left
leg."[25]

Michel was at his father's side now. A fortnight after the shooting, he
wrote a letter to the press at his father's bidding. "My father is suffering
from considerable weakness, postponing the moment when he will be
able to get out of bed" (*Le Figaro*, March 26, 1886). The wound was healing, and the family was hoping that Jules would begin to walk in a few
weeks. It was only a matter of time, for the doctors assured the Vernes

that there would be no further complications.[26] Today, a surgeon would be able to remove such a bullet, thus preventing further infection and reducing the pain. Verne's team of physicians, however, could only use morphine to ease the pain and wait.[27]

⁓◦ ◦⁓

THE COMPLICATIONS WERE TO COME, FROM REAL AND AMATEUR psychoanalysts, for whom even a healthy Jules Verne had been a source of mystery. What hidden motive had driven Gaston? Was it jealousy? Did uncle and nephew have designs on the same woman?

One writer, who found Jules Verne "very odd," compared Verne's relations with Gaston to those he entertained in the same period with Aristide Briand, the implication being that this was a crime of passion.[28] Taking off from the notion that in offering explanations for the shooting, the family seemed to have something to hide—a notion reinforced by the "internal tensions" supposedly reigning in a family "composed of children of different parents"—another scholar and amateur analyst saw Gaston Verne as Jules Verne's favorite—the young man Jules preferred to his own son. According to this curious scenario, Gaston was jealous of Aristide Briand and therefore expressed his resentment by shooting his uncle Jules.[29]

Of course no evidence links the Jules Verne of the 1880s to Briand. So we can only turn to what we know, which is what the anxious father, Paul Verne, was told about Gaston: "The district attorney and the doctors I have seen declare him absolutely *irresponsible*."[30]

It is certain that the shooting brought the prodigal son, Michel, closer to his father. It was he, not Honorine, who took over the burden of communicating with the rest of the world during the early hours of Jules's incapacity. We find him writing (on March thirteenth) to Hetzel's son. Suddenly, the condition of Verne's first and only publisher, his friend and confidant, became alarming. Hetzel was almost seventy-two, and older than his years because of illness; he had been partly paralyzed—presumably as the result of a stroke—for the past two years.[31] "I should much appreciate it if you would write to me personally in Amiens," Michel begged Jules Hetzel, "in the event you have bad news concerning Mr. Hetzel. You know how much affection my Father has for him, and it would not be without danger for him to receive alarming news abruptly."

A telegram informed Verne that Pierre-Jules Hetzel died on March seventeenth. "I never saw my father as affected as he was when told of this misfortune," Michel told Hetzel's son in a letter dispatched the same day.

"He said sadly: We were never to meet again. Since then he doesn't speak at all. Not having been there obsesses him."

And it was Michel, now, at twenty-five, on the way to becoming a sober, respectful family member, who made the journey to Paris to represent his father at Hetzel's funeral. The service was held at Saint-Germain-des-Prés church, only steps away from the rue Jacob, where Hetzel had first met Jules Verne.[32]

On the eve of the funeral, Verne picked up his pen. "These are the first lines I have been able to write until now," he told Jules Hetzel. "They are for your mother and for you. I could not be present at the last hours of your father who was my father too."[33]

Jules Hetzel was now thirty-eight years old, already a veteran publisher himself, having grown up in the job alongside his dynamo of a father. He was only fifteen when the elder Hetzel began publishing Jules Verne, so he had had plenty of time to get to know his author.

SOMBER TIMES

COMPARED TO HIS HEROES HE HAD ALREADY SEEMED A sedentary man. Now he was condemned to an armchair in Amiens. He described his condition to Léon Guillon, the husband of his youngest sister, Marie, on April thirteenth, a little over a month after the shooting. "I've always got my leg stretched out—forbidden to use it—and a hole through a bone that won't close up." He could not go anywhere as long as nature hadn't repaired the damage, and at his age—he had celebrated his fifty-eighth birthday in February—"nature is lazy," he said. Even with "the hole filled in," as he put it, he'd have to learn to walk again; he'd limp for a long, long time, consoling himself by thinking of other famous limpers, like Lord Byron.

"My poor Jules is far from cured," Honorine added in a note of her own. "His life is certainly monotonous, with only work to distract him, and I'm very afraid that with time this will weary him." She found his resignation admirable, and the fact he did not moan and groan (she was doing that for him)—"and I constantly moan the fatality that chose to strike him".

Perhaps he didn't moan, but his rancor showed all the same. He was writing to Guillon about the marriage of Léon's daughter, Jules's niece Edith. "We give them our blessing in advance, and they'll be perfectly happy, especially if they never have children," he wrote—a devastating thing to say to a bride's father (devastating also in what it said about Jules's state of mind). "It happens to be my way of seeing things—not yours apparently, since you have an infinite number of them (I don't even know how many). So God save the newly marrieds from this excess of divine blessings!"[1]

Nor did he try to fool Pierre Véron, the Parisian journalist and wit, even if Véron, as editor of the satirical magazine *Le Charivari,* was more at home with the lighter side of boulevard Paris. In a close-up portrait of his subject—surely written after a visit to the convalescent in Amiens—the journalist noted a considerable change in the famous novelist and playwright. Verne's "features . . . now show signs of weariness, which have replaced the indolent expression that used to be customary. His head, which seems weighted down by meditation, bends to one side. His gaze is clouded." The only positive note Véron observed was a "rosy complexion," but he suggested that might have been a sign that his host was running a fever.

"No transformation could ever make an exuberant or a loquacious man of Jules Verne, believe me," Véron said in summation. "But ever since his cruel accident he has become a sorrowful man."[2]

"I still have only one leg," Verne informed Alexandre Dumas in a letter dated August 24, 1886—five and a half months after Gaston's act. "They've perforated the tibia, and it takes months and months for that to heal. I therefore advise that when one is to receive a bullet in the joint of the foot, to receive it at twenty rather than at fifty-eight."[3]

He was writing to his academician friend to announce that he had sent him a copy of the first edition of *The Clipper of the Clouds.* He also had one delivered to his comrade in aviation theory, Felix Nadar. "You will find in it all your ideas about heavier-than-air flight," he advised Nadar—evidence enough that the book contained a kernel of serious anticipatory science. "I wanted to return to that question in a purely imaginary way. We were twenty-five years younger when we used to talk about these things."[4]

Perhaps it was more to kindle a journalist's curiosity than to take up a cause again, but he wrote along similar lines to his old comrade from stock market and theater days, Philippe Gille, now an editor of *Le Figaro:* "It's the real rejoinder to *Five Weeks in a Balloon.* . . . I'd be happy if this question came up for discussion again." With his one leg, he added, he resembled a heron; the doctors thought recovery would take a year, "and even after that I'll be limping for a long time."[5]

Late in October, the mayor of Amiens, Frédéric Petit, appointed Jules Verne to the management board of the regional Picardy Museum. In thanking the mayor, Verne promised to call on him as soon as his health permitted.[6] Describing his daily routine earlier that month to Jules Hetzel, now fully in charge at the rue Jacob, he explained that "if my wound still hasn't healed it's because tiny splinters are still coming out of it"; all the doctors in the world couldn't get them to out more quickly. He was getting around with a cane, walking about town, going to the theater as well as to his club. The problem now was with his good leg, which was tired after having done the work of two for several months.[7]

"I HAVE ENTERED THE SOMBER DAYS OF MY LIFE," HE AN-nounced to Jules Hetzel in a letter of December 21, 1886—a letter in which he enlisted the young publisher's support for his promotion to higher rank in the Legion of Honor. He made it clear that his own infirmity was not at the top of his list of complaints. "The future is rather threatening for me because of the affairs you know about, and I confess that if I couldn't bury myself in hard work—work that I like doing—I'd be wretched." But insofar as the Legion promotion was concerned, "don't do more than is necessary," he instructed Hetzel.[8] He might just as well have said, please do everything you can to get me promoted.

Verne was working hard, as if nothing had happened. But somber times aren't necessarily conducive to working well, and even Jean Jules-Verne in his biography of his grandfather was to call the output of these years inferior to the earlier books, saying the later work revealed a certain lassitude.[9] Fortunately, even when he wasn't working, money usually came in all the same. That fall, the roisterous *Around the World* was back on the stage. If the actors seemed less convincing than their predecessors, the scenery was freshly painted and nobody minded, or so Francisque Sarcey thought. "Success is guaranteed for this show," he wrote in *Le Temps.*[10]

One of the books betraying the lassitude of which his grandson spoke was *The Flight to France,* a patriotic tale—"very patriotic," the author informed his publisher, "of a kind I think will please readers of the *Magasin.*"[11] The hero is a young German of French Protestant origin. He is obliged to fight France under the orders of a Prussian officer who desires the same young Frenchwoman that he does. After a clash with this officer and the imposition of a death sentence, the hero makes his way to France, to serve under its colors. The story seemed good enough for *Le Temps,* which began to serialize it at the end of August 1887, and short enough to have completed its run at the end of the following month, just prior to book publication.

It was still too short for the gift format. So Jules came in with another patriotic text, this one directed against the hereditary enemy across the Channel. The short story entitled "Gil Braltar" takes the reader to Britain's rock fortress at Spain's southern tip. Clearly this citadel filled with redcoats, where no stranger could walk at night, had impressed and irritated Jules Verne in his seagoing years. His hero, a hirsute, seemingly crazed hidalgo named Gil Braltar who hides from the world in caves, has come back to chase the English from Spanish soil. He and his strange band—hundreds strong—overrun the streets of the tiny outpost; the pompous British general, when he is informed, cries out, "Gibraltar wrested from England by orange vendors! . . . That will never happen!"

When the hidalgo is subdued, it is discovered that he leads an army of monkeys. How embarrassing for the United Kingdom if its soldiers, conquerors of people in all climes, fall to a horde of simple chimps! But suddenly, the chief monkey appears and leads the creatures back into the hills. Had the hidalgo insurgent Gil Braltar managed to escape from the custody of the British?

In fact, we shall see that it is the British commander, General Mac Kackmale, who has covered himself with his captive's monkey skin to fool the animals and lure them away. (Verne adds that the general looked so much like a monkey that he convinced the real ones.) The feat will win the Crown's highest distinction for the senior officer. And from then on the British would send only the ugliest of their generals to command the fortress—since monkeys were clearly the chief threat.

"Gil Braltar" was followed by *Two Years' Holiday* (*Deux Ans de Vacances*), whose preface revealed that this was to be another Robinson Crusoe story. "Despite the infinite number of novels in the Robinson cycle," wrote Verne—as if he felt it necessary to apologize—"it seemed to me that to complete the cycle one had to show a troop of children whose ages range from eight to thirteen, abandoned on an island, struggling for survival despite conflicts due to differences in nationality—in a word, a boarding school of Robinsons."

Indeed, fifteen children, ranging in age from eight to fourteen, end up on Verne's desert island after a shipwreck. One is a competent and serious French child (in truth, the whole tribe is likable, apart from four arrogant British brats, with an American lad to maintain equilibrium). Two years go by—the two years referred to in the title—before a second shipwreck brings five criminal mutineers to the island. Fortunately, better winds bring two Americans to the rescue. This novel is remembered by Verne fans because the good French lad in the story is called Briant, seemingly a reference to Aristide Briand, the Nantes high school lad Jules had met a decade earlier.[12]

The book that helped Jules Verne fight off depression, the miracle cure in the weeks and months following the assault by Gaston and old Hetzel's death, was certainly *North Against South* (*Nord contre Sud*), an ambitious saga of Dixie during the U.S. Civil War. The setting is Florida, the hero a slave-owning Northerner waiting for the day he can free his slaves. This book provided Verne with an opportunity to display his intense feelings about slavery and his unambiguous sympathy for the abolitionist cause.

LETTERS EXCHANGED BETWEEN VERNE AND JULES HETZEL betray a subtle change in the relationship. Now Verne was the senior partner; that and his infirmity made it certain that in the near future it would be Hetzel who would travel to Amiens, not Verne to Paris.

Despite the distance between Amiens and Paris, Verne and Dumas kept up a dialogue. "You ask for news of me," Verne wrote to Dumas on January 27, 1887, well over ten months after his nephew's assault. "I'm not doing well at all. The wound or rather the operation that had required the perforation of the bone left a wound that doesn't heal. What's more, the joint has stiffened, and I shall certainly be lame." He summed up his feelings: "This accident will have changed my life entirely, and I'll never be as active as I was. But if I can carry on to the end the task I gave myself, I shall not complain."[13]

Nor were these somber times about to end. In February, Jules's mother died. "[She] simply passed away, without being ill, at eighty-seven," he wrote to Jules Hetzel. He had been expecting this news for some time, but that didn't make it less painful for him. "This breaks the link between members of our large family." He couldn't even go to Nantes for the funeral; Honorine went in his stead.[14] Only in early June would he announce some progress. The wound was healing, although his legs were still not very sturdy. "They'll improve."[15]

Certainly Hetzel could not complain about the output of his star author. At any one time, Verne was working on two or even three books in various stages; he was honoring his commitment to readers of the fortnightly magazine, keeping to the stipulated annual production. In 1887, two volumes of *North Against South* were published and the single-volume *The Flight to France,* plus the illustrated edition of his Civil War novel at gift-giving time. All the while, he continued to work on his theater projects. With two experienced theater men—another three-way split of royalties—he saw *Mathias Sandorf* to the stage of the Ambigu. A large-scale subject, it could have made a lively play, but the public didn't like what it saw and heard, and the play closed before Verne was in a condition to see it.[16]

At any rate, he used his damaged foot as an excuse for not going to Paris to see *Mathias Sandorf*.[17] But he did leave Amiens all the same, boarding a train for a quite different direction—Belgium and the Netherlands—to give a series of talks. This accomplished writer was a boring lecturer, and he obviously knew it, for he almost always read a story instead.

But sometimes even a story bored his audience. This apparently happened with the curious "Adventures of the Raton Family," which was labeled a fairy tale by its author. Apparently, Jules Hetzel never appreciated it, as he kept postponing its publication. Although the vocabulary was acceptable to adults, the text was couched in the tone of a children's bedside story, its repetitious humor fated to bore grown-ups. In this tale, a good fairy seeks to help a young man, formerly a rat, who still loves a young female rat, but she is also coveted by a wicked man, who in turn is assisted by a bad fairy. Successive transformations happen to the rat family, until they finally become humans.

"Mr. Jules Verne is not a speaker," a reporter in Liège told his readers after the author's appearance in that French-speaking city of eastern Belgium, "or he would have found material for an extremely interesting lecture on his busy career." Unaware of what was coming, the public crowded into the theater all the same. "The mountain, alas, gave birth to a mouse. Actually not a mouse but a rat—indeed a family of rats. Despite their good will the Liegeois public seemed 'only slightly' amused."[18]

PERHAPS IT WAS THE PROSPECT OF LONG YEARS OF IMMOBIL-ity, as well as the repeated rejections of his quest for status in Paris. Whatever the reason, Jules Verne was now to make a still more decisive commitment to Amiens, the town where he had chosen to spend his life seventeen years earlier. He was already a member of every private club imaginable; total involvement seemed to call for a touch of politics.

The hitch was that Amiens was snugly in the hands of the republican center, and to have any chance of winning office, Verne would have to accept its sponsorship. Robert Godefroy, the lawyer who had twice sailed aboard the *Saint-Michel,* was connected with the administration, and he agreed to open some doors for his friend.

Mayor Frédéric Petit was an energetic republican, partisan of a nonreligious France. Godefroy chose to sound him out by letter. "Ten years ago you'd have found this idea stranger than strange," he wrote to the mayor, "for this nice man, while keeping his distance from politics, hardly passed for an aggressive republican. On the contrary, I was aware of his sympathy for the Orléans dynasty. What can we do? Like so many others he is a victim of childhood memories." Verne, he explained, had grown up in the reign of Louis-Philippe, that golden age of the middle class.

Yet back in 1848, Verne had supported the incipient republic. And as an intelligent man, he now realized that democratic government was what the majority of Frenchmen demanded, Godefroy explained. Would Petit be willing to include Verne on his ticket for the city council? Godefroy suggested that perhaps the famous writer's name would attract additional support. He told Petit that when Verne asked whether he had a chance, he had replied that Verne would win by an overwhelming vote.[19]

"They accuse Mr. Jules Verne of being an Orleanist," mayor Petit's own newspaper, Le Progrès de la Somme, declared on the morning of the election. "It isn't true. Apart from his personal relations which concern nobody, Mr. Jules Verne, this glory of our city, has always behaved as a loyal republican.

"His very presence on the ticket of Mr. Frédéric Petit is a guarantee of his opinions."[20]

On the first ballot on May 6, 1888, Verne came in twelfth on the mayor's list, with 6,598 votes, not sufficient for election. But the following Sunday (May thirteenth) he received 8,591 votes (of a possible total of 14,000), assuring his victory. Mayor Petit was even further down on the first ballot, with only 6,025 votes, but he won on the second—along with everyone else on his ticket—with 6,884 votes.[21]

But after seeing how Le Progrès described his adherence to Petit's ticket, Verne fired off a letter to deny that he had ever changed anything in his political convictions, to which he had been true all of his life. He belonged to the conservative party, he insisted, and it was as a conservative that he had been accepted on the mayor's ticket "for the purpose of obtaining a purely administrative mandate." A gesture all to the honor of the mayor, said Verne.

In a letter to his childhood friend Charles Maisonneuve, Jules stressed his convictions: "My sole intention is to be useful, and to obtain certain municipal reforms," he explained. "Why always mix politics and Christianity with administrative matters?" He was all for order; he sought "a party that was reasonable, balanced, respectful of life." Of course, he regretted the exiling of the pretenders to the throne (by a law passed just two years earlier). "So what you call my 'prestige,'" he assured Maisonneuve, "can only serve respectable causes. I should add that since my in-capacity obliges me to accept a more sedentary life, it's useful for me to remain in contact with events, and with my fellow men."[22]

His role in municipal affairs was preordained. Verne specifically asked to be appointed to the committee responsible for education, fine arts, museums, theater, and festivals.[23] He actually worked at the job, and there is ample evidence of his willingness to undertake even humdrum activities, attending the dreariest of committee meetings (there was sel-dom any other kind).

IN A YEAR MARKED BY RESIGNATION, JULES VERNE ALSO LENT a hand in the choosing of a new career for his son. Michel was now re-married, and seemingly happy. Jean, Michel's son by this second mar-riage, said that his grandfather finally met Jeanne Reboul, Michel's second wife, in 1888, and that he liked this "little woman full of good sense and bright intellect." He saw in her an ally for transforming Michel into a responsible adult.[24] Further evidence of Jules's approval was the fact he accorded Michel one thousand francs a month, remitted by Het-zel from moneys due to the author.

Whether Jules encouraged Michel because he felt his son had talent or because he realized Michel was a failure in business is not known. Per-haps Michel's urge to create was irresistible and his father was merely channeling it. Family legend paints Michel as keenly desirous of a literary life. For her part, Jeanne got her husband to focus his talents. She being a musical woman, one product of her influence was an opera, the music composed by Michel.[25]

He also tried poetry, and at his father's recommendation, he had sent off a manuscript to Pierre-Jules Hetzel in February 1886, shortly before Hetzel's death.[26] One wonders whether Hetzel, even if he had been in better condition, would have been receptive to verse, even though it had been written by the son of his most profitable author.

But perhaps Michel could write like his father. Perhaps he could even *replace* his father, say in areas Jules Verne was neglecting now. Two more years went by before he tried.

Meanwhile, Michel was getting another push. A letter survives from Jules Verne to the editor of *Le Figaro*'s weekly literary supplement, ex-pressing satisfaction that the editor liked Michel's submission and was go-ing to use it. "It's so important for my son that I cannot thank you too much, and believe me that I do it from the bottom of my heart."[27] In all,

Michel wrote nine pieces for the paper, the first published on May nineteenth, three more in June, one in July, and one in August, two in September, and the last in early November. It couldn't have hurt that the series was called "Zigzags Through Science" and the author signed them with the invented name Michel Jules Verne.

It is not known how long it took Michel to write one of his *Figaro* pieces, or how much advice and editing (if any) he got from his father. However, his stories speak for themselves—they are light, interestingly written, and more than a little reminiscent of his famous father's work. Proof of that is the long-held conviction of Verne fans that *he* was the author of "An Express of the Future," actually one of Michel's *Figaro* pieces. They were encouraged to their illusion by the fact that later reprintings identified the tale as Jules Verne's. Michel—alone or in concert with his father—had decided to sign his work Michel Jules Verne for commercial reasons; from there, it was not far to *M.* Jules Verne, which allowed a troublesome ambiguity, since the *M* could be read as Monsieur. Thus, when "An Express of the Future" was reprinted five years later in the Paris magazine *Les Annales Politiques et Littéraires,* it was signed M. Jules Verne. But even the editors of this periodical were confused; the cover identified the author simply as Jules Verne, without the initial *M.*[28]

"An Express of the Future" clearly fell within the realm of anticipatory science. The setting of the story is an American railway station—in fact, the terminal of the Boston to Liverpool Pneumatic Tubes Company, for Europe is now linked to the United States by undersea tubes, through which railway carriages are driven by compressed air. In Michel Verne's story, the imaginary inventor of the system explains the technique that allows him to send passenger cars between the United States and Britain at eleven hundred miles per hour—for a trip lasting two hours and fourteen minutes.

The narrator sets off for a speedy, silent ride. But suddenly, he feels dampness on his face. He is worried that the tube has burst from the pressure of the ocean and that the sea will rush in and drown him. He calls out in panic—only to wake in his garden, where he had been napping until heavy raindrops began to fall. He had dozed off while reading a newspaper article about a proposed pneumatic tube railway, whose inventor was doubtless also dreaming.[29]

33

MEETING
NELLIE BLY

PERHAPS MICHEL VERNE WAS HAVING A GOOD DEAL MORE *FUN* than his father ever had, but he was not easy to place as a gainfully employed writer. The series of "Zigzags Through Science" in *Le Figaro* came to an abrupt end. Actually, there may have been more stories written by Michel, at least a final one: the fantasy called "The Day of an American Journalist in 2890," for example. Originally, this story was entitled "In the Year 2889." Signed by Jules Verne, it was published in English in the February 1889 issue of the New York monthly *The Forum*. And why not? Jules was sufficiently well known in the United States to be able to write and sell a story directly—provided that he use his own name on it.

The plot thickens as we scrutinize a letter Jules Verne wrote to Jules Hetzel at the time of American publication of the story: "The article I mentioned during your visit to Amiens appeared in the *Forum* in New York. After an understanding between Michel and myself, it was entirely written by him (keep this between us) and it seems to have been appreciated a great deal. As you had said, of the fee of 1000 francs I gave 500 to Michel; 500 remain to be split between us, so you can deduct 250 francs from my account."[1]

The language of the story as published in the New York magazine is clumsy; it reads like a poor translation, but nowhere did it say that it was one. "Little though they seem to think of it, the people of this twenty-ninth century live continually in fairyland," it begins. "Could they but compare the present with the past, and so better comprehend the advance we have made! How much fairer they would find our modern towns, with populations amounting sometimes to 10,000,000 souls; their streets 300 feet wide, their houses 1000 feet in height; with a temperature the same in all seasons; with their lines of aërial locomotion crossing the sky in every direction! If they would but picture to themselves the state of things that once existed, when through muddy streets rumbling boxes on wheels, drawn by horses—yes, by horses!—were the only means of conveyance."

Of course, this is reminiscent of *Paris in the Twentieth Century,* the novel vetoed by the senior Hetzel and locked away. In the 1889 story, electric power has been mastered—drawn from the sun, from water pressure, from wind, not to forget "the electricity stored in our globe." The latest wonder is the new headquarters of a newspaper called *Earth Chronicle,* founded by George Washington Smith, now run in Centropolis by his descendant Fritz Napoleon Smith. (In published French versions of the story, the paper is the *Earth Herald,* successor to the *New York Herald* founded by Gordon Benett [*sic*]; the present owner is his grandson Francis Benett. Of course, a real James Gordon Bennett founded the actual *New York Herald.*)

> Every one is familiar with Fritz Napoleon Smith's system—a system made possible by the enormous development of telephony during the last hundred years. Instead of being printed, the Earth Chronicle is every morning spoken to subscribers, who in interesting conversations with reporters, statesmen, and scientists, learn the news of the day. Furthermore, each subscriber owns a phonograph, and to this instrument he leaves the task of gathering the news whenever he happens not to be in a mood to listen directly himself.

To speak to his wife, then visiting Paris, Smith employs the "telephote." ("The transmission of speech is an old story; the transmission of images by means of sensitive mirrors connected by wires is a thing but of yesterday.") In the office, reporters read the news to subscribers, but they can also transmit images of an event. "Thus the subscribers not only hear the news but see the occurrences. When an incident is described that is already past, photographs of its main features are transmitted with the narrative."

Then there is the advertising department, which projects its messages on clouds (the sky is cloudless on the day the story takes place, so the publisher suggests the development of artificial clouds). Accounting is done on a Vernian computer: "Thanks to the Piano Electro-Reckoner, the most complex calculations can be made in a few seconds."

One passage in the story is certainly Jules Verne's contribution. In the year 2889, Great Britain is a colony of the United States, while France possesses Africa and Russia governs India. Now the only territory the English can call their own is Gibraltar.[2]

At this time, Verne was writing a workaday novel. In *A Family Without a Name* (*Famille-Sans-nom*), the curtain rises over French Canada, which has taken up arms against the dominant British. One of the rebel leaders is Jean-Sans-Nom, who with his family fights alongside fellow French Canadians to wash away the stain of treason to their cause committed by Jean's father during an earlier insurrection. An exciting story told without excitement, giving vent to the author's hostility to established authority, and above all to his Anglophobia. But the patriotism and didacticism seemed just right for the Hetzel magazine, all twenty-four numbers of which it filled in 1889. Book buyers, however, found it was something they could live without.[3]

The savant schemers of Verne's next book, *The Purchase of the North Pole* (*Sans dessus dessous*), were familiar to his readers, for in a more benign mood they had fired a cannon shot to the moon. This time, the heroes of *From the Earth to the Moon* and *Around the Moon* are strictly businessmen; incorporated as Barbicane & Co., they bid for the unclaimed territory surrounding the North Pole—acquiring this seemingly worthless property for $814,000.

What they are after is the coal buried beneath the Arctic Circle, inaccessible due to the climate of the polar region. The Gun Club's famous engineer, J. T. Maston, is to build a cannon whose recoil will be sufficient to modify the earth's axis, thereby placing the North Pole under the sun's rays; when the ice melts, the partners will be able to exploit the mineral resources of the region at leisure.

As the project progresses, fear of its consequences grows. What about the shock, the abrupt change in sea level? When the United States government launches an investigation, the promoters vanish; when Maston is found, he refuses to speak (arrested, he swallows his notes). The government learns of the plan to utilize the recoil of the powerful charge to alter the earth's position. But where will the shot be fired? Without knowing that, distressed populations cannot know which parts of the earth will be flooded, which dried out.

Finally, the investigators discover the site of the projected firing—Mount Kilimanjaro in Africa—but they are too late to prevent it. In fact, the Barbicane team will not use an actual gun—to build one large enough to do the job was beyond human capability—but a gallery bored through the mountain. In the end, the shot fails to accomplish the shift in axis.

To write his book Verne called on a specialist, a thirty-five-year-old mathematical whiz named Albert Badoureau, then a mining engineer assigned to Amiens. Verne put him to work on the logistics and the ballistics—and paid him 2,500 francs. And for the first and the only time, Verne incorporated the engineer's calculations as a supplementary chapter, giving due credit to Badoureau, who had just published a study of the current state of experimental science, Verne proudly added.

In Verne's novel, the French scientist Alcide Pierdeux—a pseudonym for Badoureau—writes a letter to *Le Temps* to explain what had gone wrong. Maston had forgotten three zeros in his calculation—because a woman who was pursuing him disturbed him with a telephone call.[4]

Purchase of the North Pole was not like the books Jules Verne had written in the past. This time science failed—rather, it was the scientists who made mistakes. Worse, their purpose had been personal gain, and had they succeeded, their achievement would have been destructive to everyone else.

A journalist privy to Verne's secrets revealed that the author had been thinking about this story for the past twenty years but hadn't been quite sure how to handle it until then. Verne had also wished to respond to the astronomer Camille Flammarion, who was at once a serious researcher and the author of popular science for the general public. Flammarion had accused Verne of basing his stories on erroneous data; hence, Verne's hiring of Badoureau, the engineer.[5]

THERE WAS PLENTY OF WORK IN AMIENS FOR A MEMBER OF the city council who took his responsibilities seriously. But one of the first acts of the new councilman had involved an avowedly personal problem. On August 17, 1888, three months after his election, Jules Verne had taken the floor to make his first formal address. "I should like to draw the attention of the administration to the passage of trains through the city of Amiens," he began. "The big question is always the smoke given off by the locomotives." He didn't know whether the railroad was required to take smoke-prevention measures; if so, "their devices are not perfect," he said.

Several times a day, acrid smoke poured from the tunnels along boulevard Longueville (which, of course, was where the Verne house stood) and boulevard Saint-Michel (now boulevard de Belfort). As a temporary expedient, the railroad could require that its engineers "keep the locomotives under pressure . . . during the crossing of the city." They would then receive a lot of steam, but steam condenses and causes no unpleasant effects. As for the inconvenience of smoke, only those living along the railroad line know what that means.

The mayor assured the council that the railroad companies were required to have smoke absorbers. He had already asked the company responsible for the line to have their engineers refrain from emitting smoke while crossing Amiens. For a while, there had been a slight improvement, and then the bad habits returned. The mayor vowed to try again.[6]

On May 12, 1889, councilman Verne addressed the annual assembly of the Caisse des Écoles, the foundation that raised and dispersed voluntary donations to deprived children in the state school system. "It's not alms from the rich," he said; "it's the gift of one brother to another." He was responsible for the fund's financial report, and he carved out this duty with apparent relish. "First of all, little boys were given 552 jackets, 794 pairs of trousers, 237 shirts. So their parents no longer had an excuse for not sending them to school—unless it was the fear, quite legitimate, that they'd get their feet wet. Don't worry, ladies, we thought of that, and 1075 pairs of galoshes now trip around. . . . As for the little girls, 698 dresses, 209 chemises, 581 smocks dress them warmly and decently," Verne reported.[7]

After years of making do with tents and shacks, the town had voted to erect a permanent building for the circus. The site happened to be place Longueville, a generously proportioned square created after demolition of a bastion along the old town ramparts, only steps away from the Verne house on rue Charles-Dubois (in fact, only steps from all three houses the Vernes were to occupy in their Amiens years).

The building that would go up became a landmark, with its multifaceted circular form, ornamented cupola, and Oriental spire. Over a century later, it is still one of the curiosities the town chooses to point out to visitors. For the inaugural concert, it seemed as if all Amiens had crowded into the new hall (in fact, three thousand heads were counted); it was for cultural councilman Verne, of course, to deliver the welcoming address.

The decision to build the permanent circus building had been made before he joined the council; its extravagance had been criticized, but Jules Verne intended to stand with the mayor and his architect, who had spent what was necessary. "And, anyway, has the present ever worried about whether the architects of the past remained within their original estimates, and will the future complain if today's architects exceeded them a little?" Verne asked. Skeptics had even criticized the soundness of the construction, spreading rumors that the roof might come crashing down. It would not, said Verne, since it hadn't collapsed that night, despite the heavy applause![8]

ELIZABETH COCHRANE WAS A PENNSYLVANIA GIRL (BORN IN a town called Cochran's Mill). Her newspaper career began innocently enough when she wrote a letter to the editor of the *Pittsburgh Dispatch* contesting a conservative article entitled "What Girls are Good For"; as feminists go, she was obviously a pioneer.[9]

By 1889, under her byline of Nellie Bly, she was at the height of her career as a journalist, about to become a world celebrity—and she was only twenty-two years old. Pertly pretty, determined in demeanor, wearing practical clothes and good walking shoes, she seemed ready for anything. Just a year earlier, on assignment for press lord Joseph Pulitzer's New York *World,* she was admitted to a notorious mental hospital on an island in the East River off Manhattan, and spent ten days there collecting information; the result was a sensational series and a book, *Ten Days in a Madhouse.*

Now, to secure the *World'*s place in a fiercely competitive New York newspaper scene ("Circulation guaranteed greater than that of any two other American newspapers combined," read the masthead boast), Pulitzer was to make use of his intrepid female reporter in a global publicity sweep. He'd send Nellie Bly around the world, the objective being to do it in less time than Phileas Fogg's eighty days. CAN JULES VERNE'S GREAT DREAM BE REDUCED TO ACTUAL FACT? asked a front-page headline in the New York *World* of November 14, 1889.

The story promised that the newspaper was about to turn a dream into reality. "Thousands upon thousands have read with interest the imaginary journey which Jules Verne, that prince of dreamers, sent his hero, Phileas Fogg, on." No one had actually accomplished the deed, so "it remains for *The World* to lead the way in this as in many other paths. Today at 9:30 o'clock Nellie Bly, so well known to the millions who have read of her doings, as told by her captivating pen, will set out as a Female Phileas Fogg."

In her own account of the adventure, the female Phileas Fogg claimed that the idea was her own; she'd been in the habit of thinking up ideas on Sunday for approval or disapproval by her editor the next morning.

Checking with a steamship company before mentioning the idea, she found that such a trip could now be accomplished in fewer than eighty days. Then she learned that her paper had already planned a round-the-world journey, to be undertaken by a male reporter. The business manager said she couldn't go without a chaperone and would have to take too much baggage to allow her sufficient mobility; further, she spoke only English. There was no use talking about it; only a man could accomplish such an exploit, she was told.

"Very well," she remembered replying in anger. "Start the man and I'll start the same day for some other newspaper and beat him."[10]

Of course, she got the assignment. It was a running story with infinite variations. Even when it didn't have a dispatch from Nellie Bly to print, the *World* could tell readers about the avalanche of letters that were coming in—some of them containing marriage proposals. Later, the paper maintained suspense by reporting on delayed trains and other inadequate connections, or the risks of shipwreck. Nellie had embarked on a ship named the *Augusta Victoria;* the ship she was originally supposed to take had been slowed by stormy seas and nearly capsized. NELLIE BLY ON THE OTHER SIDE, read the front page on November twenty-second.

THE WORLD'S GLOBE TROTTER

IS IN SOUTHAMPTON TODAY

AFTER A TEMPESTUOUS VOYAGE

MAY VISIT JULES VERNE IN FRANCE

IF SHE CAN DO SO WITHOUT LOSING TIME[11]

In legend at least, the call on Jules Verne was impromptu. Nellie Bly's version of the story was that Jules and Honorine had written to the *World*'s London correspondent asking that if possible she stop off in Amiens on her trip across the Continent. "Oh, how I should like to see them!" she had exclaimed, saying she wished there was time. "If you are willing to go without sleep and rest for two nights, I think it can be done," the correspondent (one Tracey Greaves) informed her.[12]

But later, the same newspaper's Paris correspondent, the Englishman Robert Sherard, offered a more candid version of events. "It was thought that it would give a good advertisement to the 'story' if on her way through France to Brindisi, the girl could meet Jules Verne in Amiens. I was ordered to arrange the meeting. At first the old gentleman [Jules Verne] did not at all understand what purpose could be served by such a meeting and it required some persuasion on my part to induce him to consent. The task was all the more difficult for me because I felt that we were taking advantage for our own purposes of his complacency."

So much for the unsolicited invitation by the Vernes. The meeting, in any case, was a definite success. "I had managed so to interest Verne in the scheme," recalled Sherard, "that he was good enough to come to the station at Amiens to meet the American reporter, bringing a bouquet to him to present to her."[13]

"When I saw them," Nellie remembered, "I felt as any other woman would have done under the same circumstances. I wondered if my face was travel-stained, and if my hair was tossed. I thought regretfully, had I been traveling on an American train, I should have been able to make my toilet *en route,* so that when I stepped off at Amiens and faced the famous novelist and his charming wife, I would have been as trim and tidy as I would had I been receiving them in my own home."[14] For his part, Verne was delighted to meet "this young and charming American," as he stated in a letter to *Le Temps.* "Miss Bly . . . seemed very energetic and determined; one would say a handsome young man who would have no problem accomplishing his trip within the allotted time."[15]

Jules led the way to the carriages outside the station, Nellie alongside Honorine, feeling awkward because they shared no language. "It was early evening," she would remember. "As we drove through the streets of Amiens I got a flying glimpse of bright shops, a pretty park, and numerous nurse maids pushing baby carriages about."

Jules's carriage was not far behind. "He hurried up to where we were standing and opened a door in the wall," she noted (only later did she notice his slight limp). "A large, black shaggy dog came bounding forward to greet me. He jumped up against me, his soft eyes overflowing with affection, and though I love dogs and especially appreciated this one's loving welcome, still I feared that his lavish display of it would undermine my dignity by bringing me to my knees at the very threshold of the home of the famous Frenchman."

They went up a flight of marble steps and across the tiled floor of a "beautiful little conservatory that was not packed with flowers," the young woman remarked, "but was filled with a display just generous enough to allow one to see and appreciate the beauty of the different plants." And then they proceeded to the large drawing room, where Honorine lit a fire "with her own hands."

Now the visitor had time to observe the famous Jules Verne: "His snow-white hair rather long and heavy, was standing up in artistic disorder; his full beard, rivaling his hair in snowiness, hid the lower part of his face, but the healthy color of his face and the brilliancy of his bright black eyes that were overshadowed with heavy white brows, and the rapidity of his speech and the quick movements of his firm white hands all bespoke energy—life—enthusiasm." She guessed he was about five feet five in height.

Of course, they spoke through an interpreter—Sherard. "I try to keep a knowledge of everything that is going on in America and greatly appreciate the hundreds of letters I receive yearly from Americans who read my books," Verne told her. "I know of nothing that I long to do more than to see your land from New York to San Francisco." For her part, Bly described her itinerary—from Amiens, she would return to Calais for the express to Brindisi, on Italy's heel; there she would embark for Port Said, Ismailia, Suez, Aden, Colombo, Penang, Singapore, Hong Kong, Yokohama, San Francisco, and New York.

"Why do you not go to Bombay as my hero Phileas Fogg did?" he asked her. "Because I am more anxious to save time than a young widow," she replied. "You may save a young widower before you return," Verne said with a smile. And she "smiled with a superior knowledge, as women, fancy free, always will at such insinuations."

Then it was time to go, for if she missed the train to Calais, she might just as well return to New York—as she'd lose a week. At her request, however, Jules Verne took her upstairs for a quick tour of his working quarters. "I had expected, judging from the rest of the house, that M. Verne's study would be a room of ample proportions," she remembered. "But when I stood in M. Verne's study I was speechless with surprise. He opened a latticed window, the only window in the room, and Mme. Verne, hurrying in after us, lighted the gas jet that was fastened above a low mantel."

Such a small room, she marveled; even her little den at home was nearly as big. "It was also very modest and bare. Below the window was a flat-topped desk. The usual litter that accompanies and fills the desks of most literary persons was conspicuously absent."

There was a neat pile of manuscript on the desk; Verne offered it for examination. She noted that words had been crossed out here and there but that nothing had been inserted, indicating that he improved his work by removing superfluous things, never by adding. There was a single chair in the room—his desk chair—the only other furniture being a low couch. From the latticed window, she could see the cathedral's spire. Just below was the park, and beyond that the entrance to the railway tunnel.

Now they moved into an enormous library, lined with cases from ceiling to floor. Her host produced a map, which she knew at once was Phileas Fogg's itinerary; with a pencil, he now marked out her own. She remembered saying that she expected to complete her trip in seventy-five days. "If you do it in seventy-nine days," he replied, "I shall applaud with both hands." Then he spoke in English as they touched wineglasses: "Good luck, Nellie Bly."

It was a cold night. Although Nellie begged them not to, the Vernes escorted her out through the chilled courtyard; when she looked back, she could see them waving farewell, "the brisk winds tossing their white hair."[16]

She made her connections, catching the Brindisi mail train "against fearful odds," her newspaper reported.[17] Indeed, she circled the world in seventy-two days, six hours, and eleven minutes, time zones notwithstanding.

On January 26, 1890, the front page of the *World* was all about Nellie Bly—that is, when it wasn't about Jules Verne. FATHER TIME OUTDONE, the headline declared. "Thousands Cheer Themselves Hoarse at Nellie Bly's Arrival. . . . The Whole Country Aglow with Intense Enthusiasm," the account continued in smaller type. A smaller headline announced CHEERS FROM JULES VERNE. The paper had asked "the wizard of Amiens" for a statement and now printed his telegraphed reply: NEVER DOUBTED NEL-LIE BLY'S SUCCESS. HER FEARLESSNESS MADE THAT EVIDENT. HURRAY FOR HER AND FOR THE PUBLISHER OF THE WORLD. HURRAY! HURRAY!

Even before Nellie Bly got back to New York, Robert Sherard set off for Amiens again. Verne knew the young woman had disembarked at San Francisco on January twenty-third, and he also knew that with improved service, the rail journey across the United States now took only five days. Yet he was certain that she'd find a way to beat that time, and she did, despite having to take a detour when snow blocked the direct line.

"I am very glad," Honorine Verne confided to Sherard, "if only for the reason that now my husband will have a little peace of mind. . . . Every evening he would say, 'Miss Bly must be there, or there.' Often in the evenings he would fetch out the map of the world or the globe and show me the place where Miss Bly probably was at that moment, and marked her progress on a large map upstairs with little flags every day."

"I have thought all the time about Miss Bly, as my wife says," Verne was quoted as saying. "My principal thought was—Dieu! how I wish I were free and young again! I would have been enchanted to do the same trip, even under the same conditions—rushing around the globe without seeing much; would have set off at once, and perhaps offered to escort Miss Bly." "That wouldn't have suited me," Sherard heard Honorine put in.

Asked whether he'd work Miss Bly into a story, Verne said candidly, "Doubtless, although I am not a good hand at female characters, but shall make a first attempt shortly with a book called 'Lady Franklin' [in fact, *Mistress Branican*]. Later on I shall certainly find a frame for that very pretty picture which you introduced to me only seventy odd days ago at Amiens."

Sherard's report appeared under another headline on the same front page:

VERNE'S "BRAVO"

The French Romancer in Ecstasy Over the Achievement of "The World"'s Voyager

A Great Journalistic Triumph

Verne Followed Every Step of the Journey on His Globes

His Phileas Fogg Outdone

An Extraordinarily Interesting Interview with the Wizard of Amiens—Mme Verne Joins in the Congratulations—High Compliments for "The World" and Its Representative from All Sources—This One Achievement Has Made "The World" The Best Known Journal in Existence[18]

But before Nellie Bly had even reached home base, Jules Verne was obliged to deny newspaper reports—clearly the result of misunderstanding during his meeting with Bly—that he had thought she would not be able to complete her trip in fewer than seventy-nine days. She was aiming for *seventy* days. "But . . . I told her that I thought the trip very possible within that time, if there were no delays or accidents at sea." He had also said that when a new rail line across Russia was completed, the trip would be possible in *forty* days.[19]

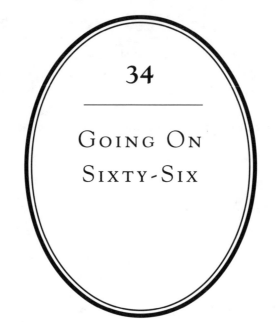

34

GOING ON
SIXTY-SIX

MICHEL VERNE HAD TOLD THE NEW YORK *WORLD*'S CORRE-
spondent Robert Sherard that his father had never in his life earned as
much as one thousand pounds a year (that would have been some 25,000
francs then, some 440,000 now). So Sherard put the question to Michel's
father. "I made an arrangement with my publishers many years ago to
supply them with two novels every year for an annual payment, which is
certainly less than the sum you mention," was Verne's reply. "Was it a
good bargain or was it a bad one? I do not know. I may add that I do not
care. If my publishers have done well out of the arrangement, *tant mieux.*
Monsieur Hetzel has always been most courteous and kind to me, and I
wish him all prosperity." Sherard decided that Jules Verne was more concerned about his literary position than his financial one and that he represented the indifference of France's men of letters. Since he had begun
to seek election to the French Academy, it had filled up every one of its
seats afresh with no nod to Verne.[1]

So Verne lost himself in his writing, which (especially when the product was less than his best) increasingly resembled any other desk job. A
book then in progress, *César Cascabel*, inspired Jean Jules-Verne to remark
later that these were years of decline, when Jules Verne simply wasn't writing as well as he used to. The only strong moments in the new novel were
unpleasant ones, Verne overlooking no occasion to speak badly of the

British—and no matter that the British paid royalties for his books, while Americans often pirated them.

The year is 1867, the place Sacramento, California. There, a family of French traveling circus performers will end its tour of America and return to France, crossing the United States in a caravan. When the money they have put aside for their ocean voyage is stolen, they decide to make an unheard-of journey to France *overland:* north to Alaska, across the Bering Strait to Siberia, and westward through Russia. The party includes César, of Norman origin; his southern French wife, their three children all born in the United States, a young lad who works for them, and an Indian girl found in the woods. They also drag along two dogs, a monkey, and a parrot.

When the circus travelers reach the polar region, the reader knows he is in familiar Verne territory. Like so many other Verne heroes, these characters have been left adrift after an ice floe has broken off from the main sheet of ice. They are saved, only to become captives. Before the adventure is over their journey is paved with gold by a Russian wanderer whom they had rescued earlier from a miserable death: It is later revealed that he is a banished prince, and then he is pardoned by the czar.

This was a book for Hetzel's *Magasin,* of course, a tale that would keep young readers interested. Its anti-British sentiments would not unsettle readers, for they were certainly in the spirit of those times (when the United Kingdom was not only France's chief rival in colonization but also a perfidious player on the European chessboard, more apt to be allied to France's enemies than to its friends). The Cascabels' daughter had been baptized Napoléone, in memory of the martyr of British captivity; Cascabel has dismissed a clown who claimed to be American but was really English; and their monkey is called John Bull because of his ugliness.

César Cascabel was followed by *Mrs. Branican,* which Verne was writing in 1890 and which would be published in *Magasin d'Education* the following January. Again, the theme is a familiar one for Verne's readers: a ship captain lost at sea. The novel is set in the South Pacific. The Branicans are Americans; after losing a child (also at sea) and suffering exploitation by a false friend, Dolly Branican survives madness and inherits a fortune, which enables her to scour the seas looking for her Captain John. There are further treasons, but her staunch will prevails; she finds John as well as her lost son.

While working on *Mrs. Branican,* Verne received discouraging news from Jules Hetzel. Books—and not only Verne's—simply weren't selling; nobody seemed to be reading. Verne thought that people did read but that what they read was inferior newspaper fiction, which kept them away from books.[2]

"I no longer travel, I don't go anywhere because of my bad legs," he complained to Alexandre Dumas early in July 1890. "I'm becoming a provincial to the bone."[3] Actually, he did move about, but only in his tiny patch of France. He crossed the Seine to camp at the d'Ennery summer hideaway at Villers-sur-Mer, just west of Trouville and Deauville. There, he spent painful weeks chewing over a theatrical version of *The Tribulations of a Chinese Gentleman*—another play that would never be produced, and this at a time when Verne so much wanted more of the easy money that in happier times had seemed to gush from the stage. After his visit at Villers-sur-Mer, Verne crossed the Seine again, this time following the coast to an even quieter Channel village, Les Petites-Dalles, whose pebble beach snuggled between protruding cliffs northeast of the better-known resort of Fécamp. Here, he met up with Michel and Jeanne.

Jules was not well that summer. In a letter to a favorite doctor, he complained of a distension of the stomach, "and with that, dizziness and ringing in my ears again." In late August, he told Jules Hetzel, illness continued to wear him down—"temporary blindness and dizziness, as violent as ever despite my diet."[4]

As always, the sparring session with d'Ennery had taken a lot out of him; perhaps that was the cause of his latest attack. In his book, Jean Jules-Verne mentions bulimia—apparently a subject of concern in the family—a condition attributed to (if not explaining) his ravenous appetite and rapid ingestion. Overeating, in turn, was later taken as an early sign, and perhaps the cause of the diabetes generally assumed to have killed him.[5]

This year of 1890 found Verne active in a new cause, the promotion of the use of French language outside of France. He was involved with an organization created only half a dozen years earlier, the Alliance Française. He became chairman of the promotional campaign for his district, and in a statement published in April 1890, he had called for "a new effort to assure the victory of the French language over English and German abroad." In July—before his trips to the shore—he had presided over a meeting where the lecturer, an Amiens high school teacher, told the audience that the Alliance Française promoted French teaching because "the French language creates French habits; French habits lead to the purchase of French products, and the foreigner who knows French becomes a client of France."

Before winter, Amiens received the visit of Pierre Foncin, founder of the Alliance Française; Jules Verne was there to introduce him. "If it is true that the birth rate is declining significantly in our country," he said, among other things, "let's train children elsewhere, in teaching them our language."[6]

A German doctor wrote to Verne from Berlin, suggesting that he contribute to mutual understanding among peoples, hence their reconciliation, by writing about Germany; specifically, he called for a novel entitled *Journey Across Germany in Thirty Days*. Verne dismissed the suggestion with scorn. If their countries were enemies, it wasn't at all for lack of knowledge, "quite the contrary, and the novel you'd like to see written would have no success," explained Verne. "Only one act of reparation could change French feelings toward Germans. I don't have to tell you what that act is, but anything done outside this framework would be vain, illusory, and unworkable." The act he alluded to would have been the return of Alsace-Lorraine, annexed by Bismarck just twenty years earlier.

Reporting Verne's reaction, *Le Temps* confessed that it agreed with him; if the French did not know Germany, they knew the Germans—too well. But the editors did regret that their countrymen possessed insufficient knowledge of its neighbor. Germans traveled in France and even resided there more often than did the French in Germany.[7]

A study of his municipal politics—including moments when the deliberations of the city council took on national and universal significance—shows Verne as a predictable conservative, opposing funds for workers seeking to create their own enterprise after losing a strike, for example, or objecting to criticism of the police, who had been accused of the excessive use of brutality in putting down a demonstration.[8]

RECONCILIATION WITH A PRESUMABLY REFORMED MICHEL Verne was soon transformed into a new intimacy between father and son, the first rapprochement since the time when Jules began to see Michel as a wayward child. The younger man was going to be helpful as a secretary, among other things. He actually acquired a typewriter and took dictation from his father—an occasional task, performed only when he happened to be in Amiens. He couldn't get there often, of course, since a succession of unhappy business ventures required that he work in Paris.[9] The best known of his forays into the business world was that of promoting a so-called universal stove, vaunted as "the only one both hygienic and inexpensive"; he sold it via prospectuses that were inserted in issues of Hetzel's *Magasin d'Education et de Récréation*.[10]

Michel's use of a typewriter would later add a complication for scholars who wished to separate novels written solely by Jules Verne from those written or rewritten by his son yet bearing Jules Verne's name. For the time being, the books that were published were unquestionably Jules Verne's and were written in his hand. He had, for example, been working on *Carpathian Castle (Le Château des Carpathes)* on and off for a half dozen years, and by 1889 it was considered to be ready for publication.[11] But room in the *Magasin* was found for this curious departure from the Jules Verne corpus only in January 1892. "I am returning the proofs," the author informed his publisher in March 1892, assuring him that he had gone over them with considerable care. "I think that there is nothing in the book that could shock readers of the *Magasin,* and I was as cautious as possible with respect to the story of the hero and the singer."[12]

One can indeed imagine that the tone as well as the subject proved disconcerting to Hetzel—and commercially risky. *Carpathian Castle* opens in the San Carlo opera house of Naples, where the final performance of the superb singer known as la Stilla is being given. She is "of an incomparable beauty, with her long gold-tinted hair, deep black eyes from which flames burst forth . . . and a form that the chisel of a Praxiteles could not have shaped more perfectly." One is reminded of the beautiful Romanian woman whom Jules Verne supposedly had within arm's reach in Amiens. In his novel, the stunning Stilla has two ardent admirers, powerful Baron de Gortz and young Count de Telek. After a final aria, the singer collapses on the stage and dies.

The scene then switches to a Transylvanian village, into which unhappy Telek wanders. Strange things have transpired in the neighboring castle, which belongs to Baron de Gortz, Telek's erstwhile rival. When *Carpathian Castle* was published, both telephone and phonograph existed. The novel shows how a mad scientist—Gortz's cohort—can place a listening device in the village and link it to the castle by copper wire. The same circuit transmits mysterious voices. And the eerie apparition of lovely la Stilla on the castle ramparts will later be explained as a projection of her portrait while the voice heard singing the closing strains of her final aria is a recording. The technology employed throughout the novel is carefully explained in the final chapter. Although by doing so Verne probably broke the spell, he turned a Gothic tale into a story fit for the most earnest of Hetzel's family readers.

Another Verne novel that would be published in time for the year-end gift season in 1892 was one the author wrote in 1890. In *Claudius Bombarnac,* the hero of the same name is a newspaper reporter describing a journey along a newly opened railroad line connecting Europe to Peking (no such line then existed). The scenario provides opportunities for de-

lightful peregrinations, as well as descriptions of colorful personalities—
suitable both for the mythical readers of Bombarnac's fictional newspaper, *The Twentieth Century,* and actual readers of the royalist daily *Le Soleil,* in which Verne's novel was first serialized.

Tension mounts along the way when a funeral coach is attached to the train; it is the well-guarded hearse of a high Chinese dignitary. In fact, the coach really hides a fabulous imperial treasure. Mongol bandits attack the convoy, while Bombarnac discovers further intrigues on board the train itself: A seemingly irreproachable traveler turns out to be an even more dangerous thief who will not hesitate to destroy the train and all its passengers in order to seize the treasure. It is a cliffhanger with a happy ending. So who would mind the many unpleasant racial, religious, and national slurs? One could still hope for readers who felt the same way about dumb Germans, arrogant Englishmen, avaricious Jews.

Foundling Mick (*P'tit Bonhomme*) a descent into pathos, was Verne's next novel. Although an homage to Charles Dickens, his neglected orphan is not English but an Irish lad. If today's audience cannot read the story with the enthusiasm of *Magasin* readers, it can appreciate something else in *Foundling Mick,* something having more to do with its author's obsessions than with his literary influences.

Jules Verne's orphan starts off in life poorer than poor, but he learns how to earn and then to save money, which he invests in increasingly profitable activities. He finally becomes wealthy enough that he can help other orphans. Was this another lecture meant for Michel?

﹏ ✑﹏

IN JULY 1892, JULES VERNE MOVED UP A NOTCH IN THE HI-
erarchy of the Legion of Honor; henceforth he could call himself an officer. His correspondence reveals, pathetically, that he had been maneuvering for the promotion for half a dozen years. In a letter written during his convalescence following Gaston's assault, he had informed Hetzel fils that Amiens's highest dignitaries, not excluding the district governor and the mayor, had been enlisted in the cause. And when the promotion came through, it was thanks to his contributions to the well-being of Amiens, not to his literary career.[13]

Then another member of the French Academy died. That gave Jules one more chance, but he'd have to go out and fight for it, as Hetzel warned him. In a letter of October 19, 1892, the publisher reminded his author of the facts of institutional life. "The old lady is delighted when someone pays attention to her, she who must take care of others, and she has a reservoir of tenderness for those who without trying to rape her—which would be unpardonable at her age—at least flirt with her regularly."[14]

But he was talking to a new Jules Verne now—or rather, to an older, disabused Jules Verne. "To *enter* the Academy between the ages of 40 and 50, fine; to *enter* when one is oneself about to *enter* one's sixty-sixth year, is no longer worth it," he replied. "I'd never consent to go to all the trouble that would be required with so little chance of succeeding, since my kind of writing appears not to be academic." He remembered when the younger Dumas had first spoken for him; that had been fifteen years earlier. Since that time, thirty-seven members of that body had died, and never once had Verne's name come up. He knew, for example, that Dumas was backing Emile Zola for the seat then vacant. (Verne didn't like Zola, but neither did the French Academy, and he would never be elected, either.)

"So nothing can be done, and if I once thought a little about the Academy, that idea has totally disappeared. I ask only to live peacefully in my provincial retreat, if possible, and to carry out my writer's task to the end, if end there be."[15] Soon he would be trying to convince one of his admirers that he had "never dreamed of standing as a candidate for the French Academy, never felt any such ambition."[16]

※ ※

FAMILY CORRESPONDENCE, WHICH SHEDS SO MUCH LIGHT ON the life of the young Jules Verne, is missing for the middle years, when Verne gained literary reknown. But there is another rich lode of letters, beginning in 1893, to draw upon. These letters were written to one of the few people in whom Jules never ceased to confide—his brother Paul, who was now turning sixty-four. This correspondence offers an intimate picture of Jules.

In large part, these letters deal with Jules's concerns about Michel. He and Jeanne had just had their third child (Jean, who later wrote a flawed but earnest biography of his grandfather). The infant was ill, and cleaner air was prescribed. Amiens and especially the house on rue Charles-Dubois were apparently sufficiently remote from big-city filth to offer the solution. Jules found Michel's wife "very proper," and her children, too. But Honorine's daughter Suzanne Lefebvre and her husband refused to see them. (Michel was divorced, of course, and had begun living with Jeanne while still married to his first wife.) The Lefebvres had also convinced others of their circle to avoid the Michel Vernes.

"Do realize," Jules told his brother, "that we never wanted to impose the young couple on anybody. . . . But if the Lefebvres and the others think they've done their duty, we are certain to have done ours." He explained himself: "There was a sick child, he had to have better air; so he came here. What we did was approved by all liberal minds and true hearts. The devil with the imbeciles."[17]

Michel's monetary situation hadn't changed. Letters he sent Jules Hetzel during this period show that he often sought early payment of the monthly stipend of one thousand francs the publisher remitted from his father's account.[18] Michel's shaky financial position did not stop him from renting a country house—actually a lonely place in Brittany, about two miles from the developing Dinard bathing resort. The property included a small guest cabin and an attached farm. "What fun for children to watch the horse walk patiently around the post that turned the threshing machine," remembered Jean (he was obviously remembering later summers, for he was just a year old then), "and what greater fun to go to the nearby beach that at the time was totally deserted!"

The isolation also pleased Michel's father. Jules spent a full summer month there in 1893, although Jean didn't remember whether he lived in the main house—there was sufficient room—or in the cabin (perhaps he used the latter only for writing). In any case, Jean believed that Jules's genuine affection for Michel's family dated from that time.[19]

If so, it coincided with a new estrangement from Honorine. Paul was also having family problems, which he dismissed, because "such is life." "Perhaps," Jules granted, "but if you are all alone in Nantes it's because you wanted it that way. Why did you let your wife settle in Paris?" Then: "In any case, you and I both committed an enormous and irreparable blunder; you know which one, without my having to be specific. Tear up this letter. But what a life we'd have had, without that blunder."[20]

Perhaps this is the key to the mature Jules Verne? He hadn't been able to live the life he had dreamed, and for that he seemed to be blaming his marriage of reason to the provincial middle class. Disappointed in marriage, he had vainly sought to compensate with substitute passions. Work, for example.

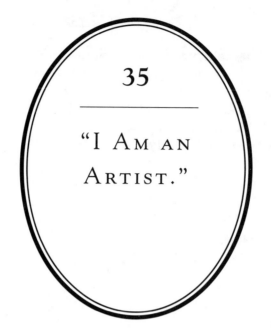

35

"I Am an Artist."

He made good use of his summer retreat at Michel's house in Brittany. The most tangible result was a good half of a new book, *Captain Antifer (Mirifiques Aventures de Maître Antifer)*, which, in accordance with the regular procedure of this calculating writer, would be ready for serialization in Hetzel's *Magasin* the following January—before the second half of the book was finished.

Captain Antifer is another sea story, and once again the novel is set on a mysterious island—this one the repository of a pasha's chest of precious stones. Antifer, whose father had saved the pasha's life during Napoléon's campaign against the Ottomans, had been told the *latitude* of a fabulous treasure island but not the *longitude*—this was promised for a later time. And now, after the pasha's death, the time has come; the secret is delivered by the Egyptian executor of the pasha's will. (The sly Egyptian will also try to make use of what he knows.)

But this is only the beginning. When Captain Antifer reaches the island, he finds only the *longitude* of a second island, and he must visit a Tunisian banker to learn the latitude; alas, the Tunisian, like the Egyptian, will try to find the treasure first. The journey from point to point continues until the travelers have completed a circle; the true treasure island is at the center of the circle, except that it has disappeared beneath the sea.

A long story leading nowhere, *Captain Antifer* is saved only by the buoyancy of its style. Jules cautioned his brother, who was reading the book, to find technical errors: "At no cost must the reader suspect the location of the treasure island."[1] This was a wasted effort, however, since the book simply didn't hold the reader's attention.

One consequence of writing to formula became clear when Verne received his next semiannual royalty statement from Hetzel. "It leaves me heartbroken," he lamented to his publisher. "The books I counted on, *Bombarnac, Carpathian Castle,* the public didn't want! It's discouraging. It is true that one cannot always be in fashion! I know that . . . and yet I haven't finished my life work, to paint the earth."[2]

The disappointment he suffered from the failure of these books made it all the more necessary to continue to collaborate on plays with d'Ennery. And yet that no longer seemed a panacea, either, as a letter to his brother indicates. Paul had said he was going to Villers. Did he mean Villers-sur-Mer on the Calvados coast? wondered Jules. If so, he might run into the famous dramatist, since he owned one of the region's great houses. Jules wanted Paul to know that he and d'Ennery were no longer on the best of terms. "After he made me go to Antibes, and then to Villers for the play [adapted from *The Tribulations of a Chinese Gentleman*], after I wrote the whole play twice, he still wanted to change things. I refused a third collaboration while leaving him free to work with someone else if he liked. So we must not be on friendly terms."[3]

THE PRECISE DATE OF ROBERT SHERARD'S NEXT VISIT TO Amiens is not known. Sherard had gone to Amiens earlier as Paris correspondent of the New York *World* to accompany Nellie Bly. He probably returned in the late autumn of 1893, since his report appeared in an American magazine the following January. Sherard's intention was to tell his readers how the famous writer actually spent his days. Perhaps other witnesses got as close to Verne in the course of his writing life; no one ever came away with as candid a portrait.

Sherard couldn't believe what he was now hearing. The famous Jules Verne, "your Jules Verne and mine, who has delighted us all the world over for so many years," was lamenting his fate, exuding gloom. His great regret, Verne said with drooped head, a ring of sadness in his voice, was that he had not achieved a rank among his country's men of letters. "I don't count in French literature," Sherard quoted him as saying. "It was in the cool withdrawing-room of the Société Industrielle at Amiens that the master said these words," reported Sherard, "and I shall never forget the tone of sadness in which he said them. It was like the confession of a wasted life, the sigh of an old man over what can never be recalled."

He found the sixty-five-year-old Verne still hale and hearty—apart from his noticeable limp, and one drooping eyelid, surely a permanent result of his facial paralysis. Still, Verne complained about his health. His eyes had weakened, so at times he couldn't guide his pen; there were days when "gastralgia [stomach pain] martyrizes him," Sherard wrote. Verne revealed that the leg wound inflicted by his nephew had never closed, and the bullet was still lodged in the bone.

The day began for Sherard when he rang the bell at the rue Charles-Dubois; readers were given a description of the house, even a look out the window at the railroad cutting immediately beneath Verne's office window and which disappeared under a public garden with its music kiosk ("a very emblem of the writer," remarked Sherard, "the rushing train, with all the roar and rattle of ultra-modernism, and the romance of the music").

"My brother Paul was and is my dearest friend," Jules told the reporter. "Yes, I may say that he is not only my brother but my most intimate friend." This seemingly gratuitous remark underscores the value of the letters to Paul that date from this time.

It was during their conversation in the house on rue Charles-Dubois that Verne brought up his great disappointment. He told Sherard that Dumas had proposed his candidacy to the French Academy fifteen years earlier; he himself had friends in that body, so there had seemed to be a chance of election "and the formal recognition of my work." But it was not to happen. Sometimes he'd get a letter from America addressing him as Monsieur Jules Verne of the French Academy; he could only smile to himself. There had been forty-two elections to seats in the Academy since his name was first proposed. "But I am passed over," he said.

He had completed the manuscript of *Captain Antifer,* and he described it briefly to Sherard. He was now working on a novel that would appear in 1895, but it was too early to talk about it. As for his life, "family ties and the quiet of the place" had kept him in Amiens: Jules Hetzel agreed that if Verne had lived in Paris, he would have written ten fewer novels. He worked mornings, read in the afternoon, exercised when he could. He enjoyed the theater, and with Honorine he saw everything staged in Amiens. (He didn't add that as the city overseer of theater, he certainly had a box of his own.) "On those days we dine [at a hotel], so as to have a little outing and to give our servants a rest. Our only child, Michel, lives in Paris, where he is married and has children. He writes ably on scientific subjects. I have only one pet; . . . it is Follet, my dear old dog."

Sherard raised the thorny question of Verne's income; he'd heard that Verne earned less from his books than an ordinary journalist did. But

Verne preferred not to talk about that. It was true that his first books were sold for a fraction of their value, but after 1875 and *Michel Strogoff,* a new contract guaranteed him a fair division of profits. He did feel that he had received less than his share of the earnings of his plays (which amounted to 10 million francs for *Around the World* and 7 million for *Michel Strogoff*). "But I am not and never have been a money-getting man. . . . A little more justice to me from my countrymen would have been prized by me more than the thousands of dollars which my books should have given me more than they did give me each year." He wanted people to see the creator behind the simple storyteller. "I am an artist."[4]

"Solid as an oak in hard ground," someone else described him at this time, "tall, with large shoulders, energetic features framed by a thick graying beard. . . ." The observer thought he resembled the "godlike head" of Victor Hugo.[5]

This was the official portrait, and perhaps the gap had never been wider between the public image of a strong Jules Verne, sure of himself and his work, and the very private one Robert Sherard had begun to perceive.

PUBLIC AND PRIVATE FACES SEEMED TO FUSE IN A REMARK-able series of letters that began at this time. Mario Turiello, an Italian student not quite eighteen years old, later to become an eminent professor of literature, was inspired by his admiration of Jules Verne to add his letters to the hundreds and hundreds Verne received from admirers each year. Certainly those from Turiello—perhaps because he had taken the trouble to pose interesting questions—called for thoughtful response.

The first reply from Verne, sent from Amiens on June 7, 1894, took note of the young Italian's obvious familiarity with the Jules Verne corpus. "I already have seventy volumes to my credit," Verne wrote, "and I have about thirty to do before my work is achieved. Will I have the time?" (In a subsequent letter, he explained that the seventy included manuscripts not yet published.)

Later that month, replying to a second letter from Turiello, Verne said, not quite candidly, "I don't know whether the Extraordinary Voyages sell more or less than in earlier times, for I don't follow the career of a book once it is done and I hate publicity." His Italian correspondent wanted to know whether Verne actually wrote all of the books appearing under his name. The rumor persisted, at least in Italy, that since the shooting attack of 1886, he was unable to write and therefore that a group of authors composed the books, collectively using the name Jules Verne. (Turiello privately found it hard to believe that the author of *Michel Strogoff* could also have written the insipid *School for Crusoes,* or the overlong *Purchase of the North Pole,* for example.) Verne insisted that he wrote every single one of his novels, from the first line to the last.[6]

IN JUNE 1894, MARIE, THE DAUGHTER OF JULES'S SISTER Anne, was married in Nantes. "I see that the wedding was very jolly," Jules wrote to Paul, who had sent a report on the festivities, "but it's precisely this merriment that is intolerable to me now. My character is deeply altered, and I received blows from which I shall never recover."

In August, it was Jules who resumed the correspondence, for he had not heard from Paul in some time. Yet the physical act of writing no longer came easily to him. "Try to read me, for I write badly with my rheumatic hand. He was working all the same, respecting the schedule: "My volumes for 1895, 1896 and 1897 are done. I'm working on 1898." The next day he wrote again, for the brothers' letters had crossed. Paul had sent some light verse, and seemed as lively as ever. "I'm not, anymore," Jules told him—as if somberness were new to him—"for with my responsibilities, the future frightens me considerably. Michel does nothing, finds nothing to do, has cost me 200,000 francs, and has three sons, and all their education is my responsibility. I'm ending badly."[7]

But there were more completed manuscripts, fulfilling his contractual obligations for three years to come. Verne had finished three books, thus fulfilling his contractual obligations for the next three years. The first, for which Paul had provided considerable expertise, was *Propeller Island (L'Île à hélice).* A French musical quartet traveling in the western United States is lured to an unknown but clearly prosperous region of electric-powered automobiles and trams, moving sidewalks, electrically stimulated agriculture—a sanitized world with every comfort money can buy. Residents don't have to go out to shop, for example; they transmit their orders by fax, which Verne calls a *télautographe.* The musicians learn that they have been taken to an autonomous city-state built on an artificial island peopled with millionaires. The mobility of their propeller-driven isle allows the happy few to sail to the best possible climate for each season of the year.

Everything seems to have been done for the comfort and pleasure of the inhabitants of this paradise. Protestants and Catholics each have their community institutions; indeed, the island is literally divided in half along religious lines. Yet harmony prevails, and everything seems to work, until a mysterious sea captain and his Maltese crew are saved from a shipwreck and taken in as guests (we can already guess, although the happy islanders apparently can't, that much evil will come of this).

When sinister Captain Sarol and his Maltese crew strike at last, assisted by savages from a remote island, the plotters are defeated, but in the fierce battle the island's beloved governor is killed. So elections are called, reviving old tensions between clans, and a Romeo and Juliet–like marriage between children of the first families on either side of the religious divide is compromised. The islanders now have two governors, who issue conflicting orders on where the island is to sail; the inhabitants discover that the effect of the action of the powerful engines on either side of the island causes them to revolve. This is too much for the power system, which explodes; it is also too much for the island's artificial foundations, which break up as the isle drifts out of control; a fierce cyclone completes the job. Finally, a cool skipper finds a way to tug detached segments of the island to safety in New Zealand. There is a reconciliation, and a marriage; perhaps a new island will be built after all.

Propeller Island is a strange, overlong, uninspired novel. The French musicians are stick figures, each with a predictable and banal reaction; nor did the author bother to breathe life into any of the other characters (the reader will never even get close enough to Captain Sarol to find out why he is so evil). In the absence of feeling, the most curious events and the most extraordinary inventions fail to move the reader. Even the ideology is predictable: There is a kindly, all-knowing exiled monarch on the island; during the final crisis, the author lets it be known that "women and children, incapable of reasoning," remain frightened even when conditions come under control.

Verne fans who read *Propeller Island* later took it for a pessimistic vision of the future, a repudiation of the author's earlier encouragement of progress. Closer reading shows that there is nothing at all wrong with the concept or the mechanics of the millionaires' island and its wondrous amenities. Only the innate flaws in human nature will destroy what should have been perfection; Jules Verne painted a beautiful picture of progress—spoiled only by the presence of his fellow men.

The next two manuscripts were never published in English, but their titles translate as *A Drama in Livonia** and *The Mighty Orinoco.*** *A Drama in Livonia,* originally planned for publication in 1895 but not published for

---

*Un drame en Livonie
**Le Superbe Orénoque

another nine years, required no expertise from Paul. *The Mighty Orinoco* was a different matter. Its protagonists cross the ocean to Venezuela. Describing piroques sailing on the great Orinoco, with its strong currents and tropical storms, called for technical help from that old sailor Paul.

The real challenge for Paul would come with *For the Flag (Face au drapeau)*, in which Jules imagines a crazed French inventor protecting his secret—an unimaginably destructive explosive—from all the world powers, including his own. For his pains, the inventor is abducted by pirates; the vessel that carries him off vanishes.

The vessel is Verne's deus ex machina, and making it credible (which means navigable) meant much to him. "Keep thinking of the phantom ship," he begged Paul in a June 1894 letter. The vanishing pirate vessel would have to plunge, but Verne wanted to avoid anything suggestive of *Twenty Thousand Leagues.*

His hero, he told Paul, was to be "a Turpin." The reference was to a real-life French scientist named Eugène Turpin, inventor of the explosive melinite, who believed he was prey to rival powers because he had been rejected by his own country's military. Verne would, of course, transform Turpin's real drama and give fictional form to the inventor's pursuers. He was, he told Paul, letting his imagination run wild, and he hoped that his brother was doing the same. "I should like to portray an astonishing Turpin," he wrote on August twenty-first.

Five days later, he was back with another plea for help. He wanted his story to unfold in "almost fantastic conditions, with madness at the climax." He suggested they talk about it at their next meeting. "At this moment my hand is in considerable pain from writing, so I can't say much more."[8] Verne's vessel is a graceful pirate yacht gliding over the waters, no sails or smokestack to explain its movement (it is drawn by a submerged tug powered by newly invented storage batteries). In the climactic scenes, a experimental British submarine is used to penetrate the pirates' island cache; the inventor nevertheless blows up the island, his stock of explosives, and himself.

The evidence is that Jules Hetzel was as conscientious a reader and an editor as his father had been; he, too, contributed to *Propeller Island* (offering pages of calculations, undoubtedly obtained from an expert consultant), as well as to *For the Flag*. But Verne didn't always accept Hetzel's suggestions, let alone his criticism, without protest. Did Hetzel want him to write *For the Flag* all over again? he asked after one such go-round. Certainly not, replied the publisher; he wished only for Verne to liven it up.[9]

Surely Hetzel realized that something was lacking in Verne's latest books; after all Verne himself had complained of being overlooked recently. "When I read all the reviews for just anything that is published," he wrote Hetzel at the time the first volume of *Captain Antifer* was released, "this makes me jealous even in the heart of my province." Then, on publication of *Propeller Island:* "I learned that the first volume has appeared because I saw it here [in Amiens] in bookshop windows. Are you waiting for a more favorable moment to announce it to the press? I read almost everything and have seen neither notice nor advertisement. Even the slightest novel is announced to the public."[10]

Replying to a question from his Italian admirer Mario Turiello, he wrote, "I can't tell you . . . which of my books is my favorite. The truth is that the one that pleases me most is . . . the one I'm writing." The aggressive young man was now preparing a study of Verne's work, and he hoped that Verne could help him place it in a French literary magazine. "I have no influence in this respect, my young friend . . . I live in the provinces, far from journalists and critics, never going to Paris, never leaving my hole."[11]

Journalists still traveled to Amiens to see him, however. A writer for London's *Strand Magazine* did just that in the autumn of 1894, remarking no fallen leaf on a lawn enhanced with baskets of flowers. In the winter garden that served as the Vernes's reception room, Marie Belloc found a man more like a gentleman farmer than an author, though he wore the small red button identifying officers of the Legion of Honor. He appeared modest all the same, but Honorine was there to speak for him, reminding the interviewer that so many of the fantastic inventions her husband had written about—which had been believed impossible at the time—had become realities. Tut-tut, Verne replied; this was simply coincidence. Honorine, showing the visitor her husband's study, explained that Jules rose each morning at five, then worked until eleven (but he was in bed by eight or eight-thirty).

Speaking for himself, Verne expressed regret that he was able to read British and American authors only in translation. Dickens was the master. But, Honorine added, Jules never looked at a line of his own work once it was published. He explained that each book was preceded by a plan; he never began a story without knowing how it would come out. The real job began with the proofs, at which time he might rewrite entire chapters; sometimes he went through eight or nine sets of proofs before he was satisfied.

He received letters from all over—surely nobody in the world received more, Mme Verne told the visitor from London. His admirers suggested plots for future stories and told of their troubles and their adventures.[12]

Some six months later, acknowledging the return of proofs Paul had corrected, he would tell his brother something about his working method—and what he said then was close to what he told Miss Belloc. Paul had gone over the technical details to be sure they conformed to what was feasible, but, Jules warned him, "It goes without saying that not a line of what you read will remain, from the point of view of style. Everything has already been rewritten, omitting the many repetitions, and with a logical correlation of sentences. But I only do this job on the second set of proofs, being too busy before that with the novel in itself."

Verne was almost joyous in such moments when he could describe his working habits, but then he quickly took himself in hand. He admired Paul's happy disposition; Paul remained young! "As for me, with my serious concerns, I am becoming horribly old, and unlike you I wouldn't take a single step in order to eat a truffle! It goes without saying that in all other respects I'm even more out of the picture."[13]

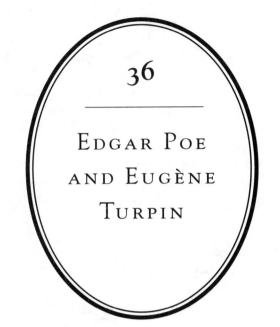

36

EDGAR POE AND EUGÈNE TURPIN

DURING THE SPRING OF 1895, JULES VERNE WAS CREATING some of his liveliest characters, his drollest scenes, with nobody outside his immediate family circle privy to his depression. Given his mental state, it is hard to believe that he was writing *Clovis Dardentor*.

Dardentor is wealthy and retired, eccentric and jovial, quite ready to accompany friends from southern France—a couple as limited in spirit as he is expansive—across the Mediterranean to Oran to help them marry their dull son to Louise, a young lady too good for him. On shipboard, Dardentor encounters Marcel and Jean, young orphans planning to enlist in the French expeditionary corps. They join Dardentor, his friends from the south, and Louise and her mother on a tour of Algeria, where they have many adventures.

On the sea crossing, Clovis Dardentor confides to Marcel and Jean that he is looking for worthy young people to adopt; from then on, they dream only of that. Indeed, Jean would have risked his life for the kindly older man (in fact, it is Dardentor who saves Jean when he falls into a stream). Then Louise shoots a lion, effectively saving Dardentor's life; Dardentor adopts *her*, so that she will inherit his fortune. As soon as he saw Louise waiting at the pier in Oran, Marcel had fallen in love with her; of course, Dardentor gives Louise to him, not to the pimply son of his friends from France. "And me?" Jean (Marcel's comrade) asks. "You'll be my nephew, my boy!" replies Dardentor without hesitation, promising a happy ending for all who deserve it.

"But, one will say, it all ends like a light comedy," concluded the author—a rare comment, within the covers of a book, on his choice of styles. "Well, what is this narrative if not a comedy, and with the obligatory marriage as the curtain rings down?" There was little else he could say about this "farce" that he had tried to write "in a merry tone," he told his young Italian admirer Mario Turiello.[1]

The irony is that when he was writing with least solemnity, he was inadvertently creating the raw material for a later controversy. In the next century, amateurs of the occult would be persuaded that *Clovis Dardentor* contains a hidden message, and a deadly serious one. They maintain that Verne prepared the story with code words—names that when parsed reveal secret meanings—as if the author had had the time or the stomach for that. One writer counted five hundred "numerical clues" in the story; another found concealed information even in the "omissions" and "silences." These writers contend that the message concealed in Verne's farce points the way to a vast hidden treasure, possibly King Solomon's, buried by the Knights Templar. Wasn't Clovis Dardentor named for the Merovingian king? In one author's view, Verne was a Freemason, if not a Rosicrucian.[2] (When published, Verne's book won few readers; perhaps this promise of treasure will attract some now.)

FRÉDÉRIC PETIT—EIGHT YEARS VERNE'S JUNIOR—DIED, UNexpectedly of a heart attack. Jules Verne had grown to admire his mayor, lay republican that he was. "It's an irreparable loss for the city," he told Paul. "I lose in this good man . . . a true friend, and this has affected me deeply. He had a magnificent funeral, unfortunately non-religious. But it couldn't have been done otherwise."[3] Such comments affirm the contradictions that underlay the political career of councilman Verne.

In further letters to Mario Turiello, who was preparing an essay on the *Extraordinary Voyages,* Jules seemed to be planting the seeds for a Verne esthetic. In April 1895, after receiving a partial text of Turiello's study, Verne called him to task for not quite comprehending his purpose, which was "the teaching of geography, the description of the earth. For each new country I had to invent a new story. The characters are only secondary, whatever you may think."[4]

In making this point, Verne seemed to be excluding the large part of his work in which anticipatory science, or character, even humor—or horror—took precedence over the teaching of geography: the moon books, for example, or *The Clipper of the Clouds.* Privately, Turiello remained unconvinced; he knew that Jules Verne's Scotland, for example, was not the geographer's, but a Scotland of the mind, inspired more by Walter Scott and other writers than by scientific observation.[5]

In this dialogue with his Italian correspondent, Verne was of course wearing his public face. He knew his books were not selling, but when in his essay on Verne, Turiello said the same thing, Verne cut him short. For one thing, since Turiello was hoping that Jules Hetzel would read and perhaps print his essay, Verne warned him that the publisher would never accept his finding that Verne was now neglected. "Especially since it isn't true—far from that, and in the crisis that bookselling is undergoing in France, because of the prodigious number of books being published— the author in question, thanks to his particular public, is one of those who has the least to complain about."[6]

Verne was certainly an optimist, or he would never have attempted his next project. That autumn found him halfway through an ambitious work in progress, nothing less than a sequel to the major work of his model Edgar Allan Poe. In *The Narrative of Arthur Gordon Pym*, Poe had unraveled a fantastic tale of shipboard mutiny en route to the South Seas, the recapture of the vessel by the survivors, their shipwreck and travails, and then their deliverance by a British schooner, which in turn is captured, her crew massacred.

In the unforgettable final pages of Poe's hallucinatory story, Arthur Pym and a fellow seaman, after escaping from savages aboard a canoe, navigate in the remote Antarctic with the help of makeshift sails. The sea becomes agitated and takes on a milky consistency; although they are drawn irresistibly southward, the water temperature rises constantly; a white powder resembling ashes falls over their boat. In the end, the water is too hot to touch, as a wall of vapor obscures the horizon, gradually taking the form of a cataract. "We were nearly overwhelmed by the white ashy shower which settled upon us and upon the canoe, but melted into the water as it fell," Pym's diary continues. The "summit of the cataract was utterly lost in the dimness and the distance. Yet we were evidently approaching it with a hideous velocity." Then as they rush into the cataract: "There arose in our pathway a shrouded human figure. . . . And the hue of the skin for the figure was of the perfect whiteness of the snow."

The reader never finds out whether the mysterious creature saves them, for the narrative ceases at that dramatic instant.

Writing about Poe more than thirty years earlier (in his long essay in *Musée des Familles*), Verne confirmed his fascination with the Pym story by retelling it, and at considerable length. Obviously, his imagination had been captured by the tale's strange and abrupt ending. "Who will take it up again?" he asked. "Someone more audacious than I, braver in adventuring into the domain of impossible phenomena."[7]

Now he obviously thought that he possessed that audacity. By October 1895, so he informed Paul, he was finishing the second (and final) volume of the book that would be called *The Mystery of Arthur Gordon Pym (Le Sphinx des glaces)*. He also let Paul know that Michel had just spent a week in Amiens and was writing a novel based on a plot suggested by Jules. Indeed, Michel's book would be, according to Jules, "a continuation of those I write."[8]

A point to remember—since Michel published under his father's name after Jules's death. Perhaps the manuscript to which Jules referred was one of these. "It certainly shows a remarkable writing facility," the proud father said of his son's work. The book could be the much-admired posthumous novel *The Thompson Travel Agency (L'Agence Thompson and Co)* to be discussed in its place.[9]

"I'm working a lot," Jules told his brother in November 1895, "but the dizziness no longer leaves me alone—a distension of the stomach, probably incurable at my age. All that smells the end," he added ominously.[10] When Paul expressed concern over his brother's letter, Jules replied, "But no, I don't work too much, I assure you. I have a distension, and I'll live more or less with this distension."[11]

His pessimism is evident in letters to Mario Turiello. "Paris isn't far," he conceded in a letter dated January 5, 1896, "but Paris doesn't tempt me anymore. Will I ever go back there for a few days? It's not at all sure."[12] The coming of spring focused his attention on Amiens, for it was time for another city council election. This time, in the absence of that supreme mediator Frédéric Petit, there was a split between the Radical Socialists and a middle-of-the-road pro bono group; by joining the latter, Verne could increase the distance between himself and the more aggressive republicans. He won four more years of municipal responsibility.

He still continued to suffer a disability with his hand. "Try to read me," he beseeched Paul in a letter dated May 8, 1896, "for I have difficult writing, which makes me desperate."[13] To his publisher, he expressed the fear that writer's cramp would drive him to the typewriter—a painful thought, for details came to him only with pen in hand.[14] All the same, he assured Paul, he was still producing an enormous quantity of work. "I don't budge any longer, and have become as much a homebody as I was active in the past. Age, lameness, worries, all that has led me to sit on my backside all day long."[15]

His industrious but curiously uninspired *Propeller Island* had been published in installments in Hetzel's *Magasin d'Education* for the preceding twelve months; now, in 1896, the shorter *For the Flag* was to run from January to June, while another short book, *Clovis Dardentor,* would finish off the year. To fulfill his commitment to the magazine for 1897, he was putting final touches to *The Mystery of Arthur Gordon Pym,* which he was now calling the counterpart to *Captain Hatteras,* although the two works shared neither characters nor story line.

He told Hetzel he wished to dedicate the book to Poe, and to "my American friends"; his wish was fulfilled.[16] Would Americans like it? he wondered aloud in a letter to Mario Turiello.[17] To Willis E. Hurd, founder of an American Jules Verne Society, he recommended his sequel to *Pym,* pointing out that it was dedicated to Poe and to his friends in the United States.[18]

In this book that had so enraptured Verne as he wrote it, the narrator, Jeorling, encounters a man convinced that Edgar Allan Poe's story of Pym is true. This man, Len Guy, claims to have found the message in the bottle described in Poe's novel, and he wishes to track down the survivors of the *Jane,* the British fishing vessel that had saved Pym, and on which he had traveled toward the South Pole. The captain of the *Jane* was Len Guy's brother.

Jeorling thinks Guy is mad, but he joins the quest; now *he* is a witness to the essential soundness of Poe's narrative. They pursue their voyage to the Antarctic, crossing a sea clear of ice within the polar circle. They also find the island described by Poe, and traces of the survivors of the *Jane.* And a sailor taken on board during a layover in the Falkland Islands reveals himself to be Dirk Peters, the faithful half-breed companion of Arthur Gordon Pym.

The search party collides with an iceberg. Their vessel requires repairs and they are left stranded by mutineers who flee in their dinghy. Then another small boat approaches, with survivors of the *Jane,* among them its captain, Guy's brother. The two parties, now one, attain the magnetic pole, only to come upon an enormous ice sphinx—highly magnetized, for their longboat is drawn to it because of its iron grapnel. There they confront the horror: the lifeless body of Pym, suspended on the magnetic sphinx by the rifle strapped to his back. Seeing this, Dirk Peters dies of heartbreak.

WHILE WRITING *FOR THE FLAG,* JULES VERNE HAD OFTEN referred to it as his Turpin story. It took the real Eugène Turpin some time to stumble upon his story in Verne's new novel, which had run in

Magasin d'Education from January to June 1896, then appeared as a book in July. Turpin didn't file a libel complaint until October.

Of course Verne denied that he had taken Turpin as the model for his mad scientist. And Jules Hetzel found him a first-class lawyer in the person of Raymond Poincaré, future prime minister and president of France. One can assume the lawyer was totally ignorant of the novelist's confessed intentions during the writing of *For the Flag;* he hadn't read the personal letters in which Verne clearly stated Turpin was the model for his protagonist.

Professing innocence to Poincaré, the veteran novelist insisted that his entire work proved that he had always placed literary considerations above personalities. Verne claimed that at his age and after publishing eighty works of fiction, he would not now choose to write a novel about a living person.[19]

At the opening of the trial in Paris in November, Turpin took the stand to present his case against Verne. Turpin's testimony is not available, for, on the grounds that national security was involved, the court banned reporting of the evidence.[20]

On November eighteenth, following Turpin's testimony, Jules Verne took the stand. "I never thought of Mr. Turpin," he said, perjuring himself, "whom I am seeing for the first time, and I leave everything to my attorney."[21] And so he did, returning to Amiens before the trial was over, confident that his reputation and Poincaré's skills would triumph over what we now know to have been the truth.

The proceedings went badly for the hapless scientist. His attorney announced that he relinquished his demand for 250,000 francs in damages, asking only for a symbolic one-franc award. In his argument, he listed similarities between Verne's mad scientist and his client. "Today," he addressed the absent Verne, "you haven't done what other authors have done in your situation. You committed a libel, you tried to dishonor a man, a very ugly thing."

Poincaré was impressive in Verne's defense. Apparently he was convinced, and he convinced the court, that Turpin had not served as Verne's model. The government attorney wasn't much help to the complainant, for he defended the author's right "to seize facts that strike his mind and to use them to create a work of pure imagination and fantasy." He then called for rejection of the complaint.[22]

The court agreed to that—albeit without quite accepting Verne's declaration that he had not had Turpin in mind. It was determined that Turpin had served as an inspiration but that Verne had not intended any harm. In the climax of the novel, noted the judges, Verne's mad scientist comes to his senses and blows up the island and its evil plotters, thus rallying to the French flag—a fine example for everybody. It was unlikely, maintained the court, that Verne had Turpin in mind when he showed his hero dying for his country, but if that had been the case, Turpin, far from complaining, should be proud that he was thought capable of such devotion.

Not only was the complaint dismissed but Turpin was ordered to pay court costs.[23] Reporting this, *Le Petit Temps* observed that if Turpin had not been the model for Verne's hero—since Verne's scientist was mad—it was also true that in the conception of the novel and of its hero, as well as in the succession of events involving the scientist, "Jules Verne took inspiration from the personality and the acts of Turpin."[24]

The luckless scientist filed an appeal, and Verne was again summoned to appear in his own defense. "Although I walk only with difficulty," he informed Poincaré, "now suffering from rheumatism of the legs, I shall be in Paris for the trial." On March seventh a second judgment was handed down, confirming the original decision: There could be no libel without an intention to harm, and that intention was not present, "which besides would be irreconcilable with the literary past and the high talent of Jules Verne."[25]

VERNE WAS AN OLD MAN AT SIXTY-NINE. DURING THE WINTER of 1897, he told his nephew Maurice that he was not well. Maurice had written to inform his uncle of his father Paul's heart condition. "I can barely move around," Jules wrote back, "rheumatism having joined up with bronchitis, and I'm just beginning to go out again." Of course confinement didn't prevent him from pursuing his activity; on the contrary, it was just what he needed to get more work done. "I am working assiduously," he informed Jules Hetzel in May 1897, "and without that what would become of me!"[26]

Writing to his young Italian admirer on May 5, 1897—"despite my rheumatisms"—he said he had a number of shorter stories ready for publication but couldn't say when they would actually appear. "This doesn't depend entirely on me . . . I only publish two volumes a year, and I have so many books ready in advance that I am now writing the book to appear in 1903."[27]

Paul, who never seemed to complain as much as his brother did, succumbed at last to his heart disease; Jules received the sad news from Maurice by telegram on August 27, 1897. His curious reply had more to do with his chronic illnesses than Paul's fatal one. "I have just now received the telegram informing me of the death of my poor brother, a death that was expected, but still atrocious," he wrote his nephew that evening. "I never thought that I'd outlive him. I'm not at all well. Since the day of your sister's marriage I've had one indigestion after another, and I stand on my feet with difficulty."

Verne expressed his sadness in a letter to Jules Hetzel. "We are deeply afflicted, and what a friend I have lost in him!" But he said he didn't think he could go to Paris for the funeral. "My health rules this out, for at any instant I can be floored by dizziness and indigestion, which has already happened several times." At best, he told Hetzel, he'd take a short summer holiday within easy reach of Amiens.[28]

Soon he was back in harness; that autumn, he assured Hetzel: "I'm working steadily as always, functioning like a machine, and I don't let the furnace cool."[29]

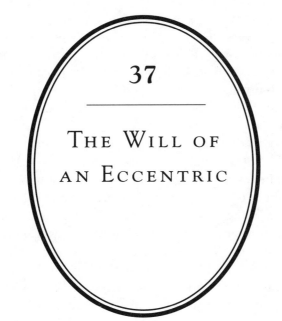

37

THE WILL OF
AN ECCENTRIC

J ULES VERNE'S SELF-EXILE CONTINUED TO SHIELD HIM FROM
the men and occasionally women of letters, usually resident in Paris, who
knew and who talked to everyone and then went home to write it all down
in their private notebooks. Diarists who did happen to meet him on one
of his rare visits to the capital didn't get sufficiently close to record their
impressions for posterity. So it was the journalists who went up to Amiens
specifically to meet him who have left a record of the public Jules Verne.
But since they knew that Verne would be reading what they wrote, their
observations are not as objective a source as one might wish.

Thus in December of that painful year—1897—the critic Adolphe
Brisson, editor of *Annales politiques et littéraires,* called at the rue Charles-
Dubois to do one of the portrait "Promenades" for which he was becoming known. The visitor found his host still lively, and Brisson was
impressed by the tranquillity of the surroundings and, once inside the
house, by the simple but obviously expensive furnishings.

Honorine Verne, explaining that their dining room was too big, showed
Brisson into a smaller room where a lunch table was set. He noted that
Verne ate eggs and greens, as if a vegetarian; his wife also had a light lunch.

The celebrated author seemed content in his isolation. Paris was only
two hours away by train now, but he no longer bothered to make the trip.
"The air you breathe here is healthy, it appeases the nerves and fortifies
the brain. . . . And then if you knew how unambitious I am!" The visitor

had to be impressed by Verne's productivity. He would soon tell readers of *Le Temps:* "The seventy-seventh volume by Mr. Jules Verne has just appeared. The seventy-eighth will blossom with the roses, the seventy-ninth will be ripe with the grapes, and if it pleases God, the hundredth, in about a dozen years, will crown the series."

The author of all these books asked not to be complimented; since he said work was his true happiness. As soon as he completed a book, he was miserable, and he felt at ease again only when he was hard at work on the next one. "Idleness is torture for me." As proof, he let Brisson look at his work in progress, the extensive notes, the draft written in pencil, to be traced in ink only when the text was ready for publication.

The journalist feigned surprise at Verne's confession that he'd never sailed beyond the Channel and the Mediterranean. Nor had Verne encountered cannibals or even Chinese. Then surely he must have practiced sports, hunted, and fished. Verne replied that he found fishing barbaric, hunted only once and hit a gendarme's chapeau, for which he received a summons to court.

They toured Amiens on foot. At three sharp, observed Brisson, Verne walked into a pastry shop, where fresh milk was kept on reserve for him; he had his daily cup. "And they say writers can be discovered in their books!" exclaimed the interviewer (to his readers).[1]

"I'm neither well nor unwell," Verne wrote to Hetzel in March, "living only on milk and eggs . . . not even vegetables." (Perhaps a necessary change from the "greens" Adolphe Brisson had watched him gobble down.) Before the year was over, he was telling Hetzel, "I no longer have legs except for what it takes to go to the Société Industrielle [a club] and the city hall every day. What do you expect when you are stupid enough to have been born under Charles X!"[2]

The family must have gotten used to his pessimism, which seemed to make it impossible for him to say anything wholly nice. His sister Marie's son was marrying. "A marriage isn't an extraordinary event in a family as large as ours," he replied to her announcement, adding, all the same, that "we wish all possible happiness to the wedding couple." Of course he was invited to join them in Nantes for the marriage, but he had to refuse. The family had spread out, making a reunion difficult, but such was the lot of large families.[3]

A letter he wrote to the secretary-general of the Geographic Society of Paris survives; apparently, he'd been asked to renew his membership. "I have reached an age when one must go into retirement," he explained; he was gradually withdrawing from all the associations with which he had been connected. His letter is dated November 24, 1898.[4]

Perhaps he simply didn't wish to pay dues to that group anymore. For just a month later the sinister Ligue de la Patrie Française—League of the French Fatherland—came into being. It was intended as a counterweight to the campaign of intellectuals on behalf of Captain Dreyfus; Jules Verne was among the first prominent sponsors. Despite such sponsors as the writer Gyp, whose pulp novels were laced with racism, and the anti-Semitic polemicist Léon Daudet, the new group was considered moderate; Francisque Sarcey of *Le Temps* was also a sponsor, along with the novelist Pierre Louÿs, the nationalist pamphleteer Maurice Barrès, and the Provençal poet Frédéric Mistral. Actually, there were worse groups.

With the publication of Emile Zola's open letter "J'accuse" in 1898, the Dreyfus Affair had flared up again. Dreyfusards now knew the identity of the real spy, Esterhazy, and so of course did the French army. But it was Zola, not Esterhazy, who was indicted for libel and subsequently convicted. He escaped going to prison by slipping away to Britain. Still, one after the other, the men who had forged the case against Dreyfus were identified. On the floor of the Chamber of Deputies Raymond Poincaré, Verne's defender in the Turpin affair, declared, "The silence of some of us at the present time would be a true act of cowardice."[5]

Writing to Mario Turiello at the end of October 1898, Verne had indicated reluctance to reply to a question about "l'affaire D." "Alas! Wouldn't it be better not to talk about this anymore? The case was judged as far as I am concerned a long time ago, and well judged, whatever may happen in the future."[6] In a letter to Hetzel in February 1899, Verne called himself "anti-Dreyfus in the soul," confessing, "I understand our Poincaré's attitude less and less!"[7] Yet the protracted process that Zola was to call "truth on the march" as now well under way, and it would end only with the rehabilitation of the accused French Jewish officer.

The paradox is that Jules's son, Michel, was "an ardent pro-Dreyfus supporter," to use the words of Jean, Michel's son, and this despite his conservative political convictions, which Jean saw as "reactionary, even royalist." Jean—only an infant at the time—later speculated that their contrary positions on the Dreyfus Affair led to a temporary rupture in relations between Jules and Michel Verne.[8] If so, it was not the only time a family split over Dreyfus.

※◎ ◎⧸

NEITHER VERNE'S HEALTH NOR THE INELUCTABLE REHABILI-tation of Captain Dreyfus seemed to slow him down. "As you know, thanks to continuous labor, I have a certain number of volumes ready for

publication," Verne wrote to Hetzel late in August 1899. "It is probable
that some of them will be posthumous."[9] "For the past month," he told
Turiello in mid-October 1899, "it seems to me that my health has been
deteriorating; I keep myself going by steady working habits."[10] A first-time
visitor who called on him now saw his office as a "peaceful sanctuary,
closed to the noise of the crowd." The visitor was the explorer Etienne
Richet, who had stopped in Amiens fresh from his discovery of the
sources of the Yukon River in northwestern Canada.[11] Verne was then
writing his novel about the Klondike mines, *The Golden Volcano (Le Volcan
d'or)*, which would not be published until a year after his death.

The last year of the century saw the serialization in Hetzel's magazine
of a tale as complicated as any Jules Verne had written up until then. In
The Will of an Eccentric (Le Testament d'un excentrique) Verne offered his
readers not just one trip, but many. And he indulged himself by depicting
the dream journey across the United States that he had never attempted.
The story begins on April 3, 1897. Following the announcement of the
death of eccentric Chicago millionaire William J. Hypperbone, six representative citizens have been invited to a public reading of his will. Once a
passionate player of the French game of goose, in which competitors proceed from square to square on successive rolls of dice, Hypperbone has
left instructions that the chosen six play the game—using the whole
United States as their board. They are to move from city to city "like
pawns on a chessboard."[12] On each throw of the dice, the precise destination will be indicated to the player, and some destinations bring penal-
ties rather than rewards. The first to complete the game will inherit
William J. Hypperbone's colossal fortune.

To create his dream trip, Verne had the benefit of a brand-new French-
language travel guide to the United States, the first Baedeker of the New
World, which ran 516 pages in the familiar red-bound compact format,
with small print to allow for every finicky detail one might need. All
American railroads , large and small, were listed, along with the kinds of
accommodation passengers could expect on arrival in a given location;
then, for each city, they could find the time it would take to get to the
next important stop, the price of the ticket, and the hotels and restau-
rants available.[13] For meticulous Jules Verne, that was almost as good as
making the trip notebook in hand.

On the lighter side, he could now find any number of books containing personal experiences of travel. One that was still new when he began
writing, for example, was a "Journey in the country of dollars," in which
the author paid particular attention to the pleasures and the dangers of
traveling by rail.[14]

Some of the players in *The Will of an Eccentric* are already affluent; others are poor but honest—like Lissy Wag, a cashier at Chicago's Marshall Field department store. Most members of the group would make pleasant traveling companions—but not all. The least sympathetic is a married couple of German origin, the Titburys. They are not only frugal but miserly, and yet a certain amount of spending will be necessary in this transcontinental contest. Paradoxically, the reactions of the contemptible Titburys are those so often heard from Verne himself. Like Jules in his own early travels, notably on the *Great Eastern* sailing to the United States, the Titbury couple "took care to choose the fastest and least costly itinerary possible"; had they been flesh-and-blood people, they might have moved from Paris to Amiens to save money. (That they are not meant to be Verne and *his* wife becomes clear when one of the likable contestants, the Quebecois painter Max Réal, calls Titbury a usurer and a "shearer of Christians.")

Then a mysterious entrant joins the fray (a codicil to the original will makes this possible); he is revealed to be the millionaire himself, who hadn't died after all. He wins the goose game, then marries Lissy's humble traveling companion, while nice Mr. Réal and modest Lissy also marry.

Describing the story to Mario Turiello (Verne called it "exceedingly whimsical"), he also let it be known that he now had twelve other volumes ready for publication in future years.[15] On publication of the illustrated edition of *The Will of an Eccentric,* in time for Christmas 1899, a newspaper offered more numbers (undoubtedly supplied by the publisher): 79 volumes published thus far, 840 separate installments having appeared in Hetzel's *Magasin.* "Pending the arrival of a new literature designed for children, which seems slow in manifesting itself, why not be satisfied by that which remains superior by its diversity and moral qualities?" asked the anonymous reviewer.[16] One can guess that the author would have preferred to see his work described in other terms.

CALENDARS SUDDENLY READ 1900. SOME THINGS CHANGED for Jules Verne, while others remained the same. Michel, for instance, was still looking for a career (he was working, but at a temporary job—for the organization putting together the Universal Exposition of 1900). Most of what is known about Michel at this time comes from his letters to his father's publisher, usually to ask for early payment of the one thousand francs his father continued to accord him monthly from his royalty account; these letters indicate a busy life.

Thus in February 1900, Michel traveled to Moscow and Saint Petersburg, presumably on Universal Exposition business, although his son wrote that Michel was involved in mining in Russia (and as far off as Siberia) as well as Romania around this time. After the 1900 fair, he became manager of a paper mill. Apparently, he was always able to afford to keep his family on the beach (albeit a pebble beach) for a month or two each summer.[17]

Meanwhile, Jules continued to ply the only trade he knew. In the course of this year, a book entitled *Second Fatherland (Seconde Patrie)*, another of his "Robinson" books (shipwreck, deserted island transformed into paradise), appeared in *Magasin d'Education* prior to book publication. The manuscript has been preserved; it is in Jules's own hand, drafted as usual in pencil; then (after a first editing process) the penciled words had been meticulously traced over in ink—all this on the left side of each manuscript page, leaving the right-hand side for insertions and corrections.[18] The book was inspired by *The Swiss Family Robinson*, and Verne thought that his version was better.[19]

He was hard at work on a new project, *The Village in the Treetops (Le Village aérien)*, which would fulfill his magazine commitment for 1901. The manuscript of this shorter work was also written in Verne's hand.[20] Yet he was writing under increasingly difficult conditions now; he could hardly read, since both eyes were affected by incipient cataracts, so he informed his faithful Italian correspondent in mid-August.[21] "I barely see enough to read, write, and eat, while waiting for the dreaded operation," he told Jules Hetzel at the beginning of October.[22] "The cataract operation hasn't been done yet because it's not yet time for it," he wrote to Turiello just before Christmas.[23]

The Vernes had decided to abandon their town house on rue Charles-Dubois, "that big house as heavy to support as it is cold," as Jules described it to Hetzel. They moved only a couple of hundred yards along the railroad track, to 44, boulevard de Longueville, the house they had lived in before moving to the corner town house. This time, there was no public garden to conceal the cutting; The Vernes saw and heard every train (Jules used a room directly above the tracks as his office).

Michel's youngest son, Jean, nine years old when his grandparents moved, was beginning to see and understand things that he'd later recall in the biography of his grandfather. He remembered how much smaller the house on boulevard de Longueville seemed after the generous proportions of the manor on the corner, how crowded with the furniture brought in from the larger house. The living and dining areas were connected; the stairway in the narrow entranceway lead to bedrooms on the upper floors and to the "holy of holies," Jules Verne's library and contiguous office, a snug room containing two tables, a high-backed, low-seated armchair, and a camp bed, where the writer slept so he could be up and at work before dawn. Jean Jules-Verne called it a monk's cell.

Jules would write his books from five in the morning until eleven, then take a walk—limping all the way—returning to wait around impatiently for lunch. The time came when he no longer had even that much patience; he'd eat before everyone else. Grandson Jean had heard stories about how Jules once ate a whole leg of mutton because he couldn't wait for late dinner guests; he'd eat six enormous artichokes from the Amiens marshland vegetable gardens.

Jean didn't pretend to have witnessed these things, nor did he ever get to know the Jules Verne remembered in the family for "fits of anger, joys and sorrows." *His* grandfather was a placid old soul. "Kindly and good, he avoided vain disputes in resorting to silence when he felt that the discussion risked becoming heated. He seemed a model of equilibrium."[24]

One tends to forget unhappy things. In 1901, for example, in the early months of his return to the boulevard de Longueville, Jules must have presented a grim face to friends and family, even to a grandchild. He was writing, but he could barely see what he was writing; the operation on his eyes had been postponed again on doctor's orders. "It seems we must wait, wait and wait," he told Mario Turiello. "It's most disheartening."[25] To his old and faithful friend Félix Nadar, who had read about his illness in the Paris press, he replied reassuringly that: The papers exaggerated—he'd only had a cold. "What they didn't say is that I'm almost blind, and will remain so until my cataract operation. I no longer recognize anyone in the street, barely see what I write, and live in a fog."[26]

The manuscript he was working on at the time (published posthumously, with revisions by Michel) provided tangible evidence of his handicap. The scholar who inventoried it noted: "The writing, very distorted, often ignores the lines of the paper."[27] In this novel, *The Chase of the Golden Meteor (La Chasse au météore)*, a self-taught scientist who has mastered the secret of energy employs his power to maneuver a meteoric mass of gold so that it will fall on the piece of ground he has chosen for it—thus exciting the greed of the civilized world and making his uncle rich. Then he scuttles the meteoroid and returns to his modest laboratory. One final time, Verne lets us see gold, then scatters or scuttles it as if so much waste (let the psychoanalysts deal with that one). It was not the kind of story Hetzel wanted for his magazine, but he did think it good enough to publish as a book, three years after the death of its author.

ON MAY 22, 1901, ANOTHER JOURNALIST TRAVELED TO AMIENS to call on Jules Verne. "The Master still erect, with his white beard, his eyes of a singular vivacity," this interviewer wrote. The visitor's mission was to obtain Verne's idea of the time it would now take to travel around the world (his answer was thirty-three or thirty-four days).

At the end of the interview, the journalist slipped in a word about the French Academy. "I'm too old to think about that!" Verne declared, dismissing the notion. Why, thought the visitor, didn't the academicians think about it *for* him?[28]

Verne would begin his ninety-ninth book the following day.

38

THE END OF
THE SERIES

While Jules Verne hardly moved from his chair, his books continued to take him everywhere. Despite an inobservant journalist's impression of the "singular vivacity" of his eyes, Verne could hardly see now, and yet he made things come to life for his readers. His new novel, *Village in the Treetops*, took them back to the fauna and flora of the most arduous of his extraordinary voyages.

Two hunters—an American and a Frenchman (Verne's favorite people)—invade the still-mysterious central African jungle. After fleeing an attack by wild elephants, they come upon the traces of a German scientist who had been seeking the link between man and monkey, à la Darwin. While the heroes—accompanied by a native guide and an African child they have rescued from a hostile tribe—fail to find the missing scientist, they are taken captive by strange monkey-men, primitive humanoids who build their dwellings high above the ground. The savages possess not only language but religion, thus providing Verne an occasion to explore the nature of man.[1]

In the elevated village, the hunters are befriended by the father of an infant they have rescued from drowning. They learn that these creatures can make fire, and boats good enough to sail on. Then they discover that the tribal king is the missing German scientist, now gone mad. Finally, the grateful father of the boy-monkey facilitates their escape. And when the hunters leave to return to Europe, father and child display another human trait: They weep.

Long since forgotten, the work that followed on the heels of *The Village in the Treetops* harkened back to Verne's great adventure stories of the high seas. In the book, whose translated title is *The Stories of Jean-Marie Cabidoulin (Les Histoires de Jean-Marie Cabidoulin)*, the untempered rivalry between French and English whalers leads to a confrontation with inexplicable phenomena that *could* be explained by the existence of sea monsters. But the author does not conclude, and doesn't let his readers conclude, which is probably why the book was quickly forgotten.

In July 1901, a visiting reporter actually got to see Jules Verne ill, and told his readers about it. A journalist from the Paris daily *Le Matin* had been assigned the job of making an around-the-world tour à la Phileas Fogg. He was to follow Fogg's route, while taking advantage of facilities not available in Fogg's time. On his return on August 1, 1901, Gaston Stiegler's race around the world was clocked at fifty-three days, ten hours, and twenty minutes. The day before Stiegler's triumphal appearance in Paris, a reporter from *Le Matin* hopped a train for Amiens to obtain Jules Verne's reactions.

"In the immobility of Amiens, which seems asleep," the reporter began, "there is a boulevard more solitary and a passion more silent, a kind of comfortable cloister from which no human sound emerges, unless it be the grumbling of a deaf servant or the discreet voice of a devoted wife." The only movement here was represented by "the Master's thought."

But now the master was abed, victim of "a spell of dizziness, above all an excess of work"; the overwork "had all but shut his eyes," and the reporter didn't hesitate to predict "forthcoming blindness." Verne had been working on his hundredth volume when floored by illness; he asked only to be able to finish it "before the darkness becomes total." The *Matin* reporter was told that the writer now dictated his novels to his wife.

Verne and the reporter from Paris talked all the same, "during moments when his headache was less severe"; out of their conversation came a moving story. Only a few months before, when the plan to send a journalist around the world became known, the *New York Journal* sent an emissary to ask Jules Verne to undertake the same journey. Of course, Verne had to reject the idea, pointing to his age and his frailty.

The brazen visitor persisted: "It's not your strength, it's your name we want. Just say yes and we'll handle everything else."

The dialogue may very well have gone that way, for the *Journal* was then personally managed by its owner, William Randolph Hearst, the bad boy of the American press, who, in waging a New York newspaper circulation war, had already helped to push the United States into war with Spain. In the face of Verne's continued reticence, Hearst's man declared, "You can set your price. Whatever you ask for I'm authorized to accept."

"All right then—give me eyes!" Verne had replied.

After he finished telling this story to the reporter from *Le Matin,* Verne seemed to fade away. Honorine took over. "You must be good and go to sleep," she told her husband softly, "if you want to be able to say goodbye to [the Paris journalist] at the station tomorrow morning." Verne closed his eyes.[2]

A month later, he was able to reassure Mario Turiello that he could still see "well enough to read and write." He hadn't been operated on for the cataracts, for his doctor didn't think they had reached the critical stage. Perhaps he'd never have the operation, he told Turiello the following January, and yet he continued to see only with great difficulty; he even feared he was going blind.[3]

⁓⊚ ⊚⁓

AT THE BEGINNING OF 1902, VERNE WAS SHEPHERDING ANother book through the publishing process—*The Brothers Kip (Les Frères Kip).*

As he so often did, Verne made the inspiration for his story clear at the outset. *The Brothers Kip,* he explained to Mario Turiello, "was inspired by the story of the Rorique brothers." (Nearly everybody in France had read about this famous murder trial; it is puzzling why Verne would think that Italians hadn't also heard about the case.)[4] The Roriques had been accused of seizing a French schooner, then killing its captain and crew. They pleaded innocent, testifying that in fact they had put down a mutiny; they said it was during the struggle for possession of the ship that the captain, his crew, and a passenger were slain.

Public opinion was on the side of the brothers, and eventually a death sentence was commuted to life at hard labor, then later reduced to twenty years. The novelized version of the case portrays evil crewmen who murder their captain and then fabricate a case against Karl and Pieter Kip (their Flemish names confirm that they are modeled on the Rorique brothers, who in fact were sons of an honorable Belgian family). In Verne's story, one shipowner believes in their innocence, and after they are convicted and sentenced to death he is able to have the sentence changed to life at hard labor (as happened in reality). When political prisoners break out of confinement, the Kip brothers are also freed, but they quickly give themselves up; this makes a favorable impression on the authorities, who, backed by public opinion, agree to a retrial. The brothers win, thanks to the enlargement of a photograph of the murder victim's face; in the pupil of an eye, the image of the real assassins—the evil crewmen—can clearly be seen.

It was typical of Jules Verne to take a true story and then add surprises of his own. The book somehow didn't impress his regular readers, though, and it is among the least likely of all the books in the Verne cycle to be found today, for it was seldom, if ever, reprinted. One remembers the book now only because a latter-day scholar, taking the lead from Verne's grandson Jean, thought he saw in it an allusion to the Dreyfus case. To accept the theory, one would have to believe that Verne had converted to the side of Captain Dreyfus—an odd notion in view of the evidence.[5] For in the very years the novelist was drafting his Kip story, he was also declaring to all who would listen that Dreyfus was *guilty*. He regretted only that misguided souls were defending Dreyfus, and he joined die-hard nationalists in a campaign specifically dedicated to the anti-Dreyfus cause.

ONE SIGN OF VERNE'S AGE WAS AN AGGRAVATED SENSE OF pessimism. When Mario Turiello egged him on to write the story of his travels, the story of his own life, Verne replied that his own career and experience weren't terribly interesting. "A writer interests his country or the world only as *writer*."[6] In a statement written expressly at the request of the *Pittsburgh Gazette*, published in that paper on July 13, 1902, he predicted that novels would not be read in fifty or a hundred years—at least not in book form; they'd be replaced by newspapers. Novels weren't necessary, he stated. When people wanted history, they would get it from the press (and then cut out and save the stories). In his opinion, even the fantastic novel was on its way out; writers of the future would work with actual facts.

He said he was writing his hundredth book, and the way things were going, he wondered if he'd ever write another after that. Because of failing sight, he could do only a page or two a day, since he also wished to save some of his sight for reading, in order to keep up with the world. So far, eighty-four of his one hundred books had been published. If they continued to come out at six-month intervals, it was likely that ten or even twenty of them would appear posthumously. But then, he added, if the long-awaited cataract operation gave him his eyesight back, he'd begin work on his *second* hundred books.

The American paper headlined its story JULES VERNE SAYS THE NOVEL WILL SOON BE DEAD.[7]

A LETTER SURVIVES THAT VERNE SENT TO THE DIRECTOR OF the Academy of Amiens on November 1, 1902, in reply to a request that he write something for that body. "Do you forget that at my age words fade away and ideas no longer come? Think about it! I was already 74 at the toll of the billionth minute of the Christian era."[8]

When a Dickens Society in England asked Verne for a brief word of homage to their idol, he replied (at the end of February 1903): "I have the highest esteem for this illustrious novelist whom I have read and read again: Study of manners, sensibility, fantasy, pity, humor, wit."[9] More improbably—perhaps another example of this resolute provincial's craving to embrace the world—he offered an unreserved endorsement of the Esperanto movement, which promoted the use of an invented universal language. The campaign (or the craze) reached Amiens in 1903; when a local chapter of the movement was established there, Jules Verne agreed to be its honorary president. He promised that he'd make the new language the theme of a future novel, and he kept his promise—in the unfinished novel *Study Trip*.

Esperanto had been invented and was being propagated by an ophthalmologist of Polish Jewish origin, Lejzer Zamenhof (the handbook on Esperanto published by the Amiens group in 1903 identified him simply as a "Russian doctor"). A character in Verne's abandoned Esperantist novel is a Russian humanist bearing the name Nicolas Vanof.[10]

"THE CONDITION OF MY EYES, MY DEAR TURIELLO, 'SHOULD not' allow me to write to you—I mean to write," Verne began a letter to his most ardent Italian admirer in mid-April. "But I don't want to leave some letters without a reply."[11] A note of optimism is detectable; he seemed to be getting better, and this without the long-awaited operation. In a letter to his sister Marie in mid-August, he dismissed a Paris newspaper's report as exaggeration. He was *not* going blind in both eyes. If his right eye had a cataract, the left one hadn't followed suit. "I read, I write, I walk, and the condition of my eyesight isn't getting any worse." He no longer seemed to require an operation. Of course he felt his age, he said. Wasn't he the family elder, "the dean of a large family so feeble and scattered?"

Honorine added her own letter to her husband's. "In having Jules reply," she began, "I wanted you to see that his eyesight even if weakened still allows him to write and as he told you to work[;] he complains of growing old, we're both in the same situation, except that he likes solitude and doesn't seek to go out. He no longer wants to travel, which I regret, for I'd so much like to see you all again."[12]

Robert Sherard had found Verne far from lighthearted on a visit to Amiens only a few weeks earlier. The English journalist talked with a Jules Verne "haunted with the fear of blindness," yet pursuing his work "manfully," resolved to carry out the contract with his publisher to the very end. Verne told Sherard that he had nine or ten manuscripts ready to go, which meant that he could supply the annual demand for two volumes for another five years.[13]

This was to be Sherard's final meeting with Jules Verne. He entered a house considerably smaller than the one he remembered (he had last been in Amiens ten years earlier, to interview Verne). At the outset, Verne made it clear that his right eye was done for—the cataract had seen to that. But since his left eye was still in rather good shape, he preferred not to risk an operation as long as he could see well enough to carry out what little reading and writing was still possible for him. He was, he said, an old man now.

He couldn't resist telling Sherard about the books that were ready for the presses; an eighty-seventh would soon appear, and thirteen more were ready. He was working on book 101, which Hetzel wouldn't need until 1910 or so. Thanks to this stock of manuscripts, it didn't matter that he was working so slowly now.

He continued to get up early (at six, he told Sherard), then work until 11:00 A.M. Afternoons, as always, he spent in the reading room of the Société Industrielle, scanning the magazines for as long as his eyes would let him. He was coy about his latest book, *A Drama in Livonia,* which he wouldn't discuss, for fear some other writer might steal the idea.

Sherard spoke of H. G. Wells—an inevitable subject at that time. Wells had burst onto the scene with *The Time Machine* in 1895; *The War of the Worlds* came three years later. By the time of Sherard's visit, both of these books and five others had been translated into French.

Verne had been sure that Sherard would ask him about Wells. Yes, he said, he had read Wells's books, which he found very curious, very English. But Wells and he could not be compared as writers, he contended, since Wells didn't concern himself with scientific principles. Verne relied on physics, while Wells employed fantasy. Verne's characters went to the moon in a cannon ball; Wells's entered space in a craft built of a metal, defying the law of gravity. Very pretty, cried Verne, but let's see that metal!

Verne and Sherard had been talking in the luxurious ground-floor salons, facing a garden filled with flowers. The visitor realized that the furnishings revealed the Vernes' expensive taste: heavy velvet wall hangings, large clocks, great mirrors, full-length portraits, Venetian glass, and rare curios. Sherard was then escorted up the two flights of stairs to the master's study and library, where he found a total absence of luxury. He was impressed by the display of Jules Verne's published books—three yards of them, with many more yards of translated editions.

Then they entered the smaller room—Verne's office. Sherard spotted a pipe stand. "But they don't let me smoke anymore," the author lamented. Here were his favorite books—all of Dickens, for example (all of translated Dickens at least).[14]

THE CONTRAST BETWEEN THIS AGING AUTHOR AND HIS EVER-youthful books was great in the last year of his life. It did not matter that the books that were being published at the time had been written earlier; Verne spoke of them as if they were fresh, and of course he kept them up-to-date by making corrections and rewriting as the books approached their publication dates. "'A Drama in Livonia' is only one volume long and this volume will come out next month," he advised Turiello, who no longer was a novice critic, but director of a Naples newspaper. "This drama presents the conflict of Slavic and Germanic peoples in the Baltic provinces. Nothing scientific. This book will be followed by another, as always; I haven't decided what to call it, but this novel, continuation and climax of *The Clipper of the Clouds*, will be the last word in automobile travel."[15]

The manuscript of *A Drama in Livonia* has been dated as early as 1892—a dozen years prior to its publication. It was dusted off in 1902, then sprang to life in successive issues of *Magasin d'Education* (from January to June 1904). Although all but forgotten today, the story is one of the strongest of Verne's last years. It is set in a Russia even more vividly drawn (because closer to real people) than the steppes of *Michel Strogoff*.

In Russia's Baltic provinces—primarily, in what is present-day Latvia—a detestable Germanic merchant class lords it over the Slavic majority, which, in turn, is protected by a distant but well-disposed czar. A courageous Russian doctor comes to the aid of a political dissenter fleeing from Siberian exile; seemingly implicated in a robbery and murder, the doctor is ruined. Before the czar's benevolence can be exercised, the doctor is murdered by the true assassin. His daughter survives to remember him, with her new husband—the former political exile, since pardoned by the czar. Once again, Verne had found a way to dramatize national tensions by portraying individual and family dramas.

To fill out the year in *Magasin,* Hetzel ran *Master of the World*—the continuation of the story of Robur and his wondrous machines. In the earlier *Clipper of the Clouds,* Robur had defied well-meaning Philadelphians who put their faith in dirigibles, abducting those who mocked him for a flight around the world in his heavier-than-air craft. In that first book, Robur's *Albatros* was destroyed, but he built another, returning to challenge the balloon enthusiasts. But he conceded, in the end, "I have come too early to win over contradictory and divided interests. . . . I therefore leave you, but I take my secret with me."

Now, in the sequel, Robur has compounded his challenge. From his base in what appears to be a volcanic crater in the Alleghenies, he employs a high-speed automobile, a racing boat, a mysterious submarine, and then a flying machine called an *aviateur,* which functions with turbine engines and flapping wings. The reader will learn that they are all one and the same diabolic machine, aptly called *The Terror.* In his arrogant defiance of the elements, Robur receives a comeuppance when lightning destroys his land-sea-air vessel. Still, Verne's hero, police inspector John Strock, wonders whether by the end of the century (and he means the twentieth) his future colleagues won't have to deal with more machines of the same kind.

This story was still running in *Magasin d'Education* when Verne received yet another English journalist, Gordon Jones. Jones would work the last full-scale portrait of Verne.

Jones's first impression of Jules Verne was a good one. He found "a man of sturdy build, somewhat below medium height, with kindly blue eyes and a short silvery beard." No hint of infirmity here, although the visitor noted that his host wore a peaked cloth cap indoors, "rendered necessary by the frequent attacks of his old enemy rheumatism." Jones, being an Englishman, was assured by Honorine that Jules had a great admiration for Jones's countrymen; indeed, Jules added, because of their independence and self-possession, the English made admirable heroes. Perhaps this little hypocrisy might be construed as politeness.

Verne reiterated that he could still see almost as well as ever with his left eye and that although doctors recommended an operation on the cataract forming on his right eye, he had decided not to take a chance at his age. He said he had another book in preparation, adding, "I feel however the time has at length come when I must rest my oars. This last production will make my one hundredth completed work, and I suppose that at any rate so far as quantity is concerned I may fairly be said to have earned my right to repose."[16]

Any future visitor calling at boulevard de Longueville would probably not have employed the word *sturdy*. "As for me," Verne informed Hetzel in October, "things go badly. If you find a new or used stomach to replace mine, send it to me."[17] Early in December, he announced that he hadn't left his house in a month—again on account of his accursed stomach. Yet he was still working; for the moment, the problem was to choose a title with just the right nuance for his story of the canal across the Sahara. "We shall speak about all this," he added optimistically.[18]

"Quite ill, more and more ill," he wrote, summing up his condition for Mario Turiello just before that Christmas of 1904. But he was still writing his own letters, and he promised that he would do so until the end.[19]

39

DEATH AND RESURRECTION

*T*HE INVASION OF THE SEA *(L'INVASION DE LA MER),* ONE MORE PANE-
gyric to the civilizing mission of the Europeans, was the last of the *Extraordinary Voyages* to be published in the author's lifetime. Hetzel began
publishing it in *Magasin d'Education* in January 1905; Jules Verne would
never actually see a copy of the book itself.

The invading sea referred to in the title is a canal dug across the Sahara. Conceived by French engineers, it will both irrigate the desert and
provide safe and rapid passage when completed. Indigenous rebels in the
French protectorate of Tunisia seek to sabotage the project; the chief villains are brigands who will no longer be able to rob caravans if the water
passage is completed. Although Jules Verne made clear in this novel that
he supported progress and bold French engineering, the book has also
been read as a story of a repressed people's struggle against their colonial
masters.[1]

At the beginning of 1905 Verne was still working. Although there is little evidence of this fact in correspondence, and none from eyewitnesses,
the manuscripts are there. Even if the books published at this time had
been written earlier, Verne, as was his practice, would be involved in the
editing process after each successive set of proofs came back from the
printers.

Then, in early March, he wrote to Hetzel, who needed two short books
that could be published together for the next year-end illustrated gift edi-

tion, "If I sent you *The Lighthouse at the End of the World* [*Le Phare du bout du monde*] it's because to my mind there is no need for changes as there will be in 'The Invasion of the Sea.' Nevertheless, since you prefer *The Secret of Wilhelm Storitz* [*le Secret de Wilhelm Storitz*] I'll send it to you Wednesday and you'll receive it Thursday. *Storitz* is the invisible, pure [E. T. A.] Hoffmann, and even Hoffmann wouldn't have dared to go so far. . . .

"As for the Klondike book, the title is *The Golden Volcano.*"[2]

That was the last letter Jules Hetzel received from Jules Verne.

JULES VERNE DEAD
Novelist Wrote Two Works Each Year
for $4000 Under Contract

This headline ran in *The New York Times,* over a dispatch from Amiens dated March twenty-fourth. How American! Jules Verne might have said of the reference to money. "Jules Verne died at 3:10 o'clock this afternoon," the report began (also in a style no French paper would copy). "His family was at his bedside. He retained consciousness until shortly before his death, his brain being the last organ to fail. He calmly awaited the end, called the members of his family to his bedside and discussed his departure."[3]

"In fact our poor Jules died of a diabetes that wasn't being watched," his sister Marie wrote home after a final visit to Amiens shortly before the end.[4] Her brother had begun to fade away less than a week after writing his last letter to Hetzel, and soon his worsening condition became a preoccupation of the international press. The *New York Herald* of March 22, 1905, announced:

> Amiens, Tuesday [March 21]—Late this evening M. Verne sustained a stroke of paralysis, affecting his right side.
>
> He has been pronounced by his physicians to be in the last stages of diabetes, and his life is despaired of.

Marie arrived in Amiens on March twenty-second; she later told her family that her brother's last words were for her. She heard him say, "I'm so happy to see you, you were right to come"; then he gripped her hand. She spoke to him, but by then his words had become unintelligible. Then she sat at his bedside as his body became immobile. When she left, she could say that "he's not our brother anymore, he's not that fine intelligence; there was only a body and a soul that was taking wing."

Honorine never left his side, of course. Marie found her sister-in-law's devotion touching. Jules's stepdaughters were also there as were Michel Verne's wife and their three sons (one can assume that Michel was traveling on business). Although Verne was still alive, the younger women begged Marie to give them the names of family members in Nantes to include in the death announcement as they didn't know the names of all the surviving relatives.[5]

There was indeed a considerable number of them; Nantes family predominated on a death notice bearing over fifty names (among them, Gaston Verne, interned for life after shooting his uncle). The family joined in announcing "the cruel loss" they had experienced.

> JULES VERNE
> Officer of the Legion of Honor
> Their husband, father, father-in-law, grandfather, great-grandfather, brother and brother-in-law, uncle and great-uncle, first cousin and cousin.
> Deceased on March 24, 1905, at the age of 77,
> Fortified with the Rites of the church.

Jules Verne was buried in the peaceful isolation of Amiens's Cemetery of the Madeleine, where his tomb was soon graced with a marble sculpture by Albert Roze, director of the district School of Fine Arts. In the voluted spirit of turn-of-the-century modern, it was more successful than the monument Roze designed for the public gardens over the railroad tunnel, within view of both the rue Charles-Dubois and boulevard de Longueville houses; here the bust of Verne seems inconsequential on its perch above amply proportioned ground-level figures (a family obviously reading Jules Verne).[6]

DEATH AS MUCH AS LIFE SHOWED THE PLACE JULES VERNE had carved out for himself in France and the world—and the bastions that had not fallen. The press spoke of his millions of readers and the reverence in which he was held in schools, where his books served as prizes for the most deserving, and in libraries, which were regularly obliged to replace worn copies of his books.[7]

Given the fact that Verne had deliberately turned away from science, it is ironic that the eulogists stressed his acute perceptions of scientific possibility. "Not only did he record scientific progress, he predicted it," observed a testimonial in Le Figaro. "We owe to Jules Verne a better idea of the world," another tribute began. "It is certain that he created the present generation of travelers, colonizers, men of action who themselves have their dream, their mirage, their ideal, and for this he was an educator of the first rank."[8]

He had indeed impressed people around the world, and he had known that. For example, a letter written on White House stationery reached Verne not long before his death, informing him that President Theodore Roosevelt, explorer, hunter, interventionist in world affairs, had read all of his books.[9]

But it appeared he had not warmed hearts. Those closest to him—the people of Amiens—appeared unmoved. No one remembered a generous act or sacrifice, not even a remembered fit of merriment—or of anger, for that matter. The romantic first-person voice of his poetry and the vigorous characters of his stories would have to speak for him.

When Victor Hugo died, a whole people rose up to join the funeral procession crossing Paris. On the death of George Sand, her peers, including Prince Napoléon, stood at her simple village graveside (and Nohant was twice as far as Amiens from the capital). Local politics have been blamed for what could be called Verne's second-class funeral—that "of a municipal councilman in a small French town," as his admirer and future biographer Charles Lemire described it. "No, Amiens did not have for Jules Verne that great enthusiasm we counted on," a professor at the local high school told Mario Turiello. "But what can we do, dear sir? Politics gets in the way of everything." A year after Verne's death, Honorine complained to Turiello that the fund-raising campaign for a monument to her husband had not been successful; she wondered whether money could be raised in Italy.[10]

No one was sent from Paris to represent the government at the funeral; but as an officer of the Legion of Honor, the deceased was entitled to a military tribute, and he did get that. In the absence of an official statement from Paris, where an unconditionally republican government was about to proclaim the definitive separation of church and state, the role of spokesman among the world leaders fell, ironically, to the emperor of Germany, the leader of the most detestable personages Verne had written into his *Extraordinary Voyages*. Kaiser Wilhelm II—at the very instant he was challenging France for colonial supremacy—was quoted as saying he would have joined the funeral procession in Amiens if he could have; he, too, had grown up reading Jules Verne.[11] (Born in 1859, the young Wilhelm would have been just the right age to have read Verne at his most anti-German period, after the Franco-Prussian War and the loss of Alsace-Lorraine.)

This was not the final irony. That came from no farther away than Paris, where the most serious and sensitive critic to pay his respects to Jules Verne, in the way he should have liked to be honored, was Léon Blum, writing in the newly founded daily organ of the Socialist party, *L'Humanité*. Blum was not only a Socialist but a Jew, a young government officer who was also gaining a reputation as a literary and drama critic.

Blum said he wished to write about Verne not only to acquit a debt—because he, too, had read the author as a child—but to act against injustice. Why deny literary value to books written for ordinary people, books for children? "His work is heroic, but of a quite rational heroism. It is also, even if the psychology of individuals and races in it seems rudimentary, both benevolent and humanitarian." Blum liked the early novels best, but he thought Verne's work should be judged as a whole, and by its influence rather than by its intrinsic qualities. "And indeed over a forty-year period it exercised an influence on the children of this country and all Europe equalled by no other work. . . . It was at once a positive tool of education and of moral development."[12]

The first biography of Jules Verne, which was published only three years after his death, was more a testimonial to a dead comrade than a biography. Its author, Charles Lemire, chose to open his book with a lengthy repudiation of the story of Verne's Jewish origins—a "stupid legend," according to Michel Verne, who supplied family documents to refute it.[13] For Michel, very much in charge now as heir to his father's papers, clearly perceived the value of preserving Jules Verne's place in the firmament—and not only for the honor of the family.

At stake was a pile of manuscripts—books written or begun by Jules Verne—that could still be published for profit by Jules Hetzel, who, in turn, would set aside a modest but still significant portion of the proceeds for Verne's estate. This simple proposition gave birth to what might be called the second Jules Verne industry. It did put Michel to work editing and rewriting (usually according to the dictates of Hetzel), and possibly to creating, as well.

The question of Michel's involvement has divided latter-day admirers. Indeed, in recent years nearly as much energy has been applied to the dissection of the posthumous Jules Verne as to the work published during his lifetime. As a result, one can see Verne's only heir as the compleat villain—mutilating his father's work in his own interest, even forging it—or as a loyal son—faithfully carrying out the will of his progenitor and unselfishly concealing his own creative role.

The controversy took fire almost before the corpse had grown cold. On

April first, a week and a day after Verne's death, an envoy from the Paris *Le Figaro* called at 44, boulevard de Longueville, to find the heirs reading through a stack of condolence letters. Was it true, Michel was asked, that his father had left several unfinished novels? Yes, five or six, he replied. He hadn't actually begun to sort out the papers, and he knew about their existence only because his father had made a brief reference to them in his final hours. He showed the visitor a final manuscript, bearing the title *Study Trip (Voyage d'études)*. It ran fifty pages, the first twenty of which contained a text inked over the pencil draft, while the remainder was in pencil only.[14]

Soon after that, stung by newspaper gossip suggesting that Jules Verne's heirs might take advantage of his name in order to publish posthumous works that hadn't even been written by him, Michel let the press know, quickly, what the family did possess. But he was careful not to mention certain titles, he told Hetzel, so that imitators wouldn't rush in to write fake Verne novels.

He separated the unpublished works into two categories: manuscripts, notes, projects, and unfinished works, which for the most part were not in genres for which Verne was known; eight novels—both finished and incomplete—intended for publication, plus the early fictional account of a trip to England and Scotland, and six short stories, two of them never published before.[15] "One must suppose a priori that manuscripts left by my father, by the very fact that they are posthumous, must have some particularity that led to postponing their publication," Michel would later say in a memorandum justifying his intervention. "Sometimes it's a matter of works of his youth that my father didn't seem determined to publish. In other cases they are books intended for publication but which didn't quite satisfy their author."[16]

At the beginning of May 1905, Michel Verne did a bold thing: He got the Hetzel contracts out of his notary's safe and examined them in detail. Then he picked up his pen to write the letter to Hetzel that his father had never written. He attacked the contract Hetzel père had gotten Jules Verne to sign back in 1875, criticizing the royalty scale and expressing shock at the discovery that his father had earned nothing for illustrated editions of books published before 1875—which happened to be the books that sold best. Even the nonillustrated editions were inadequately remunerated, and he also questioned Hetzel's 50 percent share of translation rights and prepublication newspaper rights.

While he was only a neophyte in the business, Michel thought he had better let Hetzel know how he felt. Hetzel didn't think it necessary to let

Michel know how *he* felt, at least not right then. Michel requested return of the two finished books in Hetzel's possession, *The Secret of Wilhelm Storitz* and *The Lighthouse at the End of the World*. Hetzel refused; he had gotten the manuscripts from Jules Verne, after all. Would Michel like to consult with Hetzel's lawyer?

On May tenth, Michel fired back. "If one right is sure, it's my right . . . to hold on to the posthumous manuscripts of my father, not to publish them, if I so prefer, and then to publish them after having negotiated terms of publication freely." On his deathbed, added Michel, his father had mentioned these books specifically, announcing that his son's "freedom of action was total."

Poor Jules Hetzel, the son of that wonder editor who had virtually invented commercial publishing and had found a willing author to test the system, now had to face the fact that Michel was not as passive about business matters as his father had been.

Michel had the help of the attorney who had rescued his father in the Turpin trial, the famous Raymond Poincaré (now a senator). Michel didn't want a court battle, he assured Hetzel; he'd rather make concessions than see an end to their friendly relations. But he did expect to exercise control over the books yet to be published—and Hetzel was beginning to realize that Michel meant what he said.[17]

In the end, Michel prepared the posthumous manuscripts for publication under Hetzel's guidance; there are clear indications that Hetzel was back in the driver's seat, for he knew that Michel Verne would always be short of cash. He may well have *paid* Michel to prepare his father's manuscripts for publication, in addition to the normal royalty and subsidiary rights fees.[18]

⚜ ⚜

NEW JULES VERNE STORIES IN THE RECOGNIZABLE, WELL-loved bindings appeared at intervals over the decade following the author's death.

Remarkably, some of the new books seemed more lively, richer in theme and development, than the novels published in the declining years of Jules Verne's life. In the 1970s, a bibliophile, Piero Gondolo della Riva, examined typescript copies of five unpublished Verne manuscripts; he discovered that they didn't always conform to the novels as published by Hetzel after Verne's death.

The key to this discrepancy was found in letters exchanged between Michel Verne and Hetzel, clearly indicating Michel's contractual role.

Michel agreed "to make necessary revisions and corrections on each of the volumes and to maintain as well as he could the character his father had given to these works, so as to keep the series available to Jules Verne's public." This was a noble goal, and profitable to the sons and heirs of both the great author and the famous publisher.[19]

There is no need for particular scrutiny of the first posthumous novel, *The Lighthouse at the End of the World,* which was first published in *Magasin d'Education* in mid-1905, barely twelve weeks after its author's burial. This is one of the slow-to-get-moving stories, typical fruit of Jules Verne's old age. The scene is a desolate island literally at the end of the earth, off Tierra del Fuego, at the southern tip of South America. Bandits who have amassed a treasure from shipwrecked vessels plan to attack the new lighthouse, then to escape in the next vessel unlucky enough to approach the shore.

The bad men kill two of the lighthouse keepers, but a survivor, assisted by the first mate of an American ship that had run aground on the reefs, find ways to delay the looters until the Argentine navy's relief vessel can come to their rescue, aided by the powerful lighthouse beam which is turned on just in time. "This well-planned novel contains none of the amusing scenes the author customarily introduced to liven up his work" was the severe verdict of the author's usually indulgent grandson. He called it "harsh," like the island on which the lighthouse was built.[20]

Then came *The Golden Volcano,* which Hetzel began serializing in January 1906. Noting that the book as published contains four more chapters than the version already in Hetzel's possession when Verne died, and four new characters, including two important ones, Gondolo della Riva concluded that Michel wrote them.[21] In this adventure tale, two Canadian cousins have inherited the claim to a gold mine in the Klondike; on the way to the far north, they join up with two other cousins, both attractive young women. The bad men show up later, on the site of the Klondike claim, then farther north at the Golden Mountain, an *active* volcano that ejects gold nuggets. In the end, the volcanic gold turns to dust (but not before a goldbrick kills the cousins' evil rival); the original claim makes them rich all the same—all four of them, as the cousins marry one another.

There is definitely a question of authorship regarding *The Thompson Travel Agency,* published in both original and illustrated editions in 1907. Verne's grandson was convinced that Verne himself wrote this critique of contemporary business methods, despairing of his son's succession of unhappy experiences.[22] Many Verne admirers took an opposing view, seeing this book as outside the Verne canon, wholly written by Michel during his father's lifetime (a way for the father to give his son a job).[23]

If this is true, Michel, who was forty-five years old in 1906 (date of the manuscript), was definitely a novelist in his own right. In the *Extraordinary Voyages* intrepid explorers are pitted against an inhospitable world; in *The Thompson Travel Agency,* the age of charter travel has begun. An unscrupulous travel agent—Thompson—has lured an international collection of tourists onto a grubby ship for a cruise on the cheap through the Azores and Canary Islands. Everything goes wrong, mainly because of Thompson's skimping. But among the stick figures typical of a Jules Verne comic novel, the author (whoever he was) created strong central figures; it's a British ship and crew, but the heroes are French and American.

For the first time, in a novel bearing Jules Verne's name, there is a credible love story, a totally mature relationship between a man and a woman—he is really the penniless French guide-interpreter Robert (who is concealing his true identity—that of a marquis) and the American heiress Alice. The book compares favorably with the novels of Jules Verne's best years. Recall the wearying geography of a book such as *Propeller Island,* in which scenic descriptions seem to be there only to fill the pages. In this all-new tale, the reader cares about the characteristics of the island's fauna, the singularity of each village or harbor town, for the specifics of the setting play a role in the plot. Readers looking for the typical features of a Verne novel will find a stalwart sea captain and his faithful dog; an heiress's treacherous brother-in-law, who doesn't hesitate to kill to recover his legacy; and passengers who are nouveau riche and vulgar, haughty and disagreeable. There are also savages, of course, and a shipwreck.

TWO MORE POSTHUMOUS NOVELS WERE PUBLISHED IN 1908, *The Chase of the Golden Meteor* and *The Danube Pilot.* In the case of the former, Michel added four chapters to the original seventeen, along with some lively characterizations in the manner of Jules Verne at his peak.[24] The makeover of *The Danube Pilot* had more serious consequences. The original version had only sixteen chapters; Michel was responsible for the addition of three. If he had done no more than that, his contribution might have passed unnoticed.

Verne's original title was a joke: *The Yellow Danube* (for even then the river was less blue than the song made it out to be). But the story itself contained neither humor nor depth.[25] According to the terms of a competition, Hungarian fishermen must descend the great river in a dinghy, living on what he can fish from its waters. He is joined by a Viennese gentleman who is actually a police inspector on the trail of river bandits. The bad men capture the fisherman—taking him for the inspector; the inspector thinks the fisherman is the bandit. In the end, the reader discovers that the fisherman is really a Bulgarian river pilot, tracked by the Turks; he, in turn, had been looking for his wife, who had been kidnapped by the bandits.

Michel Verne had only recently been in the Balkans, and he somehow saw fit to call the bandits' river pilot by the real name of a man he met there, Jackel Semo. The flesh-and-blood Semo, like the fictional pilot, was a Jew. The problem was that Jackel Semo was a respectable businessman whose good name was now being compromised everywhere Verne was read. Nor did Semo's lawyer fail to point out that the use of his client's name demonstrated that Michel and not Jules Verne was the real author of *The Danube Pilot*.

These "malicious insinuations" concerning the authorship of the novel were cited by a Paris court, which not only threw out Jackel Semo's complaint when it came to trial in January 1912 but also ordered that the victim pay court costs.[26] It didn't hurt that Michel Verne's attorney, Raymond Poincaré, was about to become France's prime minister *and* minister of foreign affairs (his deputy premier and minister of justice was none other than Aristide Briand). Jules Verne couldn't lose a case even when he—or his son—was caught with the goods.

The Survivors of the "Jonathan" (Les Naufragés du "Jonathan"), published four years after its supposed author's death, began as a single-volume novel; Michel managed to double its length. The scene is once more the remote Tierra de Fuego, the protagonist a mysterious anarchist who acts as benefactor to victims of a shipwreck. And he who has not wanted to be a leader must exercise authority in order to be of genuine use to the helpless survivors of the *Jonathan*. He establishes a new colony and protects it from intruders (especially when a rich lode of gold is discovered). Then, after placing a loyal acolyte in charge, he will retire to a remote lighthouse, to finish life as its keeper.

In the unfolding of his tale, Jules Verne had painted a satire of politics and government; in rewriting, expanding the story for the needs of the Verne estate, Michel Verne had inserted some of his own ideas. While puncturing the hero's utopian vision, he succeeded in tempering his father's irascibility. Jules's anarchist becomes Michel's prototype existentialist.[27]

More books would follow—and more opportunity for controversy. A smaller book appeared under Jules Verne's name in 1910; in fact, *The Se-*

cret of Wilhelm Storitz was the last manuscript Jules Verne passed on to Hetzel. As published, the novel takes place in the eighteenth century. A Parisian engineer travels to Hungary to see his brother Marc married to Myra, the daughter of a distinguished doctor there. En route, he meets a mysterious German, the son of a famous and also somewhat strange chemist. Then the engineer discovers that his German traveling companion, Wilhelm Storitz, had earlier been rejected by Myra. Preparations for the marriage are troubled by sorcery, and the wedding itself is interrupted by a mystery voice. The bride goes mad, and her groom is stabbed by an invisible assassin.

Of course it is Storitz, the chemist's son, armed with the secret of invisibility, who has troubled the marriage; now he abducts Myra and makes her invisible, too. Myra's brother finds and slays Storitz, who becomes visible as the blood flows from his body. Myra will also become visible again (thanks to a hemorrhage caused by childbirth). Her reappearance, which sophisticated readers regret, since it robs the climax of its "melancholic charm," was one of many changes made by Michel Verne. In the original version, Myra remains invisible, even after her marriage to Marc—when they will presumably be consummating their marriage. He can live with that, for he is a painter by profession and had once done an admirable portrait of her.[28]

Michel did have an opportunity—another opportunity, some would say—to write his own book. Avowedly, he began with the first section of a novel left by his father, *Study Trip*. As completed by Michel Verne and published under Jules Verne's name, it would be retitled *The Barsac Mission (L'Etonnante Aventure de la Mission Barsac)*.

Letters that Michel Verne sent from his home in Toulon to Hetzel in 1910 suggest a conspiracy between author and publisher to put something over on the public. Michel asked Hetzel for documentation on Africa, stressing that the geographic details and, above all, the accounts of exploratory voyages must not postdate 1905, "these discoveries having necessarily preceded the writing of the book."[29] In other words, he wished it to appear as if his father had actually written *The Barsac Mission*, and since Jules Verne had died in 1905, none of the background data could be more recent.

The novel Jules Verne had only begun to write concerns a French political mission to Africa. The purpose of the mission is to decide whether the French Congo is ripe for representation in the French parliament. The delegation includes two members of the Chamber of Deputies—figures of fun—and some sober personalities, including an invented Nicolas Vanof of the International Esperanto Society. This, of course, would have been the book Verne had promised advocates of Esperanto, and in his imaginary Africa, people actually *use* that invented language, a language ideal (Verne explains) for exchanges among European colonizers of different tongues.

The four chapters Jules Verne managed to finish only prepare the reader for the adventures to come, although it is already known that the deputies will decide that if the Congo gets voting rights, the ballot should be limited to Europeans.[30]

The Barsac Mission, advertised as "The Last Extraordinary Voyage", appeared in 1919 under the name of Jules Verne. The subject (Michel's, not Jules's) is the star-crossed Buxton family. One son, Lewis, is falsely accused of robbing a bank in London; another, George, is killed in combat while serving in Africa, seemingly having betrayed his flag by transforming his soldiers into bandits. But there is a Buxton sister, Jeanne, who is now in Africa looking for proof of George's innocence (she hasn't even heard about Lewis's supposed involvement in a bank robbery). She joins the Barsac mission, whose purpose remains as Jules Verne had envisioned it.

But the resemblance between Jules's beginning and Michel's full-scale effort ends there. Michel had also done away with his father's commitment to Esperanto. The Barsac mission encounters unexplained acts of sabotage and falls prisoner to a mysterious despot who controls a vast region of Africa with the help of slave labor and, more importantly, an innocent inventor unaware of the uses to which his gliders and guided missiles have been put.

Before the reader has closed the book, he learns along with Jeanne that the feared tyrant is actually the stepson of her father, Lord Buxton. Jealous of the family, the stepson has killed George and then uses George's soldiers to loot and rob. Now he holds innocent Lewis in captivity. In the end, the wayward stepson will destroy himself and his kingdom. The moral, to quote Jean Jules-Verne, is that "science can become dangerous," although he attributes this notion to his grandfather, when this final book was clearly the work of his grandfather's son.[31]

To believe some ardent Vernians—and in the absence of an original manuscript it is difficult to contest their claim—Michel alone wrote the story "The Eternal Adam," published in 1910 in the periodical *La Revue de Paris* (then later in a collection of shorter works bearing Jules Verne's name—*Yesterday and Tomorrow (Hier et Demain)*. A haunting tale, in which a future civilization finds traces of our own; earthquakes and flooding have destroyed scientific advances and they must be achieved all over again, pending the *next* natural disaster. If Michel and not Jules wrote this story, then Michel was doubly shameless, for he attached a note to it stressing his father's "rather pessimistic conclusions, contrary to the proud optimism that inspired the Extraordinary Voyages."

"The novels left by Jules Verne were a sacred trust," concluded a seasoned Verne reader, Olivier Dumas. His son should not have touched them; in doing so, even at the publisher's request, he committed a literary crime. In distorting his father's work, he changed its spirit.[32]

EPILOGUE

THE VERNE LEGACY

Death tends to leave us with a writer's books; the personality, which was probably not entirely knowable to begin with, and perhaps not even our business or our right to explore, tends to dissolve with time. In the end Verne's stories are what we want, and remember.

The best of Jules Verne's canon is part of our heritage. Without always remembering the twists and turns of plot, we remain haunted by images: the terrible and benign Captain Nemo, the purposeful and somewhat ridiculous Phileas Fogg, the terror of balloons adrift, traitorous sea captains, half-mad inventors bent on self-destruction and destruction of the universe.

Verne inspired generations of explorers and inventors, perhaps smoothing the way to solutions, surely making it easier for their discoveries to be realized. The veteran science fiction author Ray Bradbury, who also cared about nonfictional science, announced "that we are all, in one way or another, the children of Jules Verne." Among the children, of course, were the people manning actual spaceships. "Without Verne," he said, "there is a strong possibility that we would never have romanced ourselves to the moon."[1] Bradbury quoted Admiral Richard Byrd on the eve of a polar expedition: "Jules Verne guides me." William Beebe, one of the first to explore the ocean in a steel bathysphere, confessed that *Twenty Thousand Leagues Under the Sea* got him started.[2]

It is almost a cliché to compare Jules Verne's moon shot with the *Apollo*

launchings. There is no rational explanation for the coincidences between what Verne envisioned and what actually occurred a century later.
James Lovell, one of the three astronauts aboard *Apollo 8*, recalled that
during the flight he never stopped thinking of Jules Verne. He even
wanted to call the NASA spaceship—at least unofficially—the *Columbiad*,
the name of the cannon that would fire off the moon shot in *From the
Earth to the Moon*.[3] (The command module for the *Apollo 11* moon landing was called *Columbia*.) Frank Borman, who was also on that mission,
later told Jean Jules-Verne that there was no way of knowing "how many
of the world's space scientists were inspired, consciously or uncon-
sciously, by their boyhood reading of the works of Jules Verne."[4]

Actually we do know something about that.

Werner von Braun, the German-American missile scientist, also was
convinced that contemporary astronauts owed something to Jules Verne;
he cited the Russian pioneer Konstantin Tsiolkovsky, who admitted that
the first notions of rocket flight came to him from the Baltimore Gun
Club's moon shot. The American physicist Robert Hutchings Goddard
was once a kid hooked on Jules Verne, while the German rocket specialist Hermann Oberth—Werner von Braun's teacher—said that Verne
showed him the way to the utilization of rockets to guide space missiles.[5]

A monument to Jules Verne was planned for the Cape Canaveral
launching site; it was proposed by Malcolm McLouth of the Canaveral
Port Authority after the first *Apollo* missions. An association was founded
for the purpose and a model was designed by an aerospace engineer.
While there is a tribute to Jules Verne in the Air Force Space Museum
near the Kennedy Space Center, reduced funds resulted in the more ambitious project being abandoned. Port Canaveral holds a copy of the Hetzel illustrated edition of *From the Earth to the Moon*, which will be placed
alongside the monument should it eventually be built.[6]

No matter. The official map of the far side of the moon, drawn by the
Defense Mapping Agency of the U.S. Air Force's Aerospace Center in St.
Louis, Missouri, and based on photographs taken by *Lunar Orbiter* missions, includes a Jules Verne Crater, its latitude between 30° and 40°, longitude between 140° and 150° E.[7]

CLOSER TO OUR DAY, MOST OF THE NEWS ABOUT JULES VERNE
has concerned his manuscripts, including drafts of books he never published. Michel Verne died in 1925. After the death of his last surviving
son, Jean Jules-Verne, at ninety, his heirs were ready to turn over the

Verne papers to the Bibliothèque Nationale in Paris for what they termed a "reasonable" sum. Lacking the cash, the library appealed to the French president, Valéry Giscard d'Estaing, an avowed admirer of literature, but he wasn't any help. An auction was planned—with the likelihood that all, or at least the best, of the papers would go to American universities, or perhaps to private collections.

So the French government stepped in after all; Brittany and the city of Nantes acquired the lot (consisting of fifty-seven manuscripts of published works, six of unpublished prose, miscellaneous poems, letters, and other papers); the purchase price was considerably less than the reported offer from American sources.[8]

The city of Nantes also received the right to control the unpublished works, and that would prove a sore point with scholars. When Dr. Olivier Dumas, president of the Société Jules Verne, published Verne's letters to his family (from copies furnished by the heirs), the city of Nantes took him to court. After a lower tribunal in Nantes ordered the withdrawal from sale of Dumas's *Jules Verne*, the Paris appeals court held that the owner of a manuscript did *not* possess an exclusive right to publish a work no longer protected by copyright.[9] That decision, in turn, was upset by a still higher court, which in November 1993 held that only the owner of an original manuscript controls reproduction rights; possessing a copy does not signify authorization to publish.[10]

The letters, however, are now ours to read, and Nantes (presumably to underscore its copyright) has since authorized a limited edition of its manuscripts.[11] A surprise came in 1989 when the twenty-seven-year-old great-grandson of Jules Verne (the son of Jean Jules-Verne, he bears the same name as his father) was preparing to sell the family house in Toulon. He decided to open a rusting safe found in the back of the garage—on what had been Michel's property—and in it he discovered a lost manuscript.

The manuscript had once been inventoried—Michel had it in hand when he mentioned it to a reporter from *Le Figaro*. Somehow, Michel and Jules Hetzel didn't see it as publishable, any more than Pierre-Jules Hetzel had.[12] So it was locked up and forgotten for eighty-four years. On its publication in September 1994, of course, *Paris in the Twentieth Century* caused a sensation and moved to the top of best-seller lists; publishers around the world vied for the privilege of translating it. For a time, Verne was the author of the day, and those who published the novel he hadn't been allowed to publish would earn more than he ever did with a single book.

Verne's reputation has improved with time. In recent years, authors such as Michel Foucault and Michel Butor, and even that precursor of the surrealists Raymond Roussel, not only admitted to reading Verne but took him seriously and wrote about him with admiration.[13] On the one hand, Verne's readers have included serious critics seeking to plumb new territory; on the other, children who find his books on the shelves of public libraries and bookshops. But the middle ground of family readers—fathers, mothers, and their adolescent sons and daughters—had been lost to television on one hand and comic books on the other.

Yet in 1955, fifty years after the author's death, when his published work was no longer protected by copyright in France, there was a rush to reprint his best-known novels, often in formats resembling that of the Hetzel editions. And, of course, copies of the original Hetzel books are now to be found behind glass cases in antiquarian bookstores.

One of the first to produce movie versions of Verne novels was none other than Michel Verne, and the most popular of the stories were adapted again and again by successive generations in a variety of nations. *Michel Strogoff* was produced four times in the United States—in 1908, 1910, and twice in 1914—before the first French adaptation; in all, a dozen film versions have been catalogued of that book alone.[14] There was also a forgettable Verne cycle starring James Mason, including an adaptation of *Journey to the Center of the Earth,* which was released in 1959 by Twentieth Century–Fox. In the film, a young woman was added to the expedition, thereby diluting the theme of initiation that gave strength to the original story.[15]

Only television has done worse by Verne than the movies, although both media have helped keep his work alive. So have the evocations of his most popular books at the Disneyland parks (Space Mountain, inspired by *From the Earth to the Moon,* is the leading attraction at Disneyland Paris). "There can never be another Jules Verne," the science fiction writer Arthur C. Clarke concluded, "for he was born at a unique moment of time. He grew up when the steam engine was changing the material world, and the discoveries of science were changing the world of the mind." He was, added Clarke, "the first writer to welcome change and to proclaim that scientific discovery could be the most wonderful of all adventures. For this reason he will never grow out-of-date."[16]

We still read him as if we, too, are witnessing the birth of the modern world.

NOTES

Principal abbreviations utilized herein are as follows.

BN: Bibliothèque Nationale (Paris)

BN NAF: Bibliothèque Nationale, Manuscrits (Nouvelles Acquisitions françaises)

BSJV: Bulletin de la Société Jules Verne (Paris)

CDJV: Centre de Documentation Jules Verne (Amiens)

When an easily accessible published source is available, the reference is given, in preference to the original material (such as the correspondence with Pierre-Jules Hetzel in the manuscript collection of the Bibliothèque Nationale de France).

PROLOGUE: THE BALLOON

1. An English-language account appeared in an American magazine as early as 1868 (the editor suggested the story might be authentic); See *BSJV* 113 (1995): 12–13. The following year, several American book publishers were ready with an English translation (perhaps all pirated from a British edition), entitled *Five Weeks in a Balloon; or Journeys and discoveries in Africa by three Englishmen*. The subtitle read: *Compiled in French from the original notes of Dr. Ferguson [sic] (pseud.) and done into English by William Lackland.*

2. Burton's report, illustrated with thirty-seven drawings/vignettes, was published in French in 1860 in installments in the weekly *Le Tour du Monde,* then in book form early in 1862 as *Voyage aux grands lacs de l'Afrique orientale* (Paris: Hachette, 1862; announced in *Bibliographie de la France* on December 28, 1861).

3. Speke, who with Grant is credited with demonstrating that Lake Victoria was the source of the White Nile, published his *Journal of the Discovery of the Source of the Nile* in 1863 (London and Edinburgh: Blackwood); it was not translated into French by Hachette until 1864.

4. BN NAF 17000, 99–101.

5. *Le Temps* (Paris), February 17, 1863.

6. *Revue des Deux Mondes* (Paris) 43 (1863): 769.

CHAPTER 1: GROWING UP BRETON

1. Jules Verne, *Géographie illustrée de la France et de ses Colonies* (Paris: Hetzel, 1868), 357–58. At this time, Verne wrote, the port of Nantes was still receiving 60 million kilograms of sugar, coffee, cacao, rice, Scandinavian wood, and coal each year.

2. Yves Guillon, "Jules Verne et sa famille," *Bulletin de la Société Archéologique d'Ille-et-Villaine* (Rennes) 78 (1974): 121–22; Madame de Lassée, "L'Origine des Allotte de La Fuÿe," *BSJV* 11 (1969): 55–56; Marguerite Allotte de la Fuÿe, *Jules Verne: Sa vie, son oeuvre* (Paris: Hachette, 1953), 7–8. Verne's maternal family name is given variously as Allotte de la (or

La) Fuÿe (or Fuÿe). Family legend has the first Allott [*sic*] arriving from Scotland with the Scots Guard of Louis XI, who ennobled this loyal servitor, also giving him a *droit de fuÿe*—that is, the right to possess a dovecote, then a royal privilege (Lassée, in *BSJV,* 55).

3. Allotte, *Jules Verne,* 9; Charles-Noël Martin, *La Vie et l'oeuvre de Jules Verne* (Paris: Michel de l'Ormeraie, 1978), 262–63.
4. Allotte, *Jules Verne,* 9–10; Martin, *La Vie,* 266.
5. Allotte, *Jules Verne,* 11–12.
6. R. H. Sherard, "Jules Verne at Home," *McClure's Magazine,* January 1894, 118.
7. Guillon, "Jules Verne," 122–23.
8. Jean Jules-Verne, *Jules Verne* (Paris: Hachette, 1973), 25.
9. Jules Verne, "Souvenirs d'Enfance et de Jeunesse," published by Pierre-André Touttain in *BSJV* 89 (1989): 3–6.
10. Allotte, *Jules Verne,* 21–22.
11. In support of the fugue story: Jules-Verne, *Jules Verne,* 31 (who offers circumstantial evidence but nothing convincing); in firm opposition: Olivier Dumas, *Jules Verne* (Paris: La Manufacture, 1988), 22–23.
12. Sherard, "Jules Verne at Home," 118. In "Souvenirs d'Enfance," 7, Verne acknowledged that he had been criticized for inciting young boys to leave home for adventure. He was sure it had never happened—but should youngsters ever try, they'd learn much about survival in his books.
13. Verne, "Souvenirs d'Enfance," 7.
14. Ibid., 5. George Stephenson was the British engineer who invented the railroad steam engine.
15. Sherard, "Jules Verne at Home," 118.
16. Martin, *La Vie,* 20.
17. Ecole Saint-Stanislas (Nantes): CDJV, document 4374.
18. Christian Robin, *Un Monde connu et inconnu: Jules Verne* (Nantes: Centre universitaire de recherches Verniennes, 1978), 17.
19. Jules Verne, *Un Prêtre en 1839,* édition de Christian Robin (Paris: Le Cherche Midi, 1992), 201–204. Jules was of course one of the lay students who paid double tuition.
20. Martin, *La Vie,* 22–23.
21. Lucien Dubois, "Le Roman Scientifique: Jules Verne et ses oeuvres," *Revue de Bretagne et de Vendée* (Nantes) (January 1875): 17–18.
22. Jean-Louis Liters, "Jules Verne au Collège Royal de Nantes," *Cahiers du Centre d'Etudes Verniennes et du Musée Jules Verne* (Nantes) 12 (1992): 28–39; Jean Guiffan, "Le Collège Royal de Nantes au Temps de Jules Verne," in ibid., 40–41.
23. *Le Conducteur de l'Etranger à Nantes* (Nantes: Sebire, 1840), 84–86.
24. Liters, "Jules Verne," 35.

CHAPTER 2: MINOR POET

1. R. H. Sherard, "Jules Verne at Home," *McClure's Magazine,* January 1894, 118.
2. Olivier Dumas, *Jules Verne* (Paris: La Manufacture, 1988), 241.
3. Charles-Noël Martin, *La Vie et l'oeuvre de Jules Verne* (Paris: Michel de l'Ormeraie, *1978),* 24. While my English translations lack Verne's rhyme, they do try to convey the tone.
4. *BSJV* 81 (1987): 5.
5. Yves Guillon, "Jules Verne et sa familie," *Bulletin de la Société Archéologique d'Ille-et-Villaine* (Rennes) 78 (1974): 125–28; Charles-Noël Martin, "Les Amours de Jeunesse de Jules Verne," *BSJV* 28 (1973): 83–85; Dumas, *Jules Verne,* 23; Marguerite Allotte de la Fuÿe, *Jules Verne Sa Vie, son oeuvre* (Paris: Hachette, 1953), 25.
6. Allotte, *Jules Verne,* 24.
7. Dumas, *Jules Verne,* 26–27.
8. Charles-Noël Martin, "Les Amours de Jeunesse de Jules Verne," *BSJV* 29–30 (1974): 108, 110.
9. Dumas, *Jules Verne,* 27; Martin, *BSJV* 29–30, 111.
10. Dumas, *Jules Verne,* 365.
11. Martin, *BSJV* 29–30, 115–16.
12. Dumas, *Jules Verne,* 32.
13. Martin, *BSJV* 29–30, 117–20.
14. *Le Conducteur de l'Etranger à Nantes* (Nantes: Sebire, 1840), 70–72.
15. *Catalogue des Manuscrits de Jules Verne* (Nantes: Bibliothèque Municipale, 1988), 31; Martin, *La Vie,* 33.

16. Christian Chelebourg, "Les Drames de l'Aube," *BSJV* 114 (1995): 8–10.
17. Sherard, "Jules Verne at Home," 119.
18. *Catalogue des Manuscrits,* 9.
19. Verne, *Un Prêtre en 1839,* édition Christian Robin (Paris: Le Cherche Midi, 1992).

CHAPTER 3: PARIS
1. Marguerite Allotte de la Fuÿe, *Jules Verne: Sa Vie, son oeuvre* (Paris: Hachette, 1953), 22–23, 26–27.
2. "Etats de Service de Pierre Paul Verne," *Les Annales de Nantes,* 187–88 (Nantes: Société Académique de Nantes et de la Loire-Atlantique, 1978), 9.
3. Charles-Noël Martin, *La Vie et l'oeuvre de Jules Verne* (Paris: Michel de l'Ormeraie, 1978), 32.
4. R. H. Sherard, "Jules Verne at Home," *McClure's Magazine,* January 1894, 119.
5. Olivier Dumas, *Jules Verne* (Paris: La Manufacture, 1988), 35, 55.
6. Albert-Montémont, *Guide universel de l'étranger dans Paris,* 3d ed. (Paris: Garnier, 1849), 177–78.
7. Dumas, *Jules Verne,* 242–43.
8. Ibid., 164–65, 244.
9. Ibid., 253.
10. Ibid., 244–45.
11. Ibid., 246–50. Incredible as it may seem, Jules's father went through the letter with a pen to correct not only grammar but infelicitous phrasing. Was it with future publication in mind, or simply another example of his ongoing educational effort vis-à-vis Jules?
12. Ibid., 252.
13. Allotte, *Jules Verne,* 31–32.
14. Dumas, *Jules Verne,* 254–56. Author's conversation with Dr. Olivier Dumas. The colitis could also have been an early sign of diabetes, as well contributing to his later bulimia. In fact, he may not have had diabetes at all, although this disease was mentioned as the cause of his death. See also Olivier Dumas, "Jules Verne et les médecins, d'hier et d'aujourd'hui," *BSJV* 73 (1985): 11.
15. Sigmund Freud, "Character and Anal Erotism," *The Standard Edition of the Complete Psychological Works of Sigmund Freud,* vol. 9 (London: Hogarth Press, 1959), 170.
16. See chapter 24.
17. Dumas, *Jules Verne,* 254–56.
18. Ibid., 257.
19. Ibid., 258–59. At the time both Eugène Scribe and "Clerville"—Verne's error for Clairville, the nom de plume of Louis François Nicolaïe—were omnipresent on the French stage; Clairville's specialty was light comedy.

CHAPTER 4: THE LITERARY LIFE
1. Olivier Dumas, *Jules Verne,* (Paris: La Manufacture, 1988), 260–62.
2. Ibid., 264–69.
3. This is one of the letters published in a Nantes newspaper by Allotte, reprinted in Dumas, *Jules Verne,* 270. For Olivier Dumas's comments: ibid., 238.
4. Ibid., 271.
5. Ibid., 273. Cf. 167–68. Later, in a letter of March 1851, Jules indicated that his father shared his opinion of the military establishment: ibid., 289.
6. Ibid., 274, 276.
7. R. H. Sherard, "Jules Verne at Home," *McClure's Magazine,* January 1894, 119.
8. Charles Lemire, *Jules Verne (1828–1905)* (Paris: Berger-Levrault, 1908), 13. Actually, the inspiration for this text was an article published in *Le Temps* on December 29, 1897, by the journalist and critic Adolphe Brisson, following that writer's visit to Verne in Amiens; presumably, the anecdote came from Verne himself. Brisson wrote of those afternoons at Saint-Germain: "Silverware was lacking, which didn't seem to surprise the guests, but the champagne sparkled, the women were pretty, and no one minded drinking from his neighbor's glass." See "Promenades et Visites—M. Jules Verne," *Le Temps* (Paris), December 29, 1897; reprinted in Adolphe Brisson, *Portraits intimes* (Paris: A. Colin, 1899), 111–20. See also Pierre-André Touttain, "Jules Verne et les deux Dumas," in *Grand Album Alexandre Dumas* (Paris: Hachette, 1985), 173–81.
9. Dumas, *Jules Verne,* 277–78.
10. Sherard, "Jules Verne at Home," 119. Massé was born in 1822, Delibes in 1836.

11. Jules Hoche, *Les Parisiens chez eux* (Paris: Dentu, 1883), 258.
12. Dumas, *Jules Verne,* 279. Dumas points out that the original has not been found (this is one of Marguerite Allotte's contributions, and perhaps rewritings). The letter was published with the date of March 9, 1850, but it concerns the military lottery referred to in another letter of March *1849.*
13. Quoted in Charles-Noël Martin, *La Vie et l'oeuvre de Jules Verne* (Paris: Michel de l'Ormeraie, 1978), 82, and (with a slightly different text) in Marguerite Allotte de la Fuÿe, *Jules Verne: Sa Vie, son oeuvre* (Paris: Hachette, 1953), 52.
14. Georges Bastard, "Jules Verne," *Revue de Bretagne* (Vannes), (April–May 1906): 337–59.
15. Letter to Abraham Dreyfus, 1889, published in Piero Gondolo della Riva, "A Propos des *Pailles rompues,*" *Europe* (Paris), May 1980, 139, 141.
16. Ibid., 141.
17. Dumas, *Jules Verne,* 280–81.
18. W. Busseuil in *Le Courrier de Nantes,* November 8, 1850; reproduced in Christian Robin, *Un Monde connu* (Nantes: Centre universitaire de recherches Verniennes, 1978), 27.

Chapter 5: Apprenticeship

1. Olivier Dumas, *Jules Verne* (Paris: La Manufacture, 1988), 284.
2. Ibid., 285.
3. Ibid., 287–88.
4. Ibid., 289.
5. Luce Courville, "Pitre-Chevalier," *Cahiers du Centre d'Etudes Verniennes et du Musée Jules Verne* (Nantes) 6 (1986): 34–41.
6. *Musée des Familles* (Paris), April 1852.
7. Reprinted in "Avertissement," *Musée des Familles,* September 1851.
8. Dumas, *Jules Verne,* 290–91. For a rough equivalent in today's francs, multiply Verne's figures by 22.
9. Sigmund Freud, "Character and Anal Erotism," *The Standard Edition of the Complete Psychological Works of Sigmund Freud,* vol. 9 (London: Hogarth Press, 1959), 171.
10. Dumas, *Jules Verne,* 289–97.
11. Ibid., 299–300.
12. His "Moeurs du Chili" appeared in the March 1852 issue of *Musée des Familles.*
13. Jacques Arago, Souvenirs d'un Aveugle: Voyage autour du monde, vol. 5 (Paris: Delloye, 1840), i–ii, vii, 174.
14. Dumas, *Jules Verne,* 301–302.
15. *Musée des Familles,* July 1851, 304–12.

Chapter 6: New Science and Old Music

1. R. H. Sherard, "Jules Verne at Home," *McClure's Magazine,* January 1894, 120.
2. *Musée des Familles,* August 1851. Curiously, a translation into English ("A Voyage in a Balloon") of this story by a young and unknown writer was published in the United States as early as May of the following year—in a Philadelphia magazine entitled *Sartain's Union Magazine of Literature and Art;* see *BSJV* 110 (1994): 2 (from Steve Michaluk).
3. Olivier Dumas, *Jules Verne* (Paris: La Manufacture, 1988), 305–307. The play would appear to be "De Charybde en Scylla," which was never published or staged.
4. Dumas, *Jules Verne,* 50–51, 309; author's conversation with Olivier Dumas.
5. Jules Verne, "Deux Lettres inédites," *BSJV* 97 (1991): 20; Dumas, *Jules Verne* 310.
6. Jean Chesneaux, *Une lecture politique de Jules Verne* (Paris: Maspero, 1971), 11–22.
7. Dumas, *Jules Verne,* 311.
8. Ibid., 312. It took Pierre Verne over a year to bow to the inevitable; in early May 1853, he informed his son that he had found a local buyer for his law practice: ibid., 338.
9. Ibid., 314–15.
10. *Musée des Familles,* second series, vol. 18, tome 8.
11. *Musée des Familles,* June 1852, 257–71.
12. Charles-Noël Martin, *La Vie et l'oeuvre de Jules Verne* (Paris: Michel de l'Ormeraie, 1978), 75.
13. This is the viewpoint taken by Marcel Moré in *Le Très curieux Jules Verne* (Paris: Gallimard, 1960), 78.
14. Dumas, *Jules Verne,* 316.

15. *Musée des Familles,* July 1852, 301–13; August 1852, 321–35.
16. Emmanuel Le Monnier, "Une étude de la pensée politique de Jules Verne," thesis, Université de Paris XIII (Villetaneuse), October 1991. See also Jules Verne, *Le Chancellor, suivi de Martin Paz* (Paris: Hetzel, 1877).
17. Léon Poliakov, *Histoire de l'Antisémitisme,* vol. 2 (Paris: Seuil-Points, 1991), 196–97.
18. Dumas, *Jules Verne,* 317.

CHAPTER 7: PENSIONER

1. Olivier Dumas, *Jules Verne* (Paris: La Manufacture, 1988), 317. As *Monna Lisa,* it was published in 1995 by Editions de l'Herne, Paris.
2. Jean Jules-Verne, *Jules Verne* (Paris: Hachette, 1973), 47, 291–92. Jean Jules-Verne, Jules Verne's grandson, was eighty years old in 1973).
3. Dumas, *Jules Verne,* 317, 320–24.
4. Robert Pourvoyeur, "Le 'Théâtre-Lyrique' au temps de Jules Verne (1852–1855)," *BSJV* 31–32 (1974): 157–58.
5. Dumas, *Jules Verne,* 329–30, 333.
6. Ibid., 345.
7. Pourvoyeur, "Le 'Théâtre Lyrique,'" 161.
8. Michel Carré and Jules Verne, *Le Colin-Maillard* (Paris: Michel Lévy, 1853).
9. Dumas, *Jules Verne,* 329, 331–39. On Verne's work as secretary of the Théâtre Lyrique, see Piero Gondolo della Riva, "Du nouveau sur Jules Verne," *Europe* (Paris), May 1980, 143 (letter written by Jules Verne on Théâtre Lyrique stationery).
10. Dumas, *Jules Verne,* 339, 341; *BSJV* 88 (1988), 9–10.
11. Dumas, *Jules Verne,* 344, 346.
12. Ibid., 348, 350–51; Olivier Dumas, "Laurence, Le Dernier Amour de Jeunesse de Jules Verne," *Cahiers du Centre d'Etudes Verniennes et du Musée Jules Verne* (Nantes) 6 (1986): 26–31.

CHAPTER 8: ON NOT BREAKING ONE'S NECK AT AGE TWENTY-SIX

1. Edgar Allan Poe, *Contes-Essais-Poèmes,* ed. Charles Richard (Paris: Laffont/Bouquins, 1989).
2. Olivier Dumas, *Jules Verne* (Paris: La Manufacture, 1988), 355–58.
3. Ibid., 361–75; Marguerite Allotte de la Fuÿe, *Jules Verne: Sa vie, son oeuvre* (Paris: Hachette, 1953), 66–67.
4. *Les Annales de Nantes,* 187–88 (Nantes: Société Academique de Nantes et de la Loire-Atlantique, 1978), 16–17.

CHAPTER 9: THE BRIDE

1. *Musée des Familles,* March 1855, 161.
2. Olivier Dumas, *Jules Verne* (Paris: La Manufacture, 1988), 376–78.
3. *Les Compagnons de la Marjolaine* (Paris: Michel Lévy, 1855).
4. Dumas, *Jules Verne,* 379–90.
5. Ibid., 391–96.
6. H. Calland, *Guide du Voyageur à Amiens* (Amiens: Caron & Lambert, 1855), 5–6.
7. Dumas, *Jules Verne,* 397, 404. See also Cecile Compère, "Extrapolations autour d'un acte de mariage," *BSJV* 62 (1982): 211–12.
8. Dumas, *Jules Verne,* 393.
9. Ibid., 398–401.

CHAPTER 10: THE DOWRY

1. Olivier Dumas, *Jules Verne* (Paris: La Manufacture, 1988), 402–403, 405–10.
2. Jules Verne, *Dix lettres inédites* (Nantes: Société des Amis de la Bibliothèque Municipale de Nantes, 1982), 49–51.
3. Dumas, *Jules Verne,* 411–15.
4. Piero Gondolo della Riva, "Jules Verne Employé dans l'Administration des Télégraphes," *BSJV* 109 (1994): 8–10.
5. Dumas, *Jules Verne,* 417–24. It is possible that after legal complications and estate taxes, Honorine and Jules never received anything at all from her rich uncle (see Cécile Compère, "Les Héritiers de l'Oncle Riche," *Feuille de Liaison du CDJV* (Amiens) 28 (October–December 1993): 8–22.

6. Cécile Compère, "Extrapolations autour d'un acte de mariage," *BSJV* 62 (1982): 214; G. Dumas, "Le contrat de mariage de Jules Verne," *Mémoires* (Laon: Fédération des Sociétes d'Histoire et d'Archéologie de l'Aisne) 22 (1977): 80–82.

7. Marguerite Allotte de la Fuÿe, *Jules Verne: Sa Vie, son oeuvre* (Paris: Hachette, 1953), 78–79. Also on the marriage: Elisabeth Leger de Viane, "L'Entourage familiale de Jules Verne," *Visions nouvelles sur Jules Verne* (Amiens: CDJV, 1978), 22.

8. Charles-Noël Martin, *La Vie et l'oeuvre de Jules Verne* (Paris: Michel de l'Ormeraie, 1978), 110.

9. R. H. Sherard, "Jules Verne at Home," *McClure's Magazine*, January 1894, 120.

10. Dumas, *Jules Verne*, 426.

11. Leger de Viane, "L'Entourage familiale," 22.

CHAPTER 11: WRITER VERSUS BROKER

1. Olivier Dumas, *Jules Verne* (Paris: La Manufacture, 1988), 427.

2. René Lenoir, "Le Jules Verne de mes grands papas," *Visions nouvelles sur Jules Verne* (Amiens: CDJV, 1978), 5–10.

3. Marguerite Allotte de la Fuÿe, *Jules Verne: Sa Vie, son oeuvre* (Paris: Hachette, 1953), 80.

4. "Monsieur de Chimpanzé," *BSJV* 57 (1981): 11–31.

5. Robert Pourvoyeur, "Jules Verne aux Bouffes-Parisiens," *BSJV* 57 (1981): 2–10.

6. Ibid.

7. Allotte, *Jules Verne*, 83.

8. *Catalogue des Manuscrits de Jules Verne* (Nantes: Bibliothèque Municipale, 1988), 9.

9. Jules Verne, *Voyages à Reculons en Angleterre et en Ecosse* (Paris: Cherche Midi, 1989), 9–10, 18, 30–31, 99, 103, 112, 134. Verne made use of this trip in writing the *Black Diamonds* and *The Green Ray*.

10. *L'Auberge des Ardennes* (Paris: Michel Lévy, 1860).

11. Quoted in Charles-Noël Martin, *La Vie et l'oeuvre de Jules Verne* (Paris: Michel de l'Ormeraie, 1978), 118.

12. Etat-Civil, 18e arrondissement, 1861, Archives de Paris.

13. J. Verne et C. Vallut [*sic*], *Onze jours de siège* (Paris: Michel Lévy, 1861).

14. Dumas, *Jules Verne*, 429.

15. R. H. Sherard, "Jules Verne at Home," *McClure's Magazine*, January 1894, 122.

16. Olivier Dumas, "Jules Verne innocenté ou le voyage en Norvège déplacé," *BSJV* 97 (1991): 22–24. Cf. Marc Soriano, *Jules Verne* (Paris: Julliard, 1978), 100–101.

17. Elisabeth Leger de Viane, "L'Entourage familial de Jules Verne," *Visions nouvelles*, 21. The author was Suzanne's granddaughter.

CHAPTER 12: HETZEL

1. Georges Bastard, "Jules Verne," *Revue de Bretagne* (Vannes), (April–May 1906): 337–59. See also Charles Lemire, *Jules Verne (1828–1905)* (Paris: Berger-Lerrault, 1908), 15.

2. Jules Verne, *Textes oubliés* (Paris: 10/18, 1979, 183–84.

3. R. H. Sherard, "Jules Verne at Home," *McClure's Magazine*, January 1894, 120.

4. In *Le Tour du Monde* (Paris), vol. 1 (1860): 2.

5. *Le Tour du Monde*, t. 2 (1860), 305–52.

6. Sherard, "Jules Verne at Home," 120.

7. In *Le Musée des Sciences* (Paris), December 16, 1857 and January 6, 1858.

8. Marguerite Allotte de la Fuÿe, *Jules Verne: Sa Vie, son oeuvre* (Paris: Hachette, 1953), 89–90.

9. Francis Lacassin, "Les Naufragés de la Terre," *L'Arc:* "Jules Verne" (Paris: Duponchelle, 1990), 69–70. Arthur B. Evans called Verne's work "a unique brand of Industrial-Age epic literature" that helped readers come to terms with their rapidly changing world. See Arthur B. Evans, "Jules Verne and the Scientific Novel," Ph.D. dissertation, Columbia University, 1985.

10. A. Parménie and Catherine Bonnier de la Chapelle, *Histoire d'un éditeur et de ses auteurs: P.-J. Hetzel* (Paris: Albin Michel, 1953), 11–27, 30, 911–13, 152–57, 193, 316, 339, 373–94.

11. Allotte, *Jules Verne*, 91.

12. Adolphe Brisson, "Promenades et Visites—M. Jules Verne," *Le Temps* (Paris), December 29, 1897), 2.

13. BN NAF 17007, 1.

14. Parménie, *Histoire d'un éditeur*, 428. The official date of publication was January 1863.

15. Bastard, "Jules Verne."

16. Parménie, *Histoire d'un éditeur*, 102.

17. Jules Verne, "A propos du 'Géant'," *Musée des Familles,* December 1863, reprinted in Verne, *Textes oubliés,* 97–101.
18. *Le Petit Journal des Grandes Expositions* (Paris, Réunion des Musées Nationaux), June–September 1994.
19. Reproduced in Robin, *Un Monde connu* 49.
20. Evans, "Jules Verne and the Scientific Novel," 111.

CHAPTER 13: CAPTAIN HATTERAS
1. The fact that both Macé and Aristide Hignard were Freemasons led several writers to suggest that Verne himself may have been a Mason, a hypothesis carefully explored by scholar Simone Vierne, who looked for but found no evidence of Masonic affiliation. Simone Vierne, *Jules Verne* (Paris: Balland, 1986), 46–47; Vierne, "Thèses et hypothèses (Suite)," *BSJV* 61 (1982): 191–92.
2. A. Parménie and Catherine Bonnier de la Chapelle, *Histoire d'un éditeur et de ses auteurs: P.-J. Hetzel* (Paris: Albin Michel, 1953), 419–27. It does seem as if Hetzel hoped to obtain funds for the magazine through the good offices of Jules Verne, if not from Verne himself, to judge from Verne's letters to Hetzel of September 16, 1863: "The man with 40,000 francs, or say 20,000 francs, could have been me, dear friend, had it not been for the last monthly settlements on the market, where my clients got me into hot water. . . . But I'll see if some investor can be found to help you" (Parménie, *Histoire d'un éditeur*), 429.
3. Vierne, *Jules Verne,* 44–45.
4. BN NAF 17004, 1, 2.
5. Parménie, *Histoire d'un éditeur,* 429.
6. BN NAF 17007, 2. See also. Charles-Noël Martin, *La Vie, et l'oeuvre de Jules Verne* (Paris: Michel de l'Ormeraie, 1978), 140–41.
7. BN NAF 17004, 6. Reproduced in Parménie, *Histoire d'un éditeur,* 430–31. See also Olivier Dumas, *Jules Verne* (Paris: La Manufacture, 1988), 82–83; Jean-Pierre Picot, "Le Volcan chez Jules Verne," *BSJV* 111 (3, 1994): 21–22. In *The Narrative of Arthur Gordon Pym,* Edgar Allan Poe's hero finds tropical waters in the Antarctic (the book was published in French in 1858).
8. Piero Gondolo della Riva, preface to Jules Verne, *Paris au XXe siècle* (Paris: Hachette-Cherche Midi, 1994), 18.
9. Verne, *Paris au XXe siècle,* 48.
10. Piero Gondolo della Riva, "*Paris au XXe Siècle:* Réflexions du Préfacier," *BSJV* 114 (1995): 26–27.
11. Gondolo della Riva, preface in *Paris au XXe siècle,* 13–16; Gondolo della Riva, in *Un Editeur et son siècle: Pierre-Jules Hetzel* (St. Sébastien sur Loire: ACL Editions, 1988), esp. 118–19.

CHAPTER 14: INTO THE VOLCANO
1. Marguerite Allotte de la Fuÿe, *Jules Verne: Sa Vie, son oeuvre* (Paris: Hachette, 1988), 100.
2. BN NAF 17004, 9.
3. Allotte, *Jules Verne,* 101.
4. Ibid., 102–04.
5. Vivien de Saint-Martin, in *Année Géographique,* 1864 (Paris: Hachette: 1865), 270–71.
6. *Bulletin de la Société de Géographie* (Paris) 8 (July–December 1864): 510; 9 (January–June 1865): 277.
7. Jules Hoche, *Les Parisiens chez eux* (Paris: Dentu, 1883), 259–60.
8. R. H. Sherard, "Jules Verne at Home," *McClure's Magazine,* January 1894, 123.
9. Jules Verne, "Edgar Poe et ses oeuvres," *Musée des Familles,* April 1864, 193–208.
10. *Musée des Familles,* October–December 1864; Olivier Dumas, *Jules Verne* (Paris: La Manufacture, 1988), 165.
11. *Musée des Familles,* October–November 1865.
12. Jean-Pierre Picot, "Le Volcan chez Jules Verne," *BSJV* 111 (1994): 22–24.
13. Quoted in Simone Vierne, *Jules Verne* (Paris: Balland, 1986), 191.
14. A. Le Francois, *Le Temps* (Paris), December 19, 1864.

CHAPTER 15: THE HETZEL COLORS
1. Olivier Dumas, "La Correspondance Verne-Nadar," *BSJV* 97 (1991): 10.
2. Charles Clément, *Journal des Débats,* November 26, 1865.

3. Serge Robillard, "Jules Verne et la Côte d'Opale," *Visions nouvelles sur Jules Verne* (Amiens: CDJV, 1978), 12–13.
4. BN NAF 17004, 15, 16, 18.
5. Ibid., 14.
6. Pierre Terrasse, "George Sand et *Vingt mille lieues sous les mers,*" *BSJV* 22 (1972): 143–47.
7. Charles-Noël Martin, *La Vie et l'oeuvre de Jules Verne* (Paris: Michel de l'Ormeraie, 1978), 139.
8. Ibid., 153.
9. BN NAF 17004, 22. See also Christian Robin, in Verne, *L'Oncle Robinson,* Paris: Le Cherche Midi, 1991, 228–29.
10. Martin, *La Vie,* 154–55.
11. Marcus Osterwalder, *Dictionnaire des illustrateurs (1800–1914)* (Paris: Hubschmid & Bouret, 1983), 895–96.
12. Piero Gondolo della Riva, *Bibliographie analytique de toutes les oeuvres de Jules Verne,* vol. 1 (Paris: Société Jules Verne, 1977), 7, 11.

CHAPTER 16: NEW YORK

1. Charles-Noël Martin, "Recherches sur les maîtresses de Jules Verne," *BSJV* 56 (1980): 292–93. See also Jean Jules-Verne, *Jules Verne* (Paris: Hachette, 1973), 264–65.
2. Olivier Dumas, *Jules Verne* (Paris: La Manufacture, 1988), 430.
3. Ibid., 432.
4. Charles-Noël Martin, *La Vie et l'oeuvre de Jules Verne* (Paris: Michel de l'Ormeraie, 1978), 121.
5. Dumas, *Jules Verne,* 431. See also Serge Robillard, "Jules Verne et la Côte d'Opale," *Visions nouvelles sur Jules Verne* (Amiens: CDJV, 1978), 13.
6. A. Parménie and Catherine Bonnier de la Chapelle, *Histoire d'un éditeur et de ses auteurs: P.-J. Hetzel* (Paris: Albin Michel, 1953), 487.
7. As presented by Volker Dehs, who found the unpublished text by Verne, in *Cahiers* (Nantes), 7, 9; reprinted in Dumas, *Jules Verne,* 97–98.
8. Jules Verne, *Voyages et aventures du Capitaine Hatteras* (Paris: Bibliothèque d'Education et de Récréation—J. Hetzel, [1867]), 1–2.
9. Théophile Gautier, "Les Voyages imaginaires de M. Jules Verne," *Le Moniteur Universel* (Paris), July 16, 1866.
10. E. Lemoine, *Le Temps,* August 21, 1866.
11. Emile Zola, *Le Salut Public* (Paris), July 23, 1866.
12. Robert Taussat, "Le malheureux destin du *Great Eastern,*" *BSJV* 15 (1970): 138–39.
13. Jules Verne, *Voyages à Reculons en Angleterre et en Ecosse* (Paris: Cherche Midi, 1989), 221–22.
14. Taussat, "Le Malheureux destin," 139–41.
15. Quoted in Edouard Monnier, "Jules Verne et le professeur Aronnax à New-York en 1867," *BSJV* 61 (1982): 194.
16. Taussat, "Le Malheureux destin," 141; *New York Times,* April 9, 1867.
17. In a short article written on shipboard for a French shipping journal, he stressed the safety of the mammoth ship: "While the solid vessel played in a manner of speaking with the unleashed ocean, passengers took their lunch tranquilly. . . . The *Great Eastern* stood fast against the waves; one was aware of no rolling or pitching. . . ." The ship's great mass "rendered it indifferent to the sea." From article in *Le Paquebot,* "Le Great-Eastern," May 4, 1867; reprinted in Marcel Destombes, "Jules Verne et le Great Eastern, 1867," *BSJV* 56 (1980): 288, in which Verne's shipboard letter to Hetzel is published in its entirety.
18. In fact the ship left her moorings on April seventeenth (*New York Times,* April 18, 1867).
19. Destombes, "Jules Verne et le Great Eastern," 289–91.
20. Jules Verne, *Une Ville flottante* (Paris: Hetzel, 1871), 1. See also Jean-Michel Margot, "46 ans d'Expérience Maritime," *La Nouvelle Revue Maritime* (Paris) May–June 1984, 13.
21. Jules Verne, "Souvenirs d'Enfance et de Jeunesse," published by Pierre-André Touttain in *BSJV* 89 (1989): 7–8. In this memoir, written when he knew that he would never travel again, he does express regret that he'd never again see "this America that I love, and that every Frenchman can love as a sister of his own country!"
22. Monnier, "Jules Verne et le Professeur Arronax," 194–97.

CHAPTER 17: CAPTAIN NEMO

1. Olivier Dumas, *Jules Verne* (Paris: La Manufacture, 1988), 434–35.
2. Ulysse Ladet, in *Le Temps,* June 26, 1867.
3. See article on the first collection in *Le Temps,* July 14, 1867.
4. Jules Verne, *Geographie illustrée de la France et de ses colonies* (Paris: Hetzel, 1867).
5. Dumas, *Jules Verne,* 436.
6. Quoted in *Le Temps,* August 30, 1867.
7. Dumas, *Jules Verne,* 437–38.
8. Volker Dehs, "L'Affaire du *Voyage au centre de la terre,*" *BSJV* 87 (1988): 19–24.
9. M. Astier, "Le 'Nautilus' a-t-il eu un précurseur?" *BSJV* 2 (1936): 76–80.
10. BN NAF 17004, 71; quoted in Jean Jules-Verne, *Jules Verne* (Paris: Hachette, 1973), 142.
11. BN NAF 17004, 132.
12. Simone Vierne, "Jules Verne devant la critique de son temps," in *Textes et Langages,* vol. 10 (Nantes: Université de Nantes, 1984), 21.
13. Marc Soriano, "Adapter Jules Verne," *L'Arc:* "Jules Verne" (Paris: Duporchelle, 1990), 86–87.
14. In correspondence from Cécile Compère to this author.
15. Daniel Reyss, "20,000 Lieues sous les mers," *La Nouvelle Revue Maritime* (Paris), May–June 1984, 57.
16. Olivier Dumas, in ibid., 6. Pierre Vidal, in ibid., 69, counts sailing vessels in 64 novels and six stories by Verne, for a total of 259 ships in all, of which 57 are English, 44 American, 20 French. Sailing vessels are absent in only one novel in five.
17. Dumas, *Jules Verne,* 440–41.
18. Charles-Noël Martin, *La Vie, et l'oeuvre de Jules Verne* (Paris: Michel de l'Ormeraie, 1978), 176–78. Martin calls attention to the changes made since the previous contract of December 1865. A clause in the new contract stipulated that the *Illustrated Geography* was Hetzel's exclusive property, "the royalties having been paid once for all time."
19. Dumas, *Jules Verne,* 443.
20. Dumas, *Jules Verne,* 446–47. For the subsequent fate of the legacy—which was consumed before Jules and Honorine ever saw it—see Cécile Compère, "Les Héritiers de l'Oncle Riche," *Feuille de liaison du CDJV* (Amiens) 28 (October–December 1993).
21. Martin, *La Vie,* 163.
22. A. Parménie and Catherine Bonnier de la Chapelle, *Histoire d'un éditeur et de ses auteurs: P.-J. Hetzel* (Paris: Albin Michel, 1953), 489.
23. Dumas, *Jules Verne,* 176–77.
24. Eric Weissenberg, "Deux lettres inédites de Jules Verne," *BSJV* 61 (1982): 170–73; Dumas, *Jules Verne,* 140, 443–44.
25. Dumas, *Jules Verne,* 443–45.

CHAPTER 18: BACK FROM THE MOON

1. Jean Jules-Verne, *Jules Verne* (Paris: Hachette, 1973), 186.
2. Charles-Noël Martin, *La Vie et l'oeuvre de Jules Verne* (Paris: Michel de l'Ormeraie, 1978), 166.
3. Olivier Dumas, *Jules Verne* (Paris: La Manufacture, 1988), 445, 448–449.
4. Ulysse Ladet in *Le Temps,* December 19, 1868.
5. "Dr. Ordinaire," "La Littérature des Enfants et de la Jeunesse," *Le Temps,* December 25, 1868.
6. Jules-Verne, *Jules Verne,* 186.
7. Ibid., 145–50; Martin, *La Vie,* 172–75.
8. Simone Vierne, *Jules Verne* (Paris: Balland, 1986), 84.
9. Gondolo della Riva, in *Un Editeur et son siècle: Pierre-Jules Hetzel* (St. Sébastien sur Loire: ACL Editions, 1988), 122.
10. Paul de Saint-Victor in *Le Moniteur Universel* (Paris), December 17, 1872.
11. BN NAF 17004, 97.
12. Martin, *La Vie,* 176.
13. BN NAF 17004, 101–102.
14. Jules-Verne, *Jules Verne,* 131.
15. Author's conversation with Roger Pierrot.
16. BN NAAF 17007, 36–37.
17. Eugène Brandis, "Deux lettres inédites de Jules Verne," *BSJV* 48 (1978): 253; Jules-Verne, *Jules Verne,* 153–55.

18. Dumas, *Jules Verne*, 450. It was indeed the first time that a Verne novel had been divided in this way, and Verne regretted "being chopped up like that," as he told Hetzel; see Jules-Verne, *Jules Verne*, 159.

19. Vierne, "Jules Verne devant la critique de son temps," *Textes et Langages*, vol. 10 (Nantes: Université de Nantes, 1984), 16–20.

CHAPTER 19: LOVE AND WAR

1. BN NAF 17004, 139–40; Charles-Noël Martin, *La Vie et l'oeuvre de Jules Verne* (Paris: Michel de l'Ormeraie, 1978), 180; Olivier Dumas, *Jules Verne* (Paris: La Manufacture, 1988), 79.

2. Cécile Compère, "A propos du séjour de Jules Verne en Suisse," *BSJV* 65–66 (1983): 56–61. Among the legends associating Verne and his Russian translator is an unlikely story of his having joined her in Switzerland. See also Charles-Noël Martin, "Recherches sur les maîtresses de Jules Verne," *BSJV* 56 (1980): 293.

3. Martin, *La Vie*, 182.

4. Ibid.

5. Dumas, *Jules Verne*, 452.

6. Martin, *La Vie*, 179, 183.

7. Olivier Dumas, "Le Manuscrit d'*Une Ville flottante*, au destin contraire," *BSJV* 99 (1991).

8. Martin, *La Vie*, 183.

9. BN NAF, 17004, 132; Jean Jules-Verne, *Jules Verne* (Paris: Hachette, 1973), 160.

10. A. Parménie and Catherine Bonnier de la Chapelle, *Histoire d'un éditeur et de ses auteurs: P.-J. Hetzel* (Paris: Albin Michel, 1953), 520.

11. Ibid., 521; Jules-Verne, *Jules Verne*, 162. The decree was issued on August 9, 1870; information obtained from the Musée de la Légion d'Honneur, Paris.

12. Jules-Verne, *Jules Verne*, 162–63.

13. Ibid., 163–64.

14. Dumas, *Jules Verne*, 453.

15. Jules-Verne, *Jules Verne*, 164.

16. Serge Robillard, "Jules Verne et la Côte d'Opale," *Visions nouvelles sur Jules Verne* (Amiens: CDJV, 1978), 17.

17. Martin, *La Vie*, 184.

CHAPTER 20: PEACE IN AMIENS

1. Olivier Dumas, *Jules Verne* (Paris: La Manufacture, 1988), 454. Dr. Dumas thinks that the book Verne was writing was *Measuring a Meridian*. See also Jean Jules-Verne, *Jules Verne* (Paris: Hachette, 1973), 165.

2. Dumas, *Jules Verne*, 455.

3. Charles-Noël Martin, *La Vie et l'oeuvre de Jules Verne* (Paris: Michel de l'Ormeraie, 1978), 185; A. Parménie, and Catherine Bonnier de la Chapelle, *Histoire d'un éditeur et de ses auteurs: P.-J. Hetzel* (Paris: Albin Michel, 1953), 537.

4. BN NAF 17004, 163; Dumas, *Jules Verne*, 165–66.

5. Parménie, *Histoire d'un éditeur*, 547.

6. BN NAF 17004, 160; Martin, *La Vie*, 186.

7. BN NAF 17004, 162–63; Martin, *La Vie*, 186.

8. Dumas, *Jules Verne*, 456.

9. Ibid., 457.

10. BN NAF 17004, 160.

11. BN NAF 17004, 163 bis; Martin, *La Vie*, 188. A final clause of the rider stipulated that the continuation of *Celebrated Travels and Travelers*, expected to fill two volumes, would be paid for at the rate of three thousand francs per volume, to be delivered in addition to the two books expected of the author each year.

12. Daniel Compère, "1871," in *Visions nouvelles sur Jules Verne* (Amiens: CDJV, 1978), 29.

13. Volker Dehs, "En face du public: un autre Jules Verne," *BSJV* 112 (1994): 13 n.2.

14. M. Lehaguez, *Le Nouveau Paris et ses environs: Guide de l'Etranger* (Paris: Bernardin-Béchet, 1869), viii–ix.

15. Verne, "La Somme," in *Géographie illustrée de la France* (Paris: Hetzel, 1867–68).

16. *Le Courrier des Etats-Unis* (New York), April 4, 1905 (CDJV, document 4605).

17. "Notice sur la Ville d'Amiens," in *Visions nouvelles*, 33; Cécile Compère, "Je me fixe à Amiens," *BSJV* 77 (1986): 31–34.

18. Quoted in Simone Vierne, *Jules Verne* (Paris: Balland, 1986), 234–35.

19. Jules-Verne, *Jules Verne*, 173.

CHAPTER 21: AROUND THE WORLD

1. BN NAF 17004, 181.
2. Olivier Dumas, *Jules Verne* (Paris: La Manufacture, 1988), 86.
3. Olivier Dumas, "Le Docteur Ox, censuré pour Hetzel," *BSJV* 71 (1984): 98–103.
4. Dumas, *Jules Verne*, 69.
5. BN NAF 17004, 174.
6. Charles-Noël Martin, *La Vie et l'oeuvre de Jules Verne* (Paris: Michel de l'Ormeraie, 1978), 189–90.
7. Ibid., 280.
8. René Le Parquier, "Jules Verne Academicien," in *Visions nouvelles sur Jules Verne* (Amiens: CDJV, 1978), 39–41.
9. R. H. Sherard, "Jules Verne at Home," *McClure's Magazine*, January 1894, 121.
10. Edgar Allan Poe, "Three Sundays in a Week," *Contes inédits d'Edgar Poe*, trans. William L. Hughes (Paris: Hetzel, 1862), 141–53.
11. BN NAF 17004, 174; Jean Jules-Verne, *Jules Verne* (Paris: Hachette, 1973), 180–81.
12. Martin, *La Vie*, 194.
13. Paul Hippeau, "Jules Verne," in *Galerie Contemporaine Littéraire et Artistique* (Paris) no. 155 (1880): 85–86.
14. *Le Temps*, April 28, 1873.
15. *Journal d'Amiens*, September 29–30, 1873.

CHAPTER 22: ROBINSON VERNE

1. Roland Barthes, "Nautilus et Bateau ivre," in *Mythologies* (Paris: Seuil-Points, 1970), 80.
2. Christian Robin, postface to Jules Verne, *L'Oncle Robinson* (Paris: Le Cherche-Midi, 1991), 230–31.
3. Olivier Dumas and Jacques van Herp, "Un *Oncle Robinson*, une *Ile mystérieuse*, et autres, sous influence," *BSJV* 111 (1994): 39–41; Christian Chelebourg, "'Du Robinson magnifique' à *L'Ile mystérieuse:* Annales d'une création," *BSJV* 105 (1993): 11–19; Jean H. Guermonprez, "Du Navet au chef-d'oeuvre," *BSJV* 113 (1995): 5.
4. Jules Verne, *Seconde patrie* (Paris: Hetzel, 1900), ii.
5. James Fenimore Cooper, *Le Robinson américain* (Paris: Barba, 1850); *Le Cratère, ou Marc dans son île* (Paris: Passard, 1852).
6. Barthes, *Mythologies*, 80, 82.
7. Guermonprez, "Du Navet au chef-d'oeuvre," 6.
8. BN NAF 17004, 199–200.
9. R. H. Sherard, "Jules Verne at Home," *McClure's Magazine*, January 1894, 120–21.
10. BN NAF 17004, 199–200.
11. BN NAF 17004, 177–78.
12. Charles-Noël Martin, *La Vie et l'oeuvre de Jules Verne* (Paris: Michel de l'Ormeraie, 1978), 200–201.

CHAPTER 23: JULES VERNE, INC.

1. *Dictionnaire des Littératures de langue française*, (Paris: Bordas, 1987), 653–54.
2. Jean Jules-Verne, *Jules Verne* (Paris: Hachette, 1973), 180–82.
3. BN NAF 17004, 204.
4. BN NAF 17006, 1.
5. BN NAF 17004, 201. See also Christian Chelebourg, "Contre d'Ennery," *BSJV* 65 (1983): 231.
6. BN NAF 17004, 245.
7. Francisque Sarcey, "Chronique Théatrâle," *Le Temps*, November 9, 1874.
8. Sarcey, *Le Temps*, November 16, 1874.
9. Sarcey, "Chronique Théatrâle," *Le Temps*, January 4, 1875.
10. SACD (Société des Auteurs et Compositeurs Dramatiques), register of Théâtre de la Porte Saint-Martin, 1865 to July 1879, courtesy of Mme Florence Roth. On the revival of *Le Tour du Monde* at the same theater in June 1878, gross receipts continued at the same average rate. The actual amount of money received by Verne and his coauthors would have been reduced by the commission—some 10 percent—owed to the collection agency.
11. See Chapter 17.
12. All material relating to the Post-Jest Affair is from Volker Dehs, "L'Affaire du *Voyage au centre de la terre*," BSJV 87 (1988): 19–24. See also CDJV, document 7542.

13. Bibliothèque Municipale, Amiens (archives), ms. 1954D.
14. Ibid.
15. Olivier Dumas, *Jules Verne* (Paris: La Manufacture, 1988), 463.
16. BN NAF 17004, 255; Christian Chelebourg, "Contre d'Ennery," *BSJV* 65 (1983); BN NAF 17004, 255; Dumas, *Jules Verne,* 463.
17. BN NAF 17007, 6–9; Charles-Noël Martin, *La Vie et l'oeuvre de Jules Verne* (Paris: Michel de l'Ormeraie, 1978), 210–12.
18. BN NAF 17004, 262–63; Martin, *La Vie,* 211–12.
19. BN NAF 17004, 260.
20. *Miller's New York as It Is* (New York: Miller, 1866), 64–65.
21. "Around the World in Eighty Days," *The New York Times,* November 7, 1875.
22. Philippe Burgaud, "Les Spectacles de Jules Verne aux U.S.A.," *BSJV* 109 (1992): 9–11.
23. Cornélius Helling, "Jules Verne as Seen Through British Eyes," *BSJV* 3 (1936): 156–60.
24. Quoted in Martin, *La Vie,* 208.

CHAPTER 24: AFFLICTIONS

1. Elizabeth Leger de Viane, "L'entourage familiale de Jules Verne," *Visions/Nouvelles sur Jules Verne* (Amiens: CDJV, 1978), 26. The letter to Georges Lefebvre was sent from Le Tréport, where Jules Verne had docked with his *Saint-Michel* in August 1875: See "En vue du Tréport à bord du Saint Michel le 12-8-1875," *Musée des Familles,* September 1875.
2. Sigmund Freud, "On Transformations of Instinct as Exemplified in Anal Erotism," *The Standard Edition of the Complete Works of Sigmund Freud,* vol. 17 (London: Hogarth Press, 1959), 127. See also Freud, "Character and Anal Erotism," *The Standard Edition,* vol. 9, 169–75. Burness E. Moore and Bernard D. Fine, *Psychoanalytic Terms and Concepts* (New Haven: Yale University Press, 1990), 14.
3. Jacob A. Arlen, "Anal Sensations and Feelings of Persecution," *The Psychoanalytic Quarterly* (Albany, New York) 18, no. 1 (January 1949): 79.
4. Sigmund Freud, "Anal Erotism and the Castration Complex," in *The Standard Edition,* vol. 17, 72.
5. Charles Raymond, "Les Célébrités Contemporaines: Jules Verne," *Musée des Familles,* September 1875, 257–59.
6. BN NAF 1704, 269–70.
7. Jean Jules-Verne, *Jules Verne* (Paris: Hachette, 1973), 22. Verne draws on the version contained in Marguerite Allotte's biography.
8. BN NAF 17004, 178.
9. BN NAF 17004, 258–59; *Catalogue des Manuscrits de Jules Verne* (Nantes: Bibliothèque Municipale, 1988), 15.
10. *Magasin d'Education et de Recréation,* 25 (1877), 326–27.
11. Ibid., 336.
12. Ibid., 26 (1877): 293–95, 355.
13. Olivier Dumas, "Hector Servadac a 100 ans," *BSJV* 42 (1977): 54. Dumas suggests that the portrait of Isac had something to do with Jules Verne's detestation of gold, and perhaps of usurers to whom his son was indebted, which would make Michel a precocious borrower at age thirteen or fourteen.
14. BN NAF 17004, 258–59.
15. A. Parménie and Catherine Bonnier de la Chapelle, *Histoire d'un éditeur, et de ses auteurs: P.-J. Hetzel* (Paris: Albin Michel, 1953), 606.
16. Piero Gondolo della Riva, *Un Editeur et son siècle: Pierre-Jules Hetzel* (St. Sébastien sur Loire: ACL Editions, 1988), 121–22.
17. Parménie, *Histoire d'un éditeur,* 606–07.
18. Jean-Pierre Goldenstein, notes in Jules Verne, *Michel Strogoff* (Paris: Presses Pocket, 1992), 467–84.
19. Charles-Noël Martin, *La Vie, et l'oeuvre de Jules Verne* (Paris: Michel de l'Ormeraie, 1978), 203–204.
20. A. Le Reboullet, "Livres d'Etrennes," *Le Temps,* December 22, 1875.
21. René Le Parquier, "Jules Verne Académicien, in *Visions nouvelles sur Jules Verne* (Amiens: CDJV, 1978)," 40–41.
22. Jules Verne, "Une Ville idéale," *Mémoires de l'Académie des sciences, belles-lettres et arts d'Amiens* (Amiens: 1874–1875), 347–78.

CHAPTER 25: HECTOR SERVADAC

1. BN NAF 17004, 283–84.
2. Ibid., 285–86.
3. Ibid., 295.
4. A. Parménie, and Catherine Bonnier de la Chapelle, *Histoire d'un éditeur et de ses auteurs: P.-J. Hetzel* (Paris: Albin Michel, 1953), 608.
5. BN NAF 17006, 6–7.
6. BN NAF 17004, 368–69. This letter has been variously dated.
7. Charles-Noël Martin, *La Vie et l'oeuvre de Jules Verne* (Paris: Michel de l'Ormeraie, 1978), 209.
8. *Souvenirs parlés d'A. Briand, recueillis par Raymond Escholier* (Paris: Hachette, 1932), 29–34.
9. Jean Jules-Verne, *Jules Verne* (Paris: Hachette, 1973), 238. Jean Jules-Verne states that he talked to Briand in 1927, at which time Briand confirmed that Verne had been his guardian, although why Jules Verne—not often in Nantes—was chosen when Briand's own family was close at hand isn't clear. The character Briant in *Two Years' Holiday* is supposedly modeled on young Aristide Briand.
10. Georges Suarez, *Aristide Briand*, vol. 1 (Paris: Plon, 1933), 24–26.
11. Marcel Moré, *Le Très curieux Jules Verne* (Paris: Gallimard, 1960), citing a *Hommage à Jules Verne* by M. A. Gernoux.
12. Jules-Verne, *Jules Verne*, 238.
13. Note by Olivier Dumas in Jean-Michel Margot, "Dernières (?) précisions sur les rencontres Briand-Verne," *BSJV* 62 (1982): 210.
14. Olivier Dumas, "Si Verne et Briand m'étaient contés," *BSJV* 55 (1980): 270–78.
15. Marc Soriano, *Jules Verne* (Paris: Juillard, 1978), 140–48, 169–71. This author also cites those who hold the contrary view—such as Michel Serres when he writes that "woman is always the heroine of the Extraordinary Voyages, and their key."
16. BN NAF 17004, 298–301.
17. Olivier Dumas, "Le Choque de Gallia choque Hetzel," *BSJV* 75 (1985): 220–21. See also "Le Premier dénouement d'Hector Servadac" in ibid., 222–27.
18. Robert Pourvoyeur, "Verne et Offenbach," *BSJV* 20 (1972): 94–99; 21 (1972): 112–122.
19. *Le Temps*, January 28, 1877.
20. Pourvoyeur, "Verne et Offenbach," 21 (1972): 112, 117.
21. BN NAF 17004, 333–34.
22. Bibliothèque Municipale, Amiens (archives), ms. 1954D.

CHAPTER 26: MICHEL AND HONORINE

1. Informations and quotes concerning the costume ball are from: BN NAF 17004, 351; Olivier Dumas, *Jules Verne* (Paris: La Manufacture, 1988), 148–49; Jean Jules-Verne, *Jules Verne* (Paris: Hachette, 1973), 208–10; Charles-Noël Martin, *La Vie et l'oeuvre de Jules Verne* (Paris: Michel de l'Ormeraie, 1978), 216–17; René Lenoir, "Le Jules Verne de mes Grands Papas," *Visions nouvelles sur Jules Verne* (Amiens: CDJV, 1978), 4–5; *Le Progrès de la Somme* (Amiens), April 2–4, 1877; *Le Monde illustré* (Paris), April 14, 1877.
2. NAF 17006, 11.
3. Charles Lemire, *Jules Verne (1828–1905)* (Paris: Berger-Levrault, 1908), 116.
4. Piero Gondola della Riva, "Jules Verne et l'Académie Française," *BSJV* 53 (1980): 174.
5. A. Parménie and Catherine Bonnier de la Chapelle, *Histoire d'un éditeur et de ses auteurs: P.-J. Hetzel* (Paris: Albin Michel, 1953), 613.
6. BN NAF 17004, 376.
7. Parménie, *Histoire d'un éditeur*, 613.
8. BN NAF 17006, 8–10.
9. BN NAF 17004, 370–71. The letter is dated June 3, 1877.
10. BN NAF 17006, 13–14.
11. Martin, *La Vie*, 213.
12. Author's conversation with Dr. Olivier Dumas.
13. Olivier Dumas, "Hector Servadac a 100 ans," BSJV 42 (1977): 57–58.
14. Jules Verne, *Off on a Comet!* and *To the Sun* (New York: David McKay, 1878). "In one translation the pedlar's character was incredibly rehabilitated at the end of the story; in another his race was not mentioned and he was vaguely described as a Levantine," in I. O. Evans, *Jules Verne and His Work* (London: Arco, 1965), 180.
15. Emmanuel Le Monnier, "Une étude de la pensée politique de Jules Verne," thesis, Université de Paris XIII (Villetaneuse), October 1991, 83, 86.

16. BN NAF 17004, 373.
17. Ibid., 367.
18. Jules-Verne, *Jules Verne,* 213–14.
19. BN NAF 17006, 13.
20. Jules-Verne, *Jules Verne,* 213.
21. From Colette Gallois, "Mediathèque, Nantes; "Jules Verne vu par un voisin," in *Les Annales de Nantes,* 187–88 (Nantes: Société Academique de Nantes et de la Loire-Atlantique, 1978), 37.
22. BN NAF 17004, 374.
23. Jules-Verne, *Jules Verne,* 213.
24. BN NAF 17004, 372–73.
25. Information and quotes concerning the purchase of the yacht are from: Ibid., 381; Lemire, *Jules Verne,* 46–47; Georges Bastard, in *Gazette illustrée* (Paris), September 8, 1883. In his later account of a cruise to Copenhagen in 1881, Paul Verne described the yacht as "38 tons of burden in Customs, and 67 according to the standards of the Yacht-Club de France," in Paul Verne, "De Rotterdam à Copenhague à bord du yacht à vapeur 'Saint Michel,'" published in Jules Verne, *La Jangada* (Paris: Hetzel, 1881), 332. In a letter of October 14, 1877, to a shipbuilder in Le Havre, Verne sought to lower the purchase price to forty thousand francs—the most he could offer; see Olivier Dumas, "Correspondance de Jules Verne," *BSJV* 88 (1988), 12–13.
26. *Magasin d'Education et de Récréation,* 26 (1877), 352.

CHAPTER 27: ANCHORS AWEIGH
1. BN NAF 17004, 386.
2. "Deux lettres inédites de Jules Verne," *Cahiers du Centre d'Etudes Verniennes* (Nantes) 12 (1992): 5–6.
3. Serge Robillard, "Jules Verne et la Côte d'Opale," *Visions nouvelles sur Jules Verne* (Amiens: CDJV, 1978), 18.
4. Marcel Destombes, "Jules Verne à Vigo", *BSJV* 58 (1981): 52–53.
5. Charles Lemire, *Jules Verne (1828–1905)* (Paris: Berger-Levrault, 1908), 48.
6. Destombes, "Jules Verne à Vigo," 54–57.
7. Jean-Michel Margot, "Jules Verne et le Portugal," *BSJV* 61 (1982): 175–76.
8. Destombes, "Jules Verne à Vigo," 53.
9. *Le Temps,* June 10, 1878.
10. Francis Lacassin, "Le Communard qui écrivit trois romans de Jules Verne," *Europe* (Paris), November–December 1978, 94–105.
11. Jean Jules-Verne, *Jules Verne* (Paris: Hachette, 1973), 235–36.
12. Pierre Terrasse, "Jules Verne et les grandes écoles scientifiques," *BSJV* 12 (1969): 73.
13. Bibliothèque Municipale, Amiens (archives), ms. 1954D.
14. Charles-Noël Martin, A Propos de *Jules Verne en Roumanie, BSJV* 111 (1994): 7–9. Martin draws on Ion Hobana, *Jules Verne in Romania* (Bucharest: Editura Fundatiei Culturale Române, 1992).
15. "Correspondance de Michel Verne (1878–1902)," *BSJV* 103 (1992): 18–19. The letter is in the Hetzel archives, indicating that Jules Verne gave it to his publisher: BN NAF 17011, 1.
16. Olivier Dumas, *Jules Verne* (Paris: La Manufacture, 1988), 100–101.

CHAPTER 28: AUSPICIOUS DAYS
1. *Le Temps,* December 28, 1878.
2. *Le Temps,* December 30, 1878.
3. Jean Jules-Verne, *Jules Verne* (Paris: Hachette, 1973), 140–41.
4. SACD (Société des Auteurs et Compositeurs Dramatiques), register of Théâtre de la Porte Saint-Martin, 1865 to July 1879, courtesy of Mme Florence Roth. The actual royalty would have been reduced by the collection agent's commission, usually 10 percent.
5. *Le Figaro Littéraire,* December 22, 1878; full text in Emile Zola, *Les Romanciers naturalistes* (Paris: Charpentier, 1881), 356–57.
6. BN NAF 17006, 19.
7. Jules-Verne, *Jules Verne,* 234.
8. BN NAF 17006, 21.
9. BN NAF 17004, 430–31.
10. "Deux lettres inédites de Jules Verne," Cahiers du Centre d'Etudes Verniennes (Nantes) 12 (1992): 7.

11. *BSJV* 88 (1988): 13–14.
12. Charles-Noël Martin, *La Vie et l'oeuvre de Jules Verne* (Paris: Michel de l'Ormeraie, 1978), 219; Jules-Verne, *Jules Verne*, 190.
13. BN NAF 17004, 458.
14. Ibid., 464. See also Olivier Dumas, *Jules Verne* (Paris: La Manufacture, 1988), 101–102.
15. Bibliothèque Municipale, Amiens (archives), ms. 1954D.
16. BN NAF 17004, 466.
17. Ibid., 472; Cécile Compère, "Michel Verne et la Dugazon," *Feuille de Liaison du CDJV* 35/36, 1995, 24–25.
18. Ibid., 480; Compère, "Michel Verne," op. cit., 25.
19. Ibid., 483.
20. BN NAF 17006, 22.
21. Jules-Verne, *Jules Verne*, 246.
22. Pierre Terrasse, "Un centenaire: 'Michel Strogoff' au Théâtre du Châtelet," *BSJV* 56 (1980): 296–301.
23. *Le Temps*, November 19, 1880.
24. Terrasse, "Un centenaire," 306. In all, the play was performed 1,276 times in Verne's lifetime; see Volker Dehs, "Le dernier triomphe de 'Michel Strogoff,'" *Feuille de Liaison du Centre de Documentation Jules Verne* (Amiens) 27 (1993): 12.
25. *Le Temps*, February 20, 1881.
26. Jules-Verne, *Jules Verne*, 243.

CHAPTER 29: AT FIFTY-FIVE

1. Philippe Burgaud, "Les Spectacles de Jules Verne aux U.S.A.," *BSJV* 109 (1992): 10, 12. The previous year, the Kiralfys had brought *Around the World in Eighty Days* back to the stage at Niblo's Garden Theater; on opening night, the crowd "filled the house from floor to the uppermost gallery," the *New York Times* reported on August 31, 1880. The *Times* critic remarked that "Jules Verne's story, under the hands of the dramatist, may have disappeared, but in its place the Kiralfy Brothers have presented a series of beautiful pictures, and nobody complains of the liberty taken with the author. The arrival of the Suez steamer in the first scene of act first is realistic, although it develops a deplorable tendency of small steamers to large and excessively noisy whistles and much waste of steam."
2. Piero Gondolo della Riva, "Du nouveau sur Jules Verne," *Europe* (Paris), May 1980, 144.
3. According to the *Journal d'Amiens* of December 19, 1880, it was the British paper *The Theatral Novellist* that had reported Verne's death; according to this paper, Verne, disguised as a worker in order to study a new milieu, had been stabbed to death by a drunken soldier in a tawdry bar; see *BSJV* 112 (1994): 11–12.
4. A. Parménie and Catherine Bonnier de la Chapelle, *Histoire d'un éditeur et de ses auteurs: P.-J. Hetzel* (Paris: Albin Michel, 1953), 632.
5. Jean Jules-Verne, *Jules Verne* (Paris: Hachette, 1973), 246–47.
6. Paul Verne, "De Rotterdam à Copenhague à bord du yacht à vapeur 'Saint Michel,'" published with Jules Verne, *La Jangada* (Paris: Hetzel, 1881), 329–75.
7. Piero Gondolo della Riva, *Un Editeur et son siècle: Pierre Jules Hetzel* (St. Sébastien sur Loire: ACL Editions, 1988), 120–21.
8. BN NAF 17006, 26.
9. Robert Pourvoyeur, "Du nouveau . . . sur 'l'impossible'!", *BSJV* 45 (1978): 137–51; François Raymond, "Le Voyage à travers l'impossible," in *Grand Album Jules Verne* (Paris: Hachette, 1982), 126–28.
10. E. Noel et E. Stoullig, *Les Annales du théâtre et de la musique (1882)* (Paris: Charpentier, 1883), 335; quoted in Pourvoyeur, "Du nouveau," 144.
11. *Le Temps*, December 4, 1882.
12. Jules Verne et Adolphe d'Ennery, *Voyage à travers l'impossible, pièce fantastique en trois actes* (Paris: Pauvert, 1981).
13. Société des Auteurs et Compositeurs Dramatiques (SACD), register of Théâtre de la Porte Saint-Martin, August 1879–December 1885.
14. *Le Temps*, September 10, 1883.
15. Volker Dehs, "La Correspondance Verne-Dumas fils," *BSJV* 94 (1990): 16.
16. Société des Auteurs et Compositeurs Dramatiques (SACD), register of the Gaité Lyrique, May 1878–November 1883.
17. Francis Lacassin, "Le Communard qui écrivait trois romans de Jules Verne," *Europe* (Paris) November–December 1978, 96–97.

18. Georges Bastard, "Célébrité contemporaine: Jules Verne," *Gazette illustrée* (Paris), September 8, 1883, 90–92.
19. Jules Hoche, *Les Parisiens chez eux* (Paris: Dentu, 1883), 254–55.
20. Olympe Audouard, *Silhouettes parisiens* (Paris: Marpon & Flammarion, 1883), 297. For this author and others who came to Jules Verne late, his real beginnings—a dozen years before Hetzel—remained unknown.
21. Jules Claretie, *Célébrités contemporains: Jules Verne* (Paris: Quantin, 1883), 32.
22. Dehs, "La Correspondance Verne-Dumas fils", 6–18.

CHAPTER 30: LAST CRUISE

1. Jean Jules-Verne, *Jules Verne* (Paris: Hachette, 1973), 220; Cécile Compère, "Michel Verne et la Dugazon," *Feuille de Liaison du CDJV* 35/36, 1995, 28.
2. On December 1, 1884, Verne instructed Hetzel's accountant to send two hundred francs of his son's monthly one-thousand-franc stipend to Michel's abandoned wife, Thérèse, instead; see Charles-Noël Martin, *La Vie et l'oeuvre de Jules Verne* (Paris: Michel de l'Ormeraie, 1978), 235.
3. Olivier Dumas, "Jules Verne juge Verne," *BSJV* 70 (1984): 58–59.
4. BN NAF 17004, 568.
5. From *Le Journal d'Amiens* of January 17, 1884, which reprinted a report published in a Paris journal; see Volker Dehs, "En 1886," *BSJV* 113 (1995): 32–33.
6. Jules-Verne, *Jules Verne*, 192. In "Jules Verne et le Portugal," *BSJV* 61 (1982): 177, Jean-Michel Margot assumes that Gaston was the passenger, as did Dr. Olivier Dumas (conversation with the author). In *La Vie*, 219, Martin opts for Maurice.
7. All quotes from Verne's nephew's log from Marguerite Allotte de la Fuÿe, *Jules Verne: Sa vie, son oeuvre* (Paris: Hachette, 1953), 165–66. But in "Jules Verne et le Portugal," 176–77, Margot contests the veracity of this text, even though it appears within quotation marks in Allotte. He doesn't believe the anecdote about the actress, among other things.
8. *Le Charivari Oranais*, May 29, 1884, CDJV, document 12887.
9. Volker Dehs, "En face du public: Un autre Jules Verne," *BSJV* 112 (1994): 13–14. Dehs notes that Verne managed to cite Philippeville in passing in the novel he was then writing, *Mathias Sandorf*, as well as in the book he began in 1885, *The Clipper of the Clouds* (and here in quite flattering terms).
10. *Le Temps*, July 7, 1884.
11. Allotte, *Jules Verne*, 167–70; Jules-Verne, *Jules Verne*, 193–96.
12. Martin, *La Vie*, 212.
13. Jean-Pierre Picot, "Le Chef-d'oeuvre et son double: *Le Comte de Monte-Cristo*, d'Alexandre Dumas et *Mathias Sandorf*, de Jules Verne," *BSJV* 108 (1993): 50–51.
14. Simone Vierne, *Jules Verne* (Paris: Ballard, 1986), 61.
15. Jean Chesneaux, *Une lecture politique de Jules Verne* (Paris: Maspero 1971), 65.
16. A. Parménie and Catherine Bonnier de la Chapelle, *Histoire d'un éditeur et de ses auteurs: P. J. Hetzel* (Paris: Albion Michel, 1953), 644.

CHAPTER 31: GASTON

1. Guy Riegert, "Comment Jules Verne fit scandale en Grèce . . . ," *BSJV* 58 (1981): 64–66; *Le Temps*, April 18, 1885.
2. Robert Pourvoyeur, "La science chez Verne: Une thèse de Charles-Noël Martin," *BSJV* 59 (1981): 103–106. On Verne's turn away from science, see Olivier Dumas, *Jules Verne* (Paris: La Manufacture, 1988), 89–92.
3. Volker Dehs, "En 1886," *BSJV* 113 (1995): 32.
4. Volker Dehs, "La Correspondance Verne-Dumas fils," *BSJV* 94 (1990): 24.
5. *Le Journal d'Amiens*, March 9–10, 1885; *Progrès de la Somme* (Amiens), March 10, 1885; Charles-Noël Martin, *La Vie et l'oeuvre de Jules Verne* (Paris: Michel de l'Ormeraie, 1978), 227.
6. BN NAF 17004, 610.
7. Jean Jules-Verne, *Jules Verne* (Paris: Hachette, 1973), 221.
8. Elisabeth Leger de Viane, "L'Entourage familiale de Jules Verne," *Visions nouvelles sur Jules Verne* (Amiens: CDJV, 1978), 26.
9. *Le Temps*, July 6, 1885.

10. Dehs, "La Correspondance Verne-Dumas fils," 28.
11. Francis Lacassin, "Le Communard qui écrivait trois romans de Jules Verne," *Europe* (Paris), November–December 1978, 97.
12. Jules-Verne, *Jules Verne,* 260.
13. Joseph Laissus, "A propos de 'l'Albatros,'" *BSJV* 7–8 (1968): 18–19.
14. A. Parménie and Catherine Bonnier de la Chapelle, *Histoire d'un éditeur et des ses auteurs: P. J. Hetzel* (Paris: Albion Michel, 1953), 650.
15. Joseph Laissus, "La vente du 'Saint-Michel III,'" *BSJV* 1 (1967): 5–6.
16. Leger de Viane, "L'Entourage familiale," 27.
17. *BSJV* 103 (1992): 21–22.
18. Jules-Verne, *Jules Verne,* 268.
19. *Journal d'Amiens,* March 11, 1886; *L'Echo de la Somme,* March 13, 1886; *Le Temps,* March 11 and 12, 1886.
20. For example, *The New York Times,* March 11, 1886, where a report appeared on page one.
21. BN NAF 17004, 653.
22. Jules Verne, *Jules Verne,* 268.
23. Leger de Viane, "L'Entourage familiale," 24.
24. Jules-Verne, *Jules Verne,* 269.
25. R. H. Sherard, "Jules Verne at Home," *McClure's Magazine,* January 1894, 122. Cf. Daniel Compère, "L'Attentat du 9 mars 1886," *Visions nouvelles,* 48.
26. Dehs, "En 1886," 33.
27. Dumas, *Jules Verne,* 151–52.
28. Marcel Moré, *Le Très curieux Jules Verne* (Paris: Gallimard, 1960), 174–75.
29. Marc Soriano, *Jules Verne* (Paris: Julliard, 1978), 243–48.
30. Jules-Verne, *Jules Verne,* 268.
31. Pierre Véron, *Boutique de plâtres* (Paris: Dentu, 1886), 47.
32. *BSJV* 103 (1992): 22–24.
33. Parménie, *Histoire d'un éditeur,* 650.

CHAPTER 32: SOMBER TIMES

1. Olivier Dumas, *Jules Verne* (Paris: La Manufacture, 1988), 460.
2. Pierre Véron, *Boutique de plâtres* (Paris: Dentu, 1886), in Pierre Terrasse, "Trente ans après," *BSJV* 87 (1988): 15–18.
3. BN NAF 24639, 584; Volker Dehs, "La correspondance Verne-Dumas fils," *BSJV* 94 (1990): 28.
4. Olivier Dumas, "La Correspondance Verne-Nadar" *BSJV* 97 (1991): 13.
5. Volker Dehs, "En 1886," *BSJV* 113 (1995): 35.
6. *BSJV* 112 (1994): 39–40.
7. BN NAF 17005, 20–21.
8. Ibid., 30–31.
9. Jean Jules-Verne, *Jules Verne* (Paris: Hachette, 1973), 280.
10. *Le Temps,* November 22, 1886.
11. BN NAF 17005, 20–21.
12. Jules-Verne, *Jules Verne,* 273–74.
13. Dehs, "Correspondance Verne-Dumas fils," 30.
14. BN NAF 17005, 40.
15. BN NAF 17006, 54.
16. The total authors' share in November was some 300 francs nightly; in December, it varied between 150 and 400 francs, usually closer to 200; by February, the authors were dividing fewer than 100 francs on most nights, never more than 260; SACD (Société des Auteurs et Compositeurs Dramatiques), register of the Ambigu.
17. Letter of December 9, 1887, from sale catalogue, CDJV, document 3048.
18. *La Meuse* (Liège), November 28, 1887, CDJV, document 4310. Cf. Volker Dehs, "'La Famille Raton' sans ratures," *BSJV* 90 (1989): 2–4.
19. CDJV, document 7334. On Godefroy, see Anne Martin, "Robert Godefroy," *Visions nouvelles sur Jules Verne* (Amiens: CDJV, 1978), 45–46.
20. Daniel Compère, "M. Jules Verne, conseiller municipal," *L'Herne: Cahier Jules Verne* (Paris: Editions de l'Herne, 1974), 130.
21. *Bulletin Municipal de la Ville d'Amiens,* 1887, vol. 2, *Actes Administratifs* (Amiens: 1887), 160–61: CDJV.

22. Compère, "M. Jules Verne, conseiller municipal," 131. *Progrès de la Somme* noted that at its constitutive meeting on May eighteenth, when Mayor Petit ended his speech with the word *République,* everybody applauded save Jules Verne; ibid., 132.
23. Letter from Jules Verne, May 20, 1888, archives of the city of Amiens (copy in CDJV, document 3402).
24. Jules-Verne, *Jules Verne,* 277.
25. Ibid., 222.
26. Olivier Dumas, "La Carrière littéraire de Michel Verne," *BSJV* 103 (1992): 3.
27. Letter dated May 9, 1888, in *Textes et Languages,* vol. 10 (Nantes: Université de Nantes, 1984), 3.
28. *Les Annales politiques et littéraires* (Paris), August 27, 1893. Olivier Dumas points out that "An Express of the Future" appeared in Russia, Britain, and the United States under Jules Verne's name, "La Carrière littéraire," 5.
29. *Le Figaro—Supplément Littéraire* (Paris), September 1, 1888.

CHAPTER 33: MEETING NELLIE BLY

1. BN NAF 17006, 98. Olivier Dumas states that the text read by Jules Verne to the academy in Amiens was a transformation of his son's original; see *Jules Verne* (Paris: Manufacture, 1988), 506.
2. Jules Verne, "In the Year 2889," *The Forum* (New York) February 1889, 662–77. The version widely available today is "La Journée d'un journaliste américain en 2889," published in 1910 in the posthumous story collection *Hier et Demain.* By the time Verne read the story in French to the academy in Amiens, a year had gone by, and the story had been retitled "La journée d'un journaliste américain en 2890."
3. Francis Lacassin, postface to Jules Verne, *Famille-Sans-Nom* (Paris: Union Générale d'Editions—10/18, 1978), 316.
4. Charles-Noël Martin, preface, and Francis Lacassin, "Notes sur Badoureau," both in Jules Verne, *Sans dessus dessous* (Paris: Union Générale d'Editions—10/18, 1978).
5. Adrian Villart, "Chronique Amiénoise," in Verne, *Sans dessus dessous,* 241–45.
6. Volker Dehs, "Rapports et interventions au Conseil Municipal," *BSJV* 112 (1994): 40–41.
7. Ibid., 15–21.
8. Jules Verne, *Discours d'inauguration du Circle municipal d'Amiens, 23 Juin 1889,* Claude Lepagnez, ed., (Amiens: CDJV, 1989).
9. Mignon Rittenhouse, *The Amazing Nellie Bly* (New York: Dutton, 1956), 12–15.
10. *Nellie Bly's Book: Around the World in Seventy-two Days* (New York: Pictorial Weeklies Co., 1890), 3–5.
11. Rittenhouse, *The Amazing Nellie Bly,* 155.
12. *Nellie Bly's Book,* 31. Rittenhouse, *The Amazing Nellie Bly,* 155, accredits this version.
13. R. H. Sherard, *Twenty Years in Paris* (London: Hutchinson, 1905), 315.
14. *Nellie Bly's Book,* 45.
15. *Le Temps,* December 19, 1889.
16. *Nellie Bly's Book,* 45–57.
17. Rittenhouse, *The Amazing Nellie Bly,* 160.
18. *World* (New York), January 26, 1890.
19. *Le Temps,* December 19, 1889. See also *Feuille de liaison du Centre de Documentation Jules Verne* (Amiens) 26 (1993).

CHAPTER 34: GOING ON SIXTY-SIX

1. R. H. Sherard, *Twenty Years in Paris* (London: Hutchinson, 1905), 316–17.
2. Jean Jules-Verne, *Jules Verne* (Paris: Hachette, 1973), 280–81.
3. Volker Dehs, "La correspondance Verne-Dumas fils," *BSJV* 94 (1990): 30.
4. Olivier Dumas, "Correspondance de Jules Verne," *BSJV* 88 (1988): 15–16.
5. Jules-Verne, *Jules Verne,* 17.
6. Volker Dehs, "Discours et Textes divers," *BSJV* 112 (1994): 24–28.
7. *Le Progrès de la Somme,* January 11, 1891; *Le Temps,* January 11, 1891.
8. Daniel Compère, "M. Jules Verne conseiller municipal, *L'Herne: Cahier Jules Verne*" (Paris, Editions de l'Herne, 1974), 136–38.
9. Note signed Michel Jules Verne, transcription by Volker Dehs from BN NAF, 17001, 189–209, CDJV, document 8587.
10. See letters from Michel Verne to Jules Hetzel, August 29 and September 3, 1891, in *BSJV* 103 (1992): 27–28.

11. *Catalogue des Manuscrits de Jules Verne* (Nantes: Bibliothèque Municipale, 1988), 18; Olivier Dumas, *Jules Verne* (Paris: La Manufacture, 1988), 504.
12. Jules-Verne, *Jules Verne,* 302.
13. Dossier, courtesy Musée de la Légion d'honneur, Paris; Dumas, *Jules Verne,* 157–58.
14. BN NAF 17006, 57.
15. BN NAF 17005, 229.
16. Dumas, "Correspondance," *BSJV* 88 (1988): 16.
17. Dumas, *Jules Verne,* 462.
18. *BSJV* 103 (1992), 28–29.
19. Jules-Verne, *Jules Verne,* 301–302.
20. Dumas, *Jules Verne,* 463.

CHAPTER 35: "I AM AN ARTIST"
1. Olivier Dumas, *Jules Verne* (Paris: La Manufacture, 1988), 465.
2. Jean Jules-Verne, *Jules Verne* (Paris: Hachette, 1973), 302.
3. Dumas, *Jules Verne,* 463.
4. R. H. Sherard, "Jules Verne at Home," *McClure's Magazine,* January 1894, 115–24.
5. Maurice Thiéry, "Les Hommes du Nord: Jules Verne," in *Les Enfants du Nord,* vol. 11, (Paris: Chevalier, 1894).
6. Mario Turiello, "Lettres de Jules Verne à un jeune italien," *BSJV* 4 (1936): 162–68.
7. Dumas, *Jules Verne,* 466–69.
8. Ibid., 466–67, 470–71.
9. BN NAF 17006, 61–64, 68–71.
10. Jules-Verne, *Jules Verne,* 331.
11. Turiello, "Lettres de Jules Verne," 168–70.
12. Marie A. Belloc, "Jules Verne at Home," *Strand Magazine* (London), February 1895; reprinted in Jules Verne, *Textes oubliés,* (Paris: 10/18, 1979), 355–66.
13. Dumas, *Jules Verne,* 477, 479.

CHAPTER 36: EDGAR POE AND EUGÈNE TURPIN
1. Maria Turiello, "Lettres de Jules Verne à un jeune italien," *BSJV* 4, (1936): 178–79.
2. Franck Marie, *Le Surprenant message de Jules Verne* (Malakoff, France: Vérités Anciennes, 1981); Michel Lamy, *Jules Verne, inité et initiateur* (Paris: Payot, 1984); Michel Lamy, "Jules Verne et le trésor des rois de France, ou le sens caché de *Clovis Dardentor,*" *BSJV* 65 (1985): 70–74. For another decoding of this novel, see Samuel Zeitnot, "Verne tait la chose, ou les secrets de l'Orient de Jules Verne," *BSJV* 113 (1995): 14–31.
3. Olivier Dumas, *Jules Verne* (Paris: La Manufacture, 1988), 480.
4. Turiello, "Lettres de Jules Verne," 173.
5. Ibid., 174n.
6. Ibid., 175.
7. Jules Verne, *Textes oubliés* (Paris: 10/18, 1979), 151.
8. Dumas, *Jules Verne,* 481.
9. Ibid. Cf. Olivier Dumas, "La Carrière Littéraire de Michel Verne," *BSJV* 103 (1992): 5.
10. Dumas, *Jules Verne,* 482.
11. Ibid., 483.
12. Turiello, "Lettres de Jules Verne," 178.
13. Dumas, *Jules Verne,* 484.
14. Charles-Noël Martin, *La Vie et l'oeuvre de Jules Verne* (Paris: Michel de l'Ormeraie, 1978), 241.
15. Dumas, *Jules Verne,* 485.
16. Ibid., 481; BN NAF 17005, 308.
17. Turiello, "Lettres de Jules Verne," 180.
18. *BSJV* 97 (1991): 21.
19. CDJV, document 11061, from BN NAF 16018, Papiers Poincaré, vol. 27.
20. *Le Temps,* November 19, 1896.
21. Piero Gondolo della Riva, "A Propos de l'Affaire Turpin," *BSJV* 69 (1984): 37–39.
22. Ibid.; *Le Temps,* December 7, 1896.
23. Gondolo della Riva, "A Propos de l'Affaire Turpin," 39.
24. *Le Petit Temps* (Paris), December 10, 1896.
25. *Le Temps,* March 10, 1896.
26. Dumas, *Jules Verne,* 487, 158.

27. Turiello, "Lettres de Jules Verne," 181.
28. Dumas, *Jules Verne,* 488–90. Writing Maurice again on August twenty-ninth, he said that at-
    tacks of dizziness and indigestion had taken place four times in the past month.
29. Martin, *La Vie,* 242.

CHAPTER 37: THE WILL OF AN ECCENTRIC

1. Adolphe Brisson, "Promenades et Visites—M. Jules Verne," *Le Temps,* December 29, 1897;
   see also Brisson, *Portraits intimes* (Paris: A. Colin, 1899), 111–120.
2. Charles-Noël Martin, *La Vie et l'oeuvre de Jules Verne* (Paris: Michel de l'Ormeraie, 1978),
   242.
3. Olivier Dumas, *Jules Verne* (Paris: La Manufacture, 1988), 491–92.
4. Jules Verne, "Discours et Textes divers," *BSJV* 112 (1994): 9–10.
5. Jules Lemâitre, *La Patrie Française, Première conférence* (Paris: La Patrie Française, 1899), 38.
   In its statutes, the purpose of the organization was given as "to maintain and to fortify love
   of country and respect for the nation's army," ibid., 15. For Poincaré speech: Jean-Denis
   Bredin, *The Affair* (London: Sidgwick & Jackson, 1987), 363.
6. Mario Turiello, "Lettres de Jules Verne à un jeune italien," *BSJV* 4 (1936): 186–87.
7. Dumas, *Jules Verne,* 166.
8. Jean Jules-Verne, *Jules Verne* (Paris: Hachette, 1973), 324.
9. Ibid., 325.
10. Turiello, "Lettres de Jules Verne," 189.
11. Etienne Richet, "Jules Verne: Une lettre inédite," *Abeille de la Nouvelle Orléans* (New Or-
    leans, Louisiana), April 5, 1905. Richet further described the visit: "In his office there was
    a strange collection of exotic curios. It was less a work room than a museum. A Buddha I
    brought back from the ruins of Angkor had an honorable place there. Books mixed with
    portraits [of explorers]."
12. Turiello, "Lettres de Jules Verne," 188.
13. Karl Baedeker, *Les Etats-Unis avec une excursion au Mexique* (Leipzig: Karl Baedeker, 1894).
14. Emile Barbier, *Voyage au pays des dollars* (Paris: Flammarion & Marpon, 1893).
15. Turiello, "Lettres de Jules Verne," 188.
16. *Le Temps,* December 29, 1899.
17. Jules-Verne, *Jules Verne,* 221; *BSJV* 103 (1992): 31–33.
18. *Catalogue des Manuscrits de Jules Verne* (Nantes: Bibliothèque Municipale, 1988), 25.
19. Jules-Verne, *Jules Verne,* 323; Olivier Dumas, "*Seconde Patrie,* La 'Terre Promise,'" *BSJV* 108
    (1993): 26–31.
20. *Catalogue des Manuscrits,* 25.
21. Turiello, "Lettres de Jules Verne," 191.
22. Martin, *La Vie,* 242.
23. Turiello, "Lettres de Jules Verne," 193.
24. Jean Jules-Verne, "Souvenir de mon grand-père," *L'Herne: cahier Jules Verne* (Paris: Editions
    de l'Herne, 1974), 115.
25. Turiello, "Lettres de Jules Verne," 193.
26. Olivier Dumas, "La correspondance Verne-Nadar," *BSJV* 97 (1991): 14.
27. *Catalogue des Manuscrits,* 25. A typescript also exists with inserts and corrections in Michel
    Verne's hand.
28. Charles Lemire, *Jules Verne (1828–1905)* (Paris: Berger-Levrault, 1908), 102–105.

CHAPTER 38: THE END OF THE SERIES

1. Olivier Dumas, "Le secret du 'Village Aérien'," *BSJV* 53 (1980): 180–85.
2. *Le Matin,* July 31, 1901.
3. Mario Turiello, "Lettres de Jules Verne à jeune italien," *BSJV* 4 (1936): 193–94.
4. Ibid., 194–96.
5. For the best statement of their case, see Charles Porcq, "Cataclysme dans la Cathédrale
   ou le secret des Frères Kip," *BSJV* 107 (1993): 35–52; and *BSJV* 109 (1994): 36–51.
6. Turiello, "Lettres de Jules Verne," 195.
7. Jules Verne, *Textes oubliés* (Paris: 10/18, 1979), 383–86.
8. CDJV, document 16337.
9. Verne, *Textes oubliés,* 187–88.
10. Mlle Mauchien, "Jules Verne et l'Espéranto," *Visions nouvelles sur Jules Verne* (Amiens:
    CDJV, 1978), 82–83; Jean Amouroux, "Jules Verne et l'Espéranto," *Feuille de Liaison du*

CDJV Centre de Documentation Jules Verne (Amiens) 27 (1993): 2–5. See also letter from Verne in *BSJV* 88 (1988): 18.

11. Turiello, "Lettres de Jules Verne," 197.

12. Olivier Dumas, "Correspondance de Jules Verne," *BSJV* 88 (1988): 11. A few days later, Verne informed Félix Nadar that he could read, write, and walk about town. Olivier Dumas, "La correspondance Verne-Nadar," *BSJV* 97 (1991): 18.

13. R. H. Sherard, *Twenty Years in Paris* (London: Hutchinson, 1905), 317.

14. R. H. Sherard, "Jules Verne Revisited" ("Jules Verne Retrouvé"), *T.P.'s Weekly* (London), October 9, 1903; reprinted in Verne *Textes oubliés,* 387–91.

15. Turiello, "Lettres de Jules Verne," 198–99.

16. Gordon Jones, "Jules Verne at Home," *Temple Bar* (London), June 1904, 664–71.

17. BN NAF 17005, 463.

18. Ibid., 464.

19. Turiello, "Lettres de Jules Verne," 199.

CHAPTER 39: DEATH AND RESURRECTION

1. Francis Lacassin, "Jules Verne et les 'majorités opprimées,'" introduction to Jules Verne, *L'Invasion de la Mer* (Paris: Union Générale d'Editions, 1978), 9–13.

2. *BSJV* 103 (1992): 45.

3. *The New York Times,* March 25, 1905.

4. Charles-Noël Martin, *La Vie et l'oeuvre de Jules Verne* (Paris: Michel de l'Ormeraie, 1978), 250.

5. Ibid.

6. Jacques and Pierre Foucart, "Albert Roze et Jules Verne," in *Visions nouvelles sur Jules Verne* (Amiens: CDJV, 1978), 95–100.

7. Edmond Frank, "Jules Verne," *L'Illustration* (Paris), April 1, 1905, 199–200.

8. Quoted in Charles Lemire, *Jules Verne (1828–1905)* (Paris: Berger-Levrault, 1908), 97–99.

9. Ibid., 132–33.

10. Mario Turiello, "Lettres de Jules Verne à jeune italien," *BSJV* 4 (1936): 200–201.

11. Martin, *La Vie,* 250.

12. Léon Blum, "Jules Verne, *L'Humanité* (Paris), April 3, 1905.

13. Lemire, *Jules Verne,* 1–6.

14. *Le Figaro,* April 3, 1905. The manuscript consists of four completed chapters and the beginning of a fifth; *Catalogue des Manuscrits de Jules Verne* (Nantes: Bibliothèque Municipale, 1988), 26.

15. *BSJV* 103 (1992): 34–35.

16. "Note rédigée par M. Michel Jules Verne sur le differend existant entre *Le Journal* et lui," BN NAF 170011, 201; transcription by Volker Dehs, in CDJV, document 8587.

17. BSJV 103, 1992, 36–51. Michel never succeeded in getting Hetzel to renounce the earlier contracts.

18. Olivier Dumas, "La Correspondance inédite Jules Hetzel/Michel Verne," *BSJV* 104 (1992): 9.

19. Piero Gondolo della Riva, "A propos des Oeuvres Posthumes de Jules Verne," *Europe* (Paris), November–December 1978, 73–76.

20. Jean Jules-Verne, *Jules Verne* (Paris: Hachette, 1973), 347.

21. "Une Letter de Jean Jules-Verne," *Europe,* November–December 1978, 90–91. See also Gondolo della Riva, "A propos des Oeuvres Posthumes," 76.

22. Jules-Verne, *Jules Verne,* 350–51.

23. In "Une lettre," 89–90, Jean Jules-Verne acknowledges that the surviving manuscript is in Michel's hand, but he advances the hypothesis that Michel had to make this copy because Jules Verne's original was not legible enough to be used for corrections. Cf. *Catalogue des Manuscrits,* 26 ("Manuscript seemingly in Michel Verne's hand").

24. Gondolo della Riva, "A Propos des Oeuvres Posthumes," 77.

25. Olivier Dumas, "Un Roman Ironique Inédit, *Le Beau Danube Jaune,*" *BSJV* 84 (1987): 4. Dumas notes that Jean Jules-Verne in his biography (*Jules Verne,* 354) finds a lack of "the mocking good humor" one expects to find in a Jules Verne book.

26. The verdict was handed down on January 9, 1912; BN NAF 17010. See also Piero Gondolo della Riva, "Postface: L'Affaire *Pilote du Danube,*" in Jules Verne, *Le Pilote du Danube* (Paris: Union Générale d'Editions, 1979), 295–300.

27. Gondolo della Riva, "A Propos des Oeuvres Posthumes," 78–80.

28. Olivier Dumas, "Le vrai Storitz retrouvé," *BSJV* 74 (1985): 8. The Société Jules Verne in Paris has published Jules Verne's original versions of several posthumous works, including this one. One of the astonishing things they reveal is that Jules had poor grammar and sorely needed editing; it was lucky for him, therefore, that he had the Hetzels.

29. "Correspondance de Michel Verne (1910–1912)," *BSJV* 110 (1994): 13–16.

30. Jules Verne, "Voyage d'études," in *San Carlos et autres récits inédits* (Paris: Cherche Midi, 1993), 208–60 (notes by Jacques Davy).

31. Jules-Verne, *Jules Verne*, 373; Jules-Verne, "Une Lettre," 92.

32. Olivier Dumas, "Nouvelles Preuves des Manipulations de Michel Verne," *BSJV* 89 (1989): 29. See BSJV 118 (1996) for further evidence of Michel Verne's contribution to the Jules Verne corpus.

EPILOGUE: THE VERNE LEGACY

1. Foreword to William Butcher, *Verne's Journey to the Centre of the Self* (London: Macmillan, 1990), xiii–xiv.

2. Ray Bradbury, introduction to Jules Verne, *The Mysterious Island* (New York: Heritage Press, 1959), v–x.

3. *France-Soir* (Paris), February 15, 1969.

4. *International Herald Tribune* (Paris), February 6, 1969.

5. Werner von Braun and F. I. Ordway, *Histoire mondiale de l'Astronautique* (Paris: Larousse, 1968), 29, 61, 65, 73–74. See also Von Braun and Ordway, *La Fusée à travers les âges* (Paris: France Empire, 1977), 145, 148.

6. Author's correspondence with Malcolm E. McLouth, vice chairman of Port Canaveral.

7. U.S. Geological Survey, 1980, CDJV, document 7374.

8. *Le Matin* (Paris), September 13–14, 1980; *Le Monde* (Paris), October 17, 1980; Act of Sale, 1981, in CDJV, document 15831.

9. *Le Figaro*, April 24, 1991.

10. *Courrier de l'Ouest* (Anger), December 15, 1993.

11. Jules Verne, *Manuscrits nantais* (Paris: Cherche-Midi, 1991).

12. "L'Histoire du manuscrit," Hachette Référence (press release), (1994); *The New York Times*, September 27, 1994.

13. See their articles in *L'Arc: Jules Verne* (Paris: Duponchelle, 1990).

14. Filmography in Jules Verne, *Michel Strogoff* (Paris: Presses Pocket, 1992), 522–24.

15. Filmography in Verne, *Voyage au centre de la terre* (Paris: Presses Pocket, 1991), 479.

16. Arthur C. Clarke, introduction to Jules Verne, *From the Earth to the Moon* (New York: Dodd, Mead, 1962), viii.

INDEX